GW01605214

2006 Poetry Competition for 7-11 year olds

a pocketful of RHYME

Imagination for a new generation

Southern England

Edited by Young Writers

Editorial Team:
Lynsey Hawkins
Allison Dowse
Claire Tupholme
Donna Samworth
Annabel Cook
Aimée Vanstone
Gemma Hearn
Joseph Devine
Angela Fairbrace
Laura Martin

First published in Great Britain in 2006 by:
Young Writers
Remus House
Coltsfoot Drive
Peterborough
PE2 9JX
Telephone: 01733 890066
Email: youngwriters@forwardpress.co.uk
Website: www.youngwriters.co.uk

HB ISBN 1 84602 413 7

Cover design by Tim Christian
Design by Mark Rainey

FOREWORD

Young Writers was established in 1991 and has been passionately devoted to the promotion of reading and writing in children and young adults ever since. The quest continues today. *Young Writers* remains as committed to the nurturing of poetic and literary talent as ever.

This year's *Young Writers* competition has proven as vibrant and dynamic as ever and we are delighted to present a showcase of the best poetry from across the UK and in some cases overseas. Each poem has been selected from a wealth of *A Pocketful of Rhyme* entries before ultimately being published in this, our fourteenth primary school poetry series.

Once again, we have been supremely impressed by the overall quality of the entries we have received. The imagination, energy and creativity which has gone into each young writer's entry made choosing the poems a challenging and often difficult but ultimately hugely rewarding task - the general high standard of the work submitted ensured this opportunity to bring their poetry to a larger appreciative audience.

We sincerely hope you are pleased with this final collection and that you will enjoy *A Pocketful of Rhyme - Southern England* for many years to come.

A-Z OF SCHOOLS

A-Z OF AUTHORS

Name	Number
Joe McMillan (10)	465
Joe Morris-Bray (11)	503
Joe Sandwell (7)	174
Joe Smith (10)	377
Joe Williams (8)	469
Joel Derry (8)	262
Joel Livesley (10)	342
Joel Mulenga (8)	326
Johann Perera (9)	114
John Butler (10)	40
John-Paul Akoachere (8)	265
Jonathan Evans (9)	456
Jonathan Harwood-Yeo (11)	381
Jonathan Lock (8)	82
Jonathon Corke (11)	195
Jonny Howard (10)	90
Jordan Abbott (9)	268
Jordan Bailey (7)	92
Jordan Brodie (10)	408
Jordan Coleman (8)	194
Jordan Gillard (8)	190
Jordan Kane (9)	534
Jordan Mead (9)	278
Jordan Menzies (7)	269
Jordan Pamment-Gayle (11)	502
Jordan Tonico (9)	109
Jordan Van Huis (9)	89
Joseff Morgan (11)	489
Joseph Hart (9)	114
Joseph Konstam (10)	488
Joseph Lloyd (7)	87
Josh Emery (8)	153
Joshua Billups (10)	27
Joshua Denington (10)	501
Joshua Joseph (10)	410
Joshua Liddicott (9)	462
Joshua Weaver (10)	274
Josiah Lyon (8)	485
Josiah White (9)	362
Jude Conlon (8)	530
Julia Coombs (10)	328
Julia McCarthy (8)	253
Julius Lewis (7)	555
Kai Wilkinson (9)	447
Kaitlyn Sheeran (11)	334
Katherine Parkin (10)	89
Kathyann Hinchley (11)	326
Katie Boyce (10)	61
Katie Cander (8)	151
Katie Gosham (10)	552
Katie Marchant (10)	246
Katie Marsh (8)	182
Katie Moore (10)	200
Katie Moya (9)	98
Katie Reeve (9)	68
Katie Richter (10)	247
Katie Sanderson (8)	530
Katie Sharples (10)	356
Katie Tims (7)	159
Katie Vickers (8)	179
Katie Wilson (11)	411
Katie Wolford (9)	204
Katrina Francis (8)	536
Katrina Hayes-Smith (9)	237
Katy Brace (9)	282
Katy Hatter (10)	70
Kayla Leeson (7)	367
Kayleigh Gillings (9)	28
Kelly Bendall (9)	373
Kelly Holland (11)	407
Kelly Lindsay (7)	53
Kelly Neves (11)	422
Keri Mitchell (9)	36
Kerry Russell (8)	538
Keshav Palanee (10)	325
Keziah Collett (8)	481
Kiarn Eslami (10)	138
Kiera Gilbert (8)	258
Kiera Woodley (9)	183
Kieran Cheesman (10)	436
Kieran Hargreaves (8)	476
Kieran Innes (9)	49
Kieran Moore (9)	180
Kieran Trinder (7)	173
Kimberley Barnes (11)	478
Kimberley Phillips (10)	42
Kimberley Stone (9)	429
Kimberley Tugwell (9)	150
Kirstin Holloway (9)	153
Kirsty Felix (10)	205
Kirsty Jones (10)	479
Kit Steely (9)	519
Kitty Nielsen (11)	312
Kiyavash Kandar (9)	435
Kobi Norman (9)	29
Kojo Kankam (8)	347
Kunal Patel (10)	497
Kurt Hamilton (8)	193
Laila Barakat (10)	223
Lara Carey (8)	476
Lara Mills (8)	555
Lara Petty (9)	207

Reece Placzek (8)	475
Reece Powell (9)	212
Rhiannon Bullock (9)	185
Rhiannon Lewis (10)	420
Rhiannon Thomas (10)	459
Ria Willis (8)	138
Rifat Chowdhury (9)	469
Robbie Ellis (8)	348
Robbie Jenner (9)	224
Robbie Wood (10)	502
Robert Alder (10)	528
Robyn Jankowski (9)	59
Robyn Orr (11)	289
Robyn Payne (10)	331
Rohith Muhundan (9)	110
Romy Sherlock (9)	88
Ronel Kiyanga (11)	136
Ronnie Hack (8)	390
Rory England (10)	379
Rory Padfield (9)	282
Rosalie Hide (9)	314
Rose Wright (11)	106
Rosie Jones (9)	467
Rosie Lucas (9)	462
Rosie Mellish (9)	39
Rosie Payne (10)	461
Rosie Smith (10)	292
Rosie Southon (9)	217
Rosie Thomas (11)	488
Rosie Weston (11)	149
Rowan Palka (11)	105
Ruby Conlon (10)	529
Ruby Russell (8)	512
Rufus Roy (10)	359
Rumena Begum (10)	520
Rusheb Shah (10)	499
Russell Hesketh (8)	532
Ruth Leppard (11)	101
Ryan Cree (9)	386
Ryan Flew (9)	64
Ryan Foord (9)	226
Ryan Green (10)	64
Ryan Holmes (7)	86
Ryan Hopgood (7)	172
Ryan Kemish (11)	40
Ryan Lintott (9)	531
Ryan Matthews (9)	266
Ryan McWilliams (8)	513
Ryan Murphy (9)	140
Ryan Rankin (9)	207
Ryan Smith (9)	314
Ryan Steventon (11)	343
Ryan Watts (11)	391
Ryan Woods (11)	409
Ryuta Ogawa (8)	461
Saffia Dalton (7)	515
Sam Benn (9)	181
Sam Bunday (11)	82
Sam Bushell (10)	310
Sam Crane (10)	488
Sam Goodsell (8)	98
Sam Osborne (8)	351
Sam Parsons (9)	456
Sam Rose (10)	293
Sam Rowley (11)	503
Sam Wright (10)	60
Sammy Hough (8)	109
Samuel Higgs (7)	88
Samuel Hills (11)	196
Samuel Jelley (9)	508
Samuel Lloyd (7)	83
Sara Toth (8)	273
Sarah Cole (7)	542
Sarah Collier (10)	43
Sarah Corbet (10)	25
Sarah Francis (8)	74
Sarah McNally (7)	161
Sarah Pierce (9)	423
Saskia Prabhavalkar (8)	108
Satbir Mann (8)	112
Sathya Kongara (9)	62
Savannah Hayler (7)	86
Scott Davis (9)	526
Scott Goodison (10)	63
Scott Sherwood (10)	208
Scott Widnell (11)	306
Sean Edney (11)	242
Sean Michael Lindemere (10)	47
Sean Mullan (8)	354
Sean Richardson (10)	470
Sebastian Barrett (7)	159
Sebastian Pickworth (8)	457
Serene Blake (10)	324
Shane Grantham (10)	40
Shanie Barnes (9)	520
Shannon Cook (9)	34
Shannon Cutting (9)	44
Shannon Griffiths (9)	180
Shannon Guett (8)	545
Shannon Kelly (8)	154
Shannon Mills (10)	140
Shannon Sherar (9)	425

THE POEMS

The Alley Cat

He sits there staring,
Amongst the bins,
Ignoring the shouting
And the dins.
He crouches there waiting,
Ready to pounce,
Soaring through the air,
Weighing less than an ounce.
He catches the mouse,
With one swipe it's dead,
He caught its tail,
But ate its head.
He ripped it to pieces,
Guarding his prey,
The fearless alley cat,
Survived the day.

Lily-May Catling (10)

The Butterfly

I wonder why, I wonder why,
They call the butterfly, a butterfly?
This butterfly flying low,
Has no butter on it,
That I know.
Flying low, flying high
My beautiful little butterfly,
Then away you float,
With your beautiful, amazing,
Colourful coat.
I wonder why, I wonder why,
They call the butterfly, a butterfly?
This butterfly flying low,
Has no butter on it,
That I know.

Sarah Corbet (10)

The Tornado

I can start at any time, blowing away your safety
My whirling destruction will kill the world.

I can make darkness spread over your land,
I can blow you down so no one will stand.

My timing will shock you anywhere, any time.
My annoying rage will make you suffer until you can't defeat me.

I'm a whirling pool of destruction,
So beware.
Try to defeat me if you dare.

Lauren Ashley (10)

Fred The Fatty Highwayman

Fred the fatty highwayman, rode a horse
And fell off with a bump,
He tried to steal a steering wheel,
From the old place in Ma-hump.

He jumped in a bank
He realised his mistake,
His heart suddenly sank, it wasn't a bank
He had jumped into a lake.

He suddenly sneezed
And got blown away,
In the nippy wind he thought he'd be binned
And jumped into the hay.

He ran to the money-making company
And took fifty pounds,
He got hit with a club and started for the pub
Chased by twenty hounds.

He rode away
And didn't come back
Nobody knows where he went, either Kenley or Kent
But let's hope he gets sacked.

Nick Ashenden (9)
Audley Primary School, Caterham

Nigel The Nerd

Nigel the nerd
Tried to rob Robbie Williams
Robbie was sad but he didn't think Nigel was bad
He wanted Robbie's billions.

He nicked his stagecoach
All he got was a plastic brooch
Robbie slapped him on the back so his mum went *smack*
'I'll send you to London on a coach.'

He went to a pub
And got attacked by a mug
He tried to run away
But didn't get away till the end of the day
And smashed his favourite jug.

He got back on the stagecoach
With his plastic brooch
He fell off in some pee then got crushed by a tree
And ate a cockroach.

He decided to quit and fell in a pit
The snakes bit him
He drank some wine and thought
It was divine
So he decided to sit.

Joshua Billups (10)
Audley Primary School, Caterham

Simon The Incompetent Highwayman!

When Simon and Liz robbed a stagecoach
The passengers said, 'What a laugh,'
As Simon had bought a toy giraffe.

'Get off me you brute,' screeched our Simon
'Or you'll have no head, mate, I say.'
He spoke with such a fright that the poor horse took a bite
And it jumped up and sprinted away.

Now Simon he shouted at Lizzie
He thudded, screeched, bellowed and growled
And although he did his best Lizzie was quite depressed
In fact she didn't feel proud.

Simon the incompetent highwayman
Was left all alone in the rain,
He shivered and quivered, sighed and cried
And said, 'I don't want to be a highwayman again.'

Lauren Brown (9)
Audley Primary School, Caterham

Charles The Crazy Highwayman

Charles the crazy highwayman
Was staying up late at night
Eminem he would rob, for a fun job
And he would rule the world at first light

He put on his fluorescent suit
And stomped out as loud as he could
He got to Eminem's house, got scared by a mouse
And screamed as loud as he could

Eminem woke up with a start
He thought he had heard a scream
He jumped out of bed, his butler was dead
And he'd split his trouser seam

Crazy Charles stopped screaming after a while
And he climbed up into a tree
He made ghost sounds, Eminem released the hounds
And Charles started flicking peas

Charles suddenly had a thought
To pretend he was Superman
He painted himself red, in two seconds he was dead
And the hounds just ran and ran.

Kayleigh Gillings (9)
Audley Primary School, Caterham

Charlie The Chubby Highwayman

Charlie the chubby highwayman
Was walking to the bookies
Charlie had a glance and took a chance
To steal a bag of cookies.

Charlie saw the shopkeeper
Who obviously wasn't happy
The shopkeeper said, 'I'll do you for that with my bat.'
Charlie replied, 'That's too bad.'

Charlie was chased round the street
By the shopkeeper who was light on his feet
They went round and round
And Charlie took with a bound
And landed in the butcher's meat.

The meat was juicy, lovely and fat
Charlie the chubby highwayman was, of course, all that
He took a bite and had a fright
Because the meat wasn't Charlie's type.

Luke Hawkins Ruocco (9)
Audley Primary School, Caterham

Carol The Crazy Highway Lady

Carol the crazy highway lady
Was really very silly
She tried to rob but didn't do a good job
Her partner in crime was Billy.

Carol and Billy tried to be friends
Billy was silly and Carol was always chilly
So they drove each other
Round the bend.

Carol and Billy went out one night
They tried to rob a passer-by
They said, 'Hey, give me your money today,'
'I don't think so,' they said with a sigh.

Carol went out in the rain
She slipped and landed on her head
'Oh!' she cried, 'I could have died,'
And went home where her mum put her straight to bed.

Billy was alone in the dark
He had nowhere to go
'I need a mate, I'll be in a state,
My life will be really slow.'

Kobi Norman (9)
Audley Primary School, Caterham

The Highwayman

Simon, the stupid highwayman
Is as stupid as could be
He wants to fly and boy does he try
He thinks you mix coffee with tea.

Ben the brilliant highwayman
Thinks he's the best of the best
I don't know why he scoffs apple pie
He doesn't know how to put on a vest.

Jack the jealous highwayman
Is jealous of everything he sees
He wants to be the best, better than the rest
And be on all the Sky TVs.

Henry the horrible highwayman
Is as horrible as horrible gets
'Nobody's better than me but I can't get on TV
Because they're always too busy showing pets!'

Anthony Perry (9)
Audley Primary School, Caterham

Steve The Silly Highwayman

Steve the silly highwayman
Rides a brown horse *clip-clopping*
Clip-clopping along the track
He is in a rush to go shopping.

He wants some money
Sneaking behind the trees
He waits for a rich man
To rob him with ease.

Along comes a fancy carriage
The rich man wears a fine coat and rings
Steve runs out and shouts,
'Give me your valuable things!'

The man says, 'No! No!'
He shut the carriage door
On Steve's fingers, who says,
'I'm not doing this anymore!'

Steve runs away
And lives with his brother Nick
He is very kind
And finds him some work.

Amy Bee (9)
Audley Primary School, Caterham

Where Has He Gone?

(From the view of a cat)

The house is empty,
His bed is cold,
I have no food,
My milk is old,
They came a few hours ago,
When I was out,
They took him somewhere,
But now I doubt,
That he has gone
And passed away,
But me,
Where will I stay?

Hannah Cavaciuti (9)
Audley Primary School, Caterham

Highwayman

Monty the greedy highwayman
Couldn't walk a mile
He tried to walk but stood on a cork
Then did a secret trial

Laura the silly highway lady
Couldn't have a baby
When she tried the baby just died
And in the end she was just a lady

Robert the brave highwayman
Saved a stupid lady
She jumped off a cliff and said she'll be back in a jiff
And Robert got so fed up he said, 'I don't like you anymore you stupid baby.'

Penny the stupid highway girl
Couldn't walk a dog
She tried to walk it but accidentally haunted it
And fell over an old log

Joe the sly highwayman
Tried to spy on the queen
When he was young he got bought
And now he's lying in court
The queen walked up to him
And said, 'Don't ever be horrible or mean.'

Hazel McRae (9) & Hannah Lowndes (10)
Audley Primary School, Caterham

Sam The Smelly Highwayman

Sam the smelly highwayman
Tried to rob
Fernando Alonso, he thought he was a snob
So he ran away
And came back in May.

'Why are you back?
You've robbed me to bits.'
'I'm back for more
'Cause I lost all your whips.'

'I want that and this
Your necklace as well
Can I have it?'
'No, you smell!'

'Give me it
And I'll leave you forever!'
'Never! I'm really at the end of my tether!'
'Whatever!'

So Sam, he jumped out of the window
And got onto his horse,
The horse galloped away and gave a neigh
And Sam, he fell off with a force!

Nathan Hull (9)
Audley Primary School, Caterham

4AC's Colour Poem

Black is like a dark midnight sky,
As well as hair on a handsome guy,
White is like snow falling through the trees,
Chilling hands and faces when there is a cold breeze,
Blue is like the shining bright sky,
As the birds and clouds fly by,
Icicles are cold, chilly and blue,
Icicles sparkle for me and you,
Gold is like a beautiful, lost, dusty treasure,
Or like a gold medal you receive, it's a pleasure.

Class 4AC
Baden Powell & St Peter's Middle School, Poole

4KJ's Colour Poem

White is like playing alone in the snow,
Especially when you're feeling low,
White is like nothing in the air,
As quiet as the dragon's lair.

The taste of candyfloss, that is pink,
And sweets and goodies and I think,
That pink feels like something soft and warm,
And it makes me want to lie down and yawn.

The smell of orange must be,
The salty fish brought in by the sea,
The taste of orange must be like,
Delicious, nutritious, roasted pike.

Green is the colour of early spring,
Green gives everyone a real ping,
Green is a gentle sound of the rushing river,
It never ever makes people quiver.

Red is a hot burning salsa,
Red is a distrustful liar,
Beware of the dancing salsa,
It can creep into a very sore ulcer!

Yellow must be the 'Lord of the Light',
Making everything lovely and bright,
Yellow must be a fiery blaze,
That comes from the burning sun's rays.

Class 4KJ
Baden Powell & St Peter's Middle School, Poole

Fast/Slow

I am as fast as a full grown hurricane,
I am faster than a cheetah with a rocket on its back,
I am the fastest in the world,
I am as slow as a tortoise with his breaks on,
I am slower than a little ant carrying a fat human,
I am the slowest out of 400,000 people.

Alex Lang (9)
Baden Powell & St Peter's Middle School, Poole

4AC's Colour Poem

Red is like a soft, comfortable ribbon through the night sky,
Yellow is like a large ball of fire high up in the sky.
Blue is like the shimmering sky on a hot day,
Yellow is like the golden-brown hay.
Violet is like an unusual planet somewhere deep in space,
Blue is like a beaming smile on a small child's face.
Blue is like shiny water running down a stream,
Yellow is like the shining sun melting the ice cream.
Gold is like a shining car,
Brown is like an old rusty car.
Blue is like the wavy sea crashing on the rocks,
Red is like a roaring fire burning an old cupboard box.
Green is like the wet, glinting winter grass,
Bronze is like a loud trumpet made of brass.
Silver is like the glistening moon higher than the sky,
Blue is like the shining sky with clouds drifting by.
Red is like trickling water from a waterfall,
White is like a clean T-shirt from a mall.
Gold is like the shining sun glistening in the sky,
Bronze is like the glinting crown on a pillar that's very high.
Blue is like calm tears running down your face,
Black is like a little boy who can't tie his lace.

Class 4AC
Baden Powell & St Peter's Middle School, Poole

Dying In Other Countries

There's a man on the fields
He's painted by blood
Not as if he should be

Man is the most destructive
Source in the world
Try to stop

The world is now
Realising
What kind of
Harm we cause

But nothing stops
A man when
He's on a run.

Shannon Cook (9)
Baden Powell & St Peter's Middle School, Poole

4AC's Colour Poem

Blue is like the gentle breeze calmly flowing by
And white is like an aeroplane flying in the sky,
Yellow is like the yolk of shiny eggs,
Black is like a spider crawling through your legs,
White is like a ticking clock,
Grey is like a heavy big rock,
Silver is like a shining star high above the sky,
Indigo is like violets watching the world go by,
Blue is like a shining stream,
White is like smooth cream,
Red is like rosy cheeks in the cold
And green is like soft, frothy mould,
Green is like a blade of grass swaying in the breeze,
Red is like a bunch of cherries hanging from the trees,
Gold is like the sun high above the sky,
Black is like a twirling, buzzing fly,
Red is like sweet smelling bunches of cherries,
Black is like delicious, juicy blackberries,
Silver is like shining stars glinting high above the sky,
White is the fluffy clouds drifting by,
Water is a lovely clear kind of blue,
White is like a sticky glue.

Class 4AC
Baden Powell & St Peter's Middle School, Poole

The Raging Storm

The wind is howling,
The sky is dark
And ghostly figures,
Creep through the park.

The thunder booms,
With a terrible sound,
It rattles the earth
And shakes the ground.

The lightning flashes,
With a blinding light,
It sets fire to trees
And gives everyone a fright.

The rain is pouring,
Soaking all things,
Then the storm clears up
And a blue tit sings.

Victoria Joy (9)
Baden Powell & St Peter's Middle School, Poole

Blue Must Simply Be . . .

A howling wind, that is blue,
Cooking up a bitter blue stew,
Blue must simply be,
Water rushing in from the sea.

Pink is like flowers on the lawn,
Gently glinting in the light of dawn,
Pink is also something soft, I think,
It is also calming, that is pink.

Red is like the taste of fire,
Red is like a burning wire,
The smell of a liar that is red,
Smelling like a snake that is dead.

Orange is like a warming fire,
Its flames getting higher and higher,
Orange is the colour of the burning sun,
Baking me a delicious sweet bun.

Green is the colour of the never-ending sea,
Green is the sound of a buzzing bee,
If you were to taste the lovely colour green,
You would taste something spicy and mean.

Blue is the sound of cracking ice,
That is actually very nice,
Blue tastes like delicious chicken,
Especially made by Butcher Flicken.

Class 4KJ
Baden Powell & St Peter's Middle School, Poole

The Storm

The storm is a prancing cat
Pouncing on its prey
A full-grown ginger cat
Hungry all through the day
Its tail swishing from side to side
Minute by minute it creeps through the town
Waking other people with its loud
'Miaow, miaow, miaow, miaow.'

Anna Stoate (9) & Keri Mitchell (9)
Baden Powell & St Peter's Middle School, Poole

Weather

Winter
Winter is the white weather
Wrap up warm or you'll get cold
Curl up by the fire with your hot chocolate
Go to the shop where the gloves are sold.

Winter
Summer
Autumn
Spring
All different weather, on all different days.

Summer
Summer is the sunny weather
Let's all jump in the pool
In your swimming costume
And we will all be cool.

Autumn
Autumn is the colourful weather
The leaves are brown, orange, red and gold
Let's all jump in the leaves
Put a hat on just in case you're cold.

Spring
Spring is the weather with flowers
All popping out, yellow, blue and pink
A little water, a little sun
Here comes half term, no need to think.

Emily Pollard (9)
Barncroft Junior School, Bedhampton

The Playground

T he playground is so cool
H e and I play on it
E at on it too

P eople fighting and some are friends
L ay on the chairs or sit on the wall
A bird sings in the tree
Y ay the children scream when they score
G irls screaming, 'Help,' in kiss chase
R ound the playground our friends go
O ut to break we go every day
U p the climbing frame as well
N o one ever falls
D o not move when the bell goes.

Shaun Carter (10)
Barncroft Junior School, Bedhampton

The Mad Monkey - Haiku

The mad monkey swings
Up trees, eating bananas
Madly all day long.

Megan Knight (8)
Barncroft Junior School, Bedhampton

The Nibbling Hamster - Haiku

The nibbling hamster
She climbs on her cage and sleeps
I had a hamster.

Bobbi Knight (9)
Barncroft Junior School, Bedhampton

The Silly Monkey - Haiku

The silly monkey
Swinging lots from tree to tree
Silly monkey's brave.

Amy Thompsett (9)
Barncroft Junior School, Bedhampton

The Talking Parrot - Haiku

The talking parrot
Talks to the left, to the right
He's rude and smelly.

Natalie Cowdrey (9)
Barncroft Junior School, Bedhampton

The Stripy Tiger - Haiku

The stripy tiger
Running up and down on paws
It's fierce but so cute.

Georgia Bailey (9)
Barncroft Junior School, Bedhampton

The Star

The star came out bright as a light
Sparkly and glittery
And what a beautiful sight
It comes out at night
And I wish it could stay as night.

Rosie Mellish (9)
Barncroft Junior School, Bedhampton

The Funny Monkey - Haiku

The funny monkey
Swinging from the high treetops
Friendly as a fly.

Chelsea Mansfield (8)
Barncroft Junior School, Bedhampton

The Daft Dolphin - Haiku

The daft dolphin swims
Daftly round the sea quickly
Daftly and funny.

Ellie Bulbeck & Mollie Nash (9)
Barncroft Junior School, Bedhampton

The Dangerous Dog - Haiku

The dangerous dog
Growling as he is running
Very fierce and strong.

Aimee Marie Stewart (8)
Barncroft Junior School, Bedhampton

The Swinging Monkey - Haiku

The swinging monkey
Swinging from high branch to branch
He's funny and fast.

Mariah Morris (9)
Barncroft Junior School, Bedhampton

Chocolate Sundae

C hocolate sauce is the sweetest of them all
H eat melts the smooth texture
O ther flavours really colourful
C reamy like milk
O ur favourite is chocolate and toffee
L ives in a freezer
A t the top, a chocolate flake
T asting all different types
E at the flake first

S old all over the world
U ndecided children
N uts on the top
D ad spending his money
A cone shape bowl for it to rest in
E ven you can't beat a chocolate sundae.

Ryan Kemish (11)
Barncroft Junior School, Bedhampton

December

D ecorations for Christmas
E ating all the Christmas pies
C elebrating Christmas time
E veryone round for dinner
M e opening presents
B uy presents for Christmas Day
E veryone opening presents
R emember to say thank you.

Shane Grantham (10)
Barncroft Junior School, Bedhampton

The Chocolate Bar

It was as creamy as a caramel cake,
It is smooth, creamy, mouth-watering,
It was as creamy as some melted ice cream,
I fell backwards because of the taste,
You could find it at the shop,
The taste is caramel and creamy,
I could jump for that golden bar,
The world wouldn't be itself without chocolate.

John Butler (10)
Barncroft Junior School, Bedhampton

Little John

Little John was not content
Unless he played with wet cement.
One day alas in someone's yard
He stayed too long and set quite hard.
His mother didn't want him home
So he turned into a garden gnome.
When I was going out one day
My head fell off and rolled away,
But when I saw that it was gone
I picked it up and put it on.
And when I got into the street
A fellow cried, 'Look at your feet!'
I looked at them and sadly said
I've left them both asleep in bed!'

Amy Castle (10)
Barncroft Junior School, Bedhampton

Football Crazy

David Beckham scuffs the ball
Peter Crouch is really tall
Lua Lua is the best
Roy Keane plays for the west
Ronaldinho plays like Brazilians
Harry Kewell gets billions
Harry Redknapp is so bad
Because he made Pompey feel so sad.

Jamie Ashdown is so good
Thierry Henry wears a hood
People pay for the bets
To see if the balls all go in the nets.

Jake Gill (10)
Barncroft Junior School, Bedhampton

As I Was . . .

As I was swimming in a lake
A boy came up and gave me a shake
I went out and then hit the bin
A race was on and I did win.

Jody Thompsett (7)
Barncroft Junior School, Bedhampton

The Three Little Pigs

There were once three little pigs,
They left and said their goodbyes,
All three of them were triplets,
They packed their favourite fruit pies.

One pig built a house of straw,
Another built it of bricks,
Windows with a fireplace,
The other built it of sticks.

A big bad wolf attacked them
And made their happiness end,
He blew down two of the pigs' houses
And left them trying to mend.

They ran to their brother's house,
They put a pot on the fire,
The wolf climbed up onto the roof,
Then he fell into the fire.

The pigs lived in harmony,
They had a great big party,
They were so really happy,
That they were the real smarties.

Georgia Francis (9)
Barncroft Junior School, Bedhampton

I Like . . .

I like my mum's perfume as I walk in her room
The smell going up my nose
The smell is so sweet it makes me sweet as well.

I like my nan's potatoes
Warm and hot in my mouth
Munching, munching . . . the steam coming out
When I cut them with my smooth knife.

I like the sound of music singing in my ears
I'm dancing all around
My mum turns it down and says,
'Don't turn it up.'

I like to see the waves waving up and down
The stones are rolling and the sea is going
Then it comes back up
I watch the sea at night and fall to sleep smoothly.

Kimberley Phillips (10)
Barncroft Junior School, Bedhampton

Our Senses

I like the sight
Of my garden,
With leaves all over the grass,
Winter is the best,
With trees swaying in the wind.

I like the sound,
Of my cat purring in my ear,
Vibrating as I stroke her fur,
I hear the sound of her feet scampering up my stairs
And laying on my bed as I fall asleep.

I like touching
My pen
And it telling me to draw,
I like the touch of the paper,
It's so easy to tear.

I like the taste
Of honey,
It's lovely in my tummy,
I'm thankful to the bees,
For making lots of honey.

I like the smell
Of toast and jam,
It smells like heaven to me.

Carrieanne Long (10)
Barncroft Junior School, Bedhampton

Teachers Are Pests, Kids Are The Best

Teachers are mean,
Teachers are keen,
Teachers works us as if we are machines.

They eat chocolate biscuits in front of the school,
Have you ever met teachers that have been so cruel?
Teachers are bossy, they think they can rule.

Teachers are boring, they're so not cool!
Kids are cool,
Kids hate school,
Kids don't want to work or obey the rules.

They want to play games and run about all day,
But they are never allowed to get their own way.

Kids are clever, they're certainly not fools,
Kids just want to rule the schools!

Sarah Collier (10)
Barncroft Junior School, Bedhampton

At My House

I love watching the sunset
How it rises, lightens up the sky
And the birds wake up.
I like the stars shining,
Making the sky bright.
I like looking out of my window
As my mum comes in from work.

I like listening to the birds
In the morning
As the dog starts to bark.
I love the way my mum opens the gate
And her boots clatter on the concrete.

I like the couch
It is so smooth and cold in the morning
You shiver and slip down it
It's so slippery.
I like my bed
It's so soft and warm.

I like the taste of the curry
As it warms up my mouth,
As it slips down my throat
And my nan cooks her home-made roast.

Shannon Cutting (9)
Barncroft Junior School, Bedhampton

The Four Seasons And Me, The Sun

In spring I am warm,
But some showers may fall,
I can make life grow,
From March to May.

In summer it is my birthday,
Because I'm a sizzling sausage,
Children think I'm the best thing,
In the middle of the year.

In autumn my rays die down,
To a couple of little sparks,
I can still warm you up,
But not as good as last season.

In winter I'm practically dead,
Because it is my worst nightmare,
All of the clouds are now the hit of the month,
Till the start of the new year.

Bradley Sandford (9)
Barncroft Junior School, Bedhampton

Beauty And The Beast

A shining castle on a frosty night
An old beggar woman arrived
With a rose to give
The handsome prince threw the ugly woman aside.

Nearby in a village
A woman called Belle
Whose beauty shone inside and out
Spent all her days dreaming
'Oh, where are you?' she did shout.

Belle's father, Maurice
An inventor by trade
The village all thought he was mad
The hunter Gaston with his rippling chest
Thought Belle must be really quite sad.

Back at the castle, the once handsome prince
Had been turned into a ferocious beast
His servants Cogsworth and Lumiere
Were changed so all eyes did feast.

The awful Gaston hoped to win Belle's heart
But his manner destroyed all his hope
For the beautiful Belle wanted to love a great man
Who could love and treat her so.

Out walking one night
In search of her prince
Our Belle came upon a palace
She knocked at the door
Then heard a loud roar
She wondered who was being so callous.

The furious beast opened the door
And stared so deeply at Belle
Their eyes did meet
She fell at his feet
And they fell deeply in love, farewell!

Nicole Corrigan (10)
Barncroft Junior School, Bedhampton

As I Was Swimming

As I was swimming in the sea
A bumblebee came up to me
It was not very nice at all
It made a hole in my new ball.

Caitlin Tate (8)
Barncroft Junior School, Bedhampton

My Senses

I like to see
My mum and dad looking like zombies
People making breakfast
And watching telly

I like smelling
Pizza in the oven
It smells like tomatoes and pepperoni topping
I like the smell of my breakfast as well

I like tasting
The sweet taste of chocolate
And eggs for my dinner
The middle bit of it is like milk dripping everywhere.

I like to hear
50 Cent and Eminem rapping
I like hearing the crackling
Of a hot fire.

Jake Read (10)
Barncroft Junior School, Bedhampton

What I Like . . .

I like the smell of my perfume when I spray it on me,
Then I'll walk down the black, long stairs
And smell my dinner in the oven,
I like the sound of music rapping in my ears,
But then my mum turns it down.
I like to see my mum resting in peace,
Well she has done everything that she could think of.
I like the taste of orange juice swishing in my mouth.
I like the taste of my dinner sliding down my throat.

Hope Elsley (10)
Barncroft Junior School, Bedhampton

Sea Poem

As I was swimming in the sea,
A shark and fish came up to me,
They said I was not one of them,
I told them that I was their friend,
They didn't think I was so cool,
I told them that I went to school.

Yazmin Miller (8)
Barncroft Junior School, Bedhampton

Dragon In The House!

On one normal day
On a normal week
In a normal street
In a normal house
With a normal family
Something extraordinary happened.
Tim, a normal little boy
Wanted a pet
He wanted a pet dragon
He found a penny
And little Tim was set
For a wish
There was a flash
And gone was his penny
And out stepped a dragon
Tim shrieked with joy
And the dragon
The living room he went to
Tim thought he was going to the zoo!
But he saw a flame flicker round
He picked up a chew toy
Went into the garden
And threw it at the hound!
He wanted to play
But the dog just walked away
While the dragon was curious
Tim caught him too fast!
At dinner time the dragon ate with the family
At bedtime, he slept on the top bunk.

Sean Michael Lindemere (10)
Barncroft Junior School, Bedhampton

I Started To Fly One Day

I started to fly one day
Up in the cloudy sky
It seemed so beautiful from above.

I swooped down in the summery weather
To smell the lovely flowers
The smell was strong, like lavender.

I never could resist a summer's day
The smell of the flowers
Would lay in the soft warm air.

Amy Rogers (9)
Barncroft Junior School, Bedhampton

Alphabet Poem - Names

A is for Abigail who makes loads of mittens
B is for Bella who loves her twin kittens
C is for Charlie who hates PE
D is for Daniel who plays in DT
E is for Ella who is very sporty
F is for Francesca who is mostly naughty
G is for Gemma who can drive a car
H is for Harry who runs very far
I is for Isabelle who made her own map
J is for James who loves a long nap
K is for Katie who hates anything healthy
L is for Liam who likes stuff wealthy
M is for Molly who loves her mum
N is for Nathan who is very dumb
O is for Oliver who likes to play tennis
P is for Penny who is a little menace
Q is for Quentin who loves to play chess
R is for Robert who always makes a mess
S is for Sara who calls people names
T is for Tiffany who loves playing games
U is for Ulysses who had bad taste
V is for Violet who eats toothpaste
W is for William who is always watching telly
X is for Xavier who has a fat belly
Y is for Yvonne who always is lazy
Z is for Zack who is half crazy.

Lisa Jane Blandford (10)
Barncroft Junior School, Bedhampton

The Garbage Can!

The rotten, smelly garbage can,
It's always giving me swollen glands,
The flies swoop,
Suck up second-hand soup,
That's the way the trash goes out,
Broken glass all flustered,
Always dripping out smelly, old custard,
Apples lay up on the floor and rot,
The sun's burning and making them all hot,
That's the way the trash goes out,
Drips dripping disgusting slime,
Sometimes you might even find one dime,
That's the way the trash goes out!

Danny Wilkinson (10)
Barncroft Junior School, Bedhampton

My Senses

I like the smell
Of burgers sizzling on the barbeque
Dripping fat everywhere
It just lures me there, waiting to eat it.

I like the sound
Of 50 Cent rapping his tunes
The beat thumping down on the floor
So loud my mum goes insane
Everybody in the road can hear it.

I like the taste
Of bacon sandwiches bubbling on the plate
It tastes so magnificent
It's like a dream come true.

I like the view
Of snowy mountains so white and gloomy
So high and pointy
They look like cloud mountains.

Kieran Innes (9)
Barncroft Junior School, Bedhampton

A Cloud

I can be happy, peaceful and calm,
I can help the flowers grow,
I can float around the world all day long,
We all line up in rows.

I can also be angry, annoying and bad,
I can make great big storms brew,
It can be so bad nobody can go out,
You'd better watch out or it'll come after you.

I love the summer feeling,
Blue skies and seas,
My best pal, the wind,
Can make a cool breeze.

People think I'm fluffy,
Especially the birds who sit on me,
I feel famous when they look above,
A bit like Elvis Presley.

Megan Campbell (9)
Barncroft Junior School, Bedhampton

Barncroft Junior School

Barncroft is great
We play games at every break
We put our coats on the hooks
And then we read our books
My teacher's name is Mr Emery
We kids have all the energy
He thinks we're crazy
But we're really just lazy
We never punch
When we're at lunch
My best friend is Taffany at school
She is so, so, so cool
We always eat Smarties
When we're at parties
We always play football after dinner
When we do play we're all winners
After school we play sports
And our parents give us loads of support
We hate doing our SATs test
But we know we can do it because we've been taught by the best
We do loads of plays
And also games
We make perfect pairs
While organising our fairs
There are girls with all their little curls
And there's boys with all their toys
And that's why Barncroft is the best
Even better than all the rest
And don't you forget it!

Chantelle Challis (10)
Barncroft Junior School, Bedhampton

Fairy Queen

The beautiful fairy queen
Of shimmering gold and pale green
And beautiful sparkling wings
Which shine as one flies through the air
She has a diamond crown
And long, blonde hair
Her eyes are so bright and gleaming
Oh, how I wish to be a fairy queen.

Shayleigh-Maye Thorpe (8)
Barncroft Junior School, Bedhampton

As I Was . . .

As I was climbing up a tree
I fell off and hurt my knee
I did not have a parachute
I had a very big boot.

Billy Mellish (7)
Barncroft Junior School, Bedhampton

The Flapping Parrot - Haiku

The flapping parrot
Flaps up and down with its wings
He is very nice.

Louisa Bowden (8)
Barncroft Junior School, Bedhampton

As I Was Climbing

As I was climbing up a tree
I fell and cut my knee
I went to tell my mum
But she blamed it all on me.

Mollie Byles (8)
Barncroft Junior School, Bedhampton

The Galloping Horse - Haiku

The galloping horse
Gallops down the dusty road
Wild, nasty and lean.

Sherralyn Maria Miller (9)
Barncroft Junior School, Bedhampton

As I Was . . .

As I was swimming in the sea
A shark came and bit my knee
I got my head slammed in a door
Then my head felt really sore.

Deacon Clements (7)
Barncroft Junior School, Bedhampton

The Monster Creep

When you go to bed at night,
You may get a monster fright.
A monster is a terrible sight,
I found out it hates Marmite.

Once a monster crept up on me,
It looked as if it drank a cup of tea.
He said he ate a plate of peas,
That rolled down his bumpy knees.

I could tell he like playing with a ball,
A ball of fire, 'cause he was tall.
He was as fat as a bat
And he looked very much like a cat.

He had purple bumps
And loved to find food in dumps.
With big, ugly jaws
And the tallest, sharpest, scariest claws.

Sophie Read (8)
Barton Stacey CE Primary School, Barton Stacey

When I Pulled The Plug

When I pulled the plug,
My sister starts to scream,
'I'm going to meet
A monster spider.'
I just block my ears and shrug.

My mum runs and says,
'Why did you pull out the plug?'
I say, 'I did tell her,
But she did not listen,
So I gave a tremendous tug!'

There was a minute's silence . . .
Then I heard a monstrous chug
And a monster spider came out from under the plug!

Imogen Cooper (9)
Barton Stacey CE Primary School, Barton Stacey

Goblins

The goblins think you're a mouth-watering treat,
They live deep down in the sweltering heat
And have the cheesiest feet.
They're scared of the light,
It gives them a terrible fright.
They sneak out of their house
At the dead of night
And give all the children
A terrible fright.
But thank goodness
For goblin busters,
They chase all the goblins
And tickle them with dusters.
So remember the steps if you're trying to defend,
Your brother or sister or even a friend.
Remember this number,
Call the goblin buster line,
The number is 789!

Peter Goldsmith (9)
Barton Stacey CE Primary School, Barton Stacey

Dreams

Lie in bed, close my eyes
When I dream, I'll get a surprise.
I might dream
About a sunbeam
Or maybe something bad
And I'll be very sad.
I'll dream about my favourite thing
I'll feel so happy, I'll want to sing.
White clouds are floating pillows,
I dream of 'Wind in the Willows'.
Dream about something nice,
Careful, don't get pinched by mice,
Dream about birds flying sky high,
Drifting by in the bright blue sky.

Kelly Lindsay (7)
Barton Stacey CE Primary School, Barton Stacey

My Kitten Maisy

My kitten Maisy, has just caught a mouse,
We found the tail just outside our house.
She pretends to be funny and sweet and soft,
But we know she is evil 'cause she lives in the loft.

My kitten Maisy, is very, very fast,
You can hardly see her when she comes rushing past.
Even though she is small, she has very sharp claws
And whenever you go near her, she always starts wars.

My kitten Maisy, is very, very playful,
Don't try to pick her up, the result will be painful.
She is so stupid that she eats our fish food
And once she even ran into a plank of wood.

So could you understand, please, please, please?
That my kitten, Maisy, is crackers with cheese!

Jodi Marshall (9)
Barton Stacey CE Primary School, Barton Stacey

Food

Food, food is so yummy,
It can fill my big fat tummy.
Ice cream really is the best,
I also like chicken breast.

I would like some chocolate cake
And with that, a big milkshake.
Curry and rice is very nice,
It's hot and spicy, so drink something icy.

Sometimes food escapes my mouth
And goes and lives somewhere down south.
Jumping jelly beans are so funny,
But I still have a rumbling tummy!

James Burgess (9)
Barton Stacey CE Primary School, Barton Stacey

One Night

Olly came to the third tree; he turned around
To see if anybody had opened the door.
Instead of seeing someone opening the brown, wooden door,
He saw a *ghost!*
Olly ran away.
The ghost followed.
Olly could hear the autumn leaves rustling below him on the forest floor,
The ghost was wearing a black robe with a skull brooch on it.
Olly ran through the ghost, back to the door and knocked.
No one answered
And he smote upon the door again, a second time.
Still no answer.
Olly was scared.
The ghost came towards Olly with a knife,
Olly looked up at the sky above and saw the moon,
Tossed about the cloudy seas like a ship on the ocean on a stormy night.

He looked down again,
He was killed that very night.
Every year on that very night,
The moon is tossed about on the cloudy seas
Like a ship on the ocean on a stormy night.
The people of the town
Come together in the town hall and hide
From the ghost of the dead,
From many years ago . . .

Zoe Solle (9)
Bishop Tufnell CE Junior School, Bognor Regis

Whispers Of The Woods

It was cold out there in the dark, damp woods,
She stood under the arches of the old, decaying trees,
The stars were like lanterns in the blue sky,
Strong winds blew in her pale pink face,
Footsteps filled the air, someone was coming.
A scream of pain,
She was scared,
A large figure came out from behind the shadows,
A gold dagger clenched in his hand.
The moonlight shone over him,
His eyes bloodshot,
All she could do was look, look at him.

It got colder and the wind blew harder,
The wind was a torrent of darkness,
It twisted like a tornado,
The moon was hiding behind the trees,
Darkness hung over her, so cold and dark.

The wind, a lion's roar,
She heard a twig break,
The man came closer,
She spun her head round,
His dagger was on her shoulder,
The man took the blade off her,
He was gone . . .
All she could see were the trees and the birds of the woods,
She turned around and left . . .
It was cold,
It was silent,
The fog was all that was left in the dark, damp woods,
The whispers of the woods were gone . . .

Elizabeth Jarvis (9)
Bishop Tufnell CE Junior School, Bognor Regis

The Waiter

He stood boldly in the beams of moonlight
Under the jewelled sky,
As the cantering hooves came towards him,
Over the cobbled ground.
He stared down the rough track,
A black shadow was there,
Darting about in the twinkling drops of the glittering waterfall.
His cloak billowed out in a bleak wind,
As the shadow headed towards him,
Still he stayed there,
Waiting,
Waiting . . .
Suddenly, out of the black, velvety sky,
Came a snow-white horse,
His mane and tail flashing in the moonbeams;
A man was aboard this beautiful creature.
The men stayed there for a minute or two
And the horse began chewing the fresh, green ferns,
As his owner, grunting menacingly,
Handed a sack of money,
To the man who had waited for so long
And in a flash of white light
He was gone.
He stood boldly in the beams of light,
In the dusky, gloomy dawn.
A golden glow spread overhead
As the morning sun rose.
The waiter looked up to the treetops and murmured,
'He came.'
He then vanished into the morning light,
Leaving nothing, but a cloud of dust.

Amelia Waters (9)
Bishop Tufnell CE Junior School, Bognor Regis

The Sorcerer's Spells

Off the warrior went,
The sorcerer to outwit,
His hair, a horse's mane,
Blowing in the gale.

Ages it seemed, until
He reached the decaying castle;
Flying out of an open window,
A bolt flew past.

On he rode,
Over the forest's ferny floor,
Upon the bridge he rode,
The other side to reach.

Open the doors flew,
Out the sorcerer stepped,
Forward the warrior came,
Brave as a lion.

With one great strike,
Down the sorcerer fell,
All the way to the floor,
The sorcerer was dead!

Riding home the warrior went,
When he was home,
He packed his bags
And went away again!

Now he lives in the castle with his wife
And now he has a very lovely life!

Laura Wainwright (10)
Bishop Tufnell CE Junior School, Bognor Regis

The Lost Boy

The child was shaking
From head to foot;
The wind rustled the fern trees;
He stood there silently,
Perplexed and still . . .

The clouds turned as black as the night,
Rain dripped from the top of the trees high above him;
He turned to go back home, but he was lost . . .

Which way should he go?
Could he get back home?
Hard on his face, the rain was beating;
Eyes streaming with tears,
Looking this way and that,
Around the forest's black, old, rotting trees . . .

But a thought kept swimming past his mind,
Wondering, wondering where his mum was,
Though the boy kept on into the night . . .

Charlotte McCarthy (10)
Bishop Tufnell CE Junior School, Bognor Regis

Merlou's Wish

Merlou has a wish,
To swim like a fish,
To fly like a bird,
To sit on a cloud in the sky.

She wishes to get her fairy wings,
To take her to the fairy kings,
She wishes to make,
A famous angel cake.

To have a magic white dress,
To lace her dress with purple lace, which looks a mess,
To live in a chocolate house,
Eat her chocolate pet mouse.

Her wishes came true,
With an extra one too,
Little pink unicorn,
To ride off into the dawn.

Robyn Jankowski (9)
Bushy Hill Junior School, Guildford

Spiders Of Death

They are out to get you,
Why don't you say goodbye,
Unless you know what you're doing,
You will die.

They eat human beings,
They would even eat a clone,
You may escape one of them,
But they never hunt alone.

They are dangerous and fearsome
And you would never know,
If they approached you from behind
To land a painful blow.

They are the deadliest of insects,
At the top of the food chain,
When you shout loudly,
You have elected the way of pain.

Lock all doors, close all windows,
Because they strike at night,
If you don't listen to me now,
You will get a fright.

You will not ever
Want to add them to your collection,
Because when they break out of captivity,
You will need protection.

If you ever see one,
Don't try to run away,
More spider infantries will come,
Nothing will be OK.

They will always kill their prey.

Ben Stevens (10)
Bushy Hill Junior School, Guildford

In The Night

In the misty night not a sound, nothing
Just a sound of music in the town
Thinking hard, no one here
Not even a snake slithering
No one, just me
Every night sitting all alone
No one here, just me.

Sam Wright (10)
Bushy Hill Junior School, Guildford

Am I The Only One?

I feel the grass, it's itchy but smooth,
It gives me a certain freedom,
It gives me a certain groove.

I can hear people's feet touching the ground,
I don't really pay attention, but when I listen,
It sounds like a clapping sound.

I taste the sweet, red, ripe strawberries of the season,
Then I wonder why God created them,
There must be a reason.

I can smell the salty sea,
It actually smells like salt and vinegar,
You see.

In maths I'm rubbish, but you have to think,
If I could just write, my brain in my book,
I would make a good link.

But can I tell you a secret? I have a sixth sense,
It is actually exciting,
I wouldn't say it makes me tense.

I can see things before they happen, in my mind,
Sometimes it's hard to deal with,
As you might find.

I don't know if I should tell and be a freak, all over the news,
But then if I tell I might win
And never lose.

Am I the only one? I would really like to know,
Hold on, I'm getting something,
I'll have the special offer on pizza to go.

I don't know if I'm the only one out there - it's a mystery to me,
I guess if I carry on the way I'm going,
Things will get better - you'll see!

Katie Boyce (10)
Bushy Hill Junior School, Guildford

My Ted

There is Red,
My ted,
The sleepyhead,
Who sits on my toes in my bed.

David Trollope (7)
Bushy Hill Junior School, Guildford

The Three Little Pigs

The three little pigs left their mum,
Their little bodies went frozen numb,
One little pig built a house of straw,
Then the wolf came and he was no more!

Next little pig made a house of sticks,
Then he became sick, sick, sick,
Then the wolf came and gobbled him up,
The wolf burped, *'Glub, glub, glub!'*

The last little pig made a house of brick,
He wasn't thick, thick, thick, thick,
The wolf came and tried to blow it down,
But instead he blew down the whole town!

He went down the chimney but he got stuck,
Because he was covered in muck, muck, muck!
He suffocated and the pig had a bit of him for dinner
And he became much thinner.

Then the pig cut him in half,
Then there were two little pigs,
One of them was big, big, big
And that was mummy pig!

They all lived in the little brick house,
Then they all hunted for the little mouse!

Rebecca McBean (9)
Bushy Hill Junior School, Guildford

The Three Little Bears

Once, there were three little bears
Who liked eating pears.
They went away,
To build their houses of hay,
Oh, the three little bears.

Then the big bad pig,
Who was wearing a silly wig,
Came and blew their houses down
And surely, made them frown,
Oh, the three little bears.

The clever bear made his house of bricks,
But the others made them out of sticks,
The big bad pig blew the stick houses down
And laughed like a clown,
But couldn't blow the brick house down,
Oh, the three little bears.

Harri Findlay & Sathya Kongara (9)
Bushy Hill Junior School, Guildford

The Mystical Box

(Based on 'Magic Box' by Kit Wright)

I will put in the box . . .
The wonderful wonder of winter wonderland,
Love from Cupid, fresh from Heaven,
The sister of silly, seeing the sea,
The mystical magic from the magician's sleeve,
The dodo's feather, smothered in snow.

I will put in the box . . .
A whistle of winter, cold with the season,
The adder abacus, shaped like a snake,
A super snowflake from Santa,
The tremendous talent of my teacher's teaching,
The supreme sleekness of the softest snow.

I will put in the box . . .
Eight songs sung by singers,
The melting moment of a dying auntie,
The last frown of the last, lost dragon,
The horrific horror of a two-headed snake,
The swift slyness of sorrowful Sally.

I will put in the box . . .
A tenth quilt and a blinding light,
A raving rabbit riding a rodent,
A superior sea eel,
The pea from underneath the princess' mattresses
And the pillow from where Sleeping Beauty was sleeping.

My box is fashioned from ice, metal and life,
With wonderful sewing all around the corners,
Padded with leather all inside,
Filled with mystical magic,
It's a magical box and it's mine.

Holly Eade (9)
Bushy Hill Junior School, Guildford

Rapper

Hey, hey, let's write a rap,
I am going to need help, so clap, clap, clap,
Take your time, don't rush at all,
Let's make it echo all around the hall,
Shout it loud or don't shout it at all.

Scott Goodison (10)
Bushy Hill Junior School, Guildford

The Creepy Alphabet

A is for abominable snowman collecting screams
B is for bin monster floating in streams
C is for cyberman shouting *boo*
D is for Daleks chasing Dr Who
E is for Egore stealing souls
F is for Frankenstein playing with dolls
G is for green aliens from the stars
H is for Hipogriff crushing all cars
I is for Igor cooking lovely meals
J is for Jar-Jar Binks riding on wheels
K is for Kracken king of the seas
L is for London ghost who gives you wobbly knees
M is for mummy who eats your heart
N is for ninja who dresses very smart
O is for ogre jumping up high
P is for phantom wailing goodbye
Q is for Quasimodo queuing in the line
R is for red monster looks very fine
S is for soap monster, he steals all soaps
T is for triceratops who tangles with ropes
U is for unicorn who stabs you with her horn
V is for vampire he goes to bed at dawn
W is for witch who rules the west
X is for X-Man who lives in a bird's nest
Y is for yeti who rolls around like a ball
Z is for zombie who can't swim in deep pools.

Thomas Campbell & Ryan Green (10)
Bushy Hill Junior School, Guildford

Serfruiss

Serfruiss, young and brave,
Had always worked as a slave,
He was summoned by the king,
To kill a beetle with a sting
And so he went to the Sahara.

For seven hundred and twenty hours
Serfruiss fought
The dead body was not to be brought,
He killed the beast
And ate it as a feast,
Then the beetle was no longer.

Ryan Flew (9)
Bushy Hill Junior School, Guildford

My Party Invite

Dear Amy,

Everyone will be at my party,
Kate, Rachel, Jack and Barty,
My cousins, my neighbours and my dad,
Even a comedian who is never sad.

There shall be a cake,
Which took three hours to bake,
And a swimming pool too,
So there will be lots of things to do.

Bring me a present all wrapped up,
Just *please* don't buy me a china cup,
And not a girly present because I can guess,
You will probably get me a pretty pink dress.

On Saturday at 3.30pm come to my house,
And don't forget to come in fancy dress,
(You could be a mouse).

Please, please don't forget.

From
The Birthday Girl.

Rebecca Trollope (10)
Bushy Hill Junior School, Guildford

A Nursery Rap

I was walkin' in the wood
When I bumped into Little Red Ridin' Hood
I was meant to see Gingerbread Man
But I bumped into the three little pigs in their van.

I ran into Big Bad Wolf
Playing big bad crazy golf
He said he wanted to eat me
So I ran up the nearest tree
I jumped off the top and went flumpty
And landed on Humpty Dumpty
All the king's soldiers and all the king's men
Chased after me once again.

Thomas Bailey (9)
Bushy Hill Junior School, Guildford

The Three Little Pigs

There were three little pigs,
Who built some houses,
They were all separate,
Little houses.

One made out of straw,
With straw galore.
The next made out of sticks,
Held together with chocolate mix.
The last one made out of solid bricks,
Also made with solid sticks.

The big bad wolf came along,
Blew on the straw house then it was gone.
He blew on the stick house,
Which fell to bits.
The little pigs ran to their
Brother with bricks.

They were safe inside,
The solid bricks.
The big bad wolf,
Blew on the house,
But it didn't fall
To bits.

The big bad wolf
Ran out of breath,
Everyone was happy,
After his death.

The pigs built
A very big house.
And started living
In the country house.

Luke Newman (9)
Bushy Hill Junior School, Guildford

The Three Little Pigs

There were three little pigs,
Who liked eating figs,
It came to a day,
When they had to go away.

Then went to a wood
And saw Little Red Riding Hood,
They went their separate ways
And panicked for days.

They built their huts
And squirrels started throwing nuts,
One was straw and one was bricks,
The other made of lots of sticks.

But what they did not know,
There was a big bad wolf on the go,
It came to the house of straw
And knocked on the door.

'Let me in, let me in,'
'Not by the hair on my chinny, chin, chin,'
'Then I'll huff and I'll puff and blow your house down,
I have permission from a man with a crown.'

Next, he went to the house of sticks
And shouted, 'I love Weetabix,
Let me in, let me in,'
'Not by the hairs on my chinny, chin, chin,'
You know what happened then.

After he came to the house of bricks,
He said, 'I've already blown down the house of sticks,'
He tried to blow the house of bricks,
But he couldn't, not like the house of sticks.

Aaron Murdoch (10)
Bushy Hill Junior School, Guildford

The Leaf

I found a special box
Outside my house.
It was a sphere shape
Made of papier mâché.
There was a hatch - I opened it!

I saw a leaf,
An orange, browny-colour.

I sat on it and it grew.
I found myself on a tree
Then I floated to the ground.
The wind whipped us away
In its airy claws.

I held on tight
The wind dropped me
Down to the fast-flowing river
We floated down, down
To a waterspout.

I was shot into the cloudless sky
And sailed on invisible air.
Suddenly we swooped down
To a muddy hole
And slid down to where we started.

I put the leaf back into the box
Safe and sound.

Katie Reeve (9)
Charters Ancaster College, Bexhill-on-Sea

The Wonders Of The Day

The moon dances in the sky
Until the sun rises in the east
With a golden gleam.

The last star slips silently out of the picture
Leaving a clear blue sky
And the day begins.
The sun shines and rain falls.
From nowhere there appears a rainbow
A great glimmering arc.

At last the sun sets and evening closes in
The moon shines once more
Giving its silver light
And the stars dazzle and glisten.

Then the dawn dreams a wonderful dream.

Patrick Pope (9)
Charters Ancaster College, Bexhill-on-Sea

The Magic Foal

Every morning she nudges me
Shadow the horse, the magic horse.
I found her as the sun fell and the moon rose
And the darkness crept over the land.
I went outside
Owls hooted at me angrily.
Out of the shadow
A flash of light
A foal, a magic foal.
Dragons circled above
Breathing fire
On the once beautiful fields.
Then total silence
Everywhere.

Lily Harrison (11)
Charters Ancaster College, Bexhill-on-Sea

Caterpillar

A glowing, green, furry piece of string,
Munching softly and silently nibbling
Leaves disappearing.
It slowly wraps itself
Into a cocoon
Hard, brown, resting.
Then . . . crack!
Yellow, green
A swirl of bright colours
Flowing everywhere
Fluttering
The butterfly has arrived.

Louisa Kellett (8)
Charters Ancaster College, Bexhill-on-Sea

Water

Water is a snake
Curling around a jagged mountain
Like a knife.
Water is liquid
Running from a silver tap.
It is a smooth blue piece of paper
A wave dancing and roaring
And a glass showing my reflection.

Anthony Donaldson (9)
Charters Ancaster College, Bexhill-on-Sea

The Box Of Dreams

Dark black sides
With crimson lid
Look inside!

A never-ending tunnel
A world of darkness
Nothing but icicles
Made of hopeless evil dreams.
But in the snow that softly falls
Are dreams of hope and love
Each and every snowflake
Making a bright, beautiful carpet
Of soft, crisp snow.

Then the box takes me
Deeper to a volcano.
Hot bubbling lava
A place where beauty and evil
Come together as one great force
Pulling me through the heat.

I hear the birds calling
The breeze blowing through my hair
The water rippling and a tiny stream
Flowing towards a river
Where butterfly fish jump
And dolphins dive.

The trees and mountains are free
And every blade of grass has a voice
As the bright sun rises
Over the snow-covered hills.

Katy Hatter (10)
Charters Ancaster College, Bexhill-on-Sea

The Scared Monkey

The brown monkey
Swings through the trees.
Quickly it stops.
A hunter comes with a gun.
The monkey is scared.
The hunter is quick.
The monkey swings
From the hunter
With his gun.

Benjamin Wilson (7)
Charters Ancaster College, Bexhill-on-Sea

My Birthday

Today is my birthday
My present is a boring box
Which is pale and dirty.

I lift the lid
And then a mighty
Roar fills the room!
I drop the lid
But smoke lifts it again.

I jump back
Two yellow eyes open
It is a phoenix!
A flash of light coming from its ears.

'Wake up. You're late for school!' yells Mum.
'But it's my birthday!'

Declan Mason (8)
Charters Ancaster College, Bexhill-on-Sea

Grace

A sparkly fairy fluttering in the sun
Silver wings, a pink dress.
The most exciting thing I ever saw.
Emerald-green eyes and gold shoes
Creamy skin, a soft, pink pillow
As shiny as the brightest blossom of all.
A rose crown glows on her head
She holds a golden wand
With a star on top . . .
That's my sister
Grace.

George Bentley (8)
Charters Ancaster College, Bexhill-on-Sea

Three Butterflies

Three butterflies gliding through the glittering snow
With their sparkling, golden smooth wings.
They fly smoothly
Through an underwater cave
Covered with silver seashells.
They feel like silk
Running over my face.

James Burton (8)
Charters Ancaster College, Bexhill-on-Sea

The Snowy Emerald Forest

Snow dancing as it falls
From the clouds
Gently onto my hand.
A cold wet kiss swooping
As it lays on the ground
Then quickly melts
As the wind changes direction.

Beautiful trees sway in the breeze
Fresh air comes through me.
As I look around
The trees all smile at me.
The bark of the tree
Is soft and gently
Winks at me.

Beth Shearer (11)
Charters Ancaster College, Bexhill-on-Sea

Sound

Sound echoes across the world
Travelling in waves
Which shrink.

Sound echoes in tunnels
Changing into atoms
Which float.

Sound hisses through the air
Racing, dancing, terrible noises.
But the most beautiful thing in the world
Is sound.

Henry Message (9)
Charters Ancaster College, Bexhill-on-Sea

A Golden Star

A golden star brightly shining
Like a torch in the sky
Sparkling, gleaming, staring.
The star reflects its light
Beautiful and glorious
Shining golden star
Bright as it stands
In the night.

Oliver Platts (8)
Charters Ancaster College, Bexhill-on-Sea

Emotions

It was a small grey cardboard box
Strong emotions were hiding there
Amazing colours!
Red, blue, pink, green, yellow and purple.

Red was moving fast
Blue was weeping
And yellow jumping happily
But pink was calm and smiling.

Green was a mountain
Listening to the wind howling,
While the shiny purple stone
Was gliding through the deep sea.

In each corner of the box
Was the sun shining
With the promise of happiness
Forcing the night to surrender.

Isobel Kellett (10)
Charters Ancaster College, Bexhill-on-Sea

The Mystical Box

I could not sleep
I got out of bed
And saw the box
It started to rattle.
I wondered
What was in it?

Amazing!

It was a dragon
I'd never seen anything
Like it in my life.
Its scales were shiny red
Its claws as white as snow
Its eyes glistened
Yellow and black
Its stomach covered in crystal
And steam streamed out of its nose.

Danny Horton (9)
Charters Ancaster College, Bexhill-on-Sea

Dreams

Evening dreams glide through the starry night
And shine on the moonlit sky and on the rivers
Reflecting upon the dreamless world.

When darkness comes nightmares emerge.
A cold room, a dagger, a witch,
But golden dreams are alive
When angels sprinkle dreaming
Dazzling sleeping powder.

The hills are lighter
The sparkling sun rises
And warms the cold, dreary night.
The dawn appears and dreams fade away.

Jack Kitchen (9)
Charters Ancaster College, Bexhill-on-Sea

Starry Sky

Stars are a dragon's flame flaring in the dark,
Fireflies dancing in the sky.
They are dimensions to other worlds
And balloons floating up high.

Stars are candles lighting a pathway
Flashing light bulbs screwed into the night
They are wishes, which are being granted
And coins sparkling bright.

Stars are lightning bolts heading for the ground
And stars are cats' eyes looking around.

Stephen Kennedy (10)
Charters Ancaster College, Bexhill-on-Sea

Music

Music is gently round like a ball,
A river of notes
And a rainforest,
A rainbow gently swaying
To and fro.
But it is also
Thunder and lightning,
Crashing, clanging
And *banging!*

Sarah Francis (8)
Charters Ancaster College, Bexhill-on-Sea

Fire

Dancing in the night
Shiny orange, ruby red
Golden yellow flames
Hot and flickering
A spitting volcano
And dragon's breath.

Jack Bickers (7)
Charters Ancaster College, Bexhill-on-Sea

My Pets

Muffin is my pussy cat
She always wears her fluffy hat
If she wears it in the winter
She will not get those nasty splinters
From the freezing cold outside.

Tia is my puppy dog
She rolls around like a log
She is a bit loony
And reminds me of Wayne Rooney
The runner Tia.

Bosun is my Schnauzer
He is a big, soppy bouncer
If he doesn't wear his lead
He will not eat all his feed
That is him, my little Bo.

Lucie Mae Wait (11)
Chickerell Primary School, Chickerell

I Have A Pony Called Dreamer

Dreamer is a 13.3hh pony
She is a Newforest cob
She's a lovely tri-coloured
And rides like a star

She wins all the horse shows
And never gets last
Because she is so gorgeous
And is so *fast*

Dreamer has a lovely friend
Her name is Sparkie
Sparkie wins nearly every jumping class
And like Dreamer she hates the name Markie.

Natalie Howes (10)
Chickerell Primary School, Chickerell

Charlotte

Charlotte is small
With really long hair
Two skinny legs
And a face like a bear!

When she opens her mouth
She has teeth like a bunny
And as she smiles
It looks really funny!

She has big brown eyes
At the top of her head
And a tiny nose
Which is usually red!

Her ears stick out
Like a couple of plates
But not as much
As one of her mates!

I can't say who
She'll know who it is
But she's the one
That looks like a satellite dish!

Charlotte Farrell-Gaunt (9)
Chickerell Primary School, Chickerell

The Party

I went to a party
And had a cup of tea.
Then we went climbing,
Up an apple tree.

When we went climbing,
We saw a lark.
Although that doesn't really occur,
We still went to the park.

When we were at the park,
We had a sweet.
Then we sat on a bench
And began to eat.

Now it is home time,
Two hours went so fast!
It is only three o'clock,
No sorry . . . it's really half-past!

Charlotte Cox (8)
Chickerell Primary School, Chickerell

Puppies

I really want a puppy
But Mum and Dad won't let me
I will get one eventually you will see
I hope they will let me.

Hooray, puppy, puppy you are so sweet
So white and fluffy with little black feet
Your tail is so lovely, as white as snow
Oh puppy, oh puppy, I love you so.

Puppy, puppy you are so cuddly
Because your name is Bubbly
Come to me, oh come, come, come
We will have so much fun.

He will race
He will chase
He will lick you on the face
When you are tying your lace.

Jazmine Hepburn (8)
Chickerell Primary School, Chickerell

The Little Flower Fairy

A hot summer, so long, so tiring
Only one little fairy had been buzzing to each flower
She fluttered back not knowing that in her house
Was the king of dark power

When she got home she was grabbed and tortured by Goral
She was bound to the hat stand, hair over her eyes
He asked her questions but all she said was lies

He knew and took her to a prison of darkness
She cried all day, she cried all night
And suddenly there came a tremendous light

Over the gloomy hill, there came a fire-breathing dragon
As bright as a star it came, gliding over the tower
It fought the king and queen of all things sour

It picked up the trembling fairy and took her home
She was so relieved that she made him a jewelled fairy
And now all mystic creatures are wary.

Laurel Simmonds (10)
Chickerell Primary School, Chickerell

The Princess Battle

A summer's day, the princess Jane was out picking flowers
What she did not know was that the North fairy and the Corn fairy
Were watching her from the towers
She suddenly looked up
And they fluttered away
So she felt like going to the park to play
That's when the Corn fairy and the North fairy had the biggest argument
On top of the Houses of Parliament
They shouted and yelled over who should be friends with Princess Jane
The North fairy even said, 'I'm going to be friends with her
Otherwise I will hit you with a cane!'
'I bet you couldn't even pick up a cane!'
'No more than you could!'
'Look you two, you both should
Be friends with me!'
'No way!' they both shouted
I bet if you were there they would be clouted
They were not acting like fairies at all
Even though they were very small
They both had a very loud voice
If you ask me they were not making the right choice
They both went home to think about it
They both didn't want to quit
'Fine!' the Corn fairy said to her
Then she glanced at her shelf
There was a photo standing there of when the Corn fairy
And the North fairy were friends
Their friendship couldn't end
'Fine!' the North fairy said
Lying on her bed
So the next day they made friends
And told each other this wasn't the end
So in the end the Corn fairy and the North fairy were both friends with Princess Jane
And let's just say neither of them were in pain because
Neither of them got hit with a cane.

Lucy Walbridge (9)
Chickerell Primary School, Chickerell

My Dog, Charlie

My dog, Charlie
Looks like a Hovis loaf of bread,
He cuddles up on the sofa and sleeps on my bed.
He stares at the wall thinking he is cool,
But I think he is a fool because he is just a dog.

Victoria Greensit (9)
Chickerell Primary School, Chickerell

Kittens

Kittens in the bathroom,
Kittens on the stairs,
Kittens in the kitchen,
Balancing on chairs.

Some of them are ginger,
Some of them are black,
Some of them are white,
With black patches on their backs.

Kittens are very playful,
Cute and cuddly too,
They like to play with a ball of string,
Pulled along by you.

Kittens in the garden,
Having lots of fun,
They come in through the back door
And then back out they run.

On a damp, cold, winter's evening,
Snuggled on the rug,
My kitten sits in front of the fire,
All cosy, warm and snug.

Chloe Louise Baldwin (8)
Chickerell Primary School, Chickerell

Butterflies

Butterflies, butterflies in the air
Butterflies, butterflies everywhere
As light as a feather
They float around heather,
Butterflies, butterflies in the air
Butterflies, butterflies everywhere.

Butterflies, butterflies in the garden,
Butterflies, butterflies you can't harden,
They're not one colour,
Moths are much duller,
Butterflies, butterflies in the garden,
Butterflies, butterflies you can't harden.

Butterflies, butterflies in the air,
Butterflies, butterflies everywhere.

Jayme-Lee Nutman (10)
Chickerell Primary School, Chickerell

Fizzy

Fizzy is my dog
She always likes to play in the fog,
Apart from when she is being fed
She is sleeping in her comfy bed.

She plays in the mud
And eats lots of flower buds,
When it's teatime
Fizzy like to bark a little rhyme.

She does not mind having a tart
Apart from when she is being smart,
We all love her ever so much
She likes to be touched.

Hannah Woodham (11)
Chickerell Primary School, Chickerell

Wolf From Hell

I hear a noise
I flee to the hills
I see bright green eyes like the headlamps of a car
I run faster and faster away from it
It jumps towards me
I try to run away from Hell
Its nose is twenty-feet long
I fall and scream for help
The wolf from Hell takes one big swipe
I wake up and find myself lying in bed.

Christopher Southcott (12)
Claremont School, St Leonards-on-Sea

Beastie, Are You There?

Beastie, are you there?
Come out wherever you are,
I want to give you a scare,
Are you far?
Are you near?
I will find you,
As I can hear,
I can see you,
Watching now
I'm going to get you,
Watch out!
I'm here!

Emily Wilson (11)
Claremont School, St Leonards-on-Sea

Be Aware Of The Werewolf

Be aware of the werewolf,
He's very big and gorilla hairy.
His favourite food is people,
His favourite thing is to be scary.

His claws are black and sharp and long,
His eyes are gruesome red.
His teeth are yellow and sharp and strong,
He howls when we're in bed.

At dead of night he starts to creep
And tiptoe in the moonlight.
Is there anyone still not asleep?
He's feeling like a bite or two.

So go to bed and go to sleep,
As soon as you're able.
Or you will be in deep heat trouble
In a werewolf's oven.

Nahid Ahmed (11)
Claremont School, St Leonards-on-Sea

Hallowe'en's Herald

Apples falling off apple trees,
Some of the apples rotting
Due to wasps and bees.
Good ones ripped off ready for cooking,
Zzz, snap, snap, bubbling,
The apple crumble ready for Bonfire Night,
But just before was Hallowe'en
You might have had a fright that night!

Autumn draws on,
The trees become bare,
The leaves starting to rot.
As we walk through the orchard,
Leaves crackling underfoot,
Autumn comes to an end,
As winter is just beginning.

Oliver Rowlatt-Brown (11)
Claremont School, St Leonards-on-Sea

The Autumn Days

The summer sun begins to cool
And in September we go back to school.
In playgrounds children gather round
To play with the conkers that fell to the ground.
The leaves now crumple and begin to fall down
Changing colour, to red, yellow and brown
Autumn is a gorgeous season
But November 5th was the day of treason.
Feeling the fun as the first firework flashes,
Followed by rockets, bangs and crashes.
October's the month of Hallowe'en,
When ghosts and witches can be seen.
But better still than all of this
It's time to make my Christmas list.

Sam Bunday (11)
Claremont School, St Leonards-on-Sea

Autumn

Autumn leaves are falling,
Swirling to the ground,
Forming a thick carpet,
In shades of crimson, gold and brown

Gold and yellow acorns,
Berries and scarlet haws,
Ruby apples in the orchard,
The mist hangs low upon the moors

How I love the autumn,
The world is all aglow,
Oh, what a contrast,
To the whiteness of winter snow.

Oliver Slacke (11)
Claremont School, St Leonards-on-Sea

Football

Football is the best game
You win and lose and sometimes you will get the same
Liverpool are the best
I don't care about the rest
I'm watching them on TV
Do you want to watch with me?

Jonathan Lock (8)
Copthorne Preparatory School, Copthorne

Beautiful Dreamer

B eautiful girl in the sky
E ast, west I can see her
A s beautiful as the star
U sually you can see her
T he world loves her
I see her wherever I go
F orever in the sky
U nless you can't see her, look she's over there
L ove her, see her, watch her

D reams of her are beautiful
R ight now, right here, she's over there
E ver in the sky
A lovely girl in the sky
M oonlight shining all around her
E mily her name is
R emember she's always looking after you.

Harriet Brown (8)
Copthorne Preparatory School, Copthorne

The Party

T he party is fun
H ello it's only just begun
E at lots of food everyone

P resents given to me
A nd cards from everybody
R ides at parties are fun
T rifles and cakes are yum
Y elling and cheering, the fun has just begun!

Samuel Lloyd (7)
Copthorne Preparatory School, Copthorne

My Mummy

M y mummy is lovely
Y ou know you have a heart of gold

M y mummy smells of love
U nder my bedcover it's warm like her
M y mummy is sweet and kind
M eadows are green when she steps in
Y our heart will live forever.

Sofia Varela (7)
Copthorne Preparatory School, Copthorne

My Puppy

M um wants a Border terrier
Y appy is its name

P eople in the next road
U sed to have one the same
P lease can we buy him, it will be such fun
P ercy's pet shop, here we come
Y appy eats his food and barks, yum-yum!

James Cornish (7)
Copthorne Preparatory School, Copthorne

My Friends

F riends are funny, I think they are.
R emember the time when we went too far!
I love it when I can go to their house to play
E specially when we get to stay.
N obody likes it when we have no friends
D on't you remember it never ends
S o can't we be friends until the end?

Rebecca Barrie (8)
Copthorne Preparatory School, Copthorne

History

H istory is a wonderful thing to learn
I 've taken a few turns in my time machine
S eeing dinosaurs, Romans and more
T he Egyptians weren't very pleasant
O r the Stone Age - very scary
R eign of Victoria was very long
Y esterday is history now!

Luke Leszczar (7)
Copthorne Preparatory School, Copthorne

Mummy

M y lovely mum is so nice
U nder the tree we sit and read
M ummy takes me everywhere
M ummy plays in the snow with me
Y um-yum her food is scrumptious.

India Mellor (7)
Copthorne Preparatory School, Copthorne

Ancient Egypt

A ncient Egypt
N ice and hot
C ould use a drop of water
I t has a big river called the River Nile
E gypt is very interesting
N ever have you seen so many tombs
T he pyramids are huge

E gypt is where they bury mummies
G ods are there for them to worship
Y et so much sand is there as well
P apyrus paper made with reeds
T hey have scribes that can write hieroglyphics.

Melissa Davy-Ericson (7)
Copthorne Preparatory School, Copthorne

The Clock

T here's something that goes *tick-tock*
H ere's something that goes *tick-tock*
E veryone needs a clock

C locks are sometimes square
L ook at the sundial, what is the time
O ranges are round just like clocks
C ome in, it's time for tea
K eep listening to the clock go *tick-tock, tick-tock!*

Piers Toulorge (8)
Copthorne Preparatory School, Copthorne

My Mum

My mum is wonderful,
She helps me and she is kind to me,
She kisses me goodnight.

My mum is beautiful,
She plays and has fun with me,
She kisses me goodnight.

My mum is special,
She means everything to me,
She kisses me goodnight.

Sophie Miller (7)
Copthorne Preparatory School, Copthorne

My Little Sister

My sister, Hannah, goes jump, jump, jump all day long
Never tires
I think she is the cleverest 5-year-old!
She is always pretending to be an animal
She is good at maths, art and English
She is rather tall, tall like me
Her best friend is little Roselly
She is the best sister ever!

Isobel Youds (8)
Copthorne Preparatory School, Copthorne

My Stepsister

My stepsister is kind to me
She cooks my dinner sometimes
She plays with me
She's 18 years old
She plays on the computer with me
And takes me to the park
She takes me out to eat
And she loves me.

Savannah Hayler (7)
Copthorne Preparatory School, Copthorne

My Grandad

My grandad was in the Second World War
He got hit by a bomb
He was the tenth man left
He gives me cakes if I am good
He takes me to the zoo
No one could ever replace him.

Ryan Holmes (7)
Copthorne Preparatory School, Copthorne

My Granny

Granny, Granny, very handy,
She's got great spirit
With her buying me toys faster than I can run
She is wise and kind.

Harry Hickmet (8)
Copthorne Preparatory School, Copthorne

My Sister, Federica

My sister, Federica is very jolly,
She is sometimes very crazy,
When she is fun, she likes playing with me,
When she is angry, she is so, so bossy,
When she is horrible, she asks me for something
And I say, 'No!'

My sister likes to swim in the swimming pool,
She also is very good at school,
My sister likes to play with her friends,
My sister is nine years old,
She is very nice!

Veronica Williamson (7)
Copthorne Preparatory School, Copthorne

My Nanny

In the mornings we get up and bake cakes
In the night after the last meal, we get a board game out called 'Sorry',
My nanny has just had her birthday
Now she is 59,
When I am cold in the winter, Nanny will light the fire,
I love my nanny a lot.

Joseph Lloyd (7)
Copthorne Preparatory School, Copthorne

My Grandad

My grandad went to war
He survived, he survived
He gave me two medals
He's 89
He hasn't died, he hasn't died.

Jeremy Smith (7)
Copthorne Preparatory School, Copthorne

My Daddy

Daddy is kind,
Daddy is poorly,
Daddy lets me watch TV,
Daddy's leg and back hurt,
When Daddy walks he leans sideways.

Simon Hamead (7)
Copthorne Preparatory School, Copthorne

My Animals

I have a cat called Teddy,
He has a light white tail
And his body is ginger,
When he wants outside,
He is such a whinger!
He is big like a pudding,
He couldn't catch a rat,
Because he's fat,
But he's not blind, like a bat!

I have a dog called Chappie,
Whose old name was Scrappie,
He is scared of the sea,
Especially when it comes to his knees,
He once tried to bite a bee,
Which stung him on the tongue,
He yelped out in pain,
That sounded like he had been hit by a cane!

Romy Sherlock (9)
Copthorne Preparatory School, Copthorne

My Granny

My granny is the best cake maker in the world,
She taught me to play 'Uno'
And takes her time doing everything,
My granny wears glasses,
Granny has curly white hair,
My granny has a walking stick,
Granny has a very small house,
Granny has a very good patterned carpet,
She loves plants and has a big garden.

Samuel Higgs (7)
Copthorne Preparatory School, Copthorne

My Wonderful Mum

My mum is happier than anybody else,
My mum is beautiful like the stars,
When she works, she's as fast as the wind,
She cooks for me when I am hungry,
The next morning, she is active until night,
No one could ever replace her,
I love my wonderful mum!

Joanna Bartholomew (8)
Copthorne Preparatory School, Copthorne

Ellie Fat Cat

My dear, sweet cat
You are so fat
We've put you on a diet
And now you howl all day long
Instead of being quiet
Some say that you're a doorstop
Your body is so wide
You really are massive
You cannot even hide.

I don't know what has happened
You used to be so small
A lovely little ball of fluff
Now you drive me up the wall
The bed's too small for both of us
You take up all the cover
You must be eating somewhere else
I don't know why I bother.

Katherine Parkin (10)
Copthorne Preparatory School, Copthorne

My Dogs

I have two greyhounds
They're called Chester and Flynn
They sit beside me
On my lap there are two chins.
They're always dreaming, grunting in their sleep,
I often see invisible bubbles floating a couple of feet,
Normally in their bubbles I see cats,
Squirrels, mice, meat and rats.
Then, when they wake up,
I'm staring at a cute little pup,
Chester is the pup, with Flynn too,
As I look at them, I fall in love,
It's true!

Ellen Webb (9)
Copthorne Preparatory School, Copthorne

Sharks

Sharks I think are seven feet long
Two feet tall and very strong
Big, sharp teeth and shiny eyes
They jump up high into the skies.

Jordan Van Huis (9)
Copthorne Preparatory School, Copthorne

An Elephant Never Forgets

I found an elephant in my room
I really thought that I was doomed
He was like a huge monster
So I said, 'Get out you impostor!'
When he left I was really glad
Even though he was really sad

The next day I saw him again
'Please don't kick me out
I promise I won't muck about.'
Because he was nice I kept him
After a while I named him Tim
Later that night we watched 'Jaws'
It was so good we gave it applause

So we lived our lives full of laughter
Happily ever after!

Dale Smith (11)
Copthorne Preparatory School, Copthorne

Sailing Race

The wind is strong
We are having fun
The sun is out
The waves are rolling.

We are flying down the course
The sails in an oval shape
Getting wet from the water spray
The wind going through our hair.

Now we have to tack
Going past the other boats
It is an exhilarating sight
We are on the edge.

We can see the finish line
We are going to win!

Jonny Howard (10)
Copthorne Preparatory School, Copthorne

The Antelope - Haiku

Pretty all the time
The antelope is gracious
Running through the wind.

Alexandra Hunter (9)
Copthorne Preparatory School, Copthorne

The Leprechaun

I found a small leprechaun in the garden
I think it must have come from the forest
Because it is damp and green
And four-leaf clovers are still reflecting in its eyes.

I fed it many things
Like grass, onion, dandelion and different fruit
But it stared up at me as if to say,
I do not want food; I'm looking for something else.

I made it a little cave for it to sleep in
It was not like a sea cave but larger,
It is out of place here
And it walks around guilty.

If you believed in it I would come
Walking to your house and tell it in more detail,
But I want you to believe it
And tell everyone to pass.

Camilla Yavas (10)
Copthorne Preparatory School, Copthorne

Choc 'O' Horror

Dripping gooey
Sweet and chewy
Lemon, lime
Take your time

Strawberry laces
Four hundred paces
Pineapple, peach
Just for the beach

Chocolate éclair
For those who dare
Walnut Whips
Lemon dips

Ten minutes to go
Now don't you be slow
The doors will close
On your nose.

Liam Grainger (10)
Copthorne Preparatory School, Copthorne

Winter Poem

Walking on the snowy grass
Watching all the clouds go past
What a lovely snowy day
The perfect time to go and play.

Flying snowballs in the air
One just hit my snowman, there
Now it's time to sledge down the hill
Wrapped up warm against the chill.

The frozen pond, with ice on top
The falling snow will never stop
The long and cold, heavy breeze
The one that pushed back the trees.

Now the orange sun begins to set
Goodbye my friends, I have met
Once the sun has gone, it is dark
Then we begin to leave the park.

Poppy Latham (10)
Copthorne Preparatory School, Copthorne

My Pop

My pop watches TV
I play with my pop
My pop is called Bill
My pop is bald
My pop has a dog called Horace
My pop watches me play PlayStation
My pop is nice
He takes me to the park
My pop wears glasses
He gives me a snack after school.

Jordan Bailey (7)
Copthorne Preparatory School, Copthorne

Peacock

Peacock, peacock with your feathers so bright
Parading around, oh what a sight!
Peacock, peacock your cry can be heard
Throughout the garden like no other bird!
Peacocks, peacocks you are a funny lot
You gracefully swoop to a safe sunny spot!
Peacock, peacock you preen and you peck
Looking for peanuts lying on the deck!

Charlotte Varela (10)
Copthorne Preparatory School, Copthorne

The 200-Mile-An-Hour Dog

My dog Charlie loves to race,
In the park he starts the chase,
But one sad day his fun was to end,
For he got a nasty cut which had to mend.

So we took him to the vet,
Who examined my pet,
Said the vet, 'He'll need a quick repair,
To mend that really nasty tear.'

The vet stitched him up as good as new
And told us what we had to do,
Charlie had to be quiet and still,
Because he was so very ill.

Twice a day Charlie had to take a pill,
So that his leg would heal,
Soon, in time, his leg was good
And he could run as he always could.

I love my pet Charlie, he's my best friend
And I'm very happy that his leg did mend,
Even if he is sometimes a pest,
My dog Charlie, is the best.

Bethany Ward (8)
Crofton Anne Dale Junior School, Fareham

Water

Did you brush your teeth tonight?
Or did you brush your hair?
Did you ever notice, water's always there?

Did you go to the swimming pool
Or in the warm, wet bath,
Or walk by the river,
Like a watery path?

Did you have your tea
With a lovely drink?
Did you wash it down
The slippery, wet sink?

We all have lots of water
Although we have to share
But when you're near water
Always take great care.

Tabitha Wilson (8)
Crofton Anne Dale Junior School, Fareham

The Willow

He moves like a flowing river
Being caught by the wind
His long hair swishing side to side
In the breeze

He's as tall as a giraffe
But as silent as a mouse
His long arms flying everywhere
As if he's mad

His feet are paddling in a pool
He looks as if he's fishing
He's a child splashing in the water
Having lots of fun.

Harriet Wilson (11)
Crofton Anne Dale Junior School, Fareham

Leopards

Leopards fast
Leopards mean
Leopards hungry
Leopards keen
Leopards hunt into the night

Leopard cubs
Leopard males
Leopards big
And leopards frail
Leopards hunt into the night
Kill their prey with one big bite.

Charlotte Knighton (8)
Crofton Anne Dale Junior School, Fareham

My Mum's Big Race

My mum entered a race,
She went rather a long way,
She started at a slow and steady pace
And grew to get fast and speedy,
She was rewarded at the end with a mug,
I saw her go through the finish
And I congratulated her very much,
When we got home, I made her a mug of tea
In her award-winning mug!

Laura Kingston (9)
Crofton Anne Dale Junior School, Fareham

Goodnight

'Goodnight,' said the bird,
'I'm off to my nest,
Winter is coming,
It is time for my rest.'

'Goodnight,' said the squirrel,
'I've had a long day,
Collecting lots of nuts,
So, I am off to my drey.'

'Goodnight,' said the bat,
'I flew around the grave,
So, I must be off to my stony cave.'

'Goodnight,' said the fox,
'I chased a hen,
So I must be off
To my warm den.'

Phoebe Gill (7)
Crofton Anne Dale Junior School, Fareham

My Mum And Dad

My mum makes cakes,
Lots of lovely cakes,
She holds my hand,
She's the best mum in the whole of the land,
She likes pretty lights,
She likes them nice and bright.
My dad fixes things,
I think he is a king,
He takes me out
And about,
They both take me to school,
I think they are both cool!

Amelia Burrows (8)
Crofton Anne Dale Junior School, Fareham

Circle Poem

A circle is an apple
A circle is a hoop
A circle is an orange
A circle is a bottle top
But last of all and most of all
A circle is my head!

Alex Kingston (7)
Crofton Anne Dale Junior School, Fareham

Pudding Problems

There was a pudding eating contest
To be held one afternoon
When record breakers from around the world
Came with a plastic spoon

The first problem came
When half of them didn't like
The chocolate cake that had been picked
Especially that night

And when a pudding had been found
That everyone would eat
The chocolate cake was given
To a charity

The next problem came
When they were all ready to munch
They found the judge had eaten the pudding
(He thought it was his lunch)

And when a replacement had been found
For cake and judge alike
The contestants went back to the eating room
With the staff, Sally and Mike

Then they realised the German contestant
(Sick of looking at fatty food)
Had gone back to his home country
For a diet of salad and stew

So after much money had been spent
On cake as well as staff
The contest was abandoned
And they only refunded half!

Laura Macfarlane (10)
Crofton Anne Dale Junior School, Fareham

Happiness Is

Happiness is . . .
The first lick of an ice cream,
The leaves upon the trees,
The lessons in the classroom,
The honey from honeybees.

Creatures in the countryside,
Splashing in the mud,
Icing inside chocolate cake,
Forever growing buds.

Abigail Hobbins (10)
Crofton Anne Dale Junior School, Fareham

My Little Castle

In my little castle at the bottom of the garden,
I order my servants to bring me food
But all they do is bring me sticks and bark at me,
So I shout, 'You're fired!'

In my little castle at the bottom of the garden,
I order my servants to polish my crown,
But all they do is miaow and curl up on my lap,
So I shout, 'You're fired!'

In my little castle at the bottom of the garden,
My servants order me to make my bed,
Brush my teeth, tidy my room and do as I'm told,
So I say, 'In a minute!'

Beth Sadler (10)
Crofton Anne Dale Junior School, Fareham

My Friends

M y friends are loyal
Y ours should be too

F riends are always forgiving
R eal friends stick with you
I t's really fun to have friends
E verybody should
N othing's better than friendship
D on't you think friends are good?
S pecial friends will be there - remember that, everywhere!

Jessica Macfarlane (8)
Crofton Anne Dale Junior School, Fareham

Fireworks

F antastic fireworks exploding in the sky
I ncredible sparkling colours flying into the sky
R ockets blasting into the midnight sky
E xcited children watch the sky light up
W aiting to see the rockets soar up into the dark sky
O n the grass the bonfire roars, alas Guy Fawkes is no more
R emember, remember the 5th of November
K ind people help the little ones so that they can see the fun
S parklers finish the night off.

Alice Tucker (10)
Crofton Anne Dale Junior School, Fareham

Hair

Big hair
Small hair
Thin or thick
Which one would you want to pick?
Red hair
Black hair
Blonde or brown
Which one would not make you frown?
Knotty, curly
Wavy, straight
Whatever you have you seem to hate!
Bunches, ponytail
Plaits or bun
However it is
It's better than none!

Katie Moya (9)
Crofton Anne Dale Junior School, Fareham

Chocolates

C reamy texture
H eavenly taste
O pen it up and eat it up
C rinkle of the paper
O range, minty, plain and milk
L ick my lips
A nd go to the shop and buy another bar
T ummy rumbling for more
E at me every day
S avour the taste.

Sam Goodsell (8)
Crofton Anne Dale Junior School, Fareham

Sunset Sparkle

S un setting
U nforgetting
N ever too many
S unsets, but
E ven on the brightest days
T he sunset always fades away.

Jessica May Edney (9)
Crofton Anne Dale Junior School, Fareham

I Like Rabbits

I like rabbits,
I think they are cute!
They are all different shapes,
Sizes and colours too.
Some are big, some are small,
Black, brown, white and grey,
With springy legs they like to play.
Some have ears like spears,
Others flop like banana skins,
They have tails like golf balls
And teeth that crunch,
Teeth that munch.
I like rabbits, do you?

Callum Jarvis (8)
Crofton Anne Dale Junior School, Fareham

My Bunny, Honey

My bunny is called Honey
And is ever so funny
She sleeps in my bed
And she cuddles me like I'm her ted
In the morning I hear her yawning
It's oh so boring
That I go to sleep
And she goes leap, leap, leap
So I take her for a walk
And she just bunny talks
I'm still half asleep
And she's digging deep
I tell her off and she nods off.
That's the poem of my bunny called Honey.

Bethany Brown-Pitt (10)
Crofton Anne Dale Junior School, Fareham

The Foxes Who Live In My Garden

My friends, the foxes, love the dark,
Wandering unseen through garden and park,
Searching for food is their goal and aim,
Dustbins, rabbits and chickens are all fair game,
But what can I do now my foxes are tame?
I give them a bowl of dog food each night,
Especially the one who is lame.

Audrey Macleod (11)
Crofton Anne Dale Junior School, Fareham

Flies

Nasty, annoying, vile things
With buzzing sounds that are made by wings
Creatures that will drive you mad
After a day of buzzing they'll make you sad
They fly around all over the place
If they land on your head then wash your face
They're normally around during the summer terms
So watch out, they've got horrible germs.

Erin Faye Harper (10)
Crofton Anne Dale Junior School, Fareham

Dragons

There on swift wings dragon flies,
Through distant and uncharted skies,
Over mountain crags and forests old,
To guard his hoard of hidden gold,
I sought him out and called his name,
He answered with a jet of flame,
'If you be my friend, enter my lair,
If you be foe, then do not dare!'

Alexandra McRobbie (9)
Crofton Anne Dale Junior School, Fareham

I Wish . . .

I wish I was a dinosaur so I would live in the past
I wish I was a cheetah so I could be so fast
I wish I was a bird so I could fly in the air
I wish I was a whale even though they are so rare
I wish I was a penguin so I could survive the cold
But I'm happy how I'm me and I'm seven years old.

Jack Edney (7)
Crofton Anne Dale Junior School, Fareham

The Moon Has Got His Pants On

The moon has got his pants on,
He's dancing in the stars,
Showing off his boxer shorts to Jupiter and Mars,
But he better wrap up nice and tight
Or we will have no light.

Jessica Venn (10)
Crofton Anne Dale Junior School, Fareham

Winter

In the silvery moonlight she creeps,
Flaunting her frozen jewellery,
As she creeps she leaves behind a trail
Of motionless, silvery glaze.

She hears the robin sing his song,
Huddled under blankets of ice,
In the bleak and bitter winter,
Where snowflakes float like downy feather.

The river was glassy,
With skeleton trees scratching the pale sky,
Crusty snow crumbles under frozen feet,
With the icy wind ruffling my hair.

Daisy Paige-Wright (10)
Crofton Hammond Junior School, Fareham

Winter

Winter creeps down the road,
Crystalising windows as it goes,
Crunching footsteps walk along,
Hear the robin sing his song.

Winter freezes hushing trees
And stops the buzzing bumblebees,
Frozen jewellery dangles down
Like the gems inside a crown.

Winter frost clings to grass
Like glistening pieces of glass,
A spider's web turns to lace,
Jack Frost's touch in every place.

Lucy Kimbley (10)
Crofton Hammond Junior School, Fareham

Moods Of The Sea

When the waves crash violently against the cliffs,
It is a crocodile fiercely swinging his tail.
When the ripples roll onto the shore,
It is a mouse gently scurrying onto the golden sand.
When the sea is calm and peaceful,
It is a curled up cat quietly sleeping.
When the waves tumble onto the beach,
It is a tiger prowling towards its prey.

Ruth Leppard (11)
Desmond Anderson Primary School, Crawley

Moods Of The Sea

When the sea is rough and wavy
It is a curious young bear cub getting ready to pounce
When the sea is gentle and calm
It is an eagle landing swiftly on a branch
When the waves are coming onto the shore
It is a penguin smoothly sliding on the ice.

Areepha Osman-Harper (10)
Desmond Anderson Primary School, Crawley

Moods Of The Sea

When the sea is rough
It is like a stampede of elephants
When the sea is calm
It is like a starfish calmly floating on the sea bay
When the waves come rushing in
It is like a dolphin weaving in and out of the waves.

Daniel Wilcox (11)
Desmond Anderson Primary School, Crawley

Moods Of The Sea

When the waves come tumbling onto the shore
It is like a dolphin leaping into the air
When the sea falls asleep
It is like a snake slithering through the jungle
When the tide is racing out
It is like a leopard leaping at its prey.

Jade Brown (11)
Desmond Anderson Primary School, Crawley

Anger

I am full of anger and it's red-hot,
All I can smell is smoke - it really is a lot.
Ow, ow, ow, I taste hot water - boiling hot water,
Now I see a fire and I give it a leer,
Burning, burning . . . I hear burning, it's all I can hear,
Wait, I am on fire, get me out of here.

Max Wright (11)
Dorchester Preparatory School, Dorchester

Fear

Fear is black in the middle,
It tastes like blood dripping down my throat,
It smells like smoke with people smoking in a dark room,
It looks like a person putting a knife into my mum and dad,
It sounds like shouting and screaming,
It feels like a snake putting venom in me.

Charley Lester (10)
Dorchester Preparatory School, Dorchester

Happiness

My joy is yellow, when the sun is shining brightly,
I taste ice cream when my whole world feels such bliss,
When I am cheery, I smell the sweet-smelling scent of the lavender flowers,
Contentment looks like a beautiful summer's day, with a clear, blue sky,
I hear birds tweeting and a little, high laugh, 'Hee, hee,' when I am delighted.

Molly Sullivan (11)
Dorchester Preparatory School, Dorchester

Fear

My fear is black, it has dark silhouettes of men moving in the darkness,
It tastes like pepper grinding in my teeth,
It smells like chilli powder burning away,
It looks like a fire burning everything I own,
It sounds like footsteps coming closer and closer,
I feel like a fragile piece of glass smashing to pieces.

Charlotte Noyes (10)
Dorchester Preparatory School, Dorchester

The Strange Guinea Pig

There once was a young man called Robby
Who had a strange guinea pig called Nobby
They went to the park
Nobby started to bark
And said, 'Can you please call me Bobby?'

Tiffany Smith (10)
Dorchester Preparatory School, Dorchester

Rice The Cat

There once was a cat called Rice
Who thought he could look for some mice
He looked down a hole
All he found was a mole
And now he is covered in lice.

Tom Anderson (11)
Dorchester Preparatory School, Dorchester

Food

Sweet, sour, spicy or strong,
Cheeses with no smell and cheeses that pong.
Broccoli, cereal, cheese and ice cream,
Foods that make us dream and scream.

Fries go with pies but watch out for flies -
Or you will get an awful surprise!

Chocolate is scrumptious,
Chocolate is nice,
It tastes good on its own, but not with spice!

Callum Sykes (10)
Dorchester Preparatory School, Dorchester

Witch Potion To Create Chaos!

'Tis time! 'Tis time, let's mumble the rhyme
Let's make this potion thick and fine!

Tail of wolf and eye of bat
Bite of shark and tiger's fat
Paw of lynx and lava rock
Shock of quake and tooth of croc.

Crushed old slug and dragon's scale
Blood of goat and drinker's ale
Spider's web and old man's skin
Piglet's brain and rotten bin!

Leave the broth until it cools
Then the chaos will start to rule!

Thomas Dodd (10)
Durlston Court School, Barton on Sea

Bring Back The Dead Potion

You will need:
10g of snail slime
One snake tail
Four wolf's teeth
2lbs wing of drake
Newt eye
Eight tiger's claws
4kg chopped-up worms
Four horse's hooves
One spider brain
A helpless baboon's tooth
A cauldron and a blood clot
Hate, murder, death and greed
These are the things that you will need.

Slime of slug and tail of snake
Tooth of wolf and wing of drake
Eye of newt and skin of shark
Buzz of fly and flight of lark.

Tiger's claws and chopped-up worms
Chop them live and make them squirm
Spider's brain and horse's hoof
Helpless baboon, steal its tooth.

Put it all in cauldron hot
Into mixture put blood clot
Murder, death with hate and greed
Add the things that no one needs!

All that you need to do
Is pour the evil mixture over the dead person's grave.

Rowan Palka (11)
Durlston Court School, Barton on Sea

A Witch Spell

You will need:
5g of snails
Four frog's legs
One mouse
2g of louses
5oz of cheese
Handful of worms
Two goats
Lion's fur
One sheep
Three rats
2oz of spiders' fangs
Two dogs
Snake
2g of eyeball slime.

Wait till the clock chimes midnight then you must begin by chanting . . .

Tail of rat and guts of mouse
Wool of sheep and skin of louse
Toe of frog and face of cat
Drool of dog and wing of gnat

Bubble, bubble, toil and churn
Chant and stir until it's firm

Shell of snail and mouldy cheese
The eye of lion and dog's fleas
Spider's fangs and lion's tail
Worm's slime and guts of whale

Bubble, bubble, toil and churn
Chant and stir until it's firm

Grated goat and guts of worm
Chant and stir until it's firm
Eyeball slime and sting of bee
Tooth of goat and wing of flea

Throw it in the cauldron and then wait and see . . .
Before you drink this spell, stir it anti-clockwise three times . . .
This spell with turn you invisible!

Rose Wright (11)
Durlston Court School, Barton on Sea

Gruel And Spice

Ingredients:
Eye of snake
Tail of rat
Mane of lion
Mud in which it grows
Petal of enchanted rose
Spot on person's face
Trunk of elephant
Wool of sheep
Eyelid of cow
Vein of pig
Tail of dog
Grease from wig
Fat of person
Web of spider
Bark of dark
Moss from log.

The potion:
Eye of snake and vein of pig
Tail of dog and grease from wig

Lion's mane and spot of face
Fat of person overweight

Cauldron boiling, we are stirring
We all laugh when we are working

Petal of enchanted rose
Plus the mud in which it grows

Spider's web and bark of dog
Wool of sheep and moss from log

Cauldron boiling, we are stirring
We all laugh when we are working

Elephant's trunk, tiger's tongue
Cat's miaow and howlet's song

Cauldron boiling, we are stirring
We all laugh when we are working

Make your hair change to all sorts of colours!

Ellen Parsons (11)
Durlston Court School, Barton on Sea

The Witches' Spell

You will need:
One shark's fin
One rat's tail
One dog's toe
One ml of mice blood
A medium sized snail shell
A spider's fangs
Lion's tail
Crab's claw
Scorpion's sting
Lion's roar
Bat's wing.

Fin of shark and tail of rat,
Toe of dog and face of cat.

Blood of mouse and shell of snail,
Spider's fangs and lion's tail.

Claw of crab and scorpion's sting,
Roar of lion and a bat's wing.

Mix it gently, in a pot,
Making sure it's very hot!

Do make sure it's very thin,
Rub it gently on the skin.

It will go into the skin . . .
And poison the person who it is in!

Alexander Mitchell (10)
Durlston Court School, Barton on Sea

Spiders

I like spiders
Cute, small, beautiful beds of silk
And in their gorgeous home
They eat flies
How delicious!
I have a pet spider
His name is Neat
And I think he and his friends
Are really sweet!

Saskia Prabhavalkar (8)
Educare Small School, Kingston Upon Thames

Spiders

I hate spiders
Spiders are scary
Spiders are hairy
Spiders have eight legs
They have shiny black eyes
They hang off the ceiling
They eat little insects
I hate spiders
They are so ugly
The despicable pests
They leave cobwebs everywhere
They scare my hair
They go on my bike in the night
I hate spiders!

Jordan Tonico (9)
Educare Small School, Kingston Upon Thames

Spiders

I like spiders
They're black
On their back
They're friendly
And they're good
Would I like a spider?
They're ever so small and nice
Would I like a spider?
I surely would!

Helen Rice (10)
Educare Small School, Kingston Upon Thames

Spiders

I like spiders
I love spiders
Spiders are nice
Spiders are funny
Spiders are silent
Spiders are quick
I love spiders
They are cool!

Sammy Hough (8)
Educare Small School, Kingston Upon Thames

Spiders

I love spiders
My favourite type of mini-creature
They're nice and friendly on their little webs
From their silk they make webs for themselves
But they are very, very silent
One body plus eight legs
Plus one head
Equals one lovely spider!

Tobias Blackmore (8)
Educare Small School, Kingston Upon Thames

Spiders

I hate spiders
Spiders are creepy, spooky and quick
Shivers run down my spine
I hate spiders
Because they are scary, ugly and fast
One could never make me laugh.

Arthur Vie (8)
Educare Small School, Kingston Upon Thames

A Journey To The Ancient Tomb

On a dark, spooky night,
There was a terrible fight,
I ran away till I entered a room,
Inside an old, ancient tomb.

It dropped down spikes when you stepped on cotton,
If it hits you, you'll turn rotten,
It smells sandy,
Sprinkled with a bit of candy.

Suddenly I heard in the room,
Chains rattling in the entrance of the tomb,
I fell on a wall with a bit of glue,
Which made me remember that I had the flu.

My face went blue,
Which gave me a clue, to the tomb which was blue,
It reminded me of the tomb,
In my dream which made me scream!

Rohith Muhundan (9)
Elmhurst Preparatory School, South Croydon

A Racing Car

My favourite car is a racing car,
On the track it is very fast and goes far,
It refuels in the pits,
That's where it sits.

My favourite thing goes *vroom!*
No, it isn't a broom,
It pushes cars back,
All over the track.

My favourite thing is red,
Which makes the drivers go to bed,
It is shiny and slick,
I bet it can do some tricks.

I like the smell of petrol fumes,
My radio plays cool tunes,
It feels metallic to the touch,
As the driver moves the clutch.

My favourite thing reminds me of running in a race,
At a fierce pace.

James Oakley (9)
Elmhurst Preparatory School, South Croydon

The Alien Jedis

The alien Jedis are fierce and scary,
With faces that are long and hairy,
Some people say that they're cute and cuddly,
But I think they're weird and ugly.

Their lightsabers are scary,
But are they made out of jelly or Grandad's belly?
They come in different sizes and shapes and colours,
There's so many to say,
But please be scared or they'll rip off your head,
Or even worse, make you dead.

I think of my dream,
It is them,
But will they come back again?

George Webber (8)
Elmhurst Preparatory School, South Croydon

The Jungle

Deep in the jungle the lions roar
And the scream of a monkey because of a boar.

It stinks of sweat and animals dead
And with flies all over the deers' head!

The air is salty from the lake,
But there never is a snowflake.

Rough leaves scrape the animals rushing past,
The last animals follow the path.

Wild animals drink on the riverbank,
Big and small there is never a blank.

Christopher O'Sullivan (9)
Elmhurst Preparatory School, South Croydon

A Journey To Space!

A journey to space is a lovely place,
It's so cool that you must leave school,
Come to space because there's so much place to play.

Some children say that aliens are ugly and scary,
But really they are just friendly,
I say they are small and tall
But others say they are lazy and crazy,
But I think they're just fine.

The stars twinkle so beautifully,
Just like the moon shines so lovely.

Satbir Mann (8)
Elmhurst Preparatory School, South Croydon

Elmhurst School

Elmhurst is the best school,
Even though it's not that cool!
Everyone's cheerful and loves to smile
And we used to have a boy in our class called Kyle.

Out in the playground I play football,
But sometimes I bang my head on the brick wall,
I get up and I carry on,
Until the bell goes *ding-dong!*

Oliver Selby (8)
Elmhurst Preparatory School, South Croydon

All About Seasons

My seasons are very beautiful,
With some spring water gurgling pools,
My seasons have bushes with thorns
And the day the wolves were born.

In the summer people eat fish,
With curry and rice mixed in a dish,
In that warm, great sun,
You can hear the bang of a gun.

In the winter blocks of ice fall below,
While children play in the flaky snow,
In that cold, fun, snowball fight,
Polar bears crunch the snow in the night.

In the spring the leaves that are lost reappear,
In bright colours for the rest of the year,
In the day the sun is bright
And cold cool air will fill the night.

In the autumn the leaves fall down,
The floor is covered with colours,
These leaves decorate the ground,
Such a long way, that it spreads all around.

Daniel Nash (8)
Elmhurst Preparatory School, South Croydon

The Watering Hole

The animals come parading to the watering hole every day
Where the baby cubs like to play.

The lion pride lies in the shade
And what a big pride they have made.

All the baboons look for a termite
And when they do they take a bite.

The hyenas giggle and laugh
Whilst the elephants have a big massive bath.

A vulture's head has such a fluffy feather
And a giraffe's neck feels like leather.

A zebra's fur is black and white stripes
And a gazelle's horns look like pipes.

Max Beeson (9)
Elmhurst Preparatory School, South Croydon

My Pets

My pets don't look funny,
But I must mention my bunny,
He's as small as a ball,
But likes to be friendly and tall.

My two fish are called Bubble and Squeak,
One is very strong and the other is quite weak,
I've also got a precious python,
Who wants to run the London Marathon.

I've got a small hamster,
Who's not a vicious gangster,
He has a nice personality,
But his cage has not got enough gravity.

Lastly, my cat, he's left in the shed,
I'm really sad that he's dead!
Every day I go solemnly there,
So I can say my sad prayer.

Joseph Hart (9)
Elmhurst Preparatory School, South Croydon

Underwater Life

Nothing compares with the sea,
Because there are wonderful sights to see,
From the coral lands,
To the seabed of sand.

The water looks very clear
And the whales and sea creatures you will hear,
All the amazing underwater lands,
With lots of different coloured sands.

Squids as big as houses
And fish as small as mouses
Pirates sailing the seven seas,
Seaweed that looks like bees.

Spanish ships with valuable gold,
The Swallow and Amazon sailing so bold.

Johann Perera (9)
Elmhurst Preparatory School, South Croydon

A Seaside

I sit on the sandy beach,
I drink my bubbly soda and eat my peach.

I dream of going on a trip,
I would like a pirate ship.

I walk on the rocky stones
And find some pirate's bones.

I may have a clue
That there is some treasure too!

Pavan Murali (8)
Elmhurst Preparatory School, South Croydon

I Saw A . . .

I saw a parrot going vroom, vroom,
I saw a motorbike squawking,
I saw a dog running weirdly,
I saw a leopard solving a puzzle,
I saw a cheetah walking past,
I saw an elephant going fifty miles per hour down the road,
I saw a man cry,
I saw a child riding a kite,
I saw a balloon get peeled and eaten,
I saw a banana swing on trees . . .
All as I was walking past.

Brandon Kilkenny (10)
Epsom Primary School, Epsom

I Saw

I saw a teacher chase a mouse,
I saw a cat talk about maths,
I saw a man shriek loudly,
I saw a rat marry a lady,
I saw a dog laugh happily,
I saw a girl chase a rat,
I saw a cow run around,
I saw a boy eat grass,
I saw a drum visit the bees,
I saw a fly dance to the beat,
All as I was writing in class.

Nicole Batchelor (10)
Epsom Primary School, Epsom

I Saw

I saw a mountain licking itself,
I saw a cat covered in snow,
I saw a seed being fired,
I saw a gun being planted,
I saw a flag on TV
I saw Ant and Dec moving in the wind,
I saw a cake driving down a field,
I saw a car being eaten,
I saw a guinea pig eating a bone,
I saw a dog having its cage cleaned,
I saw a lion flying south for the winter,
I saw a duck eating meat,
I saw a calculator rolling in the mud,
I saw a pig doing sums,
I saw a horse eat a leaf,
I saw a snail win the Derby,
I saw a DJ eating honey from a pot,
I saw a bear mixing tunes,
I saw a pencil being drunk,
I saw a bottle being sharpened,
All as I was doing my work.

Tommaso Grant (10)
Epsom Primary School, Epsom

I Saw A . . .

I saw a clown puffing out smoke,
I saw a chimney ride a unicycle,
I saw the sun splash on the window,
I saw a raindrop pour its rays on the ground,
I saw a feather give people food,
I saw an air hostess float to the ground,
I saw a dolphin melt in the sun,
I saw a snowman leap into the air,
I saw a tooth being cut up,
I saw a cake chew the food,
I saw a balloon steal the treasure,
I saw a pirate float in the air,
I saw a mum climbing a tree,
I saw a child cook the dinner,
I saw a lion flutter on a leaf,
I saw the butterfly eat a deer,
All as I was writing in class.

Rachel Valentine (10)
Epsom Primary School, Epsom

My Poem

I saw a clown with long hair,
I saw a girl with a red nose,
I saw a frog fly into the sky,
I saw an aeroplane jump into the pond,
I saw a peacock splash on the window,
I saw a raindrop made of metal,
I saw a tiger eaten by a boy,
I saw an apple running after the deer,
I saw a cottage in the sky,
I saw a balloon made of wood,
All as I was in class.

I saw a dolphin run a race,
I saw a horse living underwater,
I saw a boy in the garage,
I saw a car walk to school,
I saw a muffin in a cage,
I saw a budgie being eaten,
I saw a child with fruits,
I saw a plant dancing in the rain,
All as I was in class.

Ravneet Jandu (11)
Epsom Primary School, Epsom

I Saw A . . .

I saw a train scream with anger,
I saw a clock speed and hoot,
I saw a child strike ten,
I saw a football joke and laugh,
I saw a raindrop get kicked out the park,
I saw a snowflake drip from the sparkling tree,
I saw a monkey peeking through the clouds,
I saw a man jump from tree to tree,
I saw a circus clown in a night club,
I saw a golden eagle doing flashy tricks,
I saw a mother pig fly in the lovely summer breeze,
I saw a baby bird giving birth,
I saw a woman having her first flight,
I saw a small child dance gracefully,
I saw a cloud talk its first word,
I saw a snake in the shape of the letter Y,
I saw a cow slide through the grass,
I saw a frog pick some grass,
I saw a madman swim underwater.

Alasdair Henderson (10)
Epsom Primary School, Epsom

I Saw A . . .

I saw a frog ride a motorbike,
I saw a Buddah jump into a pond,
I saw a machine with a fat belly,
I saw a snail speeding away,
I saw a Ferrari going so slow,
I saw an orange rev its engine,
I saw a box get juiced,
I saw a cow fall apart,
I saw a dog get milked,
I saw a cat bite a postman,
I saw a fish jump out a tree,
I saw a fly jump out the water,
All as I was working in class.

Connor Phillp (11)
Epsom Primary School, Epsom

I Saw . . .

I saw a policeman chase a herd of deer,
I saw a tiger shine up in the sunlight,
I saw the sun howl at the moon,
I saw a wolf juggling with laughter,
I saw a clown stomp through the jungle,
I saw an elephant which looked venomous,
I saw a snake oink very loud,
I saw a pig jump up and down,
I saw a kangaroo fly high in the sky,
I saw a bird make honey,
I saw a bee milking a cow,
I saw a farmer solve a crime.

Theham Subhan (11)
Epsom Primary School, Epsom

I Saw . . .

I saw an angry dog feed its babies,
I saw a bird dancing in the rain,
I saw a girl injure a rabbit,
I saw a leopard pick up a baby,
I saw a nurse cook some eggs,
I saw a chef rushing to his mother,
I saw a puppy cuddling her teddy bear,
I saw a toddler swaying in the wind,
I saw a rose driving down the road,
I saw a car chase a mad cat.

Ana Paula (10)
Epsom Primary School, Epsom

I Saw A . . .

I saw a horse on fire,
I saw a house run in a race,
I saw a chair chase a boy,
I saw a dog being sat on,
I saw a frog teach a class,
I saw a teacher jump in the lake,
I saw a ghost go shopping,
I saw a lady scare a man,
I saw a lemon ride up the road,
I saw a bike being squeezed,
I saw a baby drink a pint,
I saw a man in a cot,
I saw a fox on a leaf,
I saw a snail chase a rabbit,
All when I was working in school.

Thomas Edwards (10)
Epsom Primary School, Epsom

I Saw A . . .

I saw a pig teaching lessons,
I saw a teacher lay in mud,
I saw a bat drinking booze,
I saw a man sucking blood,
I saw a blues group having a date,
I saw a couple singing late,
I saw a frog having a fight,
I saw a cross man eat mites,
I saw a cow being great,
I saw a boy being straight,
I saw a man running a race,
But suddenly a pole went splat in his face,
I saw a mouse chase a cat,
I saw a dog chase a rat,
All as I was working.

Thomas Glynn (11)
Epsom Primary School, Epsom

Happy Deepavali

Lamps light up
Again in brilliance
As Deepavali draws near
To gather happy reflections
For another treasured year.

Pirunthuvy Sriselvarajah (10)
Epsom Primary School, Epsom

I Saw . . .

I saw a mother pig do a somersault in the blue ocean,
I saw a great white shark camouflaged in the brown sticky mud,
I saw a slithering snake munching on some cheese,
I saw a famished mouse glowing in the darkness,
I saw a poisonous scorpion rolling in the mud,
I saw a fat hippo dancing gracefully,
I saw a beautiful lady pounce on a wild pig,
I saw a black spotted leopard diving underwater,
I saw a feisty frog trotting calmly through the sparkly green grass,
I saw a golden horse gliding through the summer air,
I saw a powerful silver falcon juggling red balls of fire,
I saw a circus clown leaving its slimy silver trail of slime,
I saw a slow slug chasing a fast and innocent cat,
I saw a dangerous bulldog driving a furious red car,
I saw a sports driver giving birth in a barn,
I saw a sheep.

Avinash Ramrakka (11)
Epsom Primary School, Epsom

I Saw . . .

I saw a baby bird tuttering with its mouth,
I saw a rabbit scream and shout,
I saw a man turn into bright colourful shapes,
I saw a cloud gliding on ice,
I saw a swan running about the place,
I saw a waitress cracking its shell,
I saw a snail having a pillow fight with boys,
I saw a girl getting stuck in a web,
I saw a fly making fun of a monkey,
I saw an ape quacking about on a pond,
I saw a duck rolling in dirt getting dirty,
I saw a pig cheering at a game,
I saw a cheetah stomping around,
I saw a giant galloping around a field,
I saw a horse learn to fly by flapping its wings.

Chloe Sale (10)
Epsom Primary School, Epsom

I Saw . . .

I saw a clown eat grass,
I saw a monkey with massive shoes,
I saw a golden eagle climb from tree to tree,
I saw sharp grass fly in the lovely summer breeze,
I saw a cheetah wave in the hot sun,
I saw a multicoloured bird run as fast as the wind,
I saw a frog glide in the air,
I saw a muscled man leap high and land in a pond,
I saw an enormous dragon lift up heavy weights,
I saw a dog breathe burning fire,
I saw a white shark bite a terrified cat,
I saw a madman swim in the deep blue sea,
I saw a baby with a sharp silver knife,
I saw a frog cry with hunger,
I saw a cat jump high,
I saw a cow climb a huge tree.

Andre Leitao (11)
Epsom Primary School, Epsom

I Saw A . . .

I saw a fish climb a gigantic tree,
I saw a hungry leopard kissing a man,
I saw a woman drinking milk from a bottle,
I saw a baby eating some grass,
I saw a cow blooming in the sunshine,
I saw a rose floating in the sky,
I saw a cloud dancing in the moonlight,
I saw a lady twinkle in the midnight sky,
I saw a star swim in the crystal clear water,
I saw a mermaid hatch out of an egg,
I saw a baby bird glide in the sky,
I saw an eagle fly side to side in the sky,
I saw a plane swim in the ocean,
I saw a dolphin drive into a wall,
I saw a car swimming underwater.

Louise Bushnell (10)
Epsom Primary School, Epsom

I Saw . . .

I saw a planet blooming in the sunshine,
I saw a dog spinning around in space,
I saw a tortoise barking angrily at the thief,
I saw the sun eating healthy vegetables slowly,
I saw a leopard beaming brightly in the sky,
I saw a boy scratching an old tree viciously,
I saw a giraffe riding his mountain bike rapidly,
I saw a butterfly reaching high up the tree,
I saw the moon flutter gracefully in the sky,
I saw a rainbow shine in the sky brightly,
I saw a monkey with seven bright colours,
I saw a baby bird climb a gigantic tree,
I saw a cat trying to learn how to fly,
I saw a girl chase a terrified mouse,
I saw a shiny star pick bright, beautiful flowers,
I saw a rose twinkle in the night sky.

Micha Nirsimloo (10)
Epsom Primary School, Epsom

I Saw . . .

I saw a hungry dog hunting a lion,
I saw a young man carrying its joey,
I saw a springy kangaroo driving a sports car,
I saw a doddery man flap its wings,
I saw a colourful butterfly build a nest,
I saw a blackbird twinkling in the sky,
I saw a sparkly star win a golden medal,
I saw a pretty girl eat a dead whale,
I saw a hammer shark remove its skin,
I saw a slithery snake playing with a puppy,
I saw a white kitten shining in the sky,
I saw a twinkling star bloom in the grass,
I saw a purple tulip play football,
I saw a four-year-old boy skipping in the garden,
I saw a three-year-old girl chasing a cat.
I saw a . . .

Gurveen Jandu (11)
Epsom Primary School, Epsom

I Saw A . . .

I saw a cat chew a sweet,
I saw a man chase a rat,
I saw a clown chew a bone,
I saw a dog with a red nose,
I saw a chicken eat hay,
I saw a horse eat chicken seed,
I saw a dragon fly,
I saw a butterfly breathe fire,
I saw a house very cold,
I saw a mountain burn,
I saw a plane skip,
I saw a girl drop bombs,
I saw a boy grow,
I saw a seed learn,
I saw a turtle go fast,
I saw a car go slow,
As I was working in class.

Jack Cliffe (11)
Epsom Primary School, Epsom

My Poem

I saw a man breathing fire,
I saw a dragon swimming in the pool,
I saw a bomb walking in the sun,
I saw a zebra falling from the sky,
I saw a clown eating a zebra,
I saw a lion at a party,
I saw a frog running the marathon,
I saw a woman sitting on a lily pad,
I saw a monkey swimming in the sea,
I saw a fish hanging off a tree,
I saw a child being eaten,
I saw a deer skating on ice,
I saw a family being milked,
I saw a cow buying a house,
All as I was writing in class.

Nilema Khanam (11)
Epsom Primary School, Epsom

I Saw A . . .

I saw a teacher playing darts,
I saw Andy Fordham teach a class,
I saw a tree run into a wall,
I saw a dog 12 feet tall,
I saw a bird 2cms high,
I saw a worm touch the sky,
I saw a sale make a mess,
I saw a child at DFS,
I saw a book make a bed,
I saw a mum being read,
I saw a boy spin a web,
I saw a spider hit his head,
I saw a CD playing getting a whisk,
I saw a cake playing a disk,
I saw a man who saw these too,
He said they were weird but all were true,
All as I was working in class.

Rechard Rawoo (10)
Epsom Primary School, Epsom

I Saw A . . .

I saw a fish kiss a man,
I saw a woman eat some grass,
I saw a cow blooming in the sunshine,
I saw a rose learning to fly,
I saw a swallow having baby piglets,
I saw a pig fall out of a pear tree,
I saw a leaf learn to walk,
I saw a small child run a race,
I saw a greyhound looking like a princess,
I saw a girl laying eggs,
I saw a hen sprint after a mouse,
I saw a cat floating in the sky,
I saw a cloud dancing in the moonlight,
I saw a lady drinking from a bottle,
I saw a baby swimming in a pool.

Rachael Balchin (11)
Epsom Primary School, Epsom

My Poem

I saw a teacher jump in the pond,
I saw a frog teach the class,
I saw a person snoring,
I saw a pig exercising,
I saw a horse eat a worm,
I saw a bird in a race,
I saw a cat working,
I saw a man eat a mouse,
I saw a child sing in a concert,
I saw a pop star playing in the playground,
I saw a dog with a kilt,
I saw an old lady chase a cat,
I saw a baby with long hair,
I saw a woman drinking a bottle,
I saw a man playing dressing up,
I saw a girl going fishing.
All as I was in class.

Emma Fraser (10)
Epsom Primary School, Epsom

My Poem

I saw a prince eat a mouse,
I saw a cow sit on a throne,
I saw a car graze some grass,
I saw a snowball driving on the motorway,
I saw a fridge melt,
I saw a girl freeze some meat,
I saw a bird put on make-up,
I saw a snake flying,
I saw a pen slither on the ground,
I saw a plant ink some writing,
I saw a bomb grow petals,
I saw a teacher explode in the street,
I saw a leopard mark some books,
I saw an orange pounce on its prey,
I saw a man get peeled,
I saw a cat chop wood,
All as I was writing in class.

Chloe Simons (10)
Epsom Primary School, Epsom

I Saw A . . .

I saw a tree roll over,
I saw a pig learn to fly,
I saw a bird hit a tree,
I saw a bus explode,
I saw a grenade run like mad,
I saw a man blossom in the sun,
I saw a rose hunt mice,
I saw an eagle get blown up,
I saw a tank dance,
I saw a princess spread rapidly,
I saw a fire crash,
I saw a plane jump high,
I saw a frog open wide,
I saw a book tell the time,
I saw a clock get chopped down.

James Wild (11)
Epsom Primary School, Epsom

The Last Leaf Of The Autumn Tree

When I got up this morning
In the shining sun.
The last leaf of the bare tree,
Simply drifted down,
Onto the apple green grass.
Waving goodbye to the lonely tree
A mighty gust of wind
Blew the leaf away.
After the leaf floated in the air,
It safely landed
Onto a high hill.
Then a young boy walked up the hill,
And kicked the leaf off the edge.
It flew off to the breezy water,
The breezy water waited there,
Searching for a tide.
The leaf started to rise
And got washed away with the tide,
Ending up on the sandy shore
Gasping and panting for breath.

Jack Sharpe (11)
Fair Oak Junior School, Eastleigh

The Four Seasons

Spring is the first season
It's lovely and calm,
It sometimes rains a little
But it does us no harm.

Summer is next
It's nice and hot,
Everyone plays outside
We go to the beach a lot!

After that it's autumn
It starts to get colder,
The leaves fall from trees
Everyone is older!

Last of all it's winter
It's Christmas time,
It is also very cold
And the church bell chimes.

Hattie Waldron (10)
Fair Oak Junior School, Eastleigh

My Dog!

There once was a dog called Snoopy
Who really was quite daft
He would run around the house
After he had had a bath.

He didn't like the lightning
It made him hide and howl
He didn't like the Hoover
It made him run and growl.

He liked the taste of bathwater
And licked your wet feet dry
Then jumped up on the side
To eat your chicken pie.

At the end of the day
He'd go to sleep
On the floor right by my feet.

Hannah Bray (10)
Fair Oak Junior School, Eastleigh

Winter

In the winter you can feel
Snowballs hitting your chest like a rubber duck
An icy wind freezing your face
Snowflakes falling and melting on your hands
Water frozen by the cold night air
The warmth of your winter coat against your body.

In the winter you can hear
Screams and shouts of excited children
The wind howling through the trees
Bare trees creaking from the wind like a cello
Dead leaves crackling beneath your feet
Cars skidding along the road like out of control horses.

In the winter you can smell
The turkey roasting in the oven
New perfume wafting out the bathroom window like a puff of smoke
The cold air drifting up your nose
Candles lighting up your dinner table.

In the winter you can taste
Minuscule snowflakes dripping onto your tongue like rain
Hot chocolate trickling down your throat, warming up your entire body
The icy wind swooping into your mouth like a hurricane
The warmth of your Sunday roast in your tummy.

In the winter you can see
Children playing in the snow like mad cats in your house
Snowflakes falling all around you like balls of fluff
Trees swaying in the wind like the Mexican wave
The grass frosted up from the power of Jack Frost.

David Fisher (10)
Fair Oak Junior School, Eastleigh

After The Battle

Poisonous clouds choke the air,
Flies fight over rotting bodies,
Unfinished games of cards lie waiting to be continued,
Once joyful bodies hang limply, like rag dolls, on rusty barbed wire,
Confused horses wander the empty wasteland,
Fires blaze on uncontrollably,
Giant water craters drown dead men,
A half eaten piece of bread sits on a muddy table,
Thousands of families lie weeping in their homes,
All their lives will be changed forever.

Peter Mills (10)
Fair Oak Junior School, Eastleigh

A Wave's Journey

Trickling over the sand's hot face,
The sparkling summer sea cascades over the glistening, peaceful beach.
Frothing, bubbling, tickling every golden grain,
It twists and turns before falling back into the depths.

Floating effortlessly, a vast, diving eagle, past snowy mountain tops and sand dunes,
It swoops, glides and glistens past jungles of algae and seaweed,
Jungles where sharks are predators and everything else must be prey,
A ferocious game of wit and skill is taking place for no one can know where the enemy is lurking,
in a shady corner where the sun's golden gleam cannot reach?

But on then the sea must flow into deep, cavernous caves,
Through jet-black hideouts and demons' caves,
And over the barren landscape of dread.

Then over the crystal clear rainbow of coral and darting fish,
The jewels of the ocean in their diamond palaces,
Fiery red, sunny orange, starry yellow, vivid, poisonous green and sweet, subtle lilac and indigo.

Then the monstrous sea dragon skims back onto the sandy beach,
But is sucked suddenly and forcefully into the droughted sand.
But nobody knows nor cares,
For this is a busy world,
Too busy to worry about something as tiny and imperfect,
As a small, helpless wave.

Rachel Carter (11)
Fair Oak Junior School, Eastleigh

My Big Hairy Brother

My big hairy brother
Hear his mighty yawn
As he stamps, as he stomps on the kitchen floor
There's a party over next-door's house,
Everyone's there
Granny, Grandad and the grumpy old mare
There's balloons and crackers,
Chocolate and cakes,
Ice cream, jelly and banana milkshakes
My big hairy brother
Bends his knobbly knees
Thumps his hairy chest
As he dances with Denise!

Hannah Smyth (11)
Fair Oak Junior School, Eastleigh

Clouds Of Candyfloss

Drifting softly through the sky,
Clouds of candyfloss float by,
In high winds they rush along,
Dancing and singing their merry song.

Jumping over mountains high,
Gathering speed and on they fly,
Hanging over murky lakes,
Carrying out the journeys they make.

Suddenly the clouds gather together,
There is going to be a slight change of weather,
Bang!
Cymbals crash,
Bright lights flash,
And the rain lashes out.

The black clouds fade to grey,
And the rain slowly dies away,
The clouds turn back to candyfloss,
And the sun comes out to play!

Alice Vanstone (11)
Fair Oak Junior School, Eastleigh

Night

The night is a magician,
Ready to put on a show.
With a flick of a wand gleaming stars appear,
The sun slips away behind a dark cloth,
The moon appears to help the magician begin.
Dove magicians hang suspended waiting for their cue.
The audience watch breathing silently,
As owls hoot their song, and
Mice tiptoe across the long stage.
Children in night clothes,
Ready for bed are
Watching the doves do their part.
The show is now coming to an end.
Goodnight, goodnight is said
As they climb into bed.

Gemma McGregor (11)
Fair Oak Junior School, Eastleigh

The Butterfly

She's stuck in her own making,
Imprisoned in her cocoon.

Suddenly she breaks out free,
Prancing, dancing elegantly.

As colourful as a parrot's feathers,
Sparkling like thousands of diamonds.

Flutter, flitter, flitter, flutter
Sings the rainbow coloured butterfly.

Elegantly gliding through the air,
As the wind gently strokes her wings.

She floats down like a feather to rest,
Then she flutters off again.

Soon she will come to a rest,
But her spirit will endure.

In her little one's new life
Shh . . . flitter, flutter, flitter!

Jessica Jelley (11)
Fair Oak Junior School, Eastleigh

Autumn

The crisp, lively leaves rustled in the wind
I began to see the beginning of autumn
The wind scraped back my hair
I could see the ducks skating on ice
It made me feel as cold as a polar bear in the North Pole
The frost lay settled on the soft, dewy grass
Paths were smothered in red and golden coloured leaves
Trees reached out their long, pointy hands
As if they were going to grab me.
The plants, which were withered, glistened
As the sun began to rise
I could hear birds singing their lively songs
And could smell the fresh breeze flustering over me
Soon the lovely views will be covered in a soft blanket of snow
And all the trees and plants will have shed their leaves
Ready for the beginning of winter.

Stephanie Easton (10)
Fair Oak Junior School, Eastleigh

Hurricane!

The sun goes in
Clouds race across the sky,
Sky gets gloomy
Wind howls through the trees.

Rain shatters from the clouds,
As the wind forms,
A swirling, destructive twister
Until the rain is a flood.

They name the hurricane
Animals go silent,
Trees collapsing to the ground
Hear petrifying screams.

He pounds down the buildings
Cars thrown into the air,
But everything goes quiet
As the hurricane dies away.

Bethan Walker (9)
Fair Oak Junior School, Eastleigh

Children

Children, children, everywhere,
Screaming, shouting they don't care.

Playing games and having fun
Swimming, eating in the sun.

Laughing, dancing on the grass,
Learning, learning in the class.

As I look they're reading books,
And staring at their silly looks.

Fighting, biting, doing stupid writing,
Playing with the lighting.

How I love to see them play
Laughing, singing every day.

Meghan Phillips (10)
Fair Oak Junior School, Eastleigh

Dreams

I have a dream,
That I'll fly like a bird,
Stand up for my rights,
And make myself heard.

I have a dream,
That everybody is treated alike,
All animals live,
Like dodos, whales and pike.

I have a dream,
That oil does not exist,
And nor pollution,
Or litter, on goes the list.

I have a dream,
That snakes will keep their skin,
Tigers would keep their fur,
And hyenas keep their cheeky grin.

I have a dream,
That recycling bins were number one,
And so were bottle banks,
Dropping litter would not be done.

I have a dream
That trees were left standing,
And would not hit the ground,
With a terrible landing.

I have a dream,
That giant pandas were free to roam,
And everyone was warm and dry,
And had a friendly family and home.

I have a dream . . .

Chloe Osman (11)
Fair Oak Junior School, Eastleigh

Waterfall

The waterfall collides against the rocks,
A rampaging beast cascading over the cliff,
Before being tossed high in the air like an acrobat tumbling,
The hazy droplets of crystal splinter off the chalk rocks,
Tumbling, plummeting into the emerald waters below,
Bubbling into a whirlpool washing machine,
Forming a cloud of spray captured in the sun's grasp,
Drifting into the river beyond.

Hollie Callaway (10)
Fair Oak Junior School, Eastleigh

The Cold Winter Breeze!

The cold winter breeze:
Imprisons the trees of the thickening deep,
Passes the moonlit sky that covers over the warming sunset,
Freezes the clear meandering stream,
Travels past the shimmering glittery stars.

Glides through the lapping waves of the ocean,
Flies through the lashing downfall of snow,
Chases the crackling rainbow leaves,
Sweeps the swirling snowflakes onto the frosted glass windows.

Dances through the beckoning cornfields as they settle in the frost,
Travels through the beam of the moonlight,
Washes away the warm, radiant, luminous, summer air,
Murders the searing, blistering sun.

Kidnaps the foliage as they cry out,
The fluorescent, white clouds now damp, grey sponges,
Creates misery and illness,
But escapes before spring arrives.

Laura Archer (11)
Fair Oak Junior School, Eastleigh

The Storm

The storm is an angry football team after losing a match,
Storming back to the changing rooms,
Causing the ground to shudder violently,
Windows are smashed,
Trees fall down,
The lightning flashes,
And the thunder booms,
The children scream,
Their parents run,
But as the storm dies down,
The lightning hides,
The power lines recover,
People get back to their normal lives,
All is well in the now busy city,
Until their next defeat.

Beth Adams (11)
Fair Oak Junior School, Eastleigh

Senses!

I can see:
A great rainbow, arching gracefully through the sky's open arms,
A glorious sunset, over the laughing hills, painting the horizon as it giggles.
A roaring ocean, smashing into the brave, strong cliffs, destroying all in its murderous path,
And a velvet, midnight sky, covering the Earth lovingly, the only chinks of light coming from the distant stars.

I can smell:
Freshly cut grass, cleansing your nostrils as you breathe in the strong aroma,
Salty sea air, whipping and lashing out at you, biting and stinging you as soon as you inhale,
New, clean air, as pure as an instrument's long note, like mountain air, so sweet it is hard to take,
And the inviting smell, leading you uncontrollably to a delicious feast to devour at your own pace.

I can hear:
A fierce wind, harshly whistling in my terrified ears or a calm breeze rustling through the peaceful trees,
Waves crashing against the cliffs and the cry of sea-dwellers, battling with its home,
Leaves, frosty, crunching beneath my numb feet, cackling as they brush against each other,
And a forest symphony, conducted by the king of the jungle, the lion, while the rest create a harmony underneath.

I can touch:
A soft, eiderdown feather, resting on my tickled hand, stroking my happy palm lovingly,
Silk, as soft as a puffy, white cloud, so smooth and shiny like an ice rink just refurbished,
Animal fur or hair, as warm as a flame, encasing their bodies, a furry coat,
And clear, tranquil water, which, the moment you touch it, ripples breaking the frozen picture it has made.

I can taste:
Crispy, ice-cold snow, dripping on my shivering tongue,
Rain, so cold, that my teeth ache and chatter as it spatters the ground around me,
Chocolate, so warm and tasteful, melting in your joyful mouth,
And hot, pleasurable soup, gulping it down as it burns your insides and makes them tingle.

Content with all the world.

Laura Carter (11)
Fair Oak Junior School, Eastleigh

The Wave

The wave is wishing, wishing, wishing,
Wishing for a beach.
The wishing wave is watching, watching,
Watching for a beach.
The wishing wave is wondering,
If the beach will make things right.
The wave is wondering, watching and wishing,
And sees a glimmer of hope.
The glimmer of hope is a glitter of sand,
A beach has come in sight.
The wave descends to meet the sand,
The wave's no longer lonely,
But the sand cuts through the wave and sea,
And says goodbye forever.

Alastair Bassett (11)
Fair Oak Junior School, Eastleigh

Teacher Teacher

Teacher,
Teacher
Look at me
My best friend
Watches Dragonball Z.

Teacher
Teacher
Look at her
Her face is covered
With my kitten's fur.

Teacher
Teacher
I'm so bored
I'll buy a Ferrari
That you can't afford.

Teacher
Teacher
On the hay
I'll buy a hen
That's on eBay.

Ronel Kiyanga (11)
Gilbert Scott Junior School, South Croydon

My Family

I thought my dad was an agent
I don't know why
Or maybe he's a spy.

I think my mum is pretty
She always laughs and cries
She drops us off and picks us up
And gives us a big surprise.

I think my brother's crazy
He's so lazy,
He runs around the house,
Thinking he's a mouse.

I think my grandad is a policeman,
He drives a black and white van,
He always picks me up and throws me around,
And catches me whenever he can.

And me, I'm Whitney, I'm funny and pretty,
And as you can see very very witty.

Whitney Mendoza (7)
Gilbert Scott Junior School, South Croydon

Aliens

The aliens start off as eggs
Then face huggers emerge with eight legs,
And then they jump on someone's face
Then in that case
A chest burster comes out
And turns into a big alien no doubt.
With teeth as sharp as nails
And wiggly tails
They come from Hell.
Tell everyone our armies have fell
Then the queen alien nests down
And is in charge of the alien crown.
The eggs are laid in the hive
Nothing stays alive.
The horror lies in there,
For the aliens do not care,
That's the story of the aliens.

Bobby Hall (8)
Gilbert Scott Junior School, South Croydon

Quickly, Quickly

Quickly
Quickly
Don't want to wait
Legoland is gonna
Open the gate.

Quickly
Quickly
Let's get in line
I'm not being last
One more time.

Quickly
Quickly
Let's look around
The Lego man
Is in the playground.

Quickly
Quickly
I want to play
Make the most of it
It's only one day.

Quickly
Quickly
I don't want to play
It's time to go home
'Cause it's the end of the day.

Kiarn Eslami (10)
Gilbert Scott Junior School, South Croydon

Magic Lock

Once I saw a magic lock
On a door below a clock.

I tried to open it but it was stuck
I was out of luck
I went to bed
And I was fed.

I woke up in the morning
And I was yawning.

I went to see the lock
And the lock was not there.

I went down the stairs
And found it there.

Ria Willis (8)
Gilbert Scott Junior School, South Croydon

Teacher, Teacher

Teacher,
Teacher,
Are you sick?
You must go home
Awfully quick.

Teacher,
Teacher,
Where's my book
Over there
Go and look.

Teacher,
Teacher,
The bullies are here
Hurry over
They're pulling my ear.

Teacher,
Teacher,
In your car
Go and drive
Somewhere far.

Teacher,
Teacher,
Come back soon,
I need you
For the afternoon.

Toni Rogers (11)
Gilbert Scott Junior School, South Croydon

Hula Skirt

Behold the lion, big and hairy,
Not the slightest bit scary,
Dancing daintily like a fairy.

Does his hula skirt seem too small?
Does he always seem to crawl?
Is his dance the tiniest bit cool?

Does it matter? He always makes money,
Because he is ever so funny,
Dancing like an Easter bunny.

Chloe Chapman (9)
Gilbert Scott Junior School, South Croydon

The Day The PC Broke Down

It was worse than a volcano, worse than a boil
It was even worse than cod liver oil
Without it life is such a toil.

The day the PC broke down.

It was very very mad
My brother was sad
My mum was apparently glad.

The day the PC broke down.

My sister hit the ceiling,
My dad knew how she was feeling,
My mother was apparently gleaming.

The day the PC broke down.

Tarnya Grover (11)
Gilbert Scott Junior School, South Croydon

Dog On Skates

Behold the dog furry and sweet,
She thinks she has really big feet
But then she thinks she's lost the beat.

Do her skates seem too small?
Does she think she's going to fall?
Will her helmet slip at all?

Does it matter? There she goes
Joyful as a happy rose,
Skating on her lovely toes.

Shannon Mills (10)
Gilbert Scott Junior School, South Croydon

Wig

Behold the pig, nice and big,
Always comes out to have a dig,
With his silly and funny wig.

Does his wig seem too fat?
Will he feed it to a cat?
Does it look more like a rat?

Does it matter? There he goes,
Wiggling his happy nose,
Smelling a very lovely rose.

Ryan Murphy (9)
Gilbert Scott Junior School, South Croydon

The Day That The Computer Broke Down

It was worse than sprouts, worse than tomatoes
Worse than very old mouldy Cheerios
Worse than the supermarket when it had closed.

The day that the computer broke down.

My cousin attempted to try and nurse it
But in the end I tried to reverse it.
Then I threw up and had a big fit.

The day that the computer broke down.

I cried and cried for ever and ever
I screamed my heart out, 'Never, never.'
The computer I had was really clever.

The day that the computer broke down.

Nana Asare (10)
Gilbert Scott Junior School, South Croydon

The Day That My Laptop Broke Down

It was worse than a dog scrap, worse than a fight,
Worse than a horror film giving me a fright,
Worse than my mum in a car turning right.

The day that my laptop broke down.

My uncle said he would fix the screen,
We were all very sad, and very keen
My auntie said she would give it a clean.

The day that my laptop broke down.

My mum said, 'It has the flu'
We said, 'We are bored, what can we do?'
'Get creative with shapes, glitter and glue?'

The day that my laptop broke down.

Tara Bruce (10)
Gilbert Scott Junior School, South Croydon

Today I Saw

Today I saw a greedy pig,
On my kitchen floor.
Before he ate all my food,
I chased him out of the door.

Teresa Ward (10)
Gilbert Scott Junior School, South Croydon

The Day That The School Broke Down

We jumped for joy
But there was a boy
Who wasn't full of joy.

The day that the school broke down.

The boy rang a gas man but when he came he went insane,
The boy said, 'Oh the pain!'

Another gas man was rung
And he came along,
Cheerily singing a song.

The day that the school broke down.

The boy cried, 'Oh the pain
It's come back again,
And it's driving me insane.'

The day that the school broke down.

We all said, 'Don't be mad
Cos we'll feel sad'
But now he's gone bad!
The day that the school fell down.

Charlie Day (11)
Gilbert Scott Junior School, South Croydon

The Day That My Computer Broke Down

It was worse than a dog scrap, worse than a fight
Worse than a horror film giving a fright
Worse than a giant cobra's deadly bite.

The day my computer broke down.

My dad said he would fix the screen
My mum wasn't too keen
My mum said she would give it a clean

The day my computer broke down.

Our mum said, 'Don't worry there's homework to do,
Or something creative like glitter and glue.'

The day my computer broke down.

Stephanie Nash (11)
Gilbert Scott Junior School, South Croydon

The Day That My Computer Broke Down

It was worse than snake bites,
Worse than no sign of lights,
Worse than an itchy pair of tights.

The day that my computer broke down.

I tried to give it aid,
I even gave it shade,
I then brought in the maid.

The day that my computer broke down.

My mum told me not to panic, there's work to be done,
I said, 'No I'd rather sit on my bum,
OK I'll do one silly old sum.'

The day that my computer broke down.

What should I play for the rest of the day?
I will be bored for the rest of May,
Maybe I'll work and earn some pay.

The day that my computer broke down.

Raenée Awoonor-Gordon (10)
Gilbert Scott Junior School, South Croydon

The Future

The future has flying cars
Can instantly heal horrible scars.
A cure for the common cold,
And has never heard of green mould.

The future might not be great
Can't sing or can't skate.
The future might have a horrible fate
We might be slaves or can't hang around with your mate.

The future we never know,
It might be sunny or might just snow.
The future could be low
Everyone eaten by big crows.

The future is a mystery
Might have to build spaceships and flee.
So let the future be a big surprise
All I want is to win the number one prize.

Zawdie Campbell (11)
Gilbert Scott Junior School, South Croydon

Post

Letters to cousins, aunties and uncles
Pizzas, packages and different parcels

All arriving at the crack of dawn
Newspapers thrown all over the lawn

Here comes the prize from the cereal box
Dad's been waiting for the shed door lock

My birthday cards should be coming soon
I've been waiting ages and ages now it's noon

I wonder when my bike will arrive
My mum's special honey straight from the hive

The milkman comes and delivers my juice
My baby brother's little stuffed moose

The Chinese food is at the door
Crispy seaweed I really deplore
My grandpa's fresh breath, peppermint spray
My puppy's here, hip hip hooray.

Here comes the letter for Emily's party
My sister's paint set is really arty.

So much post, too much for me
There's heaps of it, can't you see?

Minda Lising (11)
Gilbert Scott Junior School, South Croydon

The Day My Computer Broke Down

It was worse than a storm, worse than a fight
Worse than a horror film that gave me a fright
Even worse than a really scary night.

The day my computer broke down.

My mum attempted to give it first aid
We told it we loved it and it's name was Jade
We gave it a funeral, we knelt down and prayed

The day my computer broke down.

My dad said, 'Don't worry, there's some washing up to do,
Or go do something creative with paint and glue,
And just for that there's some ironing too.'

The day my computer broke down.

Casey Lowin (10)
Gilbert Scott Junior School, South Croydon

The Day That The Computer Broke Down

It was worse than cabbage, worse than sprouts,
I'm not lying, without any doubt.
Worse than a war and worse than a flout.

The day that the computer broke down.

I tried to give it mouth to mouth
But in the end I just walked out
When my mum started to shout.

The day that the computer broke down.

I couldn't do my homework
Or fix my purple skirt,
My mum suggested to do some housework.

The day that the computer broke down.

I needed to be calm
I touched my palm
And went to the shop to get some balm

Today the computer broke down.

Melisa Parchment (10)
Gilbert Scott Junior School, South Croydon

Deliveries

Newspapers, packages, parcels and post
They all arrive while we're eating our roast

Letters, leaflets, for Mum and Dad
Pizza fliers, it's just mad.

Can you hear a knock on the door?
Maybe it could be someone I adore

Oh salespeople, salespeople selling stuff!
They make life hard and very tough

Again another knock on the door!
It's going on and on, more and more.

Great milk, orange and fresh tea!
Delivered, just for me!

Deliveries are truly sometimes great
But only if they're on time and never late!

Tara Marsh (10)
Gilbert Scott Junior School, South Croydon

Over Here, Over Here

Over here, over here,
Pass the ball
Have a shot at the goal
Before that boy makes you fall.

Over here, over here,
Dive to the left,
Don't let the ball
Go in the net.

Over here, over here,
I'm in some space,
Give me the ball,
I'll pass it to Mase.

Over here, over here,
A little flick,
I'll score a goal,
With just one kick.

Over here, over here,
Off to Jack's,
To have a party,
'Cause we won the match.

Jack Barber (11)
Gilbert Scott Junior School, South Croydon

Milkman

Here comes the milkman delivering milk
Let's hope it's creamy and as soft as silk.

There's milk for everyone and for kids,
I hope he has tightened all the lids.

They rattle and rattle
Like a herd of cattle.

But no one stops the milkman I know
I hope he drives safely and very slow.

He drives all morning
Without one warning.

He drives when it's sunny, even when it's blue,
It's hard to decide who to deliver to.

Leah Cunningham (10)
Gilbert Scott Junior School, South Croydon

Teacher, Teacher

Teacher, teacher
Got here late,
Mum was in a rush
Putting food on the plate.

Teacher, teacher
Had to feed the fish
And after that
I had to do the dishes.

Teacher, teacher
I am here.
On my way
I saw a deer.

Teacher, teacher
My head hurts,
I am going to be sick
On my favourite shirt.

Teacher, teacher
Oh goodness me,
I don't know why
My friend turned into a flea!

Jamie-Lee Martin (10)
Gilbert Scott Junior School, South Croydon

The Postman

Here comes the postman delivering the mail,
Not knowing he's leaving behind an awful trail.

Postman, postman, please give me a letter
I was ill but now I'm better.

Postman, postman, give me the mail,
Or I will put you in jail.

Letters for the rich,
Letters for the poor
Oh here he comes now knocking on the door.

Dwayne Williams (11)
Gilbert Scott Junior School, South Croydon

Mother, Mother

Mother, Mother
Got to dash
But before I go
Can I have some cash?

Mother, Mother
I've been hurt
And I've got mud
On my favourite skirt.

Mother, Mother
I'm eleven
It feels only yesterday
That I was seven.

Mother, Mother
I want a puppy
Chocolate brown
I'll call it Duffy.

Mother, Mother
Something's there
It's pulling all of
My lovely hair.

Mother, Mother
Hold my hand
I don't want to go
On the sand.

Sidney Rose (10)
Gilbert Scott Junior School, South Croydon

Rain

It's raining,
It's pouring,
It's in the morning.

It's raining,
It's pouring,
So playtime is boring.

It's raining,
It's pouring,
I'm so tired I'm snoring.

Shelley Ahmad (8)
Gilbert Scott Junior School, South Croydon

Teacher, Teacher

Teacher
Teacher
Where's my book?
Look over there
On the hook.

Teacher,
Teacher
On the wall,
Look at me
I'm going to fall.

Teacher,
Teacher
Is so cool,
Swimming far
In the pool.

Teacher,
Teacher,
Why is it me?
Well try and be good
Until tea.

Teacher,
Teacher,
Look at me,
I am turning into
A chimpanzee.

Rosie Weston (11)
Gilbert Scott Junior School, South Croydon

Sound

I like the sound of TV
Just like I like ice cream.
I wonder what it sounds like
To be on a football team.

I think it might be,
Very, very loud,
Cheers helping me on,
Coming from the crowd.

Benjamin Lloyd (10)
Gilbert Scott Junior School, South Croydon

Takeaway Man

He's got to deliver the delicious curry,
So off he rushes in a desperate hurry.

Now he's got to deliver a pizza,
All covered in his favourite meatsa!

Now he is definitely lost
This is going to make him cost.

He has got to find a phone really quick
But he knows his boss will give him the kick.

Bradley Hall (10) & Jack Dunn (11)
Gilbert Scott Junior School, South Croydon

Aeroplanes

Aeroplanes go so high,
Aeroplanes drop from the sky.

Aeroplanes land on the ground,
Aeroplanes found a pound.

Aeroplanes have got a big nose,
Aeroplanes have got a little rose.

Jack Greenwood (8)
Gilbert Scott Junior School, South Croydon

Top Hat

Behold the fly, small and shy
Flying in the sky so high,
In its top hat and little tie.

Are his hands very hairy?
Is his beloved called St Mary?
Does he think all humans are scary?

Does it matter? There he goes,
Flying with his little nose
Hopeful as a morning rose.

Kimberley Tugwell (9)
Gilbert Scott Junior School, South Croydon

Witches' Brew

(Based on Macbeth)

Double, double, toil and trouble
Fire burn and cauldron bubble.

Rotten dung of a dog, tail of a dragon, guts of a whale, an eye of a frog,
A nail of a hippo, a muscle of a human and an elephant's foot cut with a chainsaw,
All fingers of a newborn baby, body of human with the bones.

Double, double, toil and trouble
Fire burn and cauldron bubble.

A horse's head cut off with a stag beetle,
Eye of newt, a head of a dragon squashed with a wagon, rotten eye of pig,
Wing of bat cut with a knife, ear of rabbit.

Sonny Cripps (9)
Goldstone Primary School, Hove

The Witches' Evil Spell

(Based on Macbeth)

Double, double, toil and trouble
Fire burn and cauldron bubble.

Leg of spider, eye of snake,
Face of tarantulas, head of dragon,
Guts of human wriggling like worms.
Poisoned blood of scorpion caught in the desert,
Heart of goat still pumping blood,
Tooth of shark still bleeding.

Double, double, toil and trouble
Fire burn and cauldron bubble.

Stir and drink this potion o' mine,
You will not be feeling fine!

Emily Dobbs (8)
Goldstone Primary School, Hove

Untitled

Cauldron bubble but no trouble
A headless spider ridden by a tiger
Legless spider floating on a tiger
A dog's tail red as blood
Scabs cold as ice
A boy's knee scraped on a tree
A woman's hand.

Katie Cander (8)
Goldstone Primary School, Hove

A Witches' Spell

(Based on Macbeth)

Double, double, toil and trouble
Fire burn and cauldron bubble.

Burned brain of Venus flytrap from the grass in midday,
Scale of seven-headed serpent dragon pulled out with my teeth,
Crazy, dangerous car acid from a living,
Evil car, stolen from the tank in a gutsy way.

Double, double, toil and trouble
Fire burn and cauldron bubble.

The scaphoid bone of a human,
Howlet's wing,
Cat's whiskers,
Adder's fork,
Bat's venom,
Lizard's legs,
Crocodile's teeth,
Rattle of a rattlesnake,
Goat's horns and elephant's nose.

Double, double, toil and trouble
Fire burn and cauldron bubble.

Battered wings of a butterfly,
Blackbird's heart black as a bomb,
Tooth of a fox,
Dripping paint, sharp and dazzling.

Double, double, toil and trouble
Fire burn and cauldron bubble.

Caterpillar eye taken during transformation,
Squid's tentacle and dolphin's fin.

Double, double, toil and trouble
Fire burn and cauldron bubble.

Alexander Matthews (8)
Goldstone Primary School, Hove

The Witches' Spell

Scale of dragon, tail of rat,
Zombie's brain and a black bat.
Double trouble, pig's brain cut off with a knife.
Witches playing with people's lives.
Double trouble mix with ingredients.

Jimmy Dereas (8)
Goldstone Primary School, Hove

Witches' Spell

Tail of a dog chopped with an axe,
Head of a lion cut with a chainsaw,
Eye of a baby stabbed with a dagger,
Rotten guts of a pig, rotten brain of a shark,
Heart of a lizard stabbed with a dagger,
Leg of a cow chopped with an axe,
Rotten blood of a dog, eye of a goat,
Rotten tongue of a snake red as blood,
Bladder of a lion chopped out with a rock,
Enjoy, live or die.

Josh Emery (8)
Goldstone Primary School, Hove

A Death Spell

(Based on Macbeth)

Petrol-soaked mosquito,
Brain o' baby drowned in swamp,
Goblet o' fire collected at midnight.
Tooth o' a wolf grey as the moon dipped in blood,
Poison of a cobra, green as the jungle collected at dawn.

Double, double, toil and trouble
Fire burn and cauldron bubble.

Tail o' a scorpion black as night,
Acid of a car, radioactive gas spread on a green scorpion.

Double, double, toil and trouble
Fire burn and cauldron bubble.

James Evans (8)
Goldstone Primary School, Hove

The Witches' Spell

Double, double, cauldron bubble,
Fire burn which makes cauldron bubble.
Tongue of warthog ripped out with a fork.
Fillet of fenny snake in the cauldron boil and bake.
A bleeding heart of a bird pulled out with my right bare hand.
Bloodthirsty brain of a goat caught in the foggiest fog.
Head of toad as mouldy as cheese that's been in a cupboard for a year.

Kirstin Holloway (9)
Goldstone Primary School, Hove

The Ingredients For A Potion

(Based on Macbeth)

Sharp tongue of warthog got with a fork,
Moulted body of tarantula scooped with a stork.
Rotten finger of strangled babe done by vicious bloodthirsty dog,
Burnt brain of goat got in the foggiest fog.

Double, double, toil and trouble,
Fire burn and cauldron bubble.

Horrible head of dead teacher,
Spot of puss with crawling creature.
Spine of snake fresh out of the skin,
Full belly of child starved till thin.

Double, double, toil and trouble
Mix and stir, drink and die.

Shannon Kelly (8)
Goldstone Primary School, Hove

Untitled

Beating heart of a pig, head of a yellow toad,
Brain of white goat, screaming toad, its heart is beaming.

Double, double, toil and trouble,
Fire burn with cauldron bubble.

Skeleton rot on his trot, full of skeleton snot
Tooth of a wolf scooped out with a spoon.

Double, double, toil and trouble
Fire burn with cauldron bubble.

Cool it with a baboon's blood,
Then the charm is full and good.

Georgia McDonnell (9)
Goldstone Primary School, Hove

The Horrible Poem

Double, double, toil and trouble
Cats go miaow but cauldron bubble.

Paw of cat, slice off with a knife,
A mouldy tooth of the wolf which fell out of his mouth.
A heart of a tiger that melts in the pot,
The skin of a lion scraped off with a scraper.

Michaela Newing (9)
Goldstone Primary School, Hove

Witch's Spell
(Based on Macbeth)

Double, double, toil and trouble
Fire burn and cauldron bubble.

Half-eaten heart o' pig, that a stranger dug,
Guts o' elephant, bladder o' lizard,
Scale o' crocodile stolen from the Nile.

Double, double, toil and trouble
Fire burn and cauldron bubble.

Wing o' crow as black as night,
Eye o' child scooped out in the light,
Tail o' rabbit, mushy guts o' piglet stolen from a vet.

Double, double, toil and trouble
Fire burn and cauldron bubble.

Nose o' dog, fur o' polar bear as white as snow,
Tail o' kitten, beak o' swan,
Battered wing o' butterfly stolen from nature.

Double, double, toil and trouble
Mix and stir as the cauldron bubbles.

Rebecca West (8)
Goldstone Primary School, Hove

The Witches' Spell

Tongue of pig ripped off by fork,
Head of mouldy fish, pecked off by a stork,
Scattered remains of babe, collected by light of moon,
Rotten eye of kitten scooped out by a spoon.

Double, double bubble and trouble.

Scale of lizard, tail of rat,
Blood soaked by vampire bat,
Broken heart of wounded bird,
A terrified scream which nobody heard.

Double, double bubble and trouble.

Small brain of mouse, horn of rhino, beating heart of dino
Rotten skeleton rattling in the dark,
Spider legs all mangled up for a witch's spell,
Frog's tongue and cow's dung,
Fillet of fenny snake,
Claw of crab, fire of phoenix, mix, mix, mix.

Nathan Cooper (8)
Goldstone Primary School, Hove

Tudor Times

The Tudors are good, the Tudors are bad.
I'm glad that I wasn't around in the Tudor times.
Some were poor, some were rich,
The poor people were in such a hitch.
Some would tumble, some would grumble,
It was terrible living in the Tudor times.

Connor Whelan (7)
Goldstone Primary School, Hove

Friendship Poem

My name is Dan and I'm alright
I play all day and I play all night.
People really think I'm cool
So please don't treat me like a fool.
Everybody knows that I have many friends
And this is where my poem ends.

Daniel O'Neil (10)
Goldstone Primary School, Hove

I Want A Pet

I want a pet
I'm not allowed a pony,
I'm not allowed a cat,
I'm not allowed a hamster,
I'm not allowed a rat.
I'm not allowed a dog, in case it gets on my bed,
So I'll settle for a frog instead!

Amy-Jo McLellan (11)
Goldstone Primary School, Hove

I Wonder . . .

I wonder why the grass is green
And why the wind is never seen.
Who told the birds to build a nest
And made the trees stay still and rest?
Who painted a rainbow in the sky
And hung the fluffy clouds up so high?
When the moon is not quite round
Where can the missing piece be found?
I wonder.

Andile Sibanda (11)
Goldstone Primary School, Hove

Double, Double, Snake And Trouble

Claw of a crab,
A slimy gut of a teacher,
Slimy tail of a dog,
Fin of a dolphin.

Mushy foot of an elephant,
Rotten dung of a cow,
Eye of a toad and jelly,
Fin of a whale.

Body of a human and bones,
The poison of a snake,
Body of a pony.

Double, double, snake and trouble
Drink it and die.

Marianne Tettersell (9)
Goldstone Primary School, Hove

Our Spell

Huddle bubble, drink 'n' die.
Fillet of a fenny snake in the cauldron boil and bake.
Horrid heart of a lizard taken hand in hand with mine.
Monkey's tail fallen off while swinging,
Howler's wing and bee's sting for a charm of a powerful death.
Huddle bubble, drink 'n' die.
Eye of crow as black as night picked out with a spoon
And a werewolf's claw as sharp as a knife
And a scream that nobody heard.

Megan Scibberas (8)
Goldstone Primary School, Hove

The Witches' Spell

Head of mouldy toad chopped off by a knife.
Boiled brain of a babe scooped out with a spoon.
A wing of an owl taken off with a fork.
Arm of a human pulled off by hands.
Peacock's beak sawn off.
Tooth of a shark and whale mixed together, boiled under the grill.
Dog's head suffocated in the bog and whacked off with a log.
The poison is finished, *RIP.*

Lee Cox (8)
Goldstone Primary School, Hove

Strangled Baby

(Based on Macbeth)

Double, double, toil and trouble
Fire burn and cauldron bubble.

A rotten eye scooped out with a spoon.
Gooey brain of a cat stolen while sleeping.
Acid of exhaust dribbled on skin.
Breath of horrifying dangerous dragon.
Powder of gas gun.
Head of horse covered in blood.
Finger of owl, brain of dog.
Skeleton's heart, tooth of wolf.
Tongue of spider.

Daniel Fitzgerald (9)
Goldstone Primary School, Hove

Friends

My friends are very silly
My favourite one is Milly.

Milly is quite funny
Her nose is always runny.

Her favourite colour is blue
I'm sad to say she always has the flu.

My friend is very kind
She has also a great big mind.

The best thing is, I see her every day
Hooray!

Maddie Wilson (7)
Great Ballard School, Chichester

Hamsters

My hamster runs very fast
My hamster smiles when we go past.

My hamster's fluffy and always funny
My hamster's always sleepy and cuddly.

My hamster's good at making beds
My hamster loves getting fed.

But I love my hamster so, so much
Oh I forgot, it's time for his lunch.

Bryony Thomson (8)
Great Ballard School, Chichester

My Horse

My horse is greedy and fat
She has a long tail with a hat.

She smells like poo
And bucks in poo.

She likes to run all day
In her PJs in the sun.

She loves to eat
She's a breed like Pete,

She is a nincompoop!

And that is Chess, if Chess is fat,
That is that, she pokes me
She can't do that
Because that is me.

I love Chess more than a honeybee
She's cuddly like a pea.

She likes to drink beer in winter!

Katie Tims (7)
Great Ballard School, Chichester

Dinosaurs

Some dinosaurs are nice
I will give you some advice,
Diplodocuses are nice
Because they like rice.

Some dinosaurs are scary
When they go to Hell,
'Cause they turn into a fairy
Then they lose a brain cell.

Sebastian Barrett (7)
Great Ballard School, Chichester

Ducks

Ducks live in hot countries
They have big feet and beaks,
They really are greedy pigs
Don't get too close, they'll bite really big!

Megan Alvey (8)
Great Ballard School, Chichester

My Hair Clip

I fiddle with my hair clip
It feels very nice.

I diddle and daddle with it
Until I see some mice.

I use my hair clip to put up my lovely, lovely fringe
Until I see a big, big, frightening door hinge.

My hair clip is very great
Until I'm going to be late.

I've lost my hair clip
Now for good,
It seems to be in a
Great big book.

Jasmine Thomas (7)
Great Ballard School, Chichester

Elephants

Elephants are grey and dull
Elephants are noisy and big
Elephants have large trunks
Elephants have short tails.

Elephants are really nice
But they're scared of mice.

Edward Piercy (8)
Great Ballard School, Chichester

Lions

My lion is called Jack
He's allergic to cats.
He loves to play hats
So that's all of that.

He's nice and soft
But sometimes has coughs.
When he goes to bed
He loves to play with Ted.

He's really nice
And his favourite food is rice.
When he goes to sleep
He likes to cuddle up with me.

Fergus Nugent (8)
Great Ballard School, Chichester

Madagascar

Madagascar is a wonderful place
But there is only one thing,
It's face to face.

Madagascar is so mad
It has hyenas,
On mobile receivers.

I went to Madagascar
To find a currant bun,
But all I found instead
Was a loaded gun.

I went to Madagascar
To find a golden gun,
But I found a currant bun
Just to fill my tum.

William Pickles (8)
Great Ballard School, Chichester

First Place

Sandy is my horse
A great chestnut bay,
As we go to the arena
On this very sunny day.

When we jump the jump
My heart goes bump,
I had the worst face
But then I came first place.

Abi Paterson (8)
Great Ballard School, Chichester

Princess

A princess I know, she is quite slow.
A princess I know, she has a pretty glow.
A princess I know, she is a bit of a blow.
A princess I know, she has a big toe.

A princess I know, she has a good show.
A princess I know, she has a pretty bow.
A princess I know, she has a big nose.
A princess I know . . . and this is where I close.

Sarah McNally (7)
Great Ballard School, Chichester

Homework

My homework's silly
I've got a friend called Billy
He is very frilly.

My nan's rather fiddly
But also rather giggly.

I'm rather like my father
But not too much because
He eats marmalade
But I like lemonade.

My brother's a brute
But my mother's astute.

I say things twice
My dad catches mice.

George Nott (8)
Great Ballard School, Chichester

Puppies And Dogs

Mum, there is a dog on the roof
There is, there is!
Mum, there's a cheeky puppy on your bed
There is, there is!
Mum, the dog is on my bed
He is, he is!
Mum, the puppy is on the loo
He is, he is!
Mum, please believe me.
Mum said, 'No!'

Jack Lovejoy (8)
Great Ballard School, Chichester

I'm Going To Mars

I'm going to Mars
Or maybe the moon
I'm going to go soon.

I'm going to Mars
I'll go in a rocket
Or maybe a plane.

I'm going to Mars
To get some food
Because I'm in a very good mood.

Beau Hartley (7)
Great Ballard School, Chichester

People

People are cool
People are nuts,
People like living
In Pizza Huts.

People are young
People are old,
I'll tell you a secret
My friend is bald.

People are crazy
People are funny,
People like stroking
My fat bunny.

People are silly
People are kind,
People are boring
Oh no, it's pouring.

People are black
People are brown,
People can have
A very big frown.

People are slim
People are seven,
I sometimes wish
My sister was in Heaven!

People are cool
People are crazy,
People are really
Very, very lazy.

Dominic Fritche (7)
Great Ballard School, Chichester

Nits

When my mummy sees me itching
She gets the nit comb,
Out comes the shampoo
Then I start to moan.

Then when Mummy's finished
The nits run away,
Right in to the bathroom
To get right away.

Alexander Cornelius (8)
Great Ballard School, Chichester

Mars

Mars is round
It looks like it's crowned
There are little slimy people
Holding dynamite,
If I saw one
I'd have a fright.
Sometimes they're red
Sometimes they're green,
They're the strangest thing
I've ever seen
But they just always want to fight!

Mars is red
It looks like a bed
And it has got
Toffee in it too,
And I sometimes have one
With my friend Ted
Then he rushes off to the loo.

Jamie Little (8)
Great Ballard School, Chichester

Kitties

Kitties are cuddly
Kitties are cute
My kitty likes to
Hide in my boot.

Kitties are soft
Kitties are yummy
I like kitties
Because they are scrummy.

Georgina Cranfield (8)
Great Ballard School, Chichester

Shark

I wish I saw a shark
At the Brazilian sea,
Where the sharks eat sardines
But maybe not me.

I wish I saw the leeches
At the African sea,
Where the leeches eat the people
At the ocean deep.

Harry Compton (8)
Great Ballard School, Chichester

Fairies

Fairies are kind, fairies are lovely
I love their sweet song that makes me feel snugly.

I've told you they're nice, I've told you they're kind
I've told you that I've got everything signed.

I love the nice fairies, they are very sweet
I like the tooth fairy, with a tooth for a seat.

The Fairy Queen has a white and gold palace
And her favourite name is Alice.

Claudia Campbell (7)
Great Ballard School, Chichester

Slowly Glides The Snail

Slowly glides the snail
Upon the garden path.
Out comes the trail
Shining in the dark.

He is my pet, you have to admit it
But you can't take him to the vet.
I don't have a carrier case
That's what I'll have to face.

He is rather stout
You know I doubt.
He is not going to be slim
Oh poor old him.

Emily Byfield-Riches (8)
Great Ballard School, Chichester

From My Window

From my window I can see
Children playing happily.
From my window I can see
People driving madly.
From my window I can see
Dogs barking madly.
From my window I can see
Cats sleeping under my tree.
From my window I can see
Trees swaying madly.
From my window I can see
Bees buzzing madly.

Jakob Cassar-Hutton (8)
Hatch Warren Junior School, Basingstoke

From My Window

From my window I can see
Birds chirping busily.

From my window I can see
Dogs walking quickly.

From my window I can see
Trees swaying from side to side.

From my window I can see
Frogs jumping from side to side.

From my window I can see
Grass swaying in the breeze.

From my window I can see
Kittens jumping around a tree.

From my window I can see
Rabbits jumping happily.

Daisy Moore (8)
Hatch Warren Junior School, Basingstoke

Happiness

Happiness is gold and pink because it is all around you.
Happiness is like a baby being born with love.
Happiness smells like a cake being shared.
It feels like all the darkness moving from your body.
Happiness looks like everyone being kind and helpful.
It sounds like people having lots of fun.
It tastes like a pizza as hot as the sun swimming in your mouth.
Happiness reminds me of the world sharing feelings.

Natasha Gage (7)
Hatch Warren Junior School, Basingstoke

Love

Love is red and pink like roses.
It sounds joyful.
It tastes like strawberry milkshake.
It smells like cake.
It looks like red and pink hearts.
It feels like a pink squashy pillow.
It reminds me of colours.

Hannah Fairnie (7)
Hatch Warren Junior School, Basingstoke

Love

Love is red, it is like shiny purple
It sounds like music at Christmas
It tastes like chicken
It smells like blue air
It looks beautiful
It feels like furry animals' skin
It reminds me of being nice.

Courtney Eagles (7)
Hatch Warren Junior School, Basingstoke

Anger

Anger is white like a vampire
It tastes like strawberries and cream
It smells like tomato
The colour is red
It sounds like a ghost going, *'Oooooooooo!'*
It reminds me of dinosaurs and it is a pterodactyl.

Thomas Childs (7)
Hatch Warren Junior School, Basingstoke

Love

Love is red like a red, red rose
Love is very durable.
It is like a kiss between your lips and a very big hug and a pink heart.
It smells like bananas but it reminds me of a honeymoon.

Rebecca Cacace (7)
Hatch Warren Junior School, Basingstoke

Love

Love is like a red, red rose and a lollipop melting on your tongue.
It sounds like a kiss between your lips.
Love looks like a pink heart on your lips.
It reminds me of a big fluffy heart.
Love feels like a big fluffy pillow.
It smells like a big lollipop.
Love is the colour of a pink rose.

Abby Brown (7)
Hatch Warren Junior School, Basingstoke

Silence

Silence is blue like clear blue sky.
It feels like the deep sea.
It looks like a waterfall falling down.
It sounds like the tide coming in and out.
It tastes like fresh water from a river.
It smells like a chocolate cake.
It reminds me of a funeral.

Cy Brennan (8)
Hatch Warren Junior School, Basingstoke

Laughter

What does it sound like? The happiest place ever.
What does it taste like? Strawberry ice cream.
What does it smell like? Like my cheesy feet.
What does it look like? A place in America.
What does it feel like? A soft bed.
What dos it remind you of? The fastest roller coaster.
What colour is it? Bright yellow.

Nathan Barlow (8)
Hatch Warren Junior School, Basingstoke

Sadness

Sadness is blue like a big bright sky.
It reminds me of the colour of the sea.
It feels heavy and hard.
It tastes like Brussels sprouts.
It looks like rain on a grey day.
It smells like cold chicken.
It sounds like rain falling down.

Nicola Varns (7)
Hatch Warren Junior School, Basingstoke

Anger

Anger is orange like a burning fire.
It feels like you want to hurt someone you admire.
It looks like you are breathing fire.
It sounds like a giant stomping around you.
It reminds me of a fire getting hotter.
It smells like a burning candle.
It tastes of a horrible feeling.

Jane Greenwood (7)
Hatch Warren Junior School, Basingstoke

Hunger

Hunger is brown and yellow like tasty cheeseburgers.
It smells like delicious cheeseburgers.
It tastes like delicious food.
It reminds me of tasty McDonalds' Happy Meals.
It sounds like nothing.
It feels good, very good.
It looks very bad.

Frederick Coffin (7)
Hatch Warren Junior School, Basingstoke

Darkness

Darkness is green
Like an apple tree.
It smells like roses.
It sounds like a helicopter going over my head.
It looks like a monster.
It tastes like chocolate cake.
It feels like a fluffy cushion.
It reminds me of my nanny because she died.

Jack Saint (8)
Hatch Warren Junior School, Basingstoke

Silence

Silence is blue like the sky
It tastes like chocolate.
It smells like macaroni cheese.
It feels like silence.
It looks like a rabbit.
It sounds like hammering.
It reminds me of my rabbit.

Dominic Francis (8)
Hatch Warren Junior School, Basingstoke

Love

Love is red like fire.
It reminds me of tomato sauce.
It sounds like your heart is beating fast.
It looks like people kissing with their lips.
It tastes like bubbly spit.
It smells like lavender roses.
It feels like a nice big hug.

Georgia Hunt (8)
Hatch Warren Junior School, Basingstoke

Happiness

Happiness is orange like a book.
It looks like fun.
It tastes like apple.
It sounds like children.
It reminds me of my first teddy.
It smells like chicken.
It tastes like air.
It feels like fun.

Jamie Cripps (7)
Hatch Warren Junior School, Basingstoke

Fear

Fear is grey like dark clouds.
Fear reminds me of danger.
Fear looks like bullies.
Fear tastes like darkness.
Fear sounds like screeching.
Fear smells like sadness.
Fear feels like your life is over.

Leah Foster (8)
Hatch Warren Junior School, Basingstoke

Sadness

Sadness is light blue like light blue sea.
Sadness reminds me of beans and chicken.
Sadness smells like chicken in tomato soup.
Sadness looks like the waves in the sea.
Sadness tastes like really horrible water.
Sadness feels like hot chocolate.
Sadness sounds like tea dripping.

Ashley McKenzie (7)
Hatch Warren Junior School, Basingstoke

Love

Love is pink like soft candyfloss.
It looks like a cat.
It sounds like a piano.
It tastes like sweet candy.
It smells like fresh air.
Light colours remind me of having fun in the park.

Tristan Mollentze (7)
Hatch Warren Junior School, Basingstoke

Darkness

Darkness is black like a dark knight.
It sounds like screams.
It reminds me of the night.
It tastes like fear.
It looks like the dead.
It smells like dead food.
It feels like nightmares.

Haydn Ford (8)
Hatch Warren Junior School, Basingstoke

Love

Love is like pink candyfloss that smells like lovely flowers and relaxing flowers.
Love is lush like a crush.
It reminds me of a delicious cake and never a mistake.
It sounds like kittens with little mittens.
It tastes like a lonely cup of hot chocolate.

Lily Kyle (8)
Hatch Warren Junior School, Basingstoke

Darkness

Darkness is black and white like a jewel thief's scary costume.
It sounds like a noisy train.
It's like a smelly skunk.
It tastes like a dark piece of chocolate.
It reminds me of a frightening film.
It feels like someone is punching you in the stomach.

James Coster (8)
Hatch Warren Junior School, Basingstoke

Happiness

Happiness is bright red like a warm fire.
It feels like kindness.
It looks like the greatest day of your life and sounds like bells chiming merrily.
It reminds me of a bright sunny day of cosiness and warmth.
It smells like every kind of flower you can imagine.
It tastes like your favourite foods.

Alice Cockburn (7)
Hatch Warren Junior School, Basingstoke

Hunger

Hunger is like a sticky pink cotton candy.
It looks like a pink fluffy ball.
It sounds like a silence ball.
It reminds me of sweets and candy.
It smells like chocolate.
It tastes like crunchy crisps.
It feels like a soft piece of cotton wool.

Ryan Hopgood (7)
Hatch Warren Junior School, Basingstoke

Laughter

Laughter is shiny blue like the wavy sea.
It tastes like salty water.
It looks like a bumpy roller coaster.
It feels like fish are surrounding me.
It smells like fishes' bodies.
It sounds like water crashing on a rock.
It reminds me of sand.

Eddie Ayoub (7)
Hatch Warren Junior School, Basingstoke

Fear

Fear is red like a big and juicy apple.
It feels hard and round.
It tastes like nothing.
It reminds me of my doggies.
It feels like anger.
It smells like nothing.
It sounds like you're angry.

Owen Fairnie (7)
Hatch Warren Junior School, Basingstoke

Laughter

Laughter is blue like bright sky.
It feels like you're bouncing on a trampoline.
It looks like you're happy.
It sounds like kids playing.
It smells like pretty flowers.
It reminds me of red and blue.

Jodie Hinton (7)
Hatch Warren Junior School, Basingstoke

Laughter

Laughter is pink like candyfloss.
It tastes like sweet candy.
It smells like the green grass.
Laughter reminds me of cuddles.
It looks like fun.
It sounds like children playing.
Laugher feels like playing in the park.

Eleanor Stone (8)
Hatch Warren Junior School, Basingstoke

Darkness

Darkness sounds like some howling wolves.
Darkness tastes like rotten perfume.
Darkness smells like stale food.
Darkness is like being under the sea without light.
Darkness feels like a vampire's hand.
Darkness reminds me of the Dark Side.
Darkness is pitch-black.

Alex Waites (7)
Hatch Warren Junior School, Basingstoke

Hunger

Hunger is mint-green like sitting on a fresh green lawn.
It feels like a smooth grey rock, like a cupcake.
It reminds me of my mum's hot soup.
It looks like me lost in a dark forest without any food.
It smells like a fresh piece of broccoli.
It sounds like my tummy rumbling very fast.

Kieran Trinder (7)
Hatch Warren Junior School, Basingstoke

Silence

Silence is red like nobody says anything.
It sounds like nothing, no sound at all.
It reminds me of sitting doing quiet reading.
It feels like nothing.
Silence tastes like chocolate melting.
It smells like cheesy feet and smelly socks.
Silence looks like a fountain, a fountain of chocolate.

Alex Stroud (8)
Hatch Warren Junior School, Basingstoke

Hamsters

Hamsters, hamsters, fluffy and brown,
Funny, my furry friends,
They're cute and cuddly,
Very delicate.
Hamsters, hamsters, small and brown,
Sometimes naughty,
They nip with their sharp white teeth.
Hamsters, hamsters, different colours,
White, brown and golden.
Hamsters, hamsters all around,
Funny and quite fast.
Hamsters, hamsters, lovely and cool,
They're very small.
Hamsters, hamsters, sometimes long and sometimes fat.

Joe Sandwell (7)
Hatch Warren Junior School, Basingstoke

Happiness

Happiness is the colour blue all around you
When you are playing and making friends with your sister
When you are with your friend playing
You can smell the happiness in you and around you
Your friend has happiness.
It smells like raspberries and cream.
It looks like love in you.
It tastes like cream and grapes.
It reminds me of my mummy.
It sounds like fun.

Heather Webb (7)
Hatch Warren Junior School, Basingstoke

Laughter

It sounds like a river rolling down river rocks.
It tastes like strawberries in a mountain of sugar.
It smells like a piece of blossom blooming in the garden.
It looks like the sun shining on an empty beach.
It feels like a silky pair of pyjamas.
It reminds me of my friend giggling.
It is pink and pale blue.

Millie Stringer (8)
Hatch Warren Junior School, Basingstoke

Love

Love is happy and nice.
You will always be able to find it in the dark and sunlight.
It sounds like a kiss and a red rose.
Love is shaped as a heart and it makes everyone feel happy forever.
It flows through the air and makes you think of love.
When you love and smile and are kind to everyone.
It's not funny to be loved, it's nice and kind.

Nicola Sims (8)
Hatch Warren Junior School, Basingstoke

Darkness

Darkness is black like it is misty.
It sounds like big waves.
It tastes like my mum's roast dinner when it's done.
It looks like a crystal.
It feels like an ice cream.
It smells like my dad's feet (because they smell!).

Emma Scott (7)
Hatch Warren Junior School, Basingstoke

Hate

Hate is dark, dark black like nasty tiger stripes.
It reminds me of someone being really unkind.
Hate feels like people punching me.
It sounds like children shouting at one another.
It smells like dust.
It tastes like smoke drifting away in my mouth.

Jake Pearce (8)
Hatch Warren Junior School, Basingstoke

Anger

Anger is black.
It is hate, a black and grey feeling in the heart.
It smells like gas, it smells like a mouldy sandwich.
It feels like a bumpy wall and a spiky point.

Tyrell Payne (7)
Hatch Warren Junior School, Basingstoke

Hate

Hate is black like a black storm.
It feels like your heart is crushed.
It tastes like horrible, disgusting chocolate.
Hate smells like blood.
Hate feels like kicking.
Hate reminds me of people dying.

Callum Parry (7)
Hatch Warren Junior School, Basingstoke

Darkness

Darkness is very dark.
It sounds like storms.
It smells like rubbish in the dump.
It tastes like chocolate ice cream.
It looks like giants doing damage in the dark.
It feels like monsters.
It reminds me of being in the dark.

William Newcombe (7)
Hatch Warren Junior School, Basingstoke

Silence

Silence feels like a bit of fresh air.
Silence tastes like a soft and smooth tree swishing to the left and to the right.
It reminds me of quiet and silence.
It smells like the wind blowing in your face.
The colour is blue and white.

Sophie Mitchell (7)
Hatch Warren Junior School, Basingstoke

Darkness

Darkness smells like smelly socks which have been dumped in a damp puddle.
Darkness tastes like rotten mud mixed up with slugs.
Darkness looks like black treacle all around you.
Darkness feels like gooey mud that slips through your hands.
Darkness sounds like wolves scuffling through the forest.

Gawain Kinnersley (7)
Hatch Warren Junior School, Basingstoke

Sadness

Sadness is black like a dark night.
It feels like an uncomfortable bed.
It looks like a broken heart.
It sounds like people shouting at one another.
It tastes like dirty water sliding down your neck.
It smells like my dad's socks.
It reminds me of big tears running down someone's face.

Jessica Higgins (7)
Hatch Warren Junior School, Basingstoke

From My Window

From my window I can see
Birds chirping happily.

From my window I can see
Cats purring quietly.

From my window I can see
Grass swaying merrily.

From my window I can see
Trees swaying happily.

From my window I can see
Dogs chasing cats busily.

From my window I can see
A rainbow reflecting on the sea.

From my window I can see
Birds flying happily.

Ben Raeburn (9)
Hatch Warren Junior School, Basingstoke

Silence

Silence is blue like a brook in the sunlight.
It smells like a chocolate bar melting on your top.
It looks like the water rippling over the pebbles.
It sounds like the waves crashing on the shore.
It tastes like an ice cream freezing your mouth.
It feels like smooth water.
It reminds me of playing in the sea.

George Herring (7)
Hatch Warren Junior School, Basingstoke

Happiness

It feels like fun.
Happiness is blue like you are having fun.
It looks like fun.
It reminds me of me and my sister.
It sounds like people laughing.
It tastes like fun.
It smells like me having fun.

Georgia Hardy (7)
Hatch Warren Junior School, Basingstoke

Animals

Animals are very sweet,
Some animals eat meat,
Animals are fierce lions, tigers
It fills me with tears,
Animals are very friendly,
Some not, some scary,
Some animals squeak and scatter,
Some animals hop and bounce,
Animals do all different kinds of things!

Charlotte Jelley (8)
Hatch Warren Junior School, Basingstoke

Fear

Fear is tan colour like blackness at night.
It smells like a strong wind breezing through me
Like two storming lions splitting through me.
It looks like a dark black cave in the Middle East.
It reminds me of a forest with a black river flowing between.
It sounds like a fight in the open world and animals getting killed.

Luke Whorriskey (7)
Hatch Warren Junior School, Basingstoke

Darkness

Darkness is black like a creepy dark house,
It's down in the middle of nowhere,
It creeps up on towns and cities like a million-legged spider creeping up,
It feels really creepy,
Darkness is creepy, very creepy!

Alexandra Brady (8)
Hatch Warren Junior School, Basingstoke

Football Is The Best

Football is a clever sport,
Football is played a lot,
Football does rock,
Football is the best,
Now let's play that sport,
Now it's time to go to The Valley,
And watch Charlton Athletic v Sunderland,
And I support Charlton.
We win!

Bradley Sutton (7)
Hatch Warren Junior School, Basingstoke

The Sun

I watch the bright sun that turns
And watch it as it burns
It never stops going around
I think it's going to be round.

Oh sun, oh sun, will you stop spinning?
Oh no, oh no, I think he is singing
'Oh please will you stop,' I say, but he won't
Oh please, oh please don't.

I watch it as it twists and twirls
And watch it as it curls
And watch it as it goes down
And see it when it is gone beneath the town.

Simon Gray (8)
Hatch Warren Junior School, Basingstoke

Fear

Fear is a horrible thing,
Almost like a squashed potato,
Always near you,
It's almost like the flu,
But don't beat yourself up about it.
It's usually a good thing,
So be proud to have a little friend,
Who drives you round the bend!
So don't be afraid of superhero.
Fear!

Katie Vickers (8)
Hatch Warren Junior School, Basingstoke

From My Window

From my window I can see
Submarines sinking under the sea.

From my window I can see
Cats swaying sleepily.

From my window I can see
Grass growing quietly.

From my window I can see
Horses galloping next to the sea.

From my window I can see
Dogs growling angrily.

From my window I can see
Birds singing merrily.

From my window I can see
Children skipping gracefully.

From my window I can see
Frogs croaking loudly.

From my window I can see
People driving crazily.

Kieran Moore (9)
Hatch Warren Junior School, Basingstoke

Love

It sounds like romance, like a very happy day as a couple.
It smells like a diamond food as crystal in the air.
It tastes like sweet, sweet food.
It feels like a crystal ball in the air.
It looks like fun to me.
It reminds me of a happy couple and a lovely place.
It goes well every evening at home.

Shannon Griffiths (9)
Hatch Warren Junior School, Basingstoke

Darkness

Darkness is like a spooky shadow on the ground scaring people off.
Darkness feels like a shiver shivering down my spine when I am in a dark room.
Darkness reminds me of the moonlight sky covered in dark clouds shaped as a ghost.
Darkness sounds like an owl hooting in a tree with a ghost sound coming out.
Darkness tastes like a mouldy load of spinach with eyeballs.
Darkness smells like cat wee and dog pooh mixed with blood.

Louis Cox (8)
Hatch Warren Junior School, Basingstoke

The Sun

The sun is a glowing, glistening orb,
It shines all day and sometimes at night,
With delight it floats in the air,
Glaring and staring down from above.

The sun is a golden ball,
Blazing and flaring all day long,
The next poem is a song,
Hope you will sing along!

The sun is a burning hot star,
It flickers and shimmers all day long,
With its admired light and great heat,
It will sweep you off your feet.

Abhishek Dash (8)
Hatch Warren Junior School, Basingstoke

Football

Football, football is the best,
Scoring goals is part of it
And Bobby Charlton and George Best
Were our star strikers.
Tottenham, Tottenham,
I call them Tot Tots
And they are very good!
I would like to be a football player when I grow up,
I would like to be a really good footie player.

George Price (7)
Hatch Warren Junior School, Basingstoke

The Sun

The sun is like a bulb but bigger,
It bounces around like Tigger.
It's like a giant chilli pepper in the sky,
Just watch it fly.
The sun is a beautiful golden ball,
As it shines through the window in the mall.
The lovely sun isn't here at night,
Trust me it gives me a fright.
We all love the sun I know
But I think we will have to go with the flow.

Sam Benn (9)
Hatch Warren Junior School, Basingstoke

Colours

Blue is for the sky
Green is for the trees
Yellow is for the sun
Peach is for the people
Yellow and white are for daisies
Black is for the darkness
Colours are so beautiful.

Grace Honnor (7)
Hatch Warren Junior School, Basingstoke

The Sun

A glistening, sparkling, blazing hot piece of fire.
She goes a lot, lot higher
With her bright golden light and fierce heat,
No wonder she doesn't have any feet.
Oh the sun, she's a lot, lot bigger,
She bounces around a bit like Tigger!
Oh how much I want to meet her,
The sun is so big and beautiful.
I can almost hear her sing
With her diamond teeth and golden hair.
But guess what? I saw her eat a pear.
So that's the sun's story, she's never lied.
If you want to meet her, go outside!

Isabel McCarthy (8)
Hatch Warren Junior School, Basingstoke

Love

Love is very nice,
It tingles in your heart,
When I take a picture in my mind
It makes me joyful,
Love sometimes is very sad
And is sometimes happy!
I do enjoy thinking about it!
Do you?
If you believe in God, He's sure to give you a good amount of love!

Katie Marsh (8)
Hatch Warren Junior School, Basingstoke

The Wind

The wind is a moaning, rustling, disturbing dog.
It's cloudy and stormy.
When the sun goes down
The giant wind dog moans, licking his dirty paws.

When it is nightfall and it starts to snow,
He starts to look around the seas,
He lies against the cliffs,
Soon he goes to bed.

When a frisbee goes up through the clouds, he dies,
He falls and falls until he explodes.

William Davis (9)
Hatch Warren Junior School, Basingstoke

Friends

A friend is loyal and trusting
And they are kind,
They will not let you down,
You can always count on them.
If your friend back chats you or bullies you
They are not a friend,
Upsetting people does not make a friend as well.

Sophie Louden (8)
Hatch Warren Junior School, Basingstoke

From My Window

From my window I can see
Buzzing bees rushing through the trees.
From my window I can see
Birds merry for all to see.
From my window I can see
Horses neighing heavily.
From my window I can see
Grass swaying gently.
From my window I can see
Dogs walking smartly.
From my window I can see
Girls dancing beautifully.

Kiera Woodley (9)
Hatch Warren Junior School, Basingstoke

From My Window

From my window I can see
Birds chirping merrily.

From my window I can see
Grass dancing gracefully.

From my window I can see
Trees swaying quietly.

From my window I can see
Frogs bouncing crazily.

From my window I can see
Kittens purring beautifully.

From my window I can see
Dolphins leaping gently.

From my window I can see
Dogs pouncing silently.

From my window I can see
Rabbits jumping gracefully.

From my window I can see
Bugs crawling quickly.

From my window I can see
Dragonflies flying fastly.

George Anthony (9)
Hatch Warren Junior School, Basingstoke

The Wind

The wind is like an invisible ghost sneezing all over the place,
It roars and moans like a growling bear,
And thrashes through my hair.

The wind is as thick as a brick,
So you better put your hands over your ears because it will scream as loud as it can.
The wind whistles to the trees and they rustle in the breeze
'Shhh!' I shout.
'Roar!' it screamed.
I ran but suddenly I realised I was gone.

Holly Lock (8)
Hatch Warren Junior School, Basingstoke

The Sun

The sun is an orb of fire giving heat in the sky,
Blazing and golden,
As everybody sighs,
When it's a good day to play outside,
As the sun goes round and round,
And bounces up and down,
The sun is a piece of ash that stays in the sky,
It blinds my eyes as I give it an evil stare,
The sun never gives me a nightmare,
And also gives me joy,
She's like a toy to me,
The sun is always right on time,
It's like a big yellow lime,
Shining in the sky,
When the sun goes away,
We always say,
'Why sun, why did you go away?'
As the sun does its normal progress
When the sun does shine
And people say it's really mine.

Ali-Hussein Mohamed (9)
Hatch Warren Junior School, Basingstoke

The Wind

The wind is a scary roaring bear.
Black and damp.
He is growling all day long.
It is cold and dark in the sky.
It goes back and forward.
The wind blows my hair in my face, as if it is mad.
It cried and cried, it seems I've been bad.
I looked all around but it is not happy.
I don't know why.

Rhiannon Bullock (9)
Hatch Warren Junior School, Basingstoke

The Wind

The wind is like a screaming bear.
I can hear the mean, swaying wind.
I can hear the roaring, fierce wind.
The wind is like a purring cat moaning at me.
I can see the wind coming nearer with his clashing mouth snapping at me.
His jaws are big, snapping and horrible.
The wind is like a roaring lion.
The wind is like a wolf rushing past you.

Amber Webb (8)
Hatch Warren Junior School, Basingstoke

The Sun

When the sun comes out it puts a smile on my face,
But when it's not out my smile drops,
It's like a pile of burning ashes sizzling in thin air,
I look up above, it's so bright it nearly blinds.
When the sun is bright and golden,
Make the sun with gleaming, bright thread,
Everyone says, 'Where do we find it?'
It's very easy; just look up, up and even higher!

Daniella Butler (9)
Hatch Warren Junior School, Basingstoke

The Sun

The sun is like a piece of burning ash,
That sizzles in the sky.
I look above and it's like it's blinding my eyes.
Then I can hear the crackling sound,
That's gradually making the sun into fire.
Suddenly I can smell the red mean sun,
That was turned into fire by the planet Earth.
But by the end of the day it was OK,
So, I rushed inside and had a good night's sleep.

Amy McDermott (8)
Hatch Warren Junior School, Basingstoke

Fear

Fear is like your worst nightmare.
Fear sounds like people screaming.
It smells like a dead rose.
It tastes like a mouldy piece of tuna.
Fear reminds me of a dark forest.
Fear feels like you've broken your leg.
It looks like a dark crow.
Fear is like a very bad sadness.

David Sims (9)
Hatch Warren Junior School, Basingstoke

Love

Love is like a holiday on the beautiful sandy beach,
It smells like a bunch of roses,
Love looks like a big, white, fluffy cloud,
It tastes like a thick, foamy chocolate milkshake,
Love reminds me of my family,
It feels like an enormous hug,
Love sounds like peaceful, romantic music,
Love is a warm feeling around me.

Emma Kersley (9)
Hatch Warren Junior School, Basingstoke

Happiness

Happiness is like people always being friendly,
Happiness looks like playing games altogether,
Happiness smells like melting chocolate,
Happiness feels like being terribly tickled,
Happiness reminds me of being with my family all the time,
Happiness sounds like giggling and laughter,
Happiness tastes like sour sweets,
Happiness is the greatest thing ever!

Megan Ormston (9)
Hatch Warren Junior School, Basingstoke

Anger

Anger smells like a pair of slippers.
Anger feels like little bits of egg.
Anger looks like the airless vacuum of space.
Anger tastes like the sour juice of a lemon.
Anger reminds me of the heat of an oven.
Anger sounds like the loud music from a radio.

Ellena Lockwood (8)
Hatch Warren Junior School, Basingstoke

Hunger

Hunger is like a person who wants more food,
Hunger tastes like eating fresh air,
It sounds like lions roaring in your tummy.
It feels like frogs jumping in your tummy,
Hunger smells like burning fire,
It looks like a big fat monster,
Hunger reminds me of eating sweet cake,
I really hate hunger!

Tejas Chandarana (9)
Hatch Warren Junior School, Basingstoke

Darkness

Darkness is like a gigantic spooky castle.
It feels like a big teddy bear.
Darkness sounds like a roaring storm.
It looks like a gigantic vampire.
Darkness reminds me a power cut.
It smells like chocolate doughnut.
Darkness tastes like yummy chocolate.

Victoria Taylor (8)
Hatch Warren Junior School, Basingstoke

Darkness

Darkness is as dark as a haunted house.
It sounds like tu-whit tu-whoo.
I think it would feel like the softest cloud ever.
I think it would taste like air going through my mouth.
It reminds me of a haunted house at midnight.
It looks like a pitch-black haunted night.
It smells like dark, melted chocolate.

Maria Mason (8)
Hatch Warren Junior School, Basingstoke

The Wind

The gentle breeze rushed past my face
It trickled through my hair
As it flew past me like an eagle
The wind began to rattle in my mouth
Twisting, twirling, whirling and curling
It rushed through my mouth, gradually coming out
The wind ran free once again.

Megan Bowen (8)
Hatch Warren Junior School, Basingstoke

Darkness

Darkness is like a dark house with the moonlight creeping over it.
Darkness looks like a black hole riding over the Earth.
Darkness reminds me of a werewolf in front of a full moon.
Darkness sounds like a shrieking owl at midnight.
Darkness tastes like thin air running through your blood.
Darkness feels like gas blowing on your body.
Darkness smells like blood running through a dark alleyway.

Adam Claessens (9)
Hatch Warren Junior School, Basingstoke

Fear

Fear is like sadness,
Fear tastes like raw bacon,
Fear reminds me of a black hole.
Fear smells like a burning fire,
Fear sounds like a bolt of lightning.

Louis Pink (9)
Hatch Warren Junior School, Basingstoke

Hunger

It smells like a big roast dinner.
It feels like a knife and fork.
It looks like a lot of food.
It reminds me of the last dinner I had.
It sounds like my stomach rumbling.
It tastes like food.

Benjamin Bassindale (8)
Hatch Warren Junior School, Basingstoke

Darkness

Darkness is like a black, gloomy hole,
It reminds me of an alleyway with trees closing in.
It tastes like a mouldy piece of bread.
It looks like a pitch-black room,
It sounds like a hoot of an owl.
It feels like a rough piece of material.
It smells like a farm that hasn't been cleaned out for ten years.

Callum Cobbett-Payne (8)
Hatch Warren Junior School, Basingstoke

Darkness

Darkness is like a spooky house,
It feels like a cold piece of flint,
It reminds me of an alleyway of shadows,
Darkness sounds like an owl's hoot,
Darkness looks like a grizzly bear,
Darkness smells of rotten candyfloss,
It tastes of porridge and flies.

Taylor Preistley (9)
Hatch Warren Junior School, Basingstoke

Laughter

Laughter is like you are next to a friend that likes you,
It feels like you're in a warm home on a cold winter's night,
Laughter reminds you of your birthday,
It smells like a burning, warm fire,
Laughter looks like one, big, happy family,
It sounds like cheers at Christmas,
Laughter tastes like melted chocolate,
Everybody has laughter!

Alice Biddiscombe (9)
Hatch Warren Junior School, Basingstoke

Happiness

Happiness is like being excited.
Happiness reminds me of not being bad.
Happiness looks like a gigantic smile.
Happiness sounds like laughter.
Happiness smells like love.
Happiness tastes like a kiss.
Happiness feels like a sponge.

Jordan Gillard (8)
Hatch Warren Junior School, Basingstoke

Laughter

Laughter is like love,
It sounds like happiness,
It takes away your sad thoughts,
And feels like you are safe.

Laughter is cheerful,
It smells as sweet as honey.
It reminds me of the happy times
To laugh you don't pay money.

Laughter is great!
It tastes like warm cakes,
It puts a smile on my face,
Laughter is never a fake.

Laughter is brilliant,
Inside it makes me glow,
Any type of laughter's fun,
A fast laugh or a slow one.
Laughter's great!

Sophie Liming (9)
Hatch Warren Junior School, Basingstoke

Darkness

Darkness is like a dark, gloomy house,
It sounds like an owl with a bad throat,
Darkness tastes like a mouldy piece of bread,
It smells like the horrible smell of petrol,
It reminds me of a maze or a bunch of trees at night,
It looks like a dark, gloomy house with closing alleyways,
Darkness feels like slithering snakes under your feet,
Darkness is very scary and it makes me feel like I'm in danger.

Will Joyce (9)
Hatch Warren Junior School, Basingstoke

Darkness

Darkness is like a very, very spooky hole,
Darkness reminds me of falling over,
Darkness looks like a black part of town,
Darkness tastes like out of date food,
Darkness sound like one-hundred owls in a row,
Darkness feels like I'm doomed!
Darkness smells like old, rotten pizza.

Thomas Hammond (9)
Hatch Warren Junior School, Basingstoke

Laughter

Laughter is like a jolly clown,
It smells like a lovely red rose,
Laughter feels like a happy soul,
It sounds like a twinkling stream.

Laughter looks like a lovely newborn baby,
It reminds me of a hot sunny day!
Laughter tastes of a lovely fresh piece of lettuce,
Laughter is joyful!

Beccy Stanborough (8)
Hatch Warren Junior School, Basingstoke

Hunger

Hunger is like you feel very ill,
It smells like an out of date cake.
It sounds like someone has been moaning for days.
Hunger reminds me of when I throw up.
It tastes like I'm going to die.
Hunger looks like you can't walk.
Hunger feels like your happy thoughts have gone away.
Hunger is a very serious thing.

Dylan Difford (8)
Hatch Warren Junior School, Basingstoke

Love

Love is like a beautiful, shimmery, glittery heart shape.
It reminds me of my family because they love me and I love them.
Love smells like a cuddly jumper and a bunch of buttercups and daisies.
Love sounds like a piece of peaceful relaxing music.
It tastes like my favourite food and dogs' fur because my family have dogs.
Love looks like a big hug and lots of kisses.
Love feels like clothes when you huddle and cuddle up close with your family.
Love takes away your fears and bad dreams
And gives you happiness and makes your wishes come true.

Eva Wilson (8)
Hatch Warren Junior School, Basingstoke

Darkness

Darkness is like a black piece of toast.
It's hard to see at night just like a lump of mud.
It's like a dark mansion making a dark shadow.
It tastes like a dark piece of meat.
Or like a black chocolate biscuit.
It smells like a fresh pile of dirt or a horrible rubber smell.
It feels like that shivery feeling down the back of your neck.

Kurt Hamilton (8)
Hatch Warren Junior School, Basingstoke

Darkness

Darkness is like a haunted, spooky, scary mansion.
Darkness tastes of a burnt piece of bacon,
Darkness feels like sadness in my heart,
Darkness smells like a house on fire.
Darkness looks like a sad, sulky person crying,
Darkness sounds like a tsunami,
Darkness reminds me of bad times I had,
Darkness is spooky.

Harry Evans (9)
Hatch Warren Junior School, Basingstoke

Silence

Silence is all quiet and nice
It is as quiet as a mouse.
It feels like a warm-scented feeling.
Silence reminds me of my peaceful bedroom.
It looks like lots of little people all nice and silent.
Silence smells like breath.
It tastes like hot breath in your mouth.
Silence is very quiet and we all like it.

Marc Gage (8)
Hatch Warren Junior School, Basingstoke

Hate

H ate is horrid
A nd violence is cruel
T easing is really mean now,
E nd it all, right now!

Jamie Pelling (9)
Little Common School, Bexhill-on-Sea

My First Archery

I hit the middle!
I hit the middle!
I drew and it flew,
My bow bent
And the arrow went
Straight into the middle.

Jordan Coleman (8)
Little Common School, Bexhill-on-Sea

My Magic Sports Box

(Based on 'Magic Box' by Kit Wright)

I will put in my magic sports box . . .
Weight lifters six-pack,
A rugby ball kicked by Johnny Wilkinson,
And the snooker cue of Ronny O'Sullivan.
I will put in my magic sports box . . .
A hockey stick used by every hockey player,
A golf ball hit by Tiger Woods,
And my Predator Absolute football boots.
I will put in my magic sports box . . .
Xabi Alonso's super shots,
The tennis racket used by Tim Henman,
And Andy Fordham's favourite dart.
I will put in my magic sports box . . .
The cricket bat used by Kevin Pietersen,
The hinges are made of cricket ball material,
The lid is made of Djibril Cisse's neat hairstyle.
My magic sports box is sponsored by Adidas!

William Cheese (10)
Little Common School, Bexhill-on-Sea

Karate

K arate is an excellent sport,
A nd self-defence you also learn.
R un around and keep fit,
A lso needed to do this sport is discipline.
T o become a master at karate keep on learning, but remember,
E njoy yourself as well.

Alex Field (9)
Little Common School, Bexhill-on-Sea

I Will Put In My Magic Box
(Based on 'Magic Box' by Kit Wright)

I will put in my box . . .
A howling puppy
Five gold rings
And all my favourite sweets.

I will put in my box . . .
All my favourite DVDs,
The love of my mum,
And a newborn baby.

I will put in my box . . .
A bundle of fire,
A CD player with all the latest hits,
And every type of make-up in the world.

I will put in my box . . .
The best clothes in the world,
All my friends,
And all the chocolate in the world.

I will put in my box . . .
A hairdresser,
A nail machine,
And shoes.

The top is made out of bubblegum,
The hinges are made out of make-up brushes.

Catherine Terry (10)
Little Common School, Bexhill-on-Sea

Bomb

If I drop from a plane down through the sky
Ticking, tick-tock, tick-tock, what am I?
Then I hit the ground,
A great explosion, a deadly shockwave
Killing people all around,
What am I?
People crying and millions dying,
What am I?
I'm a bomb.

Jonathon Corke (11)
Little Common School, Bexhill-on-Sea

Love

Man and wife will always be together,
Love around them love forever.
They talk together until they say,
'I love you so, can you stay?'

When she goes to work he gets so sad,
Then they come home and they are really mad.
You settle her down with a glass of wine
And some food that tastes so divine.

You kiss her gently on the hand,
Then you take a walk through the silky sand.
He kisses her on the cheek,
Then she nicely goes to sleep.

Danielle Sellers (10)
Little Common School, Bexhill-on-Sea

Animals

Pets are cool,
Big and small,
Little and sweet,
With small feet,
Big and tall
They all rule.
Camels have the hump
And the kangaroos can jump.
The monkeys swing from tree to tree.
In the jungle the animals run free.

Dionne Bruce (10)
Little Common School, Bexhill-on-Sea

Fishing

Carp, roach, rudd and perch
I have caught them all
As I sit there on the bank
Waiting for the fish to bite.
Maggots, prawns and bread for bait
Sometimes I have a very long wait
Up I jump, I've got a take
Then the rod begins to shake.
I am fighting the fish, what will it be?
In the distance I can see
It is a carp so big
What a good day I have had.

Samuel Hills (11)
Little Common School, Bexhill-on-Sea

I Will Put In My Box

(Based on 'Magic Box' by Kit Wright)

I will put in my box . . .
A puppy of love,
A heart of souls,
And a swish of a wand.

I will put in my box . . .
A cat curled up to sleep,
A witch's cackle,
And a ringing mobile phone.

I will put in my box . . .
The Pussycat Dolls' album,
The glittering stars
And my lovely dogs.

I will put in my box . . .
Some grizzly tales,
A perfect picture
And my favourite slippers.

I will put in my box . . .
Sky television,
Hundreds of pounds
And a box of tissues.

I will put in my box . . .
All of my Eeyore stuff,
All of my favourite books
And some fresh fruit.

I will put in my box . . .
My computer,
My beanbag,
My mum's laptop.
My lid will be covered in roses,
My hinges will be mascara sticks.

Abbie Beale (10)
Little Common School, Bexhill-on-Sea

My Cat Fizz

I have a cat, she's oh so furry,
When I call her over she goes so purry.
All she does is play all day,
She goes for a wash every May.
She runs everywhere like a whizz,
And by the way she is called Fizz.

Ceri Hawkins (9)
Little Common School, Bexhill-on-Sea

The Sand Lady

In the dark and lonely night,
When the stars are all so bright,
She comes creeping up the street
With her sand to make you sleep.
Carrying upon her back,
Dreams of all kinds in a sack.
Though the doors are bolted still,
She can enter where she will.
And she stays, it is said
Longest by the children's bed,
Smooth their pillows, strokes their heads,
Goodnight children, tomorrow's ahead.

Matthew Booth (9)
Little Common School, Bexhill-on-Sea

Under The Sea

Deep down under the sea,
Nasty creatures lurk hiding from thee.
Whether it's shark, squid or something we don't know,
Always be careful wherever you go.

Jack Roadway (10)
Little Common School, Bexhill-on-Sea

The Game

The players kicked off,
The game began,
The striker took his chance and ran.

The crowd roared,
Number nine scored,
And the ball hit the back of the net with a whack.

The players clapped,
The whistle shrilled,
But still the crowd could not be stilled.

The stadium was empty,
The crowd was gone
But the celebrating went on and on.

Callum Hall (10)
Little Common School, Bexhill-on-Sea

How To Make A Bad, Bad Brew

Have you ever wished to make a brew
When the day is through and through?
Down in your cellar in the dead of night,
Ready to give your enemy a devilish fright?
To make your potion,
You will need,
Seventy-five thousand,
Leprechaun seeds.
Forty-six warts and a tub of toenails,
Then three goblets of dragon scales,
Tails of lizards, juice of bugs,
Carpets, furniture and hand-me-down rugs.
Goblin's shriek and baby's bawl,
Then the entire kitchen staff from the local school.
Lard, dust, saliva and grime,
Then a trail of dragon slime.
There should be a bang (this is perfectly okay),
Now leave your mixture for the next day.
Invite your enemy to your cellar,
Then into the cauldron, push that fella!
There should be a bubble and a fizz, then . . .
Your enemy shall never, ever be seen again.

Andrew Slinn (10)
Little Common School, Bexhill-on-Sea

The Magic Box

(Based on 'Magic Box' by Kit Wright)

I will put in my box . . .
The breath of a fire-breathing dragon,
The sound of a firework exploding in the air
And the bone-crunching tackles of Steven Gerrard.

I will put in my box . . .
My PSP and all the games,
The sound of snow crunching underfoot
And the slick skills of Ronaldinho.

I will put in my box . . .
The sound of West Ham's football crowd cheering.
The lid is made of sparkling red diamonds,
The hinges are made of polished bone.

Cameron Kirk (11)
Little Common School, Bexhill-on-Sea

Animals

Lots of animals have spots and stripes,
Some are vicious, some are nice,
Snakes and snails,
Frogs and dogs,
Some live inside, some live out,
Birds and bunnies hop along,
Singing their morning song,
Sheep and cows make a racket,
While the farmer wears his evening jacket.
This is my animal poem.

Katie Moore (10)
Little Common School, Bexhill-on-Sea

My Pet Rosie

Rosie is my furry cutie kitten,
She snuggles up with me like a soft mitten.
When I'm asleep I have to watch my feet,
For Rosie loves to jump and pounce, upon my mouse-like feet.

Rosie likes to go out,
But not when the foxes are out,
Because when they are my mother would roar,
'Rosie, come in now!'

Now Rosie likes to play with a ping-pong ball,
She chases it here, she chases it there,
Under the settee and into the hall,
But I would just like to say the best part of the day
Is when Rosie and I sit under the tree.

Amy Horscroft (10)
Little Common School, Bexhill-on-Sea

A Holiday In Jamaica

Jamaica, Jamaica, it's full of tourists that travel from over the seas.
Beautiful colours, red, yellows and greens.
Bunches of bananas that hang from the trees.
Clear water, golden sands,
Wonderful sunshine that burns your hands.
The evening falls and you start to yawn,
Sweet and peacefully it comes to dawn.
You wake up with glee with happiness to see,
The sun is still shining all over me.

James Park (10)
Little Common School, Bexhill-on-Sea

Sounds Of The Wake!

When I awake it's always noisy,
It's never a squeak, like a mouse,
It's just noise around the house,
There is the popping of the toast,
There is Mum cooking the Sunday roast,
My baby brother clattering his spoons against the breakfast bowls,
My bigger brother is in the garden scoring football goals
And me standing there half asleep sighing!

Emma Swan (10)
Little Common School, Bexhill-on-Sea

The Magic Box

(Based on 'Magic Box' by Kit Wright)

I will put in my box . . .
The glancing eye of an eagle,
The silky skills of Ronaldinho
And the beating rev of a Ferrari.

I will put in my box . . .
The tangy taste of an ice lolly
The gorgeous smell of apple crumble
And the chuckle of a monkey.

I will put in my box . . .
The wail of the sea crashing on the rocks,
The glorious future of Theo Walcott
And the fab tunes of Gorillaz.
The lid is made of chocolate,
The hinges are made of stars!

Oscar Hammond (10)
Little Common School, Bexhill-on-Sea

Smelly Feet

The teacher passed out and fell off her chair,
The headmaster is hiding his head,
And the plants by the window are practically dead.

There's gas in the class, it's completely her fault
And it smells like a nuclear weapons assault.
So try to remember this lesson for me,
Mrs Scales don't take your shoes off after PE!

Max Frame (10)
Little Common School, Bexhill-on-Sea

Jaguar

J aguars running through the jungle
A ttacking their prey
G urgle, gurgle as the meat goes down
U sing trees for shade
A ggressive and vicious when playing
R ancid breath always draws near.

Declan Lea-White (10)
Little Common School, Bexhill-on-Sea

Dolphins

Dolphins have blow holes, they don't use their mouth
In the summer they head for the south.
They are beautiful creatures, they greet you with a smile.
Why don't you go and swim with them for a while?
I once swam with a dolphin, it was soft
You definitely can't fit a dolphin in the loft!

Sophie Middleton (8)
Little Common School, Bexhill-on-Sea

Chelsea

C helsea are the best in the league
H ove Albion try to please
E veryone knows we are the best
L iverpol and all the rest
S coring in every game
E veryone tries to do the same
A fter all who is the best?

Luke Willard (9)
Little Common School, Bexhill-on-Sea

Rhyme

I like to rhyme
All the time.
If you don't rhyme
You have committed a crime.
I love to eat limes
But only sometimes.

Beth Chapman (10)
Little Common School, Bexhill-on-Sea

What Am I?

I don't have tusks,
But I have some flippers,
When I go to bed
I don't wear slippers.
What am I?

Answer: seal.

I carry my home on my back,
I live in the sea,
I eat seaweed
And my babies are slow just like me.
What am I?

Answer: turtle.

I live in the treetops,
I swing from tree to tree,
I say, 'ooh ooh, aah aah'
We always shout with glee.
What am I?

Answer: monkey.

I am spotty
And have a long neck,
I eat leaves
And I don't peck.
What am I?

Answer: giraffe.

Rebecca Pfaff (9)
Little Common School, Bexhill-on-Sea

Dreams

I dream and dream of custard cream,
And a bowlful of jelly in my welly.
Sweets and treats that rot my teeth,
And a kind, careful caterpillar on a leaf.
Fairies that dance and deer that prance
Dragons and beasts, bundles of feasts,
Love makes hate, hate makes love.
A lovely white dove that soars in my eyes.
Angels that sing so high in the skies.

Cherrise Woodrow (9)
Little Common School, Bexhill-on-Sea

When I Was On A Train

Cars go by when we are passing
Fields with blue streams cutting through
Long Man of Willmington gazes from the Downs
Stations appear without any sounds
Passengers are disembarking
Taxis await the lucky few
Door closes swiftly and on we go!

Harriet Tomlin (8)
Little Common School, Bexhill-on-Sea

Pizza

Pizza's great!
Pizza's ace!
Pizza puts a smile on everyone's face.
Ice cream's yummy,
Sweets are nice,
But pizza tops the very lot!

Edward Smith (8)
Little Common School, Bexhill-on-Sea

Turtles

T urtles swimming far and near
U nder the glistening blue sea
R elaxing on the beach so clear
T alking about the sea
L ittle ones by their mother's side
E ating what they find
S uch lovely creatures turtles are, they have so much pride.

Katie Wolford (9)
Little Common School, Bexhill-on-Sea

The Magical Seashore

Seashells, seashells on the seashore
Crashing gently upon the shore.
Glistening, shimmering bright!
Will shine like stars on the shore tonight.
Seagulls swooping high and low
Gathering food from down below.
Waves crashing against the shore
Making white horses that's for sure!

Charlotte Walker (9)
Little Common School, Bexhill-on-Sea

Here We Go, Here We Go

This is a poem on how football has changed,
Of the good and bad and the crowds entertained.
Way back then, when there wasn't any Sven,
The blitzed footie Brits had to wear awful kits.
They had the FA Cup but it wasn't on the telly,
Lurking in Brazil was a skilful boy named Pele.
The World Cup is coming, it's getting very near.
Let's hope the England fans cheer, cheer, cheer!
With little Mikey Owen scoring from a throw-in
And big Stevie G striking with his knee.
I hope that we can win it, for all the world to see
And when Beckham holds the cup, I wish that could be me.

Jacob Shelton (10)
Little Common School, Bexhill-on-Sea

My Mum And Dad

My mum and dad are very funny,
They make a cloudy day turn sunny.
We do lots of fun things together,
And their hugs are special to treasure.

We go for long walks along the beach,
When it's a hot sunny day it's a big treat.
We throw stones in the wavy water,
And sit on the pebbles, just Mum, Dad and Daughter.

When I am sad I can always be sure,
Mum and Dad will have a very good cure.
Lots of special words and big hugs too
My mum and dad are special, that's true!

Kirsty Felix (10)
Little Common School, Bexhill-on-Sea

Winter

The North Wind will blow
And it is now time for snow.
The sun has gone to sleep,
The weather turns to sleet.
The clouds are grey
And the blue skies have blown away.
I hear the robin sing,
He is waiting for the spring.
I saw the sun today,
Maybe spring is on its way.

Harriot Uprichard (7)
Little Common School, Bexhill-on-Sea

Dogs

Dogs are all different sizes, some big, some small
Some dogs are cute; some are not nice at all.
But my dog runs around the garden looking for her bone
She doesn't like being brushed, not even by a comb.
German Shepherds are big compared to West Highland Terriers.
They sit in their baskets waiting for their dinner
If you don't feed them, they will get thinner.
When you walk to the park, you always see a dog,
They sniff the grass, they dig big holes and when you step in them
You fall flat on your nose.
If you don't train them they will get naughty
So everyone should train their dog, even if they are forty.

Emily Vincent (9)
Little Common School, Bexhill-on-Sea

My Cat

I love my cat
She is fluffy and fat.
Happy to greet me
Purring so sweetly.

Brown and grey coat so cosy,
Yellow eyes, cute little nosey.
Loving and kind
I'm so glad she is mine.

Lydia Robinson (7)
Little Common School, Bexhill-on-Sea

My Puppy Millie

My puppy Millie is very pretty,
And she has a teddy bear called Kitty.
She always snores,
She has cheesy paws.
She loves to go out for a walk
And always tries to talk.
She has a lovely black coat
And a shiny collar on her throat.
Millie loves to chase cats
And she'll eat any rats.
I think Millie is rather great
She is my best mate.

Adam Holman (9)
Little Common School, Bexhill-on-Sea

All The Kids On Holiday

All the kids go out to play
Next thing you know they're on holiday,
Later they're on the aeroplane
They're all flying off to sunny Spain.

At the hotel they empty their cases
They run to the pool with smiles on their faces,
Some children sunbathe round the pool
And use their fans to keep them cool.

The kids are packing their cases
They all start to moan
With sadness on their faces
They all trudge on home.

Lara Petty (9)
Little Common School, Bexhill-on-Sea

Schooldays

Boys and girls go out to play,
At my school twice a day,
My teachers are nice and some are funny,
School mash potato is very runny,
Some work is hard, some work is easy,
The least of it is lemon squeezy.
Two of my friends are Jack and Scott
They are the best friends that I have got.

Ryan Rankin (9)
Little Common School, Bexhill-on-Sea

Ten Things Found In My Brother's Pocket

A hairy and sticky lollipop he's saved,
A lonely sweet from yesterday,
An unsharpened pencil from me,
A sucked rabbit rubber,
A carrot from Sunday (it's Friday now!)
A pebble (that's been coloured in),
A set of car keys, are they Mum's?
A missing, smelly, stripey sock,
A splodge of . . . I don't know!
A dog sleeping soundly.

Sophie Doick (10)
Little Common School, Bexhill-on-Sea

A Basset Hound

I have two very long ears and a long nose,
I have four small stumpy legs with big paws,
And my humongous ears drag along floors.
My tail usually gets slammed in doors,
When I run, slobber flies out of my jaws,
I am a sneaky hound,
I weigh quite a few pounds.

Scott Sherwood (10)
Little Common School, Bexhill-on-Sea

Football

F ree-kick for Arsenal
O nto Reyes' foot
O ne touch into
T hierry Henry
B ang! Into the net it goes
A ll the fans are cheering
L ast shot of the game
L ovely, we have won again.

Matthew Greenwood (7)
Little Common School, Bexhill-on-Sea

Me And My Birthday

Up early today, a badge to wear
I'm eight today but I don't care
I'm a big boy now, my life will change,
Off to school I go, in green to be seen.
'Happy birthday,' my class sing to me
I smile with a grin
Home to go, presents to open.
A birthday cake and a wish to be taken.

George Chapman (8)
Little Common School, Bexhill-on-Sea

Winter Snow

Snow is like a big, white, fluffy cushion,
Snow feels like a glowing feeling inside,
When I walk through the cold, crispy woods
I always hear a crunch from the snow,
Where the grass used to stand the snow falls without a sound.

Amelia Harmer (10)
Little Common School, Bexhill-on-Sea

Off To School

Off to school, it's early in the morning,
Got up late, I'm still yawning.
Hair's a mess, tie's undone
Got to smarten up, school's begun.

Assembly is so boring
I feel like snoring.
It's numeracy, *hooray!*
It'll take up half a day.
Oh boo, a test
In the subject I like best.

End of lesson, time for food,
I'm in a good mood.
Oh great, a really long wait
I'll get the worst plate!

Alright! It's chicken masala curry
Everyone is in a hurry.
Now, it's play
Hip hip hooray!

Back to class, now it is art,
I won't look very smart.
Blobs of paint everywhere,
Even in my hair!

It's the end of school
It is quite cool!

Asher Oliver (10)
Little Common School, Bexhill-on-Sea

My Birthday

It was fab, it was great
I spent the day with my mate.
We went bowling, we had a ball
I thought it was really cool.
We played air hockey and video games
With some weird and scary names.
We went to McDonald's for our tea
I brought my kid sister along with me.
We went to the video shop and hired a movie
It was 'Herbie Fully Loaded' the music was groovy.
I asked if my friend could stay the night
My mum said, 'Sure, that's all right.'
I had the best day being ten,
I can't wait till it's my birthday again!

Cameron Young (10)
Little Common School, Bexhill-on-Sea

Days Of Summer

As the warm air caresses me softly,
The birds fly, floating on the soft summer breeze,
Fish dance on the ocean waves as the sun reflects rainbows of colour.
Sticky puddles of what once were lollies
And empty cans of various liquids litter the promenade.
Bees buzz, stealing precious pollen from flowers in bloom.
Extended days and nights filled with joy and cheer
But hence when all had ended . . . what's left?
. . . Just a tear.

Ellen Mepham (8)
Little Common School, Bexhill-on-Sea

The Amazing Miss Keyte

There is a lady who is a treat
And you will know her from the name, Miss Keyte.
She really is the coolest teacher alive
And that is why she teaches Year 5.
She comes in each morning all happy and sunny
Ready to tell us jokes that are funny.
She gets us to learn all our times tables
And then tells us mysterious stories and fables.
But when she loses that lovely smile
You know it's time to run a mile!
If she gives you that special look
You know it's time for the behaviour book.
But never fear, before very long
That lovely smile will again come along.

Megan Roberts (9)
Little Common School, Bexhill-on-Sea

About My Family

I love my family, of course I do,
I guess you are thinking, *am I being true*?
I love parties, oh yes,
I always wear a blue dress.
My mum is very sweet, I love my mummy.
Oh yes, yes, I do love honey.
I love my brother, his name is Daniel, Daniel sucks his thumb,
He is funny, he is also very dumb.
My dad is tall, he is also cool,
He is funny; he also likes to dive into pools!

Ellie Rains (7)
Little Common School, Bexhill-on-Sea

My Dog Cassie

My dog Cassie was special to me
She was so good, I wish I had three.
She had long curly hair and dark round eyes,
She shone like a star in seven different skies.
I wish she was still around,
She never really frowned.
She always liked to smile,
It lasted for quite a long while.
My dog Cassie meant the world to me,
And to everyone else this was plain to see.

Jack Heyes (9)
Little Common School, Bexhill-on-Sea

Snowflakes

Snowflakes fall gently from the frosty sky,
Snowflakes twinkle brightly,
Snowflakes are soft and frosty,
Snowflakes are bright and white,
Snowflakes fall day and night,
We can crush them together and have a fight,
The trouble is that they do not last forever
As they melt in the warm sunlight.

William Westwood (9)
Little Common School, Bexhill-on-Sea

Snow

Crystal snow falling from Heaven,
A gift from God,
Swirling and dancing in the snow-filled sky,
Laying itself gently on the ground like a soft carpet, icy cold,
Sparkling like diamonds, nature's treasure.
Families laughing at the joy snow brings,
Building snowmen, snowball fights,
Snow tickling their bodies as it falls,
They try to catch those precious jewels,
The snow joins in the fun and flutters away,
Settling gently where it falls,
Our world is such an amazing place.

Joe Kennedy (10)
Little Common School, Bexhill-on-Sea

Football Is The Game

Football is my favourite game
Crystal Palace is the name
I watch them on the big screen telly
Eating sweets for my belly
Sometimes I watch at their ground
When they score there's not a sound
Once that ball is in the net
I shout, '*Hooray!* I won the bet.'
Crystal Palace is the name.

Reece Powell (9)
Little Common School, Bexhill-on-Sea

Down By The Woods

Close to my house there are woods where I go,
I have been there in the sun, the rain and the snow.
There are lots of big trees, squirrels, birds and a park,
But I make sure I leave before it gets dark!

Mia Cunningham (7)
Little Common School, Bexhill-on-Sea

Rain

R ain pours all day
A nd nothing can stop it
I gnorant raindrops not minding their manners
N o one can get in the way of a raindrop; it always finds its way to the ground.

Hannah Jones (9)
Little Common School, Bexhill-on-Sea

The Sun

The sun, just one ball of fire,
Floating like a bird on the sea waiting for a fish.
The sun, looking through everyone's window,
Seeing what they're watching on TV.
The sun, watching the rockets come flying past,
On their way to the moon.
The sun even when it is raining and thundering,
Always there above you, with you every day.

James Robinson (10)
Little Common School, Bexhill-on-Sea

My Cat

Lying at home, nice and warm, is my pet black cat
Going at night and back in at dawn
We are all happy when he comes back
He always walks with us to the corner shop
He waits outside until we're finished
Then he follows us back
My black cat loves me lots and always sits on my lap
My extremely cute black cat.

Jack Barfoot (9)
Little Common School, Bexhill-on-Sea

Best Mates

Now we're friends we can start again and be best mates forever.
We'll play our games and have such fun, doing things together.
Troubles may come and troubles may go,
But we'll not fall out, no never.

Beth Allen (8)
Little Common School, Bexhill-on-Sea

Love

Love tastes like melting chocolate in your mouth.
Love smells like the sweet scent of strawberry perfume.
Love looks like two kittens snuggling together on a rug.
Love feels like soft silk.
Love sounds like a nightingale singing its sweet song!

Catherine Allender (9)
Little Common School, Bexhill-on-Sea

Christmas

C hristmas is a joyful time
H ats, crackers, all fun things to play and do
R oast dinners are delicious, meat to chew
I ce skating everywhere
S nowy, snowy air
T owards the north you see the snow
M arvellous things to see like a show
A Christmas tree is normally fine
S ometimes it has a lot of pine.

Aidan Malt (9)
Little Common School, Bexhill-on-Sea

Snowflake

S lowly falling down
N o noise do we make
O n and on, on and on
W e don't know where we will land
F loating down
L ike an eagle in flight
A lways different, no two the same
K een to make the ground white
E ver so delicate, ever so white.

Mark Boorman (7)
Little Common School, Bexhill-on-Sea

The Witch In This Kitchen

Once in this kitchen
A naughty witch was itching
To make a beastly broth
For her best friend, Bert the moth!
She used a frog and an ugly dog
Not in the pot, but to fetch a spot!
Both lacked obedience but fetched the ingredients
A list of which follows below:
Firstly a spot from a child's spotty face,
A big squeezy spot to add to the taste.
An amphibian eyeball from a salamander
And from the seas of the Philippines a juicy sea cucumber.
The farmer's welly which is really, really smelly
And his wife's cheesy socks and her old dirty frocks and
A boy called Bart, because 'I want his heart,' said the witch with a cackle.

Phoebe Jones (7)
Little Common School, Bexhill-on-Sea

When I Was . . .

When I was one I sucked my thumb
When I was two I went to the loo
When I was three I hurt my knee
When I was four I climbed the door
When I was five I learnt to dive
When I was six I got my karate mitts
When I was seven I went to Devon
Now I'm eight I've got two best mates.

Jack Moyse (8)
Little Common School, Bexhill-on-Sea

The Wind

The wind can be a soft breeze
The gentle whistle in your ear
The rustle of leaves being blown along
How marvellous it is

The wind can be a wet, blustery night
With lots of strength and power
It bends the trees, like they are rubber bands
How marvellous it is.

The wind can be a killer twister
It destroys homes and cars
It tears up roads and cities
How marvellous it is.

The wind can be a great stroke of luck
Blowing a lucky lottery ticket my way
How grateful I am for the wind
How marvellous it is.

The wind can be many things
But we don't always notice it
Look after nature as nature will look after us
We should be grateful for the wind
How marvellous it is.

Andrew Leggatt (10)
Little Common School, Bexhill-on-Sea

Are We There Yet?

Are we there yet?
We've already missed lunch.
Are we there yet?
Come on Mum give us something to munch.
Are we there yet?
This isn't home.
Are we there yet?
That's not our gnome.
Are we there yet?
Is that home I see?
Yes, we're there now,
Just in time for tea.

William Carne (9)
Little Common School, Bexhill-on-Sea

Guinea Pigs

G uinea pigs are cute
U nless they puke!
I nteresting when there are fights
N either of them bites
E ven if they're scrappy
A lways, always happy!

P layful and jumpy
I n their hutch it's nice and warm
G reeting kisses when it's dawn
S o special, never grumpy!

Natasha Dupker (10)
Little Common School, Bexhill-on-Sea

Good Food, Bad Food

Bananas, bananas make me go ape
The more I eat the more I shake.

Sprouts, sprouts they make me shout
The more I shout the more I pout.

Peas, peas sound like cheese
If they were, I would be pleased!

Eggs, eggs don't make me eat them I beg
Because they give me wobbly legs.

Oh sweets, sweets give them to me
If you do I will be good for you.

Elliott Hogg (9)
Little Common School, Bexhill-on-Sea

Sisters

My name is Leah May and I am quite tall,
I sometimes drive my mum up the wall.
My sister is two and full of fun
And is always out and on the run.
She wakes up nearly every night
We think she sometimes has a fright.
My dad thinks I'm a real tomboy
But I am really his little joy.
I kick a football every day
But sometimes Amie gets in the way.
Having a sister is really fun
And lots of nice things can be done.

Leah Anderson (7)
Little Common School, Bexhill-on-Sea

Balloon Poem

B ig and round with different colours
A ll bright with many nice patterns
L ovely to play with and very enjoyable
L ike a big, round, bouncy orange
O ver, upward and onward it flies
O ut into the open blue skies
N orth of the Atlantic it goes
S oaring through the air like an albatross and then *pop!*

Daniel Ralley (9)
Little Common School, Bexhill-on-Sea

Heaven, Life And Hell

H eavenly life
E verlasting peace
A twenty-four foot gold entry gate
V ery magical place
E ndless love and happiness
N ever a dismal place

L iving is great
I mages all around
F un and laughter
E vents full of surprise

H ot and fiery
E vil all around
L ost souls
L ife lost forever.

George Carroll (10)
Little Common School, Bexhill-on-Sea

Emotions

Love is like the wind blowing in your face,
Hate is like blood crisping on your knee,
Joy is like a jack-in-the box springing out to make you jump,
Sadness is like rain drizzling down on your umbrella,
Happiness is like seeing a baby when it's still young,
Disappointment is like when Christmas is over and December is a long time to wait,
Pride is like when you have finished your homework and you are very proud of it,
Jealousy is like watching someone eat a Galaxy bar without offering you a bite.

Rosie Southon (9)
Little Common School, Bexhill-on-Sea

Suppose

Suppose a golden unicorn with ivory eyes
Came galloping down from the skies.
Suppose I climbed on its back and galloped away
To the starlight that gleams from on high.
Suppose I saw Santa in his magic sleigh,
Wrapping presents for children to open on Christmas Day.
Suppose, suppose, suppose.

Hermione Porter (8)
Little Common School, Bexhill-on-Sea

By The Sea

My name is Imogen Taylor, I live by the sea.
Although I'm not a sailor, it's where I love to be.
I sit on the wall eating my ice cream.
I play with my ball and love to daydream.
I watch ships go by and seagulls flying in the sky.
I sit with the girls and we collect lots of shells.
I love being by the sea.

Imogen Taylor (7)
Little Common School, Bexhill-on-Sea

Dolphins

D olphin, dolphins swimming around
O cean is full of them
L ooping, leaping in the sky
P opping their heads up
H appy, smiley faces
I want to swim with one
N ice and kind.

Elizabeth Terry (9)
Little Common School, Bexhill-on-Sea

The Seasons

The seasons are all different in their own way,
Because summer is bright and winter is grey.
Spring is the sign of new life coming,
Autumn is the sound of raindrops humming.
It doesn't matter if some are grey and dull,
Others are light, crimson and gold.
With sparkling sunsets and dazzling colours,
The seasons will live for eternity as brothers.

Christopher Knapp (9)
Little Common School, Bexhill-on-Sea

Bath Time Trouble

Into a foamy bath I climb and soak amongst the bubbles
When what do I hear from outside the door?
My little brother . . . *trouble!*
'Hello,' he says with a smile on his face,
'I'm having a bath with you,'
'Great!' I say and roll my eyes
This cannot be true
In he climbs - I know what's next,
He stands and looks at me.
Then grinning wide from ear-to-ear
He does a little wee!

Elliot Martin (7)
Little Common School, Bexhill-on-Sea

Lions

Lion roared and Lion snored
While lying in his den.
He wrote a letter to his friends
With his brand new pen.
And he went after school
To the local swimming pool.

Stacey Kelly (7)
Little Common School, Bexhill-on-Sea

Fairies

Fairies fly through the sky day and night.
I look out of my window hoping to catch a glimpse,
Of what people think are make-believe creatures.
Then suddenly I see one!
A beautiful pink fairy leaving a golden trail of fairy dust,
To gleam in the night sky.
I blink and rub my eyes just to check it's real,
By the fairy is still there!
I walk away and sit down to write in my secret diary.
Now every time I look out of my window,
I see a fairy then blink and rub my eyes,
Just to make sure it is my fairy friend.
It seems to turn its head and gives a little wave and a smile.

Ellen Stickland (8)
Little Common School, Bexhill-on-Sea

Another Fine Morning

It's seven o'clock, guess it's time now to rise
But I'm still so tired, I can't open my eyes
Time to fall out of bed, very slow down the stairs
It's still dark outside and cold, but who cares
Breakfast awaits me, it's Frosties and toast
And fresh orange juice which I really love most
So it's back up the stairs to get washed
And then dressed: can't find my tie, can't find my vest
My sister's still moaning cos Mummy's combing
Her hair, I don't brush mine, (don't really care).
Make my hair stand up stiff with a quick dab of gel
Then brush the teeth and rinse my mouth well.
Then it's on with my coat, gloves and a scarf
And it's out of the door with a smile and a laugh.
Scrape off the ice and into the car,
Do up the seatbelt, it's not very far.
Then out of the car to the walking bus
I'm head of the queue not making a fuss.
A quick walk to school that's all it takes
And into the playground where my friends await.
Another few minutes, my teacher appears
So it's into the classroom without any tears.

Callum Nattress (7)
Little Common School, Bexhill-on-Sea

Cats And Kittens

C ats walking on the street
A ll kittens mewing in a basket
T ails high in the air
S leeping on your bed

A lley cats howling at night
N ine lives, cats live a long time
D addy cats hunting in the night

K ittens playing with a ball of string
I nteresting fishes in a tank
T ormenting kittens playing with their mum's tail
T all, proud mummy cats
E ating bowls of cat food
N aughty cats miaowing at the window
S cared cats going to the vets.

Grace Quinn (9)
Little Common School, Bexhill-on-Sea

My Favourite Things

I like to hop, skip and jump
But sometimes I land with a bump
I like running around and around
I do it in the school playground
My favourite lesson at school is art
The pictures I make are very smart
I also like topic, science and to read
After that it's time for a feed
For lunch I love pasta bake
For pudding I have a great big cake
I love strawberries, raspberries and melon as well,
When I've finished it's time for the bell
Back to lessons, here I go
I wonder what subject it is, I don't know
It's home time, let's get in the car
Off to my house, it's not too far
My favourite programme is Drake and Josh
It's time for bed! I must have a wash
At last I'm in my favourite place
My squidgy bed is a special space
I cuddle up with Sausage, my best mate
He keeps me safe when it gets late
My favourite things are the best
Not like my mum making me wear a vest!

Rebecca Ellis (7)
Little Common School, Bexhill-on-Sea

Jungle Bells

The ducks keep quacking.
The tiger is attacking.
The monkey is swinging.
The birds keep singing.
The snake keeps eating.
The pride is at a meeting.
The parrot is always talking.
The gorilla is walking.
The rhino is charging.
The elephants keep barging.
The crucible keeps snapping.
The termite is tapping.
The bees keep stinging.
The jungle bells are ringing.

Lewis A Besbeech (9)
Little Common School, Bexhill-on-Sea

Wintertime

W oolly hats and fluffy scarves,
I n the cold winter's snow,
N o one stands around for long,
T hey rush home where they belong,
E njoy chocolate while you're warming up,
R oasting toes by an open fire,
T ime to cuddle up in bed,
I n the covers I turn my head,
M agical thoughts about my day,
E xcited about what tomorrow might bring!

Toni Littlejohn (9)
Little Common School, Bexhill-on-Sea

Cats

Cats are cute and cuddly,
I think cats are cool,
I would rather have a cat
Than a swimming pool!

Cats are cute and cuddly,
They like to play with yarn,
And catch all the mice
In the farmer's barn.

Cats are cute and cuddly,
I think cats are cool,
And anyone who doesn't like them
Is a complete fool!

Lucy Baker (9)
Little Common School, Bexhill-on-Sea

The Creatures In The Sea

Creatures swimming about
Some are nice, some are not
But all are amazing
Sharks are fierce
Turtles are gentle
Corals are colourful
Seals are plain grey
But no matter what
They are all special.

William Edwards (8)
Little Common School, Bexhill-on-Sea

Fairies

F airies fly through the sky,
A ltogether way up high
I n and out
R ound and round
I t's such fun for everyone
E ven for me and even for you
S o I would like to be a fairy too.

Jodie Henningway (9)
Little Common School, Bexhill-on-Sea

Let's Go On Holiday

Let's go on holiday to a hot and steamy beach!
At night we can't sleep because we're waiting for tomorrow's surprises.
During the day we swim in the massive green sea,
Then look in foreign shops which sell shell necklaces.

Let's go on holiday to the parasol-packed sand,
Or snorkel in the swimming pool to cool down.
We can have yummy ice cream dribbling down our wrist
And finally watch a multicoloured sunset from the dark balcony.

Let's go on holiday to a cold and icy mountain!
Where we can put on seven woolly jumpers and wish we had an eighth,
Then ski on the snow with our teeth chattering,
I can't wait for my scrummy hot chocolate to warm me up.

Let's go on holiday wearing lots of thick socks on our cold feet,
Warm gloves stop us from turning blue with all the shivering.
Beautiful snow is settling on our roofs like icing sugar!
But for now we are on the plane flying home,
With dreams of next year's holiday that awaits us.

Jemima Hipkiss (9)
Little Common School, Bexhill-on-Sea

Fairies

Fairies flying everywhere
Their wings sparkle as they go by
Fairy dust gently falls to the ground
Making wishes come true
Dancing in the flowers
Singing in the wind
Taking care of me and you.

Laila Barakat (10)
Little Common School, Bexhill-on-Sea

My Rat Reggie

My name is Reggie
And I like my veggie
I eat so much I get quite fat
It doesn't really matter
Because I am a rat.
I curl up in a ball
And look quite small
Then I open my eyes
And become alive
And I run around like a fool.

Daniel Streeter (9)
Little Common School, Bexhill-on-Sea

Lonely Hearts

Fun-loving troll dirty and smelly
With damp slimy skin and a big hairy belly,
Nice muddy fingers and grubby wet toes
Hot steamy breath and rings through each nose.

With stains in his shirt and holes in his socks
Teeth that need cleaning and knots in his locks
Tears in his trousers and scuffs on his shoe
He is waiting to meet someone lovely like you.

He likes dirty ditches and hiding in holes
He is certain to win when he fights other trolls
He is very attentive, gives gifts of roses
After he's used them to pick both his noses.

He lives on his own in a dark stinking pit
Oozing with slime and covered in spit
Now feeling lonely, he hopes there's a chance
To meet someone similar for fun and romance!

Lena Mansy (7)
Little Common School, Bexhill-on-Sea

Chelsea FC

C helsea FC are at the top of the pile
H erman Crespo makes Jose smile
E idur passes to Cole
L ampard can score some super Frankie goals
S tamford Bridge is full of dreams
E very player fights for the team
A rsen Robben has loads of steam.

Robbie Jenner (9)
Little Common School, Bexhill-on-Sea

Chocolate

C hocolate is delicious
H ungry am I for the taste
O verwhelming smells so nice indeed
C an't get enough of the texture
O oozing chocolate dribbling down my chin
L ittle chunks are not enough
A number of bars waiting in line
T ummy growling, tummy groaning
E veryone loves this treat.

Tyran Armstrong (9)
Little Common School, Bexhill-on-Sea

India

I ndia, India, it's a great place
N aughty monkeys stealing food
D resses made of rich colours and patterns
I ndia has many spicy foods
A ll Indians enjoying celebrations feasts and dancing.

Nathan Jay (10)
Little Common School, Bexhill-on-Sea

Fireworks

F aces looking excited and nervous
I nto the sky shoot colours and lights
R oaring crowds gasp as they see the amazing patterns
E xcitement mounting
W hooshing and loud bangs
O verhead the night sky vibrates
R ound and round, the Catherine wheels go
K eeping everyone's eyes fixed on them
S parklers begin to twinkle as they are lit.

Charlotte Troughton (10)
Little Common School, Bexhill-on-Sea

Sport Haiku

Sport keeps you healthy
There are lots of different kinds
It's also great fun!

Matthew Edwards (10)
Little Common School, Bexhill-on-Sea

The Elephant

E lephants plodding by
L eaves being stuffed in mouths
E ars so big they can hear for miles
P laying in the mud, squelch, squelch, squelchy,
H osing water everywhere
A baby elephant holding Mum's tail
N ow it's dark let's sleep soundly
T errific aren't they?

Nicole Maynard (10)
Little Common School, Bexhill-on-Sea

Walking In The Forest

When you're walking in the forest
And you feel a bit scared because . . .
The moon is bright
It gives you a fright
The ghosts are hiding
The witches are gliding
Werewolves are howling
Frankenstein is scowling
Owls are screeching
Rats are squeaking
Twigs are snapping
Toads are rapping
All I want is my big warm bed
But Mum says we have to walk the dog instead.

Ryan Foord (9)
Little Common School, Bexhill-on-Sea

What Am I?

What am I?
I have big fluffy ears,
I have a small round tail,
I run away from deer,
I live in a burrow.
What am I?
I have four legs
And cute blue eyes,
I have ears like pegs,
I have two thighs.
I am a rabbit!

George Stinson (10)
Little Common School, Bexhill-on-Sea

The First Day At School

I see all my friends on the first day of school,
When we write stories and swim in the pool.
We wait in the lesson until we have break
'Cause I know I'm so lucky my mum's packed me cake!
I sharpen my pencil
And draw round my stencil
And think *what a lovely way*
To start the first day.

Jodie Chennell (9)
Little Common School, Bexhill-on-Sea

A Loving Home At Last

I first lived in slimy grimy rubble with no one to cuddle
I'd wash in the dirt and bask in the sun, but it wasn't any fun.
For wet cardboard was my bed with no shelter over my head.
I have been here for many years; at night my brain is aching with hopes and fears.
For my food was a mouse, if I could catch it, I bet even that mouse had a house.
I lived off scraps that I could find, dreams of fresh fish in my mind.
I'm an old girl and my bones are aching, every day I dread waking.
To another cold and lonely day, I wish there was another way.
A family move in next door, I start to visit them more and more.
The cold winter winds start to blow, from the sky falls shimmering silver snow.
The family opened up their door and the mum said,
'Well I guess you can come in then, but please wipe your feet, don't put mud on my floor.'
They gave me a warm bed in which to sleep, brush my fur so the shine will keep.
I now know I've found my purrrfect home, where I will never be alone,
I'm fed and cared for in every way, all my dreams are real today.

Connor Whelan-Sams (11)
Little Common School, Bexhill-on-Sea

The Four Seasons

Spring, spring, it's all to do
With lambs and chicks being born anew!

Summer, summer, how I love the sun
On the beach eating my iced bun!

Autumn, autumn, leaves on the ground
Crunch, crunch, crunch getting pushed all around.

Winter, winter, frost and snow,
Gloves, hats and scarves and off we go!

Charlotte Russell (8)

Little Common School, Bexhill-on-Sea

Buster

Buster is my cat
He is lazy and he is fat
He spends all day upon my bed
And always complains he is not fed.

Buster is a tabby
Sometimes he is shabby
He likes to hunt for mice
Even though he is very nice.

Alice Rhodes (10)
Little Common School, Bexhill-on-Sea

Spooky Night

At thirteen o'clock the witches fly
As wizards watch the great black sky.
At thirteen o'clock the kids awake
Then silently they shiver and shake!
At one o'clock kids wake in the dark
Scared of their nightmare, a great white shark!
At two o'clock kids run away
Scared of the night so solemn and grey!
At three o'clock the whole house is asleep
Dreaming as huge ghosts creep!
At four o'clock the baby awakes
Sees the darkness then cries till we wake!
At five o'clock a ghost of a pope
Silently reading his horoscope!
At six o'clock men get up
Pouring their tea into their teacup!
At seven o'clock the blackbird tweets
While a group of vampires share their blood sweets!

Georgia Lea (10)
Little Common School, Bexhill-on-Sea

Unicorn

Horn that twists and gleams in the sun,
Silver hooves leaving trails of glitter,
Eyes blue as forget-me-nots shining for evermore,
Soft white fur as sleek as a seal,
Sparkling tail flicking gracefully up and down,
I am a unicorn.

Poppy Lelliott (10)
Little Common School, Bexhill-on-Sea

Underwater

U nusual fishes swimming around
N ibbling at the tasty coral they've found
D ivers watching the aquatic life
E normous shark with teeth like a knife
R eefs of life, reefs full of colour
W recks never disturbed from years ago
A hidden treasure beneath the depths below
T he dolphins ride the boats bow waves
E els lay sleeping in their underwater cave
R eally fantastic underwater world.

Jenny Whelan (9)
Little Common School, Bexhill-on-Sea

Rainforest

R ain falls gently on the trees
A nd the wind blows softly through the leaves
I n the forest animals hide
N ewts that swim, snakes that slide
F lying insects all around
O ther creatures on the ground
R eally dark and damp in there
E nter carefully and be aware
S pare the time to look around
T ell everybody what you have found.

Charlie Osborn (9)
Little Common School, Bexhill-on-Sea

Somebody

Somebody told me about love
They said it was a flying white dove.
Somebody told me about food
They said that some of it comes from a cow that mooed.
Somebody told me about school
They said most people think it's uncool!
Somebody told me about wives
They said for their cooking, buy them knives.
Somebody told me about you
I'd like to see you and say how do you do!

Ellie Harrison (10)
Little Common School, Bexhill-on-Sea

My Idol

Saturday afternoon
I'm hoping for goals galore
Keeping my fingers crossed
That my idol Henry will score

Out onto the pitch
The team appear
Up goes a roar
As all the fans cheer

The stands are covered
In shades of red and white
As Arsenal take on Chelsea
I know they will put up a fight

The whistle is blown
And the game begins
Thierry is brought down
John Terry really boots him in the shins
The ref awards a penalty
This could be our chance
Yeah, we've scored!

My idol is Thierry Henry; he is the greatest player I will ever see.

Harry Saville (10)
Little Common School, Bexhill-on-Sea

I Have A Puppy, His Name Is Hugo

He is very sweet
Just wait until you meet
He jumps up and gives you a big sloppy kiss
He is great fun
He likes to run
He likes to play
He does this all day long
He is a naughty puppy
He is a very happy puppy
He cheers you up when you are sad
He can be very bad
He likes to have hugs all the time
He likes to climb
He likes to walk all over your face while you're tucked up in bed.

Amberley Shore (11)
Little Common School, Bexhill-on-Sea

A Defender With Class

A defender with class,
Does not let strikers past,
Set pieces in his skills,
Getting the ball on his head is his will,
Stopping strikers reaching the net,
More goals from him are sure I bet,
Scored loads of goals already this season,
Chelsea nurtured him for a reason
Twenty-six is his number
John Terry is his name
Stopping strikers scoring is his game.

Lewis Kemp (10)
Little Common School, Bexhill-on-Sea

Happiness

H aving lots of great fun
A sking for something at Christmas and getting it
P ush of confidence from your friends
P erson who you don't know, then talking and making a friend
I n a wicked or nice dream
N ow your birthday or party or Christmas
E njoying an ice cream
S orting out
S ticky situations with a friend and still being friends.

George Eldridge (10)
Little Common School, Bexhill-on-Sea

Winter Poem

W inter is a cold wet season
I cicles creep up and find their own place
N obody is lonely in winter
T he children all love to make snowmen
E veryone enjoys winter
R emember to wrap up warm in a hat, scarf and gloves!

P eople open their presents
O rdering their presents into 'like' and 'hate'
E veryone is happy
M aking snowmen is great!

Emma Keall (11)
Little Common School, Bexhill-on-Sea

Seasons

I walk down the street in the hail and the sleet, I know that winter has come.
My collar is up, my hat is pulled down and I run to get dry and keep myself warm.
I look up to the sky, it seems heavy and slow, *oh no,* I think, *there might be snow.*
I look out of my window, the skies are clear and I think to myself, *spring is here.*
Daffodils bloom, primroses too, birds twitter seeming to say, 'how do you do.'
Summer arrives and with it blue skies, a great time for children's picnics and bike rides.
Cricket's the sport in everyone's thoughts, hitting the boundaries the elusive sixes constantly sought.

All too soon leaves start changing, red, yellow, russet and brown
All too quickly the sun's going down.
Birds migrating, animals hibernating, the land becoming bare.
Earth forever revolving, spinning, turning
Air being breathed to keep us all here.

Callum Guest (10)
Little Common School, Bexhill-on-Sea

My Cat Purr

My cat Purr has lots of fur,
Mainly on his back.
Bits of him are very white
But most of him is black.

At night he prowls around outside
Trying to catch mice.
He rarely catches any though
Which for the mice is nice!

In the day he sleeps a lot
Mainly on a bed
Or in a chair, or in a box
Or anywhere else instead.

Beth Harris (11)
Little Common School, Bexhill-on-Sea

Winter

W inter is magical, full of surprises
I cy lakes that we skate on all day
N uts roasted on an open fire
T alking and playing with your friends every day
E ndless snow falling to the ground
R olling up snow to make snowmen.

Winter is magical, full of surprises.

Laura Amess (10)
Little Common School, Bexhill-on-Sea

Football

F ootball is such fun
O n the field twenty-two players
O ne of them is me
T ackle players one by one
B reak away from everyone
A ttack their defence and score
L ook at me score, just one more
L oud the crowd shouts and claps, we finally win the match.

Thomas Kimber (9)
Little Common School, Bexhill-on-Sea

Friends

F riends are very important
R eally good friends stick up for you
I f you are in trouble friends will look after you
E ven if you are in a row
N one of your friends will leave you if they're good friends
D oing things with your friends is good fun
S ometimes you will break up but not for real.

Chandler Moore (9)
Little Common School, Bexhill-on-Sea

Football Haiku

Football is my goal,
Goalkeeper is my team place
Common is my team.

Cameron Smith (11)
Little Common School, Bexhill-on-Sea

Electric Eel

I squiggle and squirm
A lot like a worm
But I live under the sea
I have very sharp teeth
And I live on the reef
Can you identify me?

Ben Stiles (10)
Little Common School, Bexhill-on-Sea

Loneliness

L oneliness is one of the saddest words I know
O n my own full of grief
N obody loves me, I'm all alone
E motions are pouring out of me, I'm turning into nothingness
L ove is lost, life is melting away
I nside I feel the need of a friend
N o friends help me, I have nobody
E veryone is staring; I hold my head in my hands
S orrow of the loss of love is a never-ending feeling
S adness fills my heart as the day ends

I shelter under the trees, the leaves fall around me
S helter from the rain as cold as ice

A friend would be nice right now!

F eelings like nobody wants me
E veryone walks past me like I'm not there
E ternally life doesn't seem worth living anymore
L ove doesn't mean anything anymore
I look towards the setting sun
N obody else is around me, I'm all alone
G rief fills my heart as I think of the coming days.

Amelia Harrison (11)
Little Common School, Bexhill-on-Sea

Pets

Ralph and Katie are dogs
Katie is black and brown and very bossy
Ralph is tan and white and very stocky
Sometimes Ralph play fights with Katie
They fetch sticks, chase balls, sleep, eat and play all day.

Gus and Rumple are cats
Gus would lick your hand and likes to go out places a lot
Rumple would bring home presents like squirrels, mice and rabbits.

I have seventeen fish
Seventeen fish, white gold and black
They swim and dive and they think their names are Bob.

George Wilkie (10)
Little Common School, Bexhill-on-Sea

Happiness

H is for hugs with your mum and dad
A is for aeroplanes floating high in the sky
P is for pancakes, juicy, sloppy but scrumptious
P is for peppers, yellow, green and red
I is for igloo, small and crowded in the middle of nowhere
N is for necklace, diamond, gold and silver
E is for elephants, fat, grey but cuddly
S is for secret never to be told
S is for something! A super duper surprise!

This is happiness.

Charlie Bachellier (10)
Little Common School, Bexhill-on-Sea

Summer Days

Summer days are long,
Licking ice cream on hot days
Playing on the beach

Biking with my friends
People diving in the sea
Putting on suncream

Lovely blue rivers
Rainbow flowers at full bloom
And lovely sunsets.

Ben Profit (11)
Little Common School, Bexhill-on-Sea

Alfie

A lfie is my dog but he thinks he's a cat, he likes to play and that's a fact
L ying on a bed with his chew, he likes to chew my foot too
F aster than a runner he is, he likes to run around my trampoline
I think Alfie is made of steel when he headbutts me
E veryone calls him Badger, including me.

James Bailey (11)
Little Common School, Bexhill-on-Sea

The Fairy Ball

It is a night of June,
Under the silver moon,
Monsters creep,
Spirits leap,
The sky blackens,
The sun slackens,
Wolves cry,
Horses shy,
The fairy ball begins,
With a flutter of dainty wings,
Goblins chatter,
Footsteps patter,
The fairies start to dance,
The shadows skip and prance,
Jokers tease
And laugh with ease,
Then a swish of a silk gown,
And all seem to frown,
As the sun appears
And the dance floor slowly clears.

Vicky Turner (10)
Little Common School, Bexhill-on-Sea

Seasons - Haikus

Summer
It's baking hot now
I need more suntan lotion
To soothe the sunburn.

Autumn
The leaves are falling
Not forgetting the conkers
I've got thirty now!

Winter
It's Christmas at last
I can smell my gran's mince pies
I love Christmas time.

Spring
It's getting warmer
It is a nice temperature
Just how I like it.

George Palmer (11)
Little Common School, Bexhill-on-Sea

Birthday

B irthdays, birthdays, once a year
I am so excited with presents everywhere
R ecords playing my favourite songs
T oys to play with
H ow lucky I am
D olls to cuddle
A nd birthday cake too
Y eah, what a lucky person I am.

Katrina Hayes-Smith (9)
Little Common School, Bexhill-on-Sea

My Cat Tennant

I have a cat called Tennant
He is ginger and white and normally pleasant.
He is friendly and cuddly and purrs most of the time,
But when he is hungry he starts to whine.
He sits with me whilst I watch TV,
His favourite position is on my knee,
Into the garden he goes to play and climb,
But something frightens him from time to time.
A badger, a fox and a squirrel live nearby,
I think it is one of those that make him cry.
I brought him from London when I moved here last year,
Tenant gives my sister and I much cheer.
He plays tricks with a ball and a toy mouse which are so clever,
I love Tennant so much, I hope he lives forever.

Lucy Cunningham (10)
Little Common School, Bexhill-on-Sea

The Sea

The sea can be calm and tranquil,
The sea laps the pebbles and a huge *shhh* as the stones roll back,
Just like a teacher in quiet reading.

The sea can be a roaring emerald-green monster tearing things apart
Or like a sky-blue dolphin swimming gracefully.

The sea can have many different moods.
The sea sloshing at the side of a boat or tossing it about wildly.

The sea is so very, very beautiful, so let's keep it that way.

Alex Bedwell (9)
Little Common School, Bexhill-on-Sea

Football Haiku

Footie is a sport
I train every Tuesday night
I play in midfield.

James Vaughan (11)
Little Common School, Bexhill-on-Sea

The Four Seasons

Summer
Play out together,
The beach is joyful and free,
Sand, stones and crashing waves.

Spring
Spring is colourful,
Bright green leaves everywhere I look,
It's a happy time.

Autumn
The brown, red, green leaves
Dance to the ground with great style,
All leaves have faces.

Winter
Snow falls dreamily,
Make a snowman with a friend,
Have a snowball fight.

Emma Wright (10)
Little Common School, Bexhill-on-Sea

Dolphins

Dolphins swim in the deep blue sea,
Jumping over waves as far as you can see,
Playing and laughing, having fun,
Chasing each other in the blazing sun!
The sea is still, the sun goes down,
When all the people head to town,
But under the sea, they're still having fun,
Keeping out of trouble and avoiding the gun.
The dolphins are so wild and free,
Leaping around in the deep blue sea!

Laura Craner (11)
Little Common School, Bexhill-on-Sea

The Sea

The sea is always changing.
In summer it is calm and blue,
In winter it is dark and angry.
Sometimes the waves are tall and pounding,
Sometimes they are small and weak.
I walk along the beach collecting shells.
I listen to the seagulls cry and the sound of the waves.
The sea is always changing.

Hannah Quinn (11)
Little Common School, Bexhill-on-Sea

The Seasons

Winter is a time for fun and joy,
With laughter and singing and lots of toys,
With children playing out in the snow,
And Santa Claus shouting, 'Ho, ho, ho!'
Summer is a time for fun as well,
With people running towards the ice cream bell,
With flowers blooming all over fields,
And happy families going out for meals.
Spring is a time of new arrivals,
With lambs and calves appearing for miles,
With children picking flowers that grow quite near,
It's a really good time for happiness and cheer.
Now eventually we get to autumn time,
With the weather turning colder,
And lots of leaves falling off trees,
And people waiting for Santa, well, those who believe in him.

Lorna Piper (10)
Little Common School, Bexhill-on-Sea

Little Black Riding Hood

This is a story of Little Black who wore a bag upon her back,
She had black socks and yellow hair, when one day she ran into a bear.
The bear said, 'Hello, I am called Jack.' When the little girl whacked him with her pack.
The girl pulled him all of a sudden and locked him in her kitchen oven.
She turned the oven to one-hundred degrees when she started to cook the peas.
The bear was even more surprised when he felt the oven temperature rise
And this is why Little Riding Hood is the naughtiest girl in the wood.

Sophie Roberts (11)
Little Common School, Bexhill-on-Sea

Weather

Winter is a time for old ladies with weather-beaten faces
Dogs shivering in the cold,
Umbrellas causing a ray of colour down the street
Flowery Wellingtons on people's feet.
Mornings start to get warmer
Daffodils, crocus, primroses and bluebells shoot up.
Summer is coming, sunglasses, beach balls and costumes appear
And mummies with nothing but fear
Wondering if they have shed enough pounds to fit into the skimpy summer gear.

Emily Nolan (11)
Little Common School, Bexhill-on-Sea

Our School Trip To York

We went on a school trip to York
To learn about things we'd been taught,
As Vikings we went
From school we were sent
And clothes and pyjamas we brought.

We went to the Minster in York
Where a guide gave us a long talk,
So listened we did
As should all good kids
But ran to the shop, didn't walk!

One day we turned into Vikings
It was definitely to our likings,
We scared all the teachers
You'd be frightened to meet us
But now we're not really so frightening!

Harriet Cochrane (11)
Little Common School, Bexhill-on-Sea

Winter

W inter is the time of year when Christmas is near
I walk around in my pitch-black wellie boots
N ew fallen snow crunches around my feet
T he blurry sky as I look up is all grey and dull
E ntering the world of winter
R esting on my bench, waiting and hoping.

Emma Young (11)
Little Common School, Bexhill-on-Sea

My Twin Cam

My twin Cam likes eating ham.
We sometimes do the same things and sometimes think the same too.
But there's one thing I don't like, I don't like people guessing who's who.
It really gets on my nerves, and I don't like it.
So whoever is reading this, please don't guess who's who.

Henry Smith (11)
Little Common School, Bexhill-on-Sea

World War II

World War II was an angry giant
The angry giant's belly rumbling for his dinner was the drone of the planes overhead.
His arched eyebrows were the shape of the air raid shelters.
His stomping feet were the bombs exploding all around.
His snoring was the sound of the wailing air raid siren.
His angry roar was the roll of tanks over the ground.
His gloomy eyes were the blazing fires of houses that had been bombed.
His mouth was the deep, dark tunnel for the trains carrying evacuees.
His teeth were rows and rows of tombstones.
His hair was lines of bullets shot from machine guns.
His saliva was the water from the hoses to put out the fires.
His dark temper was the black out curtains in people's houses.
His washing flapping on the line was the barrage balloons in the city skies.
His fingers were the rows of shoppers waiting for their rations.
His toes were the lines of soldiers waiting to go to war.
World War II, an angry giant of war.

Charlotte Ellis (10)
Little Common School, Bexhill-on-Sea

Awards

I'm shining stars from the night sky,
I'm people stomping their feet when they're running the race,
I'm the crowd cheering the runners on,
I'm a delicious Christmas pudding waiting to be eaten,
I'm a smooth shiny stone being sucked up by the sea
I'm an award.

Taisie Payne (10)
Little Common School, Bexhill-on-Sea

Cam's Footie Party

Cameron's party was footie mad
I quite liked it, it wasn't bad,
We mucked around with the ball,
In this big gigantic hall,
Everyone liked it, especially me,
My favourite bit was when we had tea,
There was very yummy food,
That's what put me in a good mood.

Sean Edney (11)
Little Common School, Bexhill-on-Sea

In My Box

(Based on 'Magic Box' by Kit Wright)

I'll put in my box . . .
The sight of the glowing light from the moon
The sound of the sea bashing against the pebbles
The softness of an ostrich's feathers
The smoke from a fire burning.

I'll put in my box . . .
The brain of an eagle
The sound of an African drum
A colour from a rainbow
A vampire bite.

The lid is made from the steam of a kettle
The hinges are made from the tongue of a platypus
And it's all enclosed by magic
That's what I'll put in my box!

Jack Vincent (11)
Little Common School, Bexhill-on-Sea

The Autumn Fairy

The autumn makes the leaves come,
All crisp and golden in the sun,
A small girl with tiny wings,
With a silvery voice that really sings,
She's very special, her name is Mary,
Because she is the autumn fairy.

Nicole Carter (9)
Little Common School, Bexhill-on-Sea

Three Peas In A Pod

Three peas in a pod
Named Tim, Tom and Todd
Were walking about in the sun
When suddenly Todd, the youngest one
Said, 'Please will you buy me a cake or a bun?'
Said Tim and Tom to poor old Todd
'We are only three peas in a little green pod,
We have not the money
We know it's not funny
But it cannot be helped at all.'

That night when Tim and Tom went out
Their brother let out a terrible shout.
He had woken up from a terrible dream
And was looking all over for the rest of his team.
Then suddenly Tim, the oldest one
Came through the door holding a bun,
Todd was so happy he yelled out in joy
'This is much better than the best ever toy'
Then Tim, Tom and Todd
The three peas in a pod,
Turned off the light
And settled down for the night.

Jessica Young (10)
Little Common School, Bexhill-on-Sea

Sparkler Season

The sparkler lies with no fear,
Until the dawn of the matches come near.

The sparkler jumped to his surprise,
But he was too late and he got fried.

The sparkler's light filled up the sky,
Just before the sparkler died.

The smell of fire filled the air,
All the people began to stare.

The life of the sparkler is coming to an end,
With the sound of music in your head.

Zoe Ireo (9)
Lovelace Primary School, Chessington

Remembrance Day Poem

It's sad how many people died
But I shall hold in my tears and not cry
I'm upset about what cannot be stopped
But I think I shall not shriek
Yes, yes, I am very sad
I feel like screaming
But - bye for now love, bye-bye.

Ashley Rose (9)
Lovelace Primary School, Chessington

Seasons

Winter's cold like white frost
Spring smells like dazzling scents
Summer's hot like the sun's core
Autumn is breezy like never before
And that's what makes Earth a better place.

Chezrae Mason (9)
Lovelace Primary School, Chessington

My War Poem

Those poor old soldiers that died in the war
I feel so sorry for,
They saved our country *whoa!*
But their parents were sobbing when they did not knock on the door.
Probably because their poor old bodies were sore
They had to obey the law
The sergeant would shout a terrible roar
The army must have cried till they collapsed on the floor.

Abigail Schofield (9)
Lovelace Primary School, Chessington

Why?

Why did the war happen?
Why couldn't it end?
Why couldn't the enemies just be your friend
People are still dying every second of the day
In some poor countries miles away.

Michaela Elliott (8)
Lovelace Primary School, Chessington

Mrs Raindrop

See me in the ground about to take off
I'm so excited, I wonder what colours I will go
Now the people are lighting me up, I am about to fly, fly, fly!
I burst into a million, zillion colours and I look like rain.
I am glittering, sparkling, glowing beautifully in the deep, dark sky.
Hear me go, *whoosh, whee!*
Now here are my friends to put on an even better show!
I drop, drop, down, down until next, next time, so, bye for now!

Lucy Mozo (8)
Lovelace Primary School, Chessington

Butterfly

Butterfly, butterfly, from my little eye
May I ask, why are you shy?
You look so beautiful when you fly in the sky.

Sophia Whitelaw (8)
Lovelace Primary School, Chessington

Field Of Daffodils

I run through a field of daffodils,
I run up a steep hill
I get to the top
I have to stop
And then I stand there very still

I run down the hill of daffodils,
I run to the little tree,
I go too fast
But I am there at last,
And what lies there for me?

I run in the field of daffodils
And then I sit and lie.
My head is down
There is no frown,
Then I watch the world go by.

Lucy Alderman (10)
Lovelace Primary School, Chessington

What If?

What if air raids became music?
What if war became playtime?
What if bombs became pillows?
What if armies became villages?
What if gas masks became air?
What if trenches became flower beds?
What if tanks became cars?
What if guns became water pistols?
What if jet planes became toys?
What if . . . ?
What if . . . ?
What if . . . ?

Christopher Bone (9)
Lovelace Primary School, Chessington

We Care

Today is Remembrance Day
To remember those who went away.
War is such a dangerous place
When soldiers die they go to waste.
People sit at home and cry
While at war their family dies.
We open our hearts so that we can share
We are here to and we really care.
We can't believe such horrible things
Let's see what the future brings.

Laura Ellis (9)
Lovelace Primary School, Chessington

Schooldays

I enjoy my schooldays,
When I learn to read and write.
Maybe it's just a phase
But my teacher thinks I'm bright.
I go in every morning
With my bag and my lunch,
My lessons are not boring,
And my friends are a lively bunch.
I take part in the playground,
I join in, in the hall,
The one thing that I found
Is that life can be quite full.

Katie Marchant (10)
Lovelace Primary School, Chessington

I Feel Like . . .

I feel like the ocean smashing and bashing on the sand and stones.
I feel like the sun shining very bright in the blue, blue sky.
I feel like the clouds white as white.
I feel like me, me, me, me.

Charlotte Tighe (11)
Lovelace Primary School, Chessington

Chelsea, Chelsea

'Come on,' shouts Dad, 'it's time to go,'
I run to my room and grab my shirt.
Whee, we are waiting at the station,
The train pulls in and we all jump on.
Everyone is excited as we go through the turnstile.
I hope Wright-Phillips is playing today.
Lampard scores with a diving header,
Crespo makes it two.
Shoots and scores,
Cole makes it three.
Everyone cheers when the whistle blows
And we all get to our feet to sing.
Another win.
We are top of the league!

Mark McMillan (11)
Lovelace Primary School, Chessington

Friendship

My friends, my friends are indeed so sweet to me,
They make me feel sweet, sweet, sweet.
We laugh and play all day long,
But best of all they're my best friends, *hooray!*

Katie Richter (10)
Lovelace Primary School, Chessington

Summer Fun

In the sunshine people play, having fun every day!
Splashing in the swimming pool, running around acting cool.
Playing football while it's hot, going home or maybe not.
Laughing with all your mates, being crazy on your skates.
Having a picnic in the park, walking home when it's dark!
Then I'm getting into bed, lying down my sleepy head, dreaming of the day ahead!

Jodie Tamila (10)
Lovelace Primary School, Chessington

School Dinners

S oggy sponge and custard
C heese and tomato with mustard
H airy hamburgers and cold chips
O ily olives and apples with pips
O range jelly with gone off cream
L ate at night I thought it was a dream

D inner ladies shouting
I diots ranting
N ursery children crying
N o one's even trying
E veryone gets in a mess
R eally no one cares less
S chool dinners, it's just a guess!

Holly Nelhams (11)
Lovelace Primary School, Chessington

What A Friend Is

A friend is loyal
A friend is true
A friend is someone
Who sticks by you.

A friend does not lie
About his mate,
He does his best
At any rate.

He keeps his word
Whatever the cost,
He'd help his friend
If he were lost.

A friend will laugh
When you tell a joke,
A friend would listen
When you spoke.

A friend is someone
You can trust,
A good friendship
Will never bust.

Jack Roberts (10)
Maynards Green Primary School

My Once Best Friend

I had a best friend once
Since the day I was born
But then when we went to school
Our friendship was torn.

We met at village hall toddlers
With lots of girls and boys
But somehow we linked together
Played together on the toys.

We even went to pre-school together
Round each other's houses we would stay
But then we argued at school
And hate each other to this day.

She went off with other girls
Left me on my own
I felt like the world would end
She wouldn't even phone.

Luckily I made new friends
Of those they were the best
I had no need for her anymore
Our friendship was laid to rest.

She has just come back to me
I don't know what to say
She wants to make friends again
Maybe we will one day.

Abigail Delves (11)
Maynards Green Primary School

Baby Sister

Yes, yes, yes, as I ran up some stairs,
Is it a boy? Is it a girl?
I thought in my mind,
In about two minutes my mum's baby would be by my side,
As we opened the door my mum lay on the bed,
Holding my baby sister, my mum lying there, 'It's a girl,' she said,
I sat on the bed, so did my dad, he kissed my mum and said, 'Well done.'
He took her out of my mum's hands and kissed my baby sister,
They called her Rosie and my mum said, 'Go on Liam kiss her.'
For the first time I held her and sat next to my mum,
And I felt numb.

Liam Bourne (11)
Maynards Green Primary School

Bullying

You kick me,
You punch me,
You always hurt me.

I don't like you,
I hate you,
You always bully me.

Just leave me alone,
I don't want to be hurt,
I don't want to feel small inside.

I need to be big,
Tall and brave,
I need to let all my anger out.

So go away,
Leave me alone,
I'm big and strong now.

Don't you see?

Rebekah McGarvey (10)
Maynards Green Primary School

Spreading Your Life All Over

I remember the good times like when we went to Dover,
But now, I'm spreading your life all over.
I remember the good times like when we went to Devon
But now you're all the way up there in Heaven!

I remember the good times like when I took you for a walk,
But now I feel lonely with no reason to talk.
I remember the good times like when I had some things to say,
But now I want you to know our love'll never fade away!

I remember the good times like when we went to Dover,
But now I'm spreading your life all over.
My bright red top and your soft brown coat clashes,
But now I have a pot, full of your ashes.

I remember the good times like when we went to Dover,
But now I'm spreading your life all over.
I remember the good times like when we went to Devon
But now you're all the way up there in Heaven.

Bekki Milham (10)
Maynards Green Primary School

My Move, My Friends Or Goodbye

I'm excited and happy, moving to Spain,
Don't worry my friends, I'll come back again.
I hope you're happy as much as me,
I'm moving right across the sea!
A journey by plane, boat or car,
Exciting and fun? Oh yes, by far!
Writing to you all across the sea,
Hoping you'll write back to me.
We're still friends; I'm two hours away,
I'll see you all soon, another day!

I don't really want to leave you behind,
You are all so great, so nice, so kind.
I won't forget you if you don't forget me,
What does the future bring? Well we'll see.
I'm sad that I have to leave you here,
However, I don't think I'll shed a tear.
Can't I shove you all in my bag?
Don't worry; I don't think you'll get jet lag.
I'll be alright without you all
Make new friends, switching school.
Goodbye my friends, goodbye my enemies
I don't know how to feel,
This is not a dream, it is not false,
This adventure is for real!

Hannah Gilchrist (11)
Maynards Green Primary School

Watching Someone Getting Bullied

Watching a girl getting bullied
Standing from a distance, feeling bad,
I can't do anything otherwise they will start on me,
I wish I could do something rather than be sad.

Watching a girl getting bullied,
What can I do?
Please tell me something,
What am I to do?

Watching a girl getting bullied,
She moves school,
Nobody knows where she went,
Thank you.

Georgina Harwood (11)
Maynards Green Primary School

Five Ways Of Looking At Stars

The stars
Twinkly yellow, shiny and bright,
Gazing in my eyes.

The stars
Bringing out the night sky,
With their pretty little shape.

The stars
Tiny little dots in the night sky,
Brightly shining prettily.

The stars
Twinkly like shining sequins,
Flashing in the moonlight.

The stars
Shining brightly all over the sky,
When I look up they're everywhere.

Harriet Gibson (9)
Maynards Green Primary School

Creatures

Dragon
Sitting peacefully by his cave.
The passing phoenix
Gives a wave.
Sea serpent, gliding through the surf,
A vegetarian Hydra
Shouts in his mirth.
He has escaped Hercules
Diomedes' mares chomp
On what, I don't want to know.
Though Hercules is catching up
(We are mentioning him a lot)
And will soon catch them.
But stuck in the middle of this
Magical mess
Is . . .
Me!

Olivia McCarthy (10)
Maynards Green Primary School

Run Away!

The lion's roar is loud and scary,
The snake's hiss is sly and slick,
The moose's groan is gruff and grumpy,
The elephant's trumpet can be long and frightening,
The rotweiller's bark is sharp and petrifying,
All of these sounds are enough to make my knees knock,
But I am most scared when my mum shouts at me!

Julia McCarthy (8)
Maynards Green Primary School

Animal Land

An angry eagle killing its prey,
A baby bear sleeping on and on,
And there it will stay.

A kangaroo jumping on Australian sand,
Keep on jumping, come on,
Soon it must reach land.

A monkey swinging tree to tree,
Be quiet, be quiet,
It might see me.

A hyena running as fast as he can,
The frightened prey
Within his span.

Harry Pope (9)
Maynards Green Primary School

What Do You Want To Be?

Would you like to be a writer, or skier or dancer?
Skiing down the slopes you'd have great fun.
Or would you like to be a swimmer, or a doctor or a nurse?
Maybe you could win a prize.
Would you like to be a teacher or a racing car driver
And have the chance to go fast?
You'd enjoy it.
You could almost be anything, travelling countries, travelling space
But you don't have to choose now.

Ella Stubley (10)
Medstead CE (Controlled) Primary School, Medstead

My Favourite Things

Chocolate
Yummy, delicious,
Bite, eat, melting
Waiting to eat it,
Cocoa.

Cats,
Cute, small,
Pouncing, playing, purring,
Climbing up the curtains,
Kittens.

Ponies,
Intelligent streak,
Ride, jumping, having fun,
Galloping through the fields,
Horses.

Colours,
Bright, sparkly,
Green, red, orange,
Colours fading in the wash,
Multicoloured.

Alice Waldeck (10)
Medstead CE (Controlled) Primary School, Medstead

Playground

The school bell rings, I leap for joy,
We all line up, girl, boy, girl, boy.

In the playground children shouting,
Some little girls standing pouting.

Boys who think they're 007,
Young girls who wish they were eleven.

Footballs, basketballs in the air,
The children running everywhere.

Whispers told of weekend fun,
Stories said of things they've done.

Teachers telling off naughty boys,
Girls letting out a high-pitched noise.

Stampedes, yelling, objects flying,
Children fall and some are crying.

The school bell rings, I cringe and curl,
We all line up, boy, girl, boy, girl.

Elliot Moreton (9)
Medstead CE (Controlled) Primary School, Medstead

Love

A tear dripped down Love's ghostly cheek
She only looked ahead.
She'd ran away with nowhere to stay
Not even a tiny bed.

On Love ran in the icy wind
Her feet all cold and bare.
She weighs not a pound to get her round
No one knows or cares.

Love fell down to her shaking knees
And shrieked with all her might,
You may still hear her reappear
As she walks the lonely night.

Gina Sumner (11)
Medstead CE (Controlled) Primary School, Medstead

The Amazon

If I was in The Amazon
I would stroke the rough surface of a hairy coconut
Sleeping in the branches.

If I was in The Amazon
I would crunch the crunchy Brazil nuts.

If I was in The Amazon
I would take in the scent of the salty river and the damp mud.

If I was in The Amazon
I would witness a deadly alligator ready to kill its prey.

If I was in The Amazon
I would dream that I could slurp the everlasting river.

Greg Morris (8)
Milton Mount Primary School, Crawley

The Amazon

If I was in The Amazon
I would gaze at the dashing, fast, powerful jaguar.
If I was in The Amazon
I would look at an emerald, gliding parakeet.
If I was in The Amazon
I would see a small sharp-toothed piranha.
If I was in The Amazon
I would smell the crunchy, hard Brazil nuts
Falling to the ground.

Yasin Noormohamed (8)
Milton Mount Primary School, Crawley

The Amazon

If I was in The Amazon
I would touch a hairy chocolate shell of a coconut
That hung in the emerald trees.
If I was in The Amazon
I would breathe the air flowing through
The bright green trees.
If I was in The Amazon
I would taste a big chunk of a sweet melon.
If I was in The Amazon
I would gaze at the flowing river
With deadly piranhas in the river.
If I was in The Amazon
I would dream of going to hug a pink dolphin.

Ellie Fisher (8)
Milton Mount Primary School, Crawley

J For Jealousy

Jealousy feels like you want to be someone else because you're sick of your own life.
It stinks of mouldy spinach.
If you listen carefully it sounds like a cat miaowing, or a pig grunting.
The look of it is like a green face from the person who's jealous
It just tastes like food poisoning.
Worst of all it reminds me of a dark day and the grass goes all dark green.

Lucy Norris (9)
Milton Mount Primary School, Crawley

The Amazon

If I was in The Amazon
I would stroke the smooth fur of a spotted jaguar
As it strolled the tropical jungle.
If I was in The Amazon
I would taste a handful of lemon-yellow melons
Fresh as a rainbow.
If I was in The Amazon
I would breathe in the moist invisible air
That rustled through the emerald canopy of trees.
If I was in The Amazon
I would gaze at the beauty
Of the intelligent pink dolphins
Gliding in the sapphire seas.
If I was in The Amazon
I would gaze at the beauty of the silver capybaras
Snuggling by the flowing river.

Eleanor Terry (9)
Milton Mount Primary School, Crawley

The Amazon

If I was in The Amazon
I would touch the towering emerald green canopy.
If I was in The Amazon
I would chomp a juicy chunk of mango.
If I was in The Amazon
I would breathe the refreshing moist air.
If I was in the Amazon
I would stare at the mighty, forever growing rainforest.
If I was in The Amazon
I would dream about climbing up to the sky
And gazing at the stunning landscape.

Matthew Bale (9)
Milton Mount Primary School, Crawley

The Amazon

If I was in The Amazon
I would touch the moist green trees
High in the chocolate canopy.
If I was in The Amazon
I would taste a sweet mango
Glowing in the hot red sun.
If I was in The Amazon
I would breathe in the tender, soggy leaves in the high trees.
If I was in The Amazon
I would gaze at the lovely lemon-yellow sun
Setting in the strip of dark.
If I was in The Amazon
I would dream of being a leopard thrashing at a scattering ant.

Jake Olliffe (8)
Milton Mount Primary School, Crawley

The Amazon

If I was in The Amazon
I would breathe in the dry jade leaf floating in the sparkly water.
If I was in The Amazon
I would touch the golden mango hanging in the tallest tree,
Ready to fall down.
If I was in The Amazon I would hear the rustling of capybaras
Passing by the whole jungle.
If I was in The Amazon
I would gaze at the animals like monkeys hanging on the tallest trees.

Mujtaba Jalal (8)
Milton Mount Primary School, Crawley

The Amazon

If I was in The Amazon
I would touch the succulent crimson trees.
If I was in The Amazon
I would taste fresh sun-drenched mangoes.
If I was in The Amazon
I would breathe in a deep sniff of the jungle air.
If I was in The Amazon
I would gaze at the crimson parakeets gliding in the sky.
If I was in The Amazon
I would dream of the blue turquoise sky.

Tommy May (8)
Milton Mount Primary School, Crawley

The Amazon

If I was in The Amazon
I would grasp the tall emerald canopy which towered over me.
If I was in The Amazon
I would munch my way through a chunk of an exotic, succulent mango
Which glistened in the golden sun.
If I was in The Amazon
I would breathe in the invisible air.
If I was in The Amazon
I would gaze at a jaguar's spotted, lemon-yellow fur as it darted.
If I was in The Amazon
I would imagine handling a deadly piranha's sharp tooth
That looked like a silver, glistening spear.

Holly Talbut-Smith (9)
Milton Mount Primary School, Crawley

The Amazon

If I was in The Amazon
I would taste a fat sweet mango.
If I was in The Amazon
I would taste a fresh green leaf.
If I was in The Amazon
I would taste a chunk of a fish.
If I was in The Amazon
I would breathe the smell of the clear salty sea.

Kiera Gilbert (8)
Milton Mount Primary School, Crawley

The Amazon

If I was in The Amazon
I would touch the emerald leaves of the tallest tree.
If I was in The Amazon
I would taste the sweet juice of the tastiest mango.
If I was in The Amazon
I would breathe the fresh raindrops towering above me.
If I was in The Amazon
I would dream of flying over the sun-drenched green canopy.

Paige Johnson (8)
Milton Mount Primary School, Crawley

The Amazon

If I was in The Amazon
My hands would grasp the scaly skin
Of a deadly piranha hunting prey in the deep river.
If I was in The Amazon
I would have the pleasure to consume
The juice of the fresh mangoes on the trees
That towered over all of the wildlife.
If I was in The Amazon
I would breathe the wonderful moistened fresh air
Which drifted among the huge trees.
If I was in The Amazon
I would witness the outline of a small capybara
Which scurried about on the forest floor.
If I was in The Amazon
I would dream about clambering up
The tallest tree of the canopy
Which looked down on the beautiful forest.

Aidan Quinlan (9)
Milton Mount Primary School, Crawley

Purple Is Surprise

Purple smells like violets swaying in the midsummer breeze.
Purple sounds like a sweet wrapper being brushed in the wind.
Purple is a soft warm blanket giving you sweet dreams.
Purple looks like people playing happily.
Purple tastes like a rainbow melting into your soul.
Purple reminds me of a nine-foot-tall cake.

Anwen Shaw (9)
Milton Mount Primary School, Crawley

The Amazon

If I was in The Amazon
I would touch the soft, spotty fur on the body of a jaguar
As it strolls on the dusty path.
If I was in The Amazon
I would taste a fruity chunk of a juicy mango.
If I was in The Amazon
I would breathe in the lovely smell of the scarlet-red flowers.
If I was in The Amazon
I would gaze at the towering trees that hung above me.
If I was in The Amazon
I would dream that I had touched a smooth jaguar's spotty skin.

Ella Marsh (8)
Milton Mount Primary School, Crawley

The Amazon

If I was in The Amazon
I would touch the smooth sunset-pink skin of a dolphin.
If I was in The Amazon
I would taste the mouth-watering flame-red and yellow flesh centre of a mango.
If I was in the Amazon
I would breathe the fresh air which flowed through the over-towering trees.
If I was in The Amazon
I would gaze at the flowing river that had vicious piranhas in.
If I was in The Amazon
I would dream that I could walk on the canopy and see the never-ending rainforest.

Alice Lloyd (8)
Milton Mount Primary School, Crawley

The Amazon

If I was in The Amazon
I would touch a mouth-watering melon.
If I was in The Amazon
I would taste a chunk of succulent green leaf.
If I was in The Amazon
I would breathe in deep sniffs of a raindrop.
If I was in The Amazon
I would gaze at the pink dolphin in the flowing river.
If I was in The Amazon
I would dream of swimming with pink dolphins.

Priya Lakhani
Milton Mount Primary School, Crawley

The Amazon

If I was in The Amazon
I would touch a bunch of ruby flowers in my hands.
If I was in The Amazon
I would taste gorgeous fresh fruit that we can eat.
If I was in The Amazon
I would breathe deeply in the air.
If I was in The Amazon
I would gaze at the towering trees.
If I was in The Amazon
I would dream of meandering through the rainforest.

Michael Galvin (9)
Milton Mount Primary School, Crawley

The Amazon

If I was in The Amazon
I would touch pink dolphins swimming in unison.
If I was in The Amazon
I would taste a handful of mouth-watering fish.
If I was in The Amazon
I would smell the amazing, ruby, tropical fruits.
If I was in The Amazon
I would gaze at an emerald tooth rubber tree.
If I was in The Amazon
I would dream of having wings and flying to the top of the canopy
To grasp a chocolate coconut.

Lucas Black (8)
Milton Mount Primary School, Crawley

The Amazon

If I was in The Amazon
I would breathe the moist watery air that surrounds me.
If I was in The Amazon
I would taste the juicy flavour of a mango and smell its fresh skin.
If I was in The Amazon
I would see the lemon-yellow feathers of a parrot as it darted amongst lime trees.
If I was in The Amazon
I would gaze at the luscious emerald trees towering above my head.
If I was in The Amazon
I would imagine taking a chunk of snow-white clouds torturing the sky.

Toni Davis (9)
Milton Mount Primary School, Crawley

The Amazon

If I was in The Amazon
I would touch the dotted lemon-yellow fur of a jaguar.
If I was in The Amazon
I would taste a mouthful of mouth-watering fresh fish.
If I was in The Amazon
I would breathe in the moist air.
If I was in The Amazon
I would gaze at the high tree towering over other trees with its emerald-green leaves.
If I was in The Amazon
I would dream I would live with a helpful Indian tribe.

Jack Chappell (8)
Milton Mount Primary School, Crawley

The Amazon

If I was in The Amazon
I would touch the rich chocolate coconut shell.
If I was in The Amazon
I would hear the rustling trees swaying.
If I was in The Amazon
I would breathe in all the animals in the whole forest.
If I was in The Amazon
I would take a big chunk out of the yummy bananas and the yummy, juicy starfruit.
If I was in The Amazon
I would dream I was on a wonderful lime, large green leaf.

Eva Moore (8)
Milton Mount Primary School, Crawley

The Amazon

If I was in The Amazon
I would touch the sweet, juicy mango in the jungle.
If I was in The Amazon
I would taste the crunchy, scrumptious nuts.
If I was in The Amazon
I would breathe in all of the lovely fresh air.
If I was in The Amazon
I would gaze at all of the wildlife and environment.
If I was in The Amazon
I would dream of all the wonderful plants.

Joel Derry (8)
Milton Mount Primary School, Crawley

The Giant Amazon

If I was in The Amazon
I would listen to the rippling river.
If I was in The Amazon
I would sniff the luscious fruit.
If I was in The Amazon
I would touch a rose as red as crimson.
If I was in The Amazon
I would savour a taste of The Amazon for home.
If I was in The Amazon
I would stare at the maroon Indians.
I think it must be beautiful.

Beth Hicks (8)
Milton Mount Primary School, Crawley

The Amazon

If I was in The Amazon
I would gulp down the scrummy fruit.
If I was in The Amazon
I would stroke the trees.
If I was in The Amazon
I would see the scampering animals.
If I was in The Amazon
I would hear dolphins splashing in the clear water.
If I was in The Amazon
I could smell the strong smell of coffee beans.

Connor Grant (9)
Milton Mount Primary School, Crawley

The Amazon

If I was in The Amazon
I could hear rippling water.
I could smell luscious fruit.
I would crunch a taste of a bright yellow banana skin.
I would touch rich green leaves hanging from trees.
If I was in The Amazon
I could feel pink dolphins swimming in the river.
If I was in The Amazon.

Ayesha Hussain (8)
Milton Mount Primary School, Crawley

My Trip To The Amazon

If I was in The Amazon
I would touch the rustling leaves and the bark from the Brazil nut tree.
If I was in The Amazon
I would smell the golden maize that the Indians were eating.
If I was in The Amazon
I would taste the flesh of the jaguar that the Indians had killed.
If I was in The Amazon
I would see the pure beauty of the flowers.
If I was in The Amazon
I would hear the noisy parakeets swooping in the trees.
I love The Amazon.

Sophie Webster (9)
Milton Mount Primary School, Crawley

Anger Is Evil

Anger looks like a ghostly bull charging from nowhere.
Anger feels like a sword plunging in your back.
Anger smells of moulding meat and unwashed hair.
Anger tastes of out of date yoghurts and out of date custard.
Anger sounds like a chamber of death.
Anger reminds me of an awful horror film about a mad chef.
The head of anger is strong and
The tread of anger is long
And the red light of anger is blinding!
Anger is evil.

Joe Gardiner (10)
Milton Mount Primary School, Crawley

My Amazon Adventure

If I was in The Amazon
I would touch the back of a wild piranha and stroke a sleek black jaguar.
I would taste the golden air and inhale the orchid's fumes.
I would see the emerald rubber trees and the sharp spine of a fish.
I would hear the rich chirping sounds of beautiful birds
And the rushing of the angry wind.
I would smell the overpowering scent of the finest flowers
And the tang of fresh-drawn blood.
Suddenly, I woke up hot and bothered in the bath!

Jack Webster (9)
Milton Mount Primary School, Crawley

The Amazon Adventure

When I walked in The Amazon
I saw the magnificent parrots,
That flew from tree to tree.

When I strolled in The Amazon
I smelled the scent of the flowers
Dancing in the breeze.

When I stripped in The Amazon
I touched the alligators
That were as prickly as a knife.

When I tiptoed in The Amazon
I felt the mud
Gathering and oozing under my feet.

When I crawled in The Amazon
I heard the parrots
Soaring in the sky.

If I was in The Amazon again
I would dream of having another adventure.

John-Paul Akoachere (8)
Milton Mount Primary School, Crawley

My Poem About The Amazon

If I was in The Amazon I would feel the soft fruit.
If I was in The Amazon I would feel the skin of a jaguar.
If I was in The Amazon I would fly with the toucans.
If I was in The Amazon I would hear the whistling of the trees.
If I was in The Amazon I would smell the lovely lilies and all kinds of flowers.
If I was in The Amazon I would taste different nuts.

Bradley Bell (8)
Milton Mount Primary School, Crawley

Amazon Poem

If I was in The Amazon I would see the ruby flowers.
If I was in The Amazon I would sniff the flavour of the delicious juicy fruit.
If I was in The Amazon I would feel the red, red roses the colour of crimson.
If I was in The Amazon I would hear the rippling water.
If I was in The Amazon I would swallow a taste of air for home.
It will always be in my heart.

Laura Fielder (9)
Milton Mount Primary School, Crawley

My Poem

If I was in The Amazon
I would hear the rainfall dripping on the water.
If I was in The Amazon
I would hear parrots squawking.
If I was in The Amazon
It would be dark.
If I was in The Amazon
I would scurry through it.
If I was in The Amazon
I would munch on the food.
If I was in The Amazon
I would hear the swaying of the trees.

Jason Pirie (8)
Milton Mount Primary School, Crawley

If I Was In The Amazon

If I was in The Amazon
I would dash into the damp rainforest.
If I was in The Amazon
I would smell the beautiful flowers.
If I was in The Amazon
I would munch on all of the food.
If I was in The Amazon
I would scuttle to drink all of the rain.
If I was in The Amazon
I would watch all of the rain coming down.
If I was in The Amazon
I would swing from tree to tree.

Ryan Matthews (9)
Milton Mount Primary School, Crawley

Amazon Adventure

If I was in The Amazon
I would feel the scaly and wrinkly anaconda, as powerful as a giant's finger.
If I was in The Amazon
I would taste the mouth-watering avocados.
If I was in The Amazon
I would smell the luxurious scented lotus flower.
If I was in The Amazon
I would hear the silent whistle of trees swaying in the cold wind.
If I was in The Amazon
I would see the vicious jaguar lying on a tree waiting for its prey.

George Ferguson (9)
Milton Mount Primary School, Crawley

My Amazon Dream

If I was in The Amazon
I would touch the smoothness of a juicy watermelon.
I would smell the scent of a luscious lovely lotus flower.
I would taste the best vegetables and the finest juices.
I would hear the multicoloured parakeets squawking in the distance.
I would see the alligators eating a parrot for their dinner.
If only I was there.

Charlie Towning (9)
Milton Mount Primary School, Crawley

If I Was In The Amazon

If I was in The Amazon
I would sniff the scent of fiery flowers,
I would smell the aroma of the fruit
And whiff the tang of the fresh water.

If I was in The Amazon
I would feel the skin of the slithery snake,
I would feel the short fur of the jaguar
And touch the back of a long alligator.

If I was in The Amazon
I would taste freshly picked fruit
And the rhythm of the beautiful river.

If I was in The Amazon
I would hear the birds squawking
And the waves of the water splashing.

If I was in The Amazon
I would see the lush tall trees rustling
And see the pink dolphins diving down deep into the sapphire river.

Charlotte Warnes (8)
Milton Mount Primary School, Crawley

The Amazon

If I was in The Amazon
I would hear the rubber man chopping the trees.
I would see the crimson-red rose and damp green grass.
I would look at the pink dolphin going down the river bank,
The jaguar looking around for its prey.
The colour of the rain is a sapphire-blue and the fresh fruit is on a tree nearby.
I think it looks amazing.

Chailey Collins (9)
Milton Mount Primary School, Crawley

Home And Away

When I walked through The Amazon
I got a whiff of scent from a ruby lily pad.
When I ran through The Amazon
I saw a snake plunge down from a golden canopy tree.
When I swam through The Amazon
I stroked a pink dolphin splashing me with water.
When I canoed through The Amazon
I caught a piranha with sparkling sea salt skin.
When I crept through The Amazon
I heard an Indian singing mysterious songs.
When I walked through Crawley
I saw none of these things.

Jordan Abbott (9)
Milton Mount Primary School, Crawley

The Amazon Is In My Heart

The Amazon is in my heart,
I can smell rich, moist earth,
I can touch the rich, olive-green, luscious leaves,
I can swim with pink dolphins,
I can hear the birds humming,
I can see the parrots flying in the air,
I can smell the scent of beautiful flowers,
The Amazon is in my heart.

Liam Woodvine (9)
Milton Mount Primary School, Crawley

If I Was In The Amazon

If I was in The Amazon
I would smell the sweet and sharp tropical fruit of the rainforest.
If I was in The Amazon
I would taste a bit of the cherry sun like a red-hot chilli on my tongue.
If I was in The Amazon
I would feel the piranhas' teeth on my long thin arms
And stroke the lush pink dolphins swimming by me.
If I was in The Amazon
I would hear the squawking multicoloured parrots in the huge trees
With rusty green leaves.
If I was in The Amazon again my dreams would come true.

Reagan Muir (8)
Milton Mount Primary School, Crawley

At The Seaside

On the pebbles,
Teenagers wrestling,
Children charging,
Parents bathing.

By the water,
Toddlers splashing,
Beach balls bouncing,
Kids playing.

In the water,
Men sailing,
Families snorkelling,
Adults diving.

Sounds amazing, but what is it like on the pier?

On the rides,
Children screaming,
Cable cars bumping,
Roller coasters screeching.

By the railings
Seagulls sitting,
People chatting,
Stallholders selling.

In the café,
Adults smoking,
Teenagers eating,
Families drinking.

Sounds amazing, but what is it like on the pier?

Jordan Menzies (7)
Milton Mount Primary School, Crawley

Last Night I Went To The Amazon

Last night I went to The Amazon
I flew with the parrots and touched the sky
I swam with the pink dolphins in the silver river
I smelt the fresh smell of the ruby lilies
I heard the gentle rain coming down from the sapphire sky
I saw the cherry sun set down
I suddenly found myself in the garden, in the pond soaking wet in my pyjamas.

Amy Johnson (8)
Milton Mount Primary School, Crawley

If I Went To The Amazon

If I was in The Amazon
I would dash and dart in the water,
I would stroke the hypnotic water,
I would swim with the dolphins.

If I was in The Amazon
I would fly with the scarlet parakeets,
I would smell the crimson orchids,
I would scurry through the rainforest.

If I was in The Amazon
I would pounce with the jaguar,
I would experience the finest fruit,
I would bathe in the fresh water of the river.

If I was in The Amazon
I would pick the red lilies,
I would see creatures that no one had ever seen before,
I would find things in the topaz trees.

If I was in The Amazon
I would sail along the river,
I would speak with the Indians,
I would compare The Amazon with my home
And truly The Amazon is the best.

Emily Hawkins (8)
Milton Mount Primary School, Crawley

If I Swam In The Amazon

If I swam in The Amazon
I would feel piranhas biting me
And pink dolphins chasing me
And alligators laying their eggs
And burying them in deep water
And when I devour all the food into my stomach
Like creamy bananas
And juicy fruits
I hear a jaguar,
Prowling away and toucans screeching
And monkeys swinging from trees
The piranhas are crimson
As blood and birds
As scarlet as piranha
And ant armies scamper to their nests
The rainforest is as damp as soggy clouds.

Ben Sra (8)
Milton Mount Primary School, Crawley

At The Seaside

On the rides,
People screaming,
Roller coasters screeching,
Children playing.

By the railings,
Couples chatting,
Seagulls swooping,
Babies crying.

In the café,
Families eating,
Adults talking,
Toddlers crawling.

Sounds amazing, but what is it like on the beach?

On the pebbles,
Women sunbathing,
Children charging,
Teenagers joking.

By the water,
Volleyballs dancing,
Sandcastles building,
Beach balls darting.

In the sea,
Youngsters surfing,
Families sailing,
Fishes jumping.

Naseem Bouchhar (7)
Milton Mount Primary School, Crawley

Amazon

As I walked through The Amazon
I would feel the bumpiness of the alligator.
If I went to The Amazon
I would hear the multicoloured parrots screeching to other flocks.
If I went to The Amazon
I would taste the luscious avocados.
If I went to The Amazon
I would gaze upon the freshwater dolphins.

Bailey Lamb (8)
Milton Mount Primary School, Crawley

At The Seaside

On the pebbles,
Women sunbathing,
Children charging,
Teenagers joking.

By the water,
Volleyballs dancing,
Sandcastle building,
Beach balls darting.

In the sea,
Youngsters surfing,
Families sailing,
Fishes jumping.

Sounds amazing, but what is it like on the pier?

On the rides,
Boys bumping,
Girls screaming,
Dads chewing.

On the railways,
Seagulls squawking,
Families laughing,
Babies crying.

In the café,
Tea drinking,
Donut eating,
Strangers talking.
Sounds amazing, but what is it like at the seaside?

Billy Towning (7)
Milton Mount Primary School, Crawley

Love

Love feels like soft cuddly fur and strong, loving arms keeping me safe.
Love sounds like happy and jolly singing, ringing through echoing corridors.
Love tastes like a steaming, soft, bouncy sponge pudding waiting to be eaten.
Love smells like a delicious chocolate fudge pudding steaming by the oven.
Love looks like a happy couple on their anniversary.
Love reminds me of a jolly happy person walking in the sunset on the beach.

Lucy Presland (9)
Milton Mount Primary School, Crawley

At The Seaside

On the pebbles
Drinks bubbling,
Families picnicking,
Adults tanning.

In the waves
People snorkelling,
Youngsters sailing,
Professionals body-boarding.

By the water's edge
Teenagers bathing,
Mates volleyballing,
Men fishing.

Sounds amazing, but what is it like on the pier?

On the rides
Children screaming,
Adults laughing,
Teenagers giggling.

By the railings,
Seagulls swooping,
Pigeons pecking,
Birds cooing.

In the café
Families eating,
Toddlers chomping,
Fanta fizzing.

Sounds amazing, but what is it like on the beach?

Sara Toth (8)
Milton Mount Primary School, Crawley

Fear

Fear sounds like a scream,
Fear sounds like fast breathing,
Fear sounds like hearts beating,
Fear tastes like blood,
Fear feels like a spider,
Fear looks like darkness.

Alexander Gilbert (9)
Milton Mount Primary School, Crawley

The Dark Corridor

Sad feels like your heart has sunk down onto the floor for what you have done.
Sad smells like nothingness except for minty fresh air.
Sad looks like a dark hall, identical to a tunnel.
Sad sounds like nothing . . . just silence . . .
Sad tastes like the most disgusting thing that you've ever eaten,
You can't eat for hours even when it's your favourite.
Sad is the colour greyish-blue that glues you to the ground.
It reminds me of when my grandad had lung cancer and died.

Abigail Bala (10)
Milton Mount Primary School, Crawley

The Colour Of Evil Is Black

The colour of evil is black
The look of evil is a dark shadow
It is as dismal and lifeless as marrow
The sound of evil is like someone dying or someone lying; even worse
The taste of rotten eggs or raw eggs with cheese.
The feel of evil is very sharp and rough, can't you see it is very tough.
Evil, enchanted feeling, fills you with a dastardly deed that you must complete.
Makes horrified people horrific
But makes evil people feel terrific.

Joshua Weaver (10)
Milton Mount Primary School, Crawley

The Guilty Poem

Guilty is a colour of green.
Guilty feels like there's no dawn.
Guilty sounds like a lot of people are talking to you at once.
Guilty smells of a skyscraper on fire.
Guilty looks as there's no way out.
Guilty tastes as people grassing you up.

Lewis Mitchell (9)
Milton Mount Primary School, Crawley

Emotions

Pink is the colour of nice
I feel nice when the moon shines bright
I don't feel nice when I have been horrible
Cold bowls of ice are kind of nice
The sun is so, so bright.

Haleigh Lembergs (9)
Milton Mount Primary School, Crawley

At The Seaside

On the sand,
People bathing,
Fanta fizzing,
Children chuckling.

By the water,
Volley players,
Rackets hitting,
Beach balls bouncing.

In the sea,
Surfers boarding,
Dolphins diving,
Fishes flipping.

Sounds amazing, but what is it like on the pier?

On the rides,
Teenagers talking,
Bumper cars bumping,
Children screaming.

By the railings,
Lovebirds gazing,
Families playing,
Fathers joking.

In the café,
Sausages sizzling,
Children chomping,
Adults slurping.

Amber Keighron (8)
Milton Mount Primary School, Crawley

Jealousy

Green is the colour of jealousy.
Jealousy feels like my sister and me fighting over my Game Boy.
Jealousy makes you feel guilty.
Jealousy feels like another team winning The World Cup.
Jealousy feels like someone hogging your favourite food.
Jealousy is like your brother being the president.
Jealousy makes me sad.

Thomas Greenwood (9)
Milton Mount Primary School, Crawley

At The Seaside

On the pebbles,
Kites flying,
Eating ice cream,
Seagulls squawking.

By the water,
Children laughing,
People on the shore,
Sand swirling.

In the sea,
Swimmers snorkelling,
Swimmers gliding,
Waves crashing.

Sounds amazing, but what is it like on the pier?

On the rides,
Children screaming,
Adults shouting,
Teenagers cheering.

By the railings,
Seagulls squawking,
People chatting,
Babies crying.

In the café,
Families eating,
Children drinking,
Adults talking.

Sounds amazing, but what is it like on the beach?

Eleanor Taylor (7)
Milton Mount Primary School, Crawley

Happy!

Pink is the colour of happy.
Happy smells like a chocolate cake just being baked.
Happy feels like kittens' fur just been brushed.
Happy sound like my little sister laughing.
Happy tastes like a scoop of chocolate ice cream.
Happy looks like someone smiling.
Happy reminds me of my friends and family.

Hollie Lloyd (9)
Milton Mount Primary School, Crawley

At The Seaside

On the sand,
Teenagers wrestling,
Children charging,
Parents bathing.

By the water,
Toddlers splashing,
Beach balls bouncing,
Kids skipping.

In the sea,
Brave men sailing,
Families swimming,
Adults diving.

Sounds amazing, but what is it like on the pier?

On the rides,
Teenagers screaming,
Toddlers giggling,
Families laughing.

By the railings,
Seagulls soaring,
Friends chatting,
Teenagers joking.

In the café,
Lovers dreaming,
Toddlers slurping,
Adults eating.

Sounds amazing, but what is it like on the beach?

Hollie Martin (8)
Milton Mount Primary School, Crawley

Happiness

I am happy all of my life,
I am happy, I'm always pink,
I'm really happy, keep me going,
I need a scoop of chocolate cake,
I like the feel of soft fur,
I like happy, it is pink,
I'm always happy, yeah! Yeah! Yeah!
Be happy.

Jodie Cashman (10)
Milton Mount Primary School, Crawley

At The Seaside

On the sand,
Parents sunbathing,
Seagulls flying,
Crabs sidewalk.

In the sea,
Colourful fish,
Children splashing,
Men surfing.

By the water's edge,
Water whipping up,
Shells washing up,
Footprints everywhere.

Sounds amazing, but what is it like on the pier?

On the rides,
Toddlers jumping,
Families screaming,
Babies crying.

By the railings,
Teenagers eating,
Seagulls gliding,
Lovebirds laughing.

In the café,
Parents chatting,
Donuts sitting,
Couples eating.

Sounds amazing, but what is it like on the beach?

Sophie Mansfield (8)
Milton Mount Primary School, Crawley

The Amazon

If I was in The Amazon I would touch a jaguar.
If I was in The Amazon I would smell an exquisite flower.
If I was in The Amazon I would nibble the smooth soft fruit.
If I was in The Amazon I would see the magnificent rainbow.
If I was in The Amazon I would hear the cry of a dolphin.

Jordan Mead (9)
Milton Mount Primary School, Crawley

At The Seaside

On the rides,
People giggling,
Swaying their hands,
People screaming.

By the railings,
Families giggling,
Babies crying,
People talking.

In the café,
Families chatting,
Teenagers eating,
Men serving.

Sounds amazing, but what is it like on the beach?

On the pebbles,
Fanta fizzing,
People sunbathing,
Children messing.

By the water,
Volleyball players jumping,
Rackets hitting,
Beach balls bouncing.

In the sea,
People diving,
Babies floating,
Men surfing.

Sounds amazing, but what is it like on the pier?

Tyler Hyatt (8)
Milton Mount Primary School, Crawley

Boredom

Boredom feels like you have nothing left in the world to do.
Boredom sounds dull.
Boredom tastes like crackers with no cheese.
Boredom smells of nothing.

Nick Downton (9)
Milton Mount Primary School, Crawley

At The Seaside

On the pebbles,
Fanta fizzing,
Children whizzing,
Sausages sizzling.

By the water,
Playing volleyball,
Waves breaking,
Water skiing.

In the sea,
People swimming,
Bells ringing,
Women singing.

Sounds amazing, but what is it like on the pier?

On the rides,
Roller coasters roaring,
Cable cars crashing,
Children shoving.

By the railings,
Teenagers talking,
Lovers walking,
Friends chatting.

In the café,
Adults ordering,
People drinking,
Others thinking.

Sounds amazing, but what is it like on the beach?

Thomas Owen (8)
Milton Mount Primary School, Crawley

Love

Love tastes like rich chocolate melting in your mouth.
Love feels like wrapping your arms around someone and never letting go.
Love sounds like romantic music.
Love smells like fresh crimson roses.
Love reminds me of my family all together.
Love looks like a couple at the cinema watching a romantic movie.
Love smells like chocolate candles burning in the living room.
Love sounds like a cute puppy barking.
Love tastes like devouring into rich, creamy chocolate fudge cake.

Sian Atkins (9)
Milton Mount Primary School, Crawley

The Raging Wind

I saw you help the gliders fly,
Higher and higher in the sky,
I saw you toss away the rain,
I saw you give it to the grain.

Oh wind, you are so very cold
And you are so terribly bold,
I saw you toss shaped leaves around,
All about the tough ragged ground.

I heard you scream so very loud,
Nowhere near as soft as a cloud,
I saw you puff away the mould,
So far away which is so old.

Hallam Earl (9)
Ninfield CE School, Ninfield

The Wind

I saw you toss leaves on high
And blow balloons up in the sky
And all around I heard you spin
Lots of hurricanes in the wind

I heard you howl like wolves at night
I held my teddy very tight
You rattled on my windowpane
And you made me run down the lane.

Oliver Greene (9)
Ninfield CE School, Ninfield

The Wind

I saw you blow the leaves up high,
Like fairies flying in the sky,
I saw you blow a sheet at night
And you gave me a great big fright,
I sometimes see you rustle a bush,
You get them over with a push,
I see you creak an old oak tree,
You push until you set it free.

Abigail Nixon (10)
Ninfield CE School, Ninfield

Christmas Is Over

Brown is like the bark on the old Christmas tree as it stands in the garden,
Green is like the pine needles now lying on the ground,
Silver is like the blade of the axe as it chops through the branches,
Orange is like the dancing flames of a fire as it eats through the wood,
Grey is like the billowing smoke as it rises from the fire,
White is like the papery ashes scattering over the ground,
Red is like the glowing embers of the dying fire,
Black is the charred remains of our lovely Christmas tree.

Rory Padfield (9)
Ninfield CE School, Ninfield

Wind Poem

I saw you blow across the trees,
Where squirrels hide beneath the breeze,
I saw you blow the windmill's sails,
You sometimes walk as slow as snails.

I cannot see you, you're so clear,
I know you're blowing something near,
I felt you blowing in the night,
You made me hold my clothes so tight.

I saw you blow the ladies' hair,
I heard you here, then you were there,
I saw you push the clouds that pass,
You are so strong, you'll always last.

Matthew Newnham (9)
Ninfield CE School, Ninfield

Colours

Pink is like a pretty flower blossoming in the spring,
Yellow is like the bright shining sun,
White is like the soft fluffy clouds in the sky,
Black is like the darkness of the stormy, cold night,
Orange is like the flickering glow from an open fire,
Grey is like the cold, wet dirty mist,
Red is like the sweet-smelling petal of a rose,
Blue is like the big crashing salty sea
And purple is warm and cosy, just like my duvet!

Katy Brace (9)
Ninfield CE School, Ninfield

The Wind

I saw you pick the leaves from trees
Like bees fluttering in the breeze.
I saw leaves blowing in the sky
Like blackbirds playing with a fly.

I breathed the warm, soft, smooth air
Like a big, furry, grizzly bear.
I saw the big, hot, steaming sun
Like a huge, scorching hot cross bun.

Oh wind, you blow the leaves from trees
Like air blowing them in the breeze.
Some leaves are brown, some leaves are green
Some leaves are red, some leaves are seen.

Nicky Hewson (10)
Ninfield CE School, Ninfield

Colours Around The World

Blue is like swirling waves in the salty sea,
Green is like the ruffling trees,
Red is like prickly bunches of garden roses,
Pink is like the fashion catwalk poses,
Silver is like twinkling stars around the shining, cheesy moon,
Orange is like a massive volcano erupting,
Going *kaboom!*

Amy Boyd (8)
Ninfield CE School, Ninfield

The Wind

I saw you play in the salty sea
I saw you make the towels flee
I heard you make the palm tree shake
I heard you make the chimney break

I watched you play with rubbish bins
I watched you kick the Tesco tins
I knew you made the lamp post fall
I knew you made the wolf pack call

I felt you blow my scarf up high
I heard you give a boring sigh
I knew you were calling the sun
I knew you blew a hot cross bun.

Vanya Askew (9)
Ninfield CE School, Ninfield

The Wind

I saw you toss the clouds away
And watched the sun come out to play,
Are you cross? Do you go slowly?
Are you very, very holy?

I saw the different things you made,
A meadow where the cattle laid,
I felt you kick, I heard you roar
And bring back England's sunny shore.

I saw you bend the pushing trees,
As if they were a swarm of bees,
I heard you buzz, I heard you soar,
Like you were very, very poor.

I saw you fly past like a plane
And fall down to a water drain,
Sometimes you sound like a dog's growl,
I heard you scream, I heard you howl.

Tamsyn Maile (8)
Ninfield CE School, Ninfield

Colours

Blue is like the morning sky,
Orange is like a round juicy tangerine,
Yellow is like the hot burning sun,
Green is like the soft grass,
Red is like a ruby, shining beautiful jewels,
Black is like coal burning in the fire,
Pink is like a flamingo standing on one leg,
Brown is like an angry bear.

Jasmine Gann (8)
Ninfield CE School, Ninfield

The Wind

I saw the large leaves whirling round
I felt the trees shake in the ground
I don't know if you are slim or wide
But I know you sway side to side.

I don't know if you are weak or strong
But I know you are very long
I really want to hold you tight
But I know you are very light.

James Webb (9)
Ninfield CE School, Ninfield

Colours

Yellow is like the hot beaming sun on a steaming hot summer's beach,
Black is like a funeral of crying souls,
Orange is like oranges; sweet and juicy ripe,
Pink is like my bed, all camouflaged and warm,
Purple is like my bedroom, all welcoming when I enter,
Green is like the grass swaying in the breeze,
Red is like a strawberry full of juicy flavour,
White is like a cloud, all fluffy and white,
Blue is like the Caribbean Sea, all wavy and shimmering when the sun shines on it.

Chloe Saunders (9)
Ninfield CE School, Ninfield

The Wind

I saw you blow boxes up high
Gusting way up in the sky.

You made my shoulder very cold
You looked so bold and very old.

I saw you howl and blow the leaves,
You sounded like the bumblebees.

I saw you blow the grass on high
I have to go home now, bye-bye.

Milo Moussalli (8)
Ninfield CE School, Ninfield

My Colour Poem

Red is the colour of Italian red wine
My dad's friend gives us.
Blue is the colour of the seas
Where penguins live in the North Pole.
Gold is the colour of the 2006 one pound coins.
Silver is the colour of my mum's saucepans
That she cooks porridge in.
Purple is the colour of our new school bus
The one I travel on.
Black is the colour of my dad's 80s jacket.
Brown is the gravy that swims on my plate.
Yellow is like the colour of the organic lemons
That my dad buys.

Aziz Bourner (9)
Ninfield CE School, Ninfield

Colour Poem

Orange is like the crackling fire,
Yellow is like the gleaming sand in the sunlight,
White is like the snow-covered ground at Christmas time,
Red is like the poisonous berries on the bush,
Purple is like my Bratz chair that I sit in,
Brown is like my chest of drawers with my clothes in,
Blue is like the river flower gently on a hot summer's day,
Black is like my house at night when all the lights are out,
Silver is like the stars twinkling at night.

Emma Taylor (9)
Ninfield CE School, Ninfield

The Wind

I watched the clouds fly past the sky
While Mum was making an apple pie
When you're darting across the trees
Just tossing like the bumblebees

I saw you run from here to there
I saw you dance at the funfair
I saw you blow the twirling leaves
And give a loud call out to me

I felt your cold breeze on my face
While I was walking pace by pace
I felt you blowing the cold air
While I was eating juicy pears.

Bryony Pegge (8)
Ninfield CE School, Ninfield

My Colour Poem

Red is like red-hot fire burning wood,
Emerald is like the shimmering spring grass,
Black is as black as the moonless winter's night,
Orange is like the beautiful sunset,
Blue is as blue as the Caribbean sea,
Gold is like the bright shine of Tutankhamen's gold mine,
Pink is like the colour of the bricks on my wall,
White is like frost on an early winter's morning.

Mohammad Bourner (10)
Ninfield CE School, Ninfield

The Deep, Dark, Deadly Sea

The sea, she dragged me down as I struggled
Like a fish in a net,
Her slippery hand injected me with anaesthetic,
I tried to escape but it was whipping me painfully,
She made a death signal to her shark slaves,
The sharks sang a murderous song,
She ordered them to bite me,
Their teeth unleashed a deadly smile,
I lost all hope as the Peggy Sue, sails flapping,
As if to say goodbye, sailed on.

Emily Browne (10)
Ninfield CE School, Ninfield

My Colour Poem

Red is like the juice from strawberries I eat,
Blue is like the sky on a hot summer's day,
Black is like looking into a dark cave,
Silver is like the twinkling stars at night,
Yellow is like sunflowers growing in the fields,
Green is like the leaves growing on the trees,
White is like the snow on a Christmas Day,
Orange is like a goldfish swimming in a fish tank.

Holly Scott (8)
Ninfield CE School, Ninfield

Deep, Dark, Deadly Sea

The sea salt was burning my eyes,
Like someone had blinded me with fire,
Her waves were hands tossing me about,
The darkness was like a virus spreading everywhere,
Her waves were blinding me with fear,
The sharks smiled at me with their white, sharp teeth,
The darkness was a never-ending hole,
The sharks were like cats scavenging
And in the darkness, I could see the Peggy Sue sailing away.

Carmelle Askew (10)
Ninfield CE School, Ninfield

Deep, Dark, Deadly Sea

Her waves tossing me about like a floppy fish in the freezing ice,
The saltwater stung my eyes as though I was peeling off a layer of skin,
The sharks dancing around me,
Once they had finished they took a bow
And slipped under the freezing cold water,
The rain shot down on me as though a million guns were attacking me
And in the distance I saw Peggy Sue sailing on without me . . .

Lauren Sharp (10)
Ninfield CE School, Ninfield

Deep, Dark, Deadly Sea

The sea was twinkling like stars in the pitch-black sky,
The froth was galloping horses jumping over the waves,
Tails as white as snow,
Her waves are like a stampede of zebras,
Trampling over my head, dragging me under
And in the distance I can see the Peggy Sue sailing away.

Jessica Mitchell (10)
Ninfield CE School, Ninfield

Deep, Dark, Deadly Sea

The sea's watery tongue swallowed me down its throat,
The hunched crabs grabbed me, trying to pull me down to the depths of the sea,
She was darker than the ebony of night,
I tried to stand on a giant fish, but sadly nothing came to help me,
The sharks did their death dance,
They knew flesh was around,
After all that, I saw the Peggy Sue gone forever.

Zak Barton (10)
Ninfield CE School, Ninfield

The Sea

The sea was an underwater prison
With the waves pulling you down,
She is like thunder clapping against the rocks
As the waves roll in,
She is a million hands trying to hold anyone who lands in the sea,
The waves are like a stampede of zebras trying to run over you,
I'm alone in the blackness
And in the distance, I see the Peggy Sue sail on.

Jasie Berry (11)
Ninfield CE School, Ninfield

The Deep, Dark, Dangerous Sea

The sea,
She swallows me down in her air-ridden depths,
Her waves slap me around the face like a whip across a white horse's hind quarters,
The air was tight around my neck, strangling me with its freezing breeze,
The coldness of the water was an anaesthetic,
The waves were salmon, competing with each other to see who could get the highest,
It was the beginning of death,
Her salt blinded my eyes like splinters,
I swallowed a mouthful of shards of glass,
The water chewed at my skin until I was soaked through,
My legs gave up hope
And in the distance I saw my last hope sail away with the Peggy Sue.

Jamie Trimmer (11)
Ninfield CE School, Ninfield

Deep, Dark, Deadly Sea

Her waves spiral around me as if I'm stuck in a tornado,
I am surrounded by the darkness in a cemetery,
Her sharks dance around me,
The rain hits me like a million sharp knives,
A blank hole grabs me and pulls me under,
It's like being in the middle of the sea
And in the distance I see the Peggy Sue sail on . . .

Robyn Orr (11)
Ninfield CE School, Ninfield

The Deep, Dark, Deadly Sea

The sea,
She took me down as if I were an anchor,
A piece of driftwood,
Her waves crashing quickly over my head
As hands push me down underneath the booming waves,
The air was around my neck, strangling me with its inclement breeze,
The waves were like white horses galloping away from the whip,
Salt sticking to me, blinding me,
The smell of loneliness coming closer and closer . . .
My legs gave up hope, knowing that I was going down . . .
And in the distance I saw Peggy Sue sail on . . .

Molly Boyd (10)
Ninfield CE School, Ninfield

The Deep, Dark, Deadly Sea

The sea,
She hauls me down like an anchor sinking to the sea's salty cemetery,
Her waves lash my chilly cheeks like a white stallion being whipped in the wind,
Her servant's fin was a chopping knife cutting carefully through the water's surface,
The sea was smirking as she saw me sink under the shark infested water
And in the distance I see the Peggy Sue sail on . . .

Poppy Brace (11)
Ninfield CE School, Ninfield

Deep, Dark, Dangerous Sea

The sea was the centre of all evil,
The sharks were her living demons eating away at my soul,
She foamed at the mouth as she slapped my fragile body,
Her icy water sprayed into my eyes like arrows,
She pulled me under,
Her evil laugh filled my mind,
The sea,
The waves were white horses stampeding over my tired body,
My paralysed body was forced to move to stay above her icy depths,
The air was tight around my neck, strangling me with its freezing climate,
She forced me down, down
And in the distance I saw the Peggy Sue sail on . . .

Nicola Palmer (11)
Ninfield CE School, Ninfield

Deep, Dark, Deadly Sea

The sea,
It floods my body with its salty water,
The crashing of its waves are like needles stabbing in my legs,
The shark's smirk is deadly, as it lurks beneath me,
As the water shoots up my nose,
A headache lurks like a hunting ghost
And in the distance I see the Peggy Sue sail away.

Mattie White (10)
Ninfield CE School, Ninfield

Deep, Dark, Deadly Sea

The sea,
Her waves are a crashing machine throwing me around into tiny pieces,
She is a whirlpool playing and chewing my frozen flesh,
Her waves are like a washing machine tumbling until I'm clean,
Her waves are like a thousand bees stinging me,
Her waves slap me in the face,
She is a slash of grit smashing against me,
Her waves tumble against me as if someone is pushing me,
Her waves are like a python choking me in a coil of death
And in the distance I see the Peggy Sue sail on . . .

Jodie Freeman (10)
Ninfield CE School, Ninfield

The Deep Dark Ocean

The sea,
The waves were tossing me around like a tennis ball,
The sharks sniff me out like dogs searching for rabbits,
The darkness was an everlasting black hole,
The air is colder than ice,
Its salty spray was splintering my eyes,
The wave was pouncing on me like a cheetah
And in the distance I see hope fade away into the distance.

Daniel Lowry (11)
Ninfield CE School, Ninfield

The King Of The Sea

She is pulling me, sucking me into a Hoover,
The waves are like tumbling eyes, going round and round,
She is stirring the sea for her supper, making a whirlpool,
It is like a washing machine spinning me,
Like twisting on a roundabout in the park,
The rocks are like the muscles of the great sea,
The waves tumble me as if someone is pushing from side to side,
The giant hand crushing me to death,
The waves are like a python choking me in a pool of death
And in the distance I see the Peggy Sue sail on.

Hayden Boyce (10)
Ninfield CE School, Ninfield

Deep, Dark, Deadly Sea

The sea,
The sea is a whole pool playing and chewing at my frozen flesh,
The waves are like splinters of smashed glass blinding me,
Her waves are like a python choking me in a coil of death,
She sucks me down into her icy depths,
Her waves are like thousands of bees stinging me,
The waves are like an icy bath
And there I sink
And in the distance I see the Peggy Sue sail on . . .

Jessie Williams (11)
Ninfield CE School, Ninfield

The Sea

The waves were a crashing machine throwing me around into tiny pieces,
She slapped me like a lunging whip scarring me for life,
The waves are like a washing machine tumbling me till I'm clean,
The waves are like a python choking me in a coil of death,
The sea is a whirlpool playing and chewing my frozen flesh and blood,
She was a slash of grit smashing against me,
The waves are like a thousand bees stinging me
And in the distance I see the Peggy Sue sail on . . .

Jessica Reid (10)
Ninfield CE School, Ninfield

Deep, Dark, Deadly Sea

The sea,
Her waves tossed me like an acrobat in a circus,
She was as strong as an ox throwing me about like people playing volleyball,
Her white horses danced around me as if they were in a competition,
She sucked me through her dark hole trying to drown me,
The rain shot down at me like an automatic machine gun,
Her salt stung my eyes like waxing your eyebrows
And in the distance I saw the Peggy Sue sail on . . .

Rosie Smith (10)
Ninfield CE School, Ninfield

Deep, Dark, Deadly Sea

The sea pulled me away from the surface like sinking sand in the jungle,
The sea is as angry as a teenager throwing a tantrum,
The darkness pressed down on me, trapping me in its claws,
It's like thunder clapping against rocks as the water rolls in
And in the distance I see the Peggy Sue sail on . . .

Olivia Sztyber (10)
Ninfield CE School, Ninfield

Deep, Dark Sea

The sea,
She numbs my legs by injecting them with anaesthetic,
Her icy waves feel like poisonous snakes squirting venom
Into my warm-blooded body,
The fear inside me was heard from the growl of the waves,
Her waves are sharp as a shark's tooth,
Biting into me with laughing gas
And in the distance I see the Peggy Sue sail on.

Ellie Whiting (10)
Ninfield CE School, Ninfield

Deep, Dark, Deadly Sea!

The sea,
Her icy, cold sea is like a nurse injecting me with anaesthetic,
My energy draining away like a funnel full of water,
Foam on her sea was froth from a bitter flavoured cider,
Power of currents slash debris into my body like sharp needles,
Depths of the ocean like a black diamond mine,
The waves feeling like poisonous snakes injecting venom
Into my warm blooded nerves
And in the distance I see the Peggy Sue sail on . . .

Nicole Donno (10)
Ninfield CE School, Ninfield

The Sea

She pulls me down into her frozen mouth,
The sea is like wolves howling a hypnotising tune,
To lead me to their lair,
I am in the darkness
And I am all alone,
In the distance, I see the Peggy Sue sail away.

Sam Rose (10)
Ninfield CE School, Ninfield

Deadly, Dark Sea

The sea,
Her waves are like a poisonous snake injecting venom into my warm blooded nerves,
She pulls me deep into the cold, icy depths,
The sea,
The depths acting like black diamond mines,
A headache lurks likes a haunting ghost,
I can feel my energy draining like a funnel of water,
The sea,
Her foam is like the froth from a bitter flavoured cider,
The hands of the sea throwing me around
And the noise of the waves like the cheer from a football stadium,
But in the distance my parents sailed away on board the Peggy Sue.

Hannah Harmer (9)
Ninfield CE School, Ninfield

The Deep, Dark, Deadly Sea

The sea,
The night's darkness was beaming onto the wandering waves,
Sharks were circling me, like a hand on a clock,
The sea was a racehorse with its jockey unseated,
Galloping aimlessly across the beaten track,
She was as fierce as a charging rhino, attacking everything in view,
The ocean was smirking as it saw me sink under the shark infested water,
Suffering a slow, painful death
And in the distance I see the Peggy Sue sail on . . .

Elizabeth Evans (10)
Ninfield CE School, Ninfield

Deep, Dark, Deadly Sea

The sea froth is galloping white horses
Slapping my face furiously with their snow-white tails,
Her waves are like gigantic hands reaching out
And dragging me under the stone cold sheet of water,
The sea twinkles like stars in the night sky,
The sea is a huge, underwater tornado
Trying to swallow me whole
And in the distance I see the Peggy Sue sail on.

Sophie Roller (9)
Ninfield CE School, Ninfield

Not For The Squeamish

This tale is not for the squeamish,
It is meant for the very brave,
So please don't go on and read,
Or you'll be sent to an early grave.

The tale is all about cannibals
And very ugly witches,
That walk around bubbling cauldrons
And have some deadly kisses.

Once upon a time,
In Gonna-Kill-You land,
Some bratty little children,
Were playing on the sand.

The witches came to take them
And of course, they did succeed,
Those little kids got all tied up,
The witches made their way back and Aggie took the lead.

When they got back to the witches' house,
The kids were put into a large cage,
One of the witches ate a mouse
And the other read a spell from a large brown page.

In one moment, a group of cannibal people
Came to eat them up,
One of them said that girls taste better with treacle
And boys were turned to a mushy pulp and drunk from a very large cup.

So that was the end of the bratty kids,
The ones that deserved to die,
So the moral of this sick and twisted story is,
Don't be a bratty young child!

Iesha Godden (11)
Oakfield Primary School, Southampton

My Pet Elephant

My pet elephant is very hairy
And really, really, really scary.
He crushes all my bestest friends
And won't stop till the world ends.
He always thinks he's really big,
But looks a bit stupid in his Afro wig.
Then suddenly, something blew off his hat
And a lorry came and squashed him flat!

Jack Freemantle (10)
Oakfield Primary School, Southampton

Back In Time

I went back in time
Just to say this rhyme.
I landed with the Greeks
And it really does reek!
I was in with the cattle
And now the battle.
I had better run
Because it is not fun.
Knives and swords
Like cats' claws.
Hercules, come save me
Otherwise I won't be.
Please wake me up
Before I break this cup.
I saw a great wall
It was really tall.
I think I've moved on
To a big time bomb.
I am in the Blitz
I am calling it quits.
I think I'm going back to the time
Where I started this rhyme.
It was just a dream
Now that was my theme.

James Farmer (11)
Oakfield Primary School, Southampton

Sleeping Elephants

Sleeping elephants on the floor,
We would like them so much more,
If all they did was sleep and sleep,
Then all we'd do is eat and eat,
From the mass of flesh and bone,
To their terrible, trumpeting moan,
Killing them with our very big arrows,
We would eat them with lots of marrows,
Marrows, marrows, everywhere,
They would start to fill the air,
But if those elephants were to wake,
They would cause a giant quake,
Then all of us would surely die,
So let sleeping elephants lie!

Thomas Nagel (10)
Oakfield Primary School, Southampton

Humpty Dumpty

You probably know Humpty Dumpty's fall,
But the wall he sat on was 200 metres tall,
It all started a year ago,
When we all went with the flow
And then Humpty climbed up on a wall,
A certain wall that was very, very tall,
He went to see the spectacular view,
He thought he'd see other people too,
When he thought the view was extremely cool,
He forgot himself and started to fall,
The next thing we heard was a splat,
When everybody saw him, he was crushed flat,
The king sent for his special men,
To fix Humpty Dumpty back up again,
They didn't want Humpty to go to waste,
So they let everybody have a taste,
So this is a risk you shouldn't take,
If you do, it's a very big mistake,
So never climb a very big wall!

Christopher Woodman (11)
Oakfield Primary School, Southampton

On The Playground

On the playground there isn't a sound
Except for the children playing around.
As I look there is a child on the ground,
Is he hurt? Or what has he found?

On the playground there is a swing,
Around which the children sing.
The chains on the swing always ching,
Until it's time for the bell to ring.

On the playground there stands a lonely tree,
Everyone thinks it is heavenly.
Playing, little ones run around it with glee,
Hide-and-seek, hoping to see.

On the playground is a climbing frame,
On which everyone has a good game.
If you climb to the top, there is instant fame,
But if you fall, oh, what a shame!

Aston Marsh & Hannah Patching (10)
Oakfield Primary School, Southampton

The Three Little Pigs And The Big, Tall Wolf

You know the three little pigs' story or at least you think you do
This is the true story from my point of view,
I was just a lonely wolf with a very bad cold
And because I'm very big and tall, everyone thought I was old.

I was walking outside in the freezing cold
I knocked on someone's door trying to be bold,
I said, 'Please, please, please let me in?'
The pig said, 'Not by the hairs on my chinny-chin-chin!'

I mean, what cheek, I was saying please
Then all of a sudden, I started to sneeze,
The house started to shake and it fell to the floor
Well, I couldn't help it, it was made of straw.

I walked constantly for two miles straight
Quite a while later, I reached a gate.

I said, 'Please, please, please let me in?'
The pig said, 'Not by the hairs on my chinny-chin-chin!'
That's not nice, I was on my knees
Then all of a sudden, I started to sneeze.

The house fell down in a few ticks
Well, I couldn't help it, it was made of sticks,
Then suddenly, I saw, or is this a trick?
I saw a house made of bricks,
I said, 'Please, please, please let me in?'
The pig said, 'Not by the hairs on my chinny-chin-chin!'

The cops came and locked me in a cell.

Aaron Roulstone (10)
Oakfield Primary School, Southampton

Our Playground

On the playground you can play,
There is not even a price to pay,
You can play a fast game of football,
Or maybe even a game of nail-biting netball.

You can talk to your favourite friends,
Or drive the teachers round the bend,
All the children are very loud,
It's like I can hear no other sound.

On the playground a boy fell to the ground,
He made a very sad, moaning sound,
The girls were constantly talking,
Which made them stop walking.

Eleanor Pugh (11)
Oakfield Primary School, Southampton

My Pet Cheetah

My pet cheetah is very scary,
But really she is as soft as a fairy,
She has big, pointy claws,
They curl out from her paws.

My pet cheetah is very angry,
But only when she is exceptionally hungry,
Now and then she gets in a mood,
So I always offer her food.

My pet cheetah is very pretty,
Just like a cute, fluffy kitty,
She has very long, dark eyelashes,
Which protect her from bright flashes.

My pet cheetah is very ticklish,
Especially when she is chewing on fish,
When I start to tickle her,
I guarantee she will start to purr.

Chloe Reynolds (10)
Oakfield Primary School, Southampton

Silence

Silence is white
Like silk and lace
Silence is light
It's breathtaking in any case

Silence sounds
Like an undiscovered world
Silence is sweet
Like sugar and tea

Silence feels
Like you're in a large, white room
With no one around you
But the lovely sound of a mellow tune

Silence tastes
Like cheesecake
On a china plate
Or sparkling water from a flowing lake.

Lauren Scammell (10)
Oakfield Primary School, Southampton

Humpty Dumpty's True Story

You think you've heard the true story
Of Humpty Dumpty - it was actually very gory.
Get prepared for the truth
You don't need to be a sleuth.

I was walking far along
When I started to sing a song
I went - 'Bling, bling, bling.'
I wish I hadn't started to sing.

I was in the forest covering my ears
When I saw this man drinking some beers
He tried to offer me some
So I then started to run.

I suddenly found a giant wall
One that was 20 metres tall
I started to climb and climb
I was really running out of time.

When I got up there, I looked at the view
I seriously needed the loo
Suddenly, I started to fall
From the top of the 20 metre wall.

Down, down, down and down
I felt like I was falling through the ground
I thought I'd broke my leg
But I gave everyone some scrambled egg!

Crash!

Cem Mollaahmetoglu (10)
Oakfield Primary School, Southampton

My Friend, Alfred

I have a secret friend, who is different from most,
He loves to play the piccolo and dance on the coast,
Alfred is a special name and everything he does is a big game!
Like fishing for the biggest fish, then flipping it onto a big dish!
He even dances when the night is young,
Without telling his ghoulish mum!
Alfred wears a pointy hat
And he has a huge, fluffy, black cat.
Alfred's friends do lots of things
And all look like great big kings,
As they dance on the moon,
Alfred left, saying, 'I shall see you all very soon!'

Bethany Luxton (10)
Oakfield Primary School, Southampton

Anger!

Anger looks like a flash of lightning,
Anger is very, very frightening.

Anger is like a boiling kettle,
Anger will never settle.

Anger is bright, bright red,
Anger will never go to bed.

Anger smells like burning fire,
Anger feels like electricity wires.

Anger thinks it is the best,
Anger will never take a rest.

Alice Donovan (11)
Oakfield Primary School, Southampton

My Magic Unicorn

My magic unicorn flies around the sky,
Like a fluttering butterfly.
She is as white as snow,
You would love to see her horn glow.
Her hooves sparkle like silver glitter,
Her name is May Chitter.
I will always keep May,
I will never ever give her away.

Amy Lovell (11) & Jodie Thorp (10)
Oakfield Primary School, Southampton

Little Red Riding Hood

Little Red Riding Hood did all she could
She took food to her nan, who she called her gran
On her way, she skipped and did play.

She thought the wolf was really cool
But actually, he was a fool
She skipped along the path
And the wolf began to laugh
He said, 'Fetch me a cup of tea
As I'm your nanny!'

Lauren Halstead (11)
Oakfield Primary School, Southampton

My Friend, Wilfred

My friend, Wilfred, is cooler than you think,
He likes to make boats that always sink,
His favourite food is snails,
He also has friends which are whales,
He has lots of stories to tell,
He is a male
Who's been in jail!

Tom Marsh (10)
Oakfield Primary School, Southampton

My Dog Oscar

My dog Oscar
He was a lot of fun
We'd walk him every weekend
Happy days spent in the sun.
Every day after school
My brother Christian and me
Would come home to play with him
For hours before our tea.

Then as I grew up, he grew up
He drank water from a bowl
And I drank water from a cup
But then his old legs gave up.
After that he got very ill
And started to lie quite still.

When I came home from school one day
Mum began to say, 'Dad took Oscar to the vet and he was put down.'
I started to frown
And looked down,
I was very sad, not glad,
Because I didn't get to say goodbye
Which was bad.
Then nothing happened until 2003
When I got a new baby brother
Who is now nearly three!

Jacob Andriesz (10)
Oakhyrst Grange School, Caterham

My Brother And Me

My brother and me
Not a great pair you see
We kick, we scream
He always hogs the TV screen

We make terror around the house
He scares me with a mouse
I try to lock him in his room
But he threatens me with the broom

But really he loves me
And that is the key
To the relationship
Between my brother and me.

Jodie Mackintosh (9)
Oakhyrst Grange School, Caterham

Maths

What's cruel? What's annoying?
What's so hard, it's boring?
What do you do on a summer's day?
Do you laze about and play?
We do maths.

Our teacher shouts and shouts,
She never stops moving her mouth,
If we don't do everything right,
She makes us stay in, all the night!

Do you know nine times nine?
If we don't, it's a crime!
We have a test every week
And everyone is quiet and meek.

The boisterous boys,
The quiet girls,
The horrible bully as well,
They never do anything wrong
In maths!

Emily Galvin (10)
Oakhyrst Grange School, Caterham

Best Friends

A best friend is like a soulmate,
Not someone you love or hate,
Someone you can trust
And not get into a huff,
You can tell them a secret
And they will keep it,
You can talk to a best friend
And they will understand.

I go round to her place
And she puts make-up on my face,
When I did this to her, she wore a frown,
Because I made her look like a clown!
We put music on so loud,
So loud we have to shout,
Sometimes we argue,
This is very true,
But we will always be best friends,
Right until the very end.

Anna Kristina Gibson (9)
Oakhyrst Grange School, Caterham

My Friend, Tree

I have a friend called Tree
He's part elf and part gnome, you see
He's got big, blue eyes
And a liking for mince pies
He has a little green hat
And his tummy's very fat
Yes, that's my friend, Tree!

He is never silent, always loud
Never bothered by a dark cloud
He can't sit still, always fidgets
He's very rude he called my teachers midgets!
The thing about Tree, you see
He can only be seen and heard
By me!

Georgina Candy (10)
Oakhyrst Grange School, Caterham

My Birthday Present

'Happy birthday sweetie!'
Said my mum as I came through the door.
I waited until I heard, 'Presents,'
But the presents she seemed to ignore.

'So where are my presents then Mum?'
I asked as I walked to the snug.
'They're all up in your bedroom!
They're lying up there on the rug.'

'*Oooh!* How many are there?'
I gasped as I ran to my room.
'One,' said Mum and I sighed,
One? What? Oh, the gloom.

Yes, only one present,
But it practically took up my flat!
I ran to it squealing,
Mum said, 'It took ages to wrap!'

Was it my own TV
Or was it a new bouncy bed?
Was it a new computer?
So many ideas in my head!

I need a TV now I'm 15,
Well, I'm nearly there,
So I cut off the ribbon, ripped all the paper,
And guess what?

A teddy bear!

Fiona Lynn (11)
Oakhyrst Grange School, Caterham

My Teddy Bear

My teddy bear's name is Magic,
If I lost her, it would be tragic,
Her best friend's name is Pinky,
My Magic is very twinkly.

On my fourth birthday I opened my door,
To see my little Magic
Sitting on the floor,
Around her neck sparkled a chain
And in the shape of a panda,
It said, *Happy Birthday Miranda!*

Miranda Batki-Braun (9)
Oakhyrst Grange School, Caterham

Vindaloo And Spice

Vindaloo and spice,
Hot and very nice,
I prefer it with rice,
Do you?

You can't let it grow old
And get covered in mould,
That's not the way it's sold,
To you!

Everyone I know
Doesn't like it so,
Especially when outside it snows,
It's warm!

It's nice with some chilli,
Some people think I'm silly,
Especially Millie,
Off I storm!

Vindaloo and spice,
Hot and very nice,
I prefer it with rice,
Do you?

Adam Giles (10)
Oakhyrst Grange School, Caterham

The Gnome

The little gnome sits in my garden
And comes alive at night.
He scares the cat
And he scares me.

He climbs into my house
And the stair boards creak
When he comes up the stairs.

When it is the morning
He's back outside again
Back to stone again.

Scott Widnell (11)
Oakhyrst Grange School, Caterham

My Last Evening Of Being . . . Ten!

My last evening of being ten
I can't believe it's come,
Tomorrow I'm eleven,
At home with Dad and Mum.

My favourite guest though, is my nan,
She's sleeping over tonight,
In the spare bedroom - lucky thing,
My hamsters might give her a fright!

When I *was* ten - one year ago,
I was really excited, oh yes,
I opened my presents in the lounge,
The wrapping paper *was* such a mess!

I opened some presents today,
My dad was a bit annoyed,
He said my birthday was not till tomorrow,
What the heck! I'm overjoyed!

Philippa Downs (11)
Oakhyrst Grange School, Caterham

My Friend, Lauren

Well, Lauren is Lauren and always will be
She is as funny and as happy as a dancing bee
If I am most unhappy, she will always be with me.

Her hair is as brown as a chocolate bar
And chocolate is my lucky star
I won't eat her hair, don't you fear
The thought was just floating around the atmosphere.

Her eyes are as blue as a beautiful sky
And this I definitely can't deny
And this is Lauren for you
She is also rather tall too!

Stephanie Lindo (9)
Oakhyrst Grange School, Caterham

Sports

Netball is such fun,
It is best to play in the sun.

Swimming is so wet,
I have not won yet.

Football is for boys,
I would rather play with my toys.

Lacrosse makes me cross,
I keep losing my ball in the moss.

Running makes you fit,
I only like it a little bit.

Badminton is cool,
But sometimes I act a fool.

Tennis is a mess,
I like it less and less.

And that's what I think about sports!

Rebecca English (11)
Oakhyrst Grange School, Caterham

At The Bottom Of The Garden

At the bottom of the garden
Where the daffodils blow
Little fairies can be found, sitting in a row
'Come down to us,'
They used to call
'Come down to us and we'll have a ball
With the flowers and the trees
And the mice and the bees.'

So come down to the bottom of the garden
Whenever you are feeling blue
Because your frown will be turned upside down
And the fairies will be waiting for you.

Jaimee Welsh (11)
Oakhyrst Grange School, Caterham

Lessons

Maths, maths, what a pain,
Drives my friends insane.
I don't blame them, they're totally right,
Even though they're pretty bright.

Games, games, such good fun,
Especially today in the sun.
It's better today because it's hockey
And it's with Mr Wockey.

Art, art, very bad
And the teachers are very mad.
I suppose it can be OK,
But I really don't like using clay.

Overall, lessons are good
But what I don't like is the work.
My friends get As or Bs
Whilst all the time I get Cs.

Harry Hopkins (10)
Oakhyrst Grange School, Caterham

Homework Excuses

Homework, what a pain
I've forgotten it again
I'll say I left it at home
I'll say it was eaten by my gnome
I'll say it was gobbled by the dog
Or it fell in a bog
I'll say it fell down the loo
Maybe I'll say it's stuck in glue
I'll say it flew really far away
Or that it totally decayed.

I tried all nine excuses
Teacher exclaimed, 'What a nuisance!'
Maybe she believed that it decayed
But my hopes were shattered when she said,
'You've told these before, so I thought I'd mention
You've earned a month's detention!'

Alexander Niemira (11)
Oakhyrst Grange School, Caterham

My Guinea Pig

She was fat and round, that's all I can say
She was not very jolly and just wouldn't play.

Her name was Tulip, funny I know
She liked the sunshine, but hated the snow.

She loved having cuddles, strokes and tickles too
But whenever I held her, she just did a poo!

The end of my poem to me is quite sad
You see, Tulip died and that makes me feel bad.

So, now she's in Heaven with her guinea pig chums
She's probably happy, but I still feel glum.

Sam Bushell (10)
Oakhyrst Grange School, Caterham

Sports

Rugby, football,
Cricket and hockey,
You can play these sports with your doggy,
I wish I could play these sports 24/7,
Even when I'm one hundred and eleven!

I play sports when I'm at school,
At home, even in the pool,
I've been playing sports since I was five,
I love sports,
Because sports are my life.

Declan McDougall (11)
Oakhyrst Grange School, Caterham

My Tiger

My tiger is orange and black,
Now he lives in my rucksack,
Sometimes he cries
And I have to wipe his eyes,
I love him truly,
But he loves his girlfriend, Julie,
And we are best friends,
So this is where my poem ends!

Emily Ruiz (10)
Oakhyrst Grange School, Caterham

When It Comes To Holidays

I sometimes am at home,
When it comes to holidays,
Or sometimes I could roam.

I'm more likely to be abroad,
When it comes to holidays
Enjoying myself on the road.

I'll always be having fun,
When it comes to holidays,
I'll be lying in the sun.

I might be alone,
When it comes to holidays,
But I'll always come back home.

Zarah Saumtally (10)
Oakhyrst Grange School, Caterham

You And Me!

You and me what a sight
Going round the Eiffel Tower
It's just so right.
At school we learned history
It was about the Saxons
It was great!
I went home
I played with my friend
That was nice.
After that lovely day
It's time to have a good night's sleep
Goodnight!
Zzzzz!

Natasha Duursma (8)
Ocklynge Junior School, Eastbourne

If You Were An Animal What Would You Be?

If you were an animal what would you be?
A tall giraffe or a busy bee?
A fluffy kitten or a bird in a tree?
I'll tell you what I'd rather be, me!

If you were a plant what would you be?
A pretty flower or a yucky weed?
A giant tree or a tiny seed?
I'll tell you what I'd rather be . . . me!

Esme Wood (7)
Ocklynge Junior School, Eastbourne

The Bully

B ullies are nasty, bullies are cruel
U naware of what they'll do to you makes you feel small
L iving in a world of pain
L osing out in every game
I f you're worried or you're feeling rather sad
E very time a bully comes it makes you feel bad
S adness is a terrible thing that also makes you mad

A ny person black or white
R eally doesn't deserve to fight
E mptiness never feels quite right

N ame him and shame him
O bviously he lives a life of sin
T ogether we can win

N icking your money
I don't think that's funny
C ramming rubbish in your locker
E ven kicking you in soccer

The bully won't get the best of you
'Cause we all know what you can do.

Michelle Turner (11)
Ocklynge Junior School, Eastbourne

The Night Flight

When you go to bed
Inside your head
A world is formed
To be performed

Of colours and light
And angel flight

But one night it changed
I was all alone
In a world of evil and fear
I changed a gear
Inside my head
Before I knew it, I was being lead
To dread by Satan and evil men
There were ten
Ten big holes and I fell down and down

And I was sitting in my bed!

Kitty Nielsen (11)
Ocklynge Junior School, Eastbourne

Seal Girl

'I'm a little seal girl
In my little seal world
And it's so hard to get by
Cos seals can't even cry'

When I'm swimming in the sea
Everything seems blue to me
I feel the tears come to my eyes
But though I try and try and try
I simply cannot cry

So I looked for Oz the octopus
I said to him, 'Oh, please don't fuss,'
But deep inside I knew he was
A friend that I could trust

He fixed my problem in a tick
It really was so very quick
I tried to cry, but then I laughed
So seals still don't even cry
Isn't that daft!

Jasmine Colkett (7)
Ocklynge Junior School, Eastbourne

A Good Dream

Last night I had an exquisite dream,
I dreamt of golden wrapped presents,
With all range of colours.
What stood out, was the Christmas tree,
With lights shining like stars
And little gold and green,
Surprisingly dazzling baubles.
All the presents laid out with little labels
With beautiful handwriting
And bright decorations.
Then suddenly, on the highest spot
Of the Christmas tree,
I saw a dazzling looking angel.
I knew it was early in the morning
Because everyone was awake,
Laughing and cheering,
I felt really happy,
It was Christmas Day.

Paul Blackwell (9)
Ocklynge Junior School, Eastbourne

What Am I?

I wake up in the morning,
Jump straight out of bed,
I'm a really good hopper and love to jump,
I'm a real vegetarian,
I eat lots of grass,
Do you know what I am yet?
If not, here's a clue,
I have great, big, floppy ears and whiskers,
I have a small, twitchy nose,
I have a little fluffy tail,
Do you know what I am?

Shannon Thomas (9)
Ocklynge Junior School, Eastbourne

Spooks

S pooks are simply frightful
P opping up they find delightful
O oooooooo and *aaarrrggghhhh* they yell
O h dear, I'm under a magic spell
K eep your distance, never speak
S pooks I would never like to meet

Argh! I'm spooked!

Rosalie Hide (9)
Ocklynge Junior School, Eastbourne

Football Poem

I like football it's my favourite game
I want to hear the crowd shout out my name.

I run with the ball
I get tackled and fall
But even in pain
I get up again.

When I score a goal
I shout and cheer
But it only happens
Once a year!

I love my team
They are the greatest
Arsenal is their name
They always win the game.

Ryan Smith (9)
Ocklynge Junior School, Eastbourne

My Friend Mollie

My friend Mollie had wonderful eyes that shone like crystals
I remember the day she played with her favourite water pistols
Everyone liked her made-up games
When it was Bonfire Night she was clever not to go too near the sizzling flames
Oh Mollie, oh Mollie, you had such pretty hair
And you always played fair
I remember the way you danced, the way you skipped and smiled
All day long until the sun went down and you would never frown
But Mollie now you are gone, it's so dull and grey
You're not near me now
But God's with you, I know.

Pascale Smith (9)
Ocklynge Junior School, Eastbourne

Cinderella

So you think you know this story
But it is not full of glory
When young Cinderella's mother died
Her father cried
But when Cinderella began to cry
Her stepmother shot her father in the eye
So Cinderella worked day and night
While her stepsisters got into a fight
When Prince Charming came to the door
Cinderella fell flat on the floor
She slowly pulled out her sharp dagger
And plunged it into his bladder
So she did not marry the handsome prince
Instead she married Jar Jar Binks!

Madeleine Jackson (9)
Ocklynge Junior School, Eastbourne

I Had A Dream

I had a dream, a weird dream,
About a dragon who liked to ski,
A rabbit who liked to dance
And a snake who liked to eat leaves!

I had a dream, a weird dream,
Where there were eggs at Christmas
And tinsel at Easter.

I had a dream, a magnificent dream,
Where all of this came true.

Georgina Whatley (9)
Ocklynge Junior School, Eastbourne

Toy Magic

The toys each cast a magic spell
And made sad Puppet feel all well.

Doll made her lips sparkle brightly.
Train made her face blush kindly.

Teddy made her hair twirl neatly
Jack-in-the-box made her smile twinkle brilliantly.

Dog made her shoes shine wonderfully
Spider-Man made her cheeks glow beautifully.

Chloe Andrews (8)
Ocklynge Junior School, Eastbourne

Toy Magic

The toys each cast a magic spell
And made the sad puppet feel all well.

Doll made her smile twinkle brightly,
Dog made her skin sparkle lightly,
Teddy made her eyes twinkle delicately,
Jack-in-the-box made her hair flow nicely,
Car made her cheeks glow beautifully,
Train made her shoes shine golden,
Teddy made her arms move gracefully.

Catriona Houston (8)
Ocklynge Junior School, Eastbourne

Toy Magic

The toys each cast a magic spell
And made sad Puppet feel all well.

The big teddy made her cheeks blush brightly,
The dog made her dress twinkle lightly,
The doll made her hair shine nicely,
The Spider-Man made her toes point clearly,
The Jack-in-the-box made her smile shine sweetly,
The train made her eyes blink cutely.

Laura McKenzie (7)
Ocklynge Junior School, Eastbourne

Little Dragon

Little dragon wants to play,
So he walks off to the bay.
He sees a seal,
(His father's meal)
So the seal runs away.

Little dragon runs along,
Till he smells a very bad pong!
He sees some wolves, a very big pack,
Unfortunately his uncle's snack.

He's flying fast through the sky,
When he hears a loud cry!
It's some parrots, a whole bunch,
Of course they're his grandad's lunch.

Little dragon running through the green
Then he sees something mean.
A spotted lizard, it's really speckly,
Luckily they're his mother's brekkie.

Dragon then climbs up a tree
Finally he feels free
He sees a bear, a big papa
This of course is his aunt's supper.

Little dragon goes to crouch
He steps on a thorn and shouts, *'Ouch!'*
He sees a cheetah, the running winner
This turns out to be Grandma's dinner!

He runs back home, says, 'Papa play!'
His papa turns round to say,
'Rrrrrraaaaaahhhhhh!'

Lazar Liebenberg & Ziggy Smith (10)
Ocklynge Junior School, Eastbourne

Slowly

Slowly the lion devours his prey
Slowly April melts into May
Slowly the ship sails the sea
Slowly the mother pours the tea.

Slowly the tadpole turns to a frog
Slowly the moss appears on the log
Slowly the dusk fades into night
Slowly I write this poem in candlelight.

Frances Timberlake (11)
Ocklynge Junior School, Eastbourne

Paint Palette

Green
Reminds me of leaves and peas,

Red
Reminds me of traffic lights and tulips,

Yellow
Reminds me of summer and ice cream,

Pink
Reminds me of babies and flamingos,

Blue
Reminds me of a clear sky and forget-me-nots,

Orange
Reminds me of ice lollies and a winter fire,

Purple
Reminds me of jewels and crocuses,

Multicolours
Reminds me of fireworks and an *everlasting rainbow!*

Naomi Nunn (11)
Ocklynge Junior School, Eastbourne

Puppies

Puppies, puppies,
Cute and cuddly
And very bubbly,
Really funny,
Just like a bunny.

Puppies, puppies,
Are such fun
And can be as fat as a bun,
They love to play games,
Even ones that include their names.

Puppies, puppies,
Love to chase their tails round and round,
They chase it like a hound,
Now they curl up into bed,
Awaiting the new day ahead.

Sophie Beer (10)
Ocklynge Junior School, Eastbourne

Strawberry Jam (Naughty Pixie)

A basketful of strawberries,
Red, sweet and small,
Tip them in a fairy pot,
Stalks and leaves and all,
Pour Mr Wild Bee's honey in,
Stir it round and round,
Cook it on a fire of sticks,
Built upon the ground.
Bubble, bubble!
Now the jam is baking and cooking,
Bubble, bubble!
Could anybody be peeping or looking?
Could a little hungry fairy who hasn't had tea,
Take a tiny taste of *my* jam,
Would anybody see?
A basketful of strawberries,
Cook and stir and skim,
Get little acorn cups and fill to the brim,
Fairy jam pots acorns made with a leaf for a lid,
Stand them in a row to cool.
This the fairy did,
Trouble! Trouble! A fairy is seeking,
Trouble! Trouble! Someone is creeping,
Here is a little fairy now,
Who hasn't had her tea,
Takes a pot of jam,
Did anyone see?
Another basketful of strawberries,
Red, sweet and small,
Tip them in a fairy pot,
Stalks, leaves and all!

Niloufar Safari (10)
Ocklynge Junior School, Eastbourne

The Park In The Dark

Come on down into the park
To hear the trees' leaves rustle in the dark
The wolves are howling
The fox is growling
And the hedgehog is running
Up and down the field
The spooky ghost
That some people believe is
Coming down our street
That I would not like to meet.

Toby Ware (8)
Otterbourne CE Primary School, Winchester

The Sphinx

In a tomb in the Far East
Lays an ancient, daring beast.
Behold this creature
Big and bold
From stone to bone
Behold the Sphinx.
Guarding the heart of a god called Mart.
The Sphinx lives on - behold the Sphinx.
The Sphinx will die after thousands of years
Behold the Sphinx.

Bonnor Sullivan (8)
Otterbourne CE Primary School, Winchester

Fairyland

Fairies are always busy,
Fairy babies and their mothers
Hovering in and out of the toy shops,
Flower fairies sprinkling fairy dust over the flowers,
Tooth fairies flying back and forward with coins and teeth,
Water fairies fluttering in and out of the waterfall,
They move so quickly and fast,
You can't see them,
They are just a dot of sparkle.

Ella Morgan (8)
Otterbourne CE Primary School, Winchester

One Winter's Day

I got out of bed one winter's day
It was snowing on that day
I put on my gloves and went out to play
Making snowballs round and hard
Hitting the windows with a crash

Making snowmen rolling about
Throwing snowballs at the house
Shouting all about.

Andrew Budd (8)
Otterbourne CE Primary School, Winchester

The Dragon

'I saw a dragon,' said the boy one day
'Sleeping in his cave, very gentle
You can tickle him when he is asleep.
But when he is awake, he is very fierce and angry
He has got sharp teeth and he can blow fire very fast like a cheetah
His tail is long and pointy, it swings round in circles
His eyes, blue and shiny, they can see people far away.'

Fabrìce Ali-Fogarty (7)
Otterbourne CE Primary School, Winchester

I Wish I Could Go To Fairyland

If I could go to fairyland
I wonder what I could see
Maybe a big, big castle or a big, big tree
I wonder if we could go to fairyland
Just you and me.

Isobel Bloomfield (8)
Otterbourne CE Primary School, Winchester

When I Go To St Mary's

When I go to St Mary's
I hear cheering, lots of it,
Suddenly, I hear booing
And then, *wow* a goal for the Saints!
Yippee!
It's 1-0
Now an amazing save by Paul Smith,
It's a corner,
Well defended by Claus Lundekvam,
Up to Ricardo Fuller, he's scored!
Now it's 2-0
Yippee!
The full time whistle,
We've *won!*
Yippee!

Matthew Moody (8)
Otterbourne CE Primary School, Winchester

Busy Fairies

We are the fairies
We run, jump and play.
Always are busy
Getting very, very dizzy
And bumping into
Other fairies' way.

Sweet shops
Everywhere
Yum, yum, yum.
I love chocolate
I love sweets.
Every fairy I know
Loves chocolate
And sweets.

Now it's time
For a fairy ball
I got new jewellery today.
A new dress
Slipping and sliding
I try to keep
Out of the way.

Anna Creagh (7)
Otterbourne CE Primary School, Winchester

At St Mary's

It's a big match; I get in, smells horrible,
Coke, crisps on the floor, finally the whistle blows,
Two teams came out, one by one,
The team I cheer for is Southampton!
Kick-off!
Southampton pass to each other
Till they get to the goal
Boom! Goal!
1-0
Then kick-off for the other team
A midfielder sprints up the pitch,
He strikes!
Anti Neami saves it, corner.
He puts it on the spot, takes the corner.
A player heads it,
Goal!
For the other team.
We sadly drew in the end.

William Day (8)
Otterbourne CE Primary School, Winchester

One Winter's Day

One winter's day
I went out to play
Because it was snowing
Hip hip hooray!
It's slippery and slidy
You just can't keep tidy
'Cause you keep on sliding away
Hooray!

Abi Bundy (7)
Otterbourne CE Primary School, Winchester

My Best Friend

He is a ticking clock all on the go,
He is an active cheetah,
He is an overflowing jungle,
He is a noisy aeroplane,
He is the early morning.

Evandale Meade (9)
Purley Oaks Primary School, Croydon

My Best Friend

She was the comforting sofa
She was a friendly Staffordshire bull terrier
She was the swing in the park
She was the sound of the howling wind
She was the smiling sun.

Zoe Brown (10)
Purley Oaks Primary School, Croydon

My Best Friend

He is dozy like a pillow
He is slow like a giraffe
His brain is like a jungle
His sound is a jolly clown
He is lunchtime at school.

Brandon Aung-Mya (10)
Purley Oaks Primary School, Croydon

Going Away

I can feel the dull atmosphere,
Everyone hanging their heads low,
I can see a small girl,
Who appears to have lost her doll,
'I want dolly,' she cried,
'We will find her,' her mother said,
Looking unsure.
As I stand here, the piercing whistle
Hits my ear like a raging bull,
I can smell the steam rising from the steam train
As it pulls to a halt at the track,
The children began to cling to their parents,
Like leeches on your skin.
The children's eyes looked like glass,
As they were about to get on the train.
I could taste their tears
As if they were pouring them into my mouth.
The little girl was not moving without her doll,
Her mum was begging the little girl to move,
Worried that if she stayed
Something bad would come.
The girl stood
As if someone had glue-gunned her feet to the floor,
Finally, she gave in.
As the children were off on the train,
A sudden outburst of tears hit the parents,
As staying strong was no longer important . . .

Summer Penfold (11)
Purley Oaks Primary School, Croydon

My Best Friend

She is a comfy sofa
Silky and soft
She is a bouncy bear
Really cuddly
She is a bubble bath
Lovely and warm
She is a thunderstorm, very loud
She is a rushing morning, very awake.

Serene Blake (10)
Purley Oaks Primary School, Croydon

Home From School

Eating popcorn chicken, so spicy in my mouth,
Ketchup dribbling down the hamburger,
Also with chips that are salty.

Eating hot pizza oozing with cheese,
With sweets, all kinds of flavours.

Drinking bubbly Pepsi,
Straight from the shop.

Smelling burgers from the oven and pizza
Entering every single room
Popcorn chicken trying to be recognised.

Hearing people chatting as the party began,
Hearing cats miaowing as loud as they can,
All the children sleeping, now it's quiet.

Megalie Wansongi (9)
Purley Oaks Primary School, Croydon

Gone Away

I can see the children
On the train
Everyone is rushing like a machine
Children are crying
Like a waterfall
The children are scared
Like a mouse
Mums are crying crystals
In the corner of their eyes
The children disappear
Into the train
Children saying goodbye.

Keshav Palanee (10)
Purley Oaks Primary School, Croydon

Happy

Happy is the colour of pink and orange
Happy is the taste of hot roast beef
Happy is the smell of apple pie
Happy is the pony that you look at
Happy is the sound of gentle waves crashing
Happy is the fluffy carpet that you feel.

Cierra Gray (7)
Purley Oaks Primary School, Croydon

Love

The colour is like a burning red like a love heart beating really fast
It tastes like red jelly wobbling on your plate
It smells like melted Belgian chocolate coming towards you
It looks like people kissing on a bench in a park
It sounds like a bluebird singing its bestest song
It feels like an angel just touched you on the arm
And has given you the strength you never had.

Jade Miriam Reid (10)
Purley Oaks Primary School, Croydon

Home From School

Eating delicious BBQ chicken with hot sauce
Eating crispy fried fish fingers with chips
Eating crunchy nuggets with spicy ketchup
Drinking juicy passion fruit with lemon
Smelling the fresh smell of shampoo
Smelling a fruity fresh passion
The smell of BBQ chicken with sauce,
You can hear the frosty wind.

Joel Mulenga (8)
Purley Oaks Primary School, Croydon

Far Away

The train is coming
Tears also coming down like a big sea flowing
With lots of diamonds
I can smell
The burning of coal
The children rushing
To the train
Doors slamming
Everyone rushing to a chair
The children's heads
Out of the window
The train went off
With a flash
Mum's eyes were packed with tears
At the corner of Mum's eyes
You could see
Two diamonds at the end.

Kathyann Hinchley (11)
Purley Oaks Primary School, Croydon

Home From School

Eating crispy chicken smothered with gravy
Eating vanilla ice cream in the sun
Eating BBQ chicken with hot beefburgers
Eating rich chocolate
Drinking fizzy cola in the shade.

Smelling perfume that smells like roses
Smelling toffee when I open the wrapper.

Hearing my mum singing as she cooks
Hearing my brother banging on his toys
Hearing my mum singing to my baby cousin.

Tamara John (8)
Purley Oaks Primary School, Croydon

Evacuation

E is for evacuation to the countryside
V is for very sad
A is for all leaving the station
C is for continuously shooting other people
U is for united soldiers getting shot
A is for attacking Germany sneakily
T is for terrible feeling, I'm missing my mum
I is for ignore the war, it is terrible
O is for on the train to a safer place
N is for no going back home.

Conor Wilkinson (11)
Purley Oaks Primary School, Croydon

Home From School

Eating the best handmade lasagne that can be made
Eating glorious pepperoni pizza
Eating shepherd's pie with mince on the side
Eating soft vanilla ice cream
And at the bottom of the cone, melted chocolate.

Smelling freshly baked cake straight out of the oven
Smelling sweet fruit that has just come from the store
Smelling wet, cold rain from the day before.

Hearing my mum's beautiful voice
Heaving my mum on the phone.

Janique Hutson-Ayim (8)
Purley Oaks Primary School, Croydon

The Floods Are Coming

The floods are coming!
Erupting like a volcano
Rushing, rampaging and ramming like rhinos
Engulfing all in its path.
It is storming in at the speed of light
The valley is being filled like a container
The emerald-green valley is being submerged
It is like a slow but painful death
The leaves float to the top like a rose bath
Soon all was gone, covered with murky, brown water
It is like a great war has just ended
Demolished!

The creatures are upright after hearing the whooshing water coming
Their eyes quaking in their sockets
Their hair was up in the air as if they had just been electrocuted
Feet rooted into the ground like a great oak tree
The creatures were immobilised by fear . . . soon rushing frantically everywhere
Fleeing, retreating like an army who were defeated, carrying their cubs away
Rocketing out of everywhere like shooting stars, the atmosphere was . . . static
Making all sorts of noises, trumpeting and cries, the creatures like hailstones
Vanished!

Tharsan Rathakrishnan (11)
Purley Oaks Primary School, Croydon

The Charmed Ones

The Charmed Ones is their name,
Fighting demons is their game.

First, there's Prue, she was the oldest,
She was always the boldest.

Next, there's Piper,
Later on, she has to change the diaper.

Then there's Phoebe, she's so small,
Phoebe also loves to shop in the mall.

Prue dies, it's so sad,
Piper feels so bad.

Then there's Paige, the young half-sister,
Piper and Phoebe almost dismissed her.

Once again they are the Charmed Ones,
Piper carried on the generation by having two sons.

Julia Coombs (10)
Purley Oaks Primary School, Croydon

Gone Away

What's going on?
My mummy standing
Beside me
I feel glum
I hear the steam train
Whistling
My eyes are like waterfalls
Gushing down
Hitting off rocks
Why does this have to happen?
I feel in my pocket for a coin
That my mummy gave me
I can't get on that train
I won't!
Suddenly I hear a voice
A deep voice
Like a trombone playing
It's a conductor
It's like the conductor wants us
To leave our mums and families
I'm about to walk onto the train
My tears are gushing down
Properly now
I wish my life could be
Peaceful
I want to be with my mum and family again.

Charlotte Fitzsimons (10)
Purley Oaks Primary School, Croydon

Happy

It sounds like chocolate melting
It feels soft, cuddly
It is yellow
It looks like a rainbow
It tastes nice and yummy
It smells nice
Happy is great!

Sharic Morton-Johnson (8)
Purley Oaks Primary School, Croydon

Floods

The flood is coming!
It's speeding up, getting faster
And hits the valley like a herd of elephants!
Smashing into trees like a big army truck,
As the valley starts to *demolish!*
The green grass
Starts getting trampled on,
As the water starts to rise up
It looks like a bath full of roses.

The animals start hearing the water,
As it gets closer, the animals' mouths drop open,
Like flying saucers' doors opening.
The animals start seeing the water,
Then they start to run really fast,
Until it is out of sight,
The animals look back and the valley is
Gone!

Akil Atkins (11)
Purley Oaks Primary School, Croydon

Evacuation

My mum is here
Next to me
Is it possibly
Good to be evacuated?
I'm clinging on for dear life
Feeling crushed and heartbroken
By rocks . . .
Hanging on my mum's skin
I'm so scared it's piercing very hard
Off we go
I'm on the train
Bye-bye Mum, see you soon
Gone . . .
I'm feeling dejected and crestfallen
We arrive at the station
Smelling of thick vapour . . .

Calum Graves (11)
Purley Oaks Primary School, Croydon

Far Away

As the people hear the train
The children's faces start to cry
Their mothers' faces are red
The tears are rushing out as fast as a cheetah
As the tears come out
You can see crystals
The boy has to go now
The sound of the other children
Makes him depressed
Choo-choo!
Goes the train
As the boy goes in
He glances over his shoulder
To take a last look
The train goes off
And that is it.

Leroy Parkinson (11)
Purley Oaks Primary School, Croydon

Do I Have To Go?

Do I have to go?
Mum is putting me on this
Massive monster
Tears are running down my face
Like the sea
The train is whistling
Doors are slamming
Like an elephant stamping on the floor
Children shout
I don't want to go
The taste of coal is sickly
Every other child is waving
But I'm not, I'm crying
The wheels turn
Like a leopard running
I know my mum is crying
But I just can't see her
Mum is getting harder to see
As I go further
And further
Goodbye
Goodbye
I will miss you, Mum.

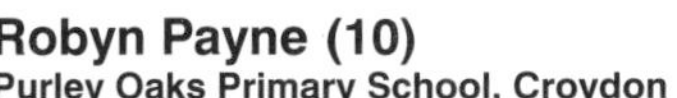

Robyn Payne (10)
Purley Oaks Primary School, Croydon

Evacuation

My tears ran down my face
Like a river overflowing.
I felt my heart
Beat,
Faster and faster.
I clung to my mother,
Like a crab
Biting her,
But not
Ever!
Wanting to let go
I could see my mother's
Light blue,
Crystal tears
Sadly rolling down her red, cold cheeks.
I could hear the
Piercing
Whistle getting closer.
The enormous puffing machine,
It had come.
The taste and smell of the burning coal,
It made we want to cry
I heard doors slamming
Mothers' heads were down,
Trying to hide their feelings
The sight of my mother,
It made me sob.

Aaliyah Binnie (10)
Purley Oaks Primary School, Croydon

Leaving Home

The children rush into the station
Adults tugging like a tug of war
The train whistling
Like a bird in the sky
People are sobbing
I see kids clinging to their mothers
Like a crab's claw locked
I hear the whistling of the train
Like a Spitfire going past your ear
Big children saying, 'No, no, please Mum!'
Little children saying, 'Yes, yes, hurry up sister!'
Like little kids in a candy shop
I am glad I am not young
It would have been scary.

Logan Mander Bremridge (11)
Purley Oaks Primary School, Croydon

Evacuation

Why did this happen?
My tears fell
Like silver crystals.
My heart pounded
Like someone beating a drum.
The salty tears
Ran down my mum's face.
I clung to my mum's coat
Wishing it was all a dream.
The taste of burning coal
Made me giddy.
My anger was like a volcano
About to blow.
I was petrified!
The whole world flickers past my eyes.
No!
This couldn't happen to me
Like I was a slave.
My tears fell like rain from the cloud
Automatically.
My insides were burning like fire.
I was pulled onto the train
Bye-bye!

Nazifa Hossain (10)
Purley Oaks Primary School, Croydon

Leaving

Sobbing all around me
The steam making an ear-piercing sound
The doors closing like *thunder!*
Children screaming
Clinging on like a predator to its carcass
Children petrified
Of losing their mum
People coughing
Because of the steam
They're still clinging on, they won't let go!
I see one child
Three years old with nobody
Lost in the crowd.

Matthew Aldridge (10)
Purley Oaks Primary School, Croydon

Evacuation

Children flooding the platform,
Pushing to get on a train to take them away
To their new homes and lives.
Mothers crying, children waving,
The children safe from the war,
Living in the countryside.

Trees and fields go speeding by,
Houses come and go,
Children realising what is happening now,
They are afraid and alone.
Getting their suitcases and belongs,
Ready to get off the train
At their new homes.

Children crying now,
Missing their parents now that they've gone,
Getting chosen by a new family,
Strangers take them home.
Worried who will be chosen first,
Worried if they will be last.

New home more scary,
Not knowing what to do.
Can't wait to go home,
But that will be too long.
It's upsetting writing letters to parents
Who are no longer there, at home.

Kaitlyn Sheeran (11)
Purley Oaks Primary School, Croydon

The War Is Coming

I don't want to go
I'm so tearful
Everyone rushing
I feel invisible like a ghost
The train is piercing steam
Mum's head down like a funeral
I hang onto my mum like a leech
Suitcases crashing around
Doors smashing together
I'm shaking like I'm going to be killed
I get on the train with fear.

Georgina Macdonald (10)
Purley Oaks Primary School, Croydon

The Evacuation Poem

It was terrible
I felt sorry for her
She was shaking
Nervously
Her mum told her not to worry
It will be alright
The little girl tried hard
Not to let her feelings out
But her tears
Came gushing out like a
Waterfall of tears
The mum looked ashamed
And I knew that in her head
She was confused
Didn't know what to do
Her daughter dropped her dolly
Clung to her mum tight
The girl was shocked with fear
Saying, 'Mummy, that machine
Is scaring me
It looks like a monster
Taking away children!'
'Calm down,' the mum whispered
'You will meet other children
On the train and you can
Make friends with them.'
I wondered about the voices
That were following me around my head
They were saying *poor little girl*
Poor little girl
Poor little girl . . .

Joanne Matheson (11)
Purley Oaks Primary School, Croydon

Why Do I Have To Go?

I feel very sad
I am worried
Because my mother has to stay.
I do not know
Where I am going.
Sometimes I am crying
My head is downcast.
I do not know
When I will see my mother.
I will sleep with her picture.

David Milarski (10)
Purley Oaks Primary School, Croydon

There's A Flood In The UK

There's a flood in the UK
The people are running
The flood's all over
And nothing is burning.
There's a flood in the UK
The water is going high
And no one is eating pie.
There's a flood in the UK
No one is panicking
But everyone is sleeping.

There's a flood in the UK
The dogs are dead
And the rats are fed.
There's a flood in the UK
People are screaming
And no one is dreaming.
There's a flood in the UK
The men are laughing
And the women are barking.
There's a flood in the UK
The help has arrived
And the people are saved.

James Jugghoo (11)
Purley Oaks Primary School, Croydon

Home From School

Eating scrumptious pancakes with sweet maple syrup
Eating loving scrumptious grated carrots
Eating crispy macaroni and cheese served in a pint bowl
Eating lovely croissants with cheese inside.

Smelling chunky chicken soup
Smelling BBQ chicken smothered with BBQ sauce
Smelling sweet toffee
Smelling fresh shampoo.

Hearing the sound of the TV
Hearing the sound of a bird singing
Hearing the sound of fresh water in the bath.

Carlisa Hinchley (9)
Purley Oaks Primary School, Croydon

Home From School

Eating wet, smooth, mouth-watering pasta covered with melted cheese
Eating lovely chicken nuggets buried in cold, fizzy salt.

Drinking ice-cold Fanta straight from the fridge ready to drink
Eating frozen strawberry ice cream, smothered in sprinkles and strawberry sauce.

Smelling sweet Domino's pizza covered with hot cheese
Smelling a sweet bar of Galaxy chocolate that's just been opened
Smelling my nan's home-made Welsh cakes with raisins baked in them
And sugar sprinkled over them
Smelling sweet English saveloy with salt mashed in.

Hearing the loudest TV, coming from the neighbours
Hearing noisy trains that rattle the house
Hearing loud doors crashing onto the latches
Hearing the loudest cry, coming from my baby brother.

Thomas Shepherd (9)
Purley Oaks Primary School, Croydon

There's A Flood In The City!

There's a flood in the city!
Everyone is fleeing
The flood's coming closer
Everyone is screaming!
As the flood's coming
People are shouting
And people are running!
Now the flood's really getting bigger
Now people are getting frightened
As it's getting thicker.

Now the army is here
Pushing the water
Now there is less fear
Now there are tears of joy
As the flood is going
And now kids can go outside
And play with their toys
People aren't crying
Being sarcastic
Pretending to be crying
And are actually lying.

Alessio Valenza (10)
Purley Oaks Primary School, Croydon

Flood In The City

There's a flood in the city
People are fleeing
There is nowhere to go
Only on higher ground
Until it rises above
The water is getting closer
The diseases are moving in
So that it can catch the people
Please save us from this sin
People dying any minute now
They can't believe their eyes
To find that their homes are ruined
Oh, what a horrible surprise
There is a flood in the city
People are trying to escape
To run away to other countries
To live in misery all day
The houses are shaking
For it is too late
Oh, please save us
From this horrible fate.

Nicola Rogers (10)
Purley Oaks Primary School, Croydon

Evacuation Poem

Mums and dads are crying
Little boys and girls are saying, 'Look at that amazing train.'
Older kids know, but little kids don't know
They're being evacuated.

'Get on the train, get on the train.'
The wardens are shouting as loud as they can.

The train is screeching
The children are jumping on
'Goodbye Mummy, goodbye Daddy.'
'Goodbye darlings, I'll miss you.'

Anne-Marie Akiwumi (10)
Purley Oaks Primary School, Croydon

War, War

War, war
What's it worth fighting for?
Bombs are falling from the sky,
They fall in the blink of an eye.
Children are getting evacuated,
The Germans are getting more hated.
Guns are shooting,
Bang, bang, bang,
The Germans are killing every man.
Oh no, my next-door neighbour's house is being bombed,
I think Britain is being conned.
Oh wait, it looks like the prime minister has an army,
Galalalalalala, boom, boom, crash, bang,
Wallop, niioowww! (Aeroplane noise)
Britain has won!

Lenina Aung-Mya (11)
Purley Oaks Primary School, Croydon

Evacuation

My dad got sent to France
Mum doesn't stand a chance
I was sent away
I miss them every day
I hope this war will stop
But somehow I think not.

Leigh McLaughlin (11)
Purley Oaks Primary School, Croydon

Evacuation

E vacuation, you are for us to remember
V ery sour, so sour that it will never be
A rrive again as we have the stamina
C onstantly to prevent it still
U nfairly torn by my wicked foster mother
A t the time, where were you
T ill the very end of the world
I s going to get evacuated
O bject lesson we all have to learn
N o, no more of that horrible evacuation.

Fabi Peerbux (10)
Purley Oaks Primary School, Croydon

The Evacuation

The air raid is coming
Evacuate the children!
Children want to go back
Because they've forgotten to get something.

As they wave their goodbyes
The train pulls out
And the train got slowed.

They're finally here
Might they get someone good?
Or they might get a bad one
Let's only drink beer.

Gokul Raj (10)
Purley Oaks Primary School, Croydon

Happy

I am happy when I play with Morgan
Happy sounds like laughing
Happy is yellow and pink
Happy smells like orange
Happy feels soft and cuddly
Happy looks great!

Hinano Koyama (8)
Purley Oaks Primary School, Croydon

I Saw . . .

I saw a postman delivering mail
I saw a baby kitten with a small tail
I saw a fly swallow a cat
I saw a night creature and it was a bat
I saw a cat chasing a mouse
I saw a man lifting a house
I saw a girl who got everything right
I saw a boy who is scared of the night.

Morgan Payne (7)
Purley Oaks Primary School, Croydon

Evacuation

As the train puffs into the station my heart beats wild
As the doors open I know I have to say goodbye I try and try
Then I hear my mum start to cry, I try not to cry
I sit down next to my friends to cheer myself and my friends up
Our parents are sending us away for our own good to get away from the bombs
What about them? They might get bombed
Will they go somewhere for safety?

Lauren Fowler (10)
Purley Oaks Primary School, Croydon

Evacuation Poem

My dad has gone to war
And I have been evacuated to London
I am on the train with my brother
I miss my friends and they have gone to Selsdon
We write to each other once a week
Letters tell me something sad
But when I left my mum she was crying
Blast.
But I tried not to cry.

Gurpreet Ubi (10)
Purley Oaks Primary School, Croydon

Evacuation Poem

War started, children were sent away from their mums and dad
And people were sick of the war.

Children are evacuated
Mum doesn't know where they are sent
Far away from home
And mums are crying
Dads are fighting for their lives
We can hear sounds like
Bang, bang, bang
The Germans are killing everyone
Even their people
The people scared for their lives
The bombs are dropping, banging and crashing
And the shops are bombed
The factories are closed
Now everything is quiet.

Amarjargal Batkhuyag (11)
Purley Oaks Primary School, Croydon

Evacuation

I'm getting evacuated,
I'm leaving home,
I'm going to leave my mum all alone,
I'm going to travel somewhere up north,
To leave the city where I might die,
Children will leave on a train,
The younger ones will be a pain,
The countryside they will be,
In the city where the Germans will be,
The sirens will go off
And bombs will drop,
People will die and the Germans won't stop.

Joel Livesley (10)
Purley Oaks Primary School, Croydon

The Evacuation

The air raid is coming
Everyone evacuating their children
They want to go home
Because they want their mums
The noises get louder
As they wave goodbye
Then the train pulls out
Then everyone cries
The train slows down
They have a sad life
And want to go home.

Tafazdwa Zama (10)
Purley Oaks Primary School, Croydon

I Saw . . .

I saw someone with lots of candy
I saw someone who's got something handy
I saw someone with a swimming pool
I saw someone going to the mall
I saw someone telling the time
The time is mine!

Somer Wigger (7)
Purley Oaks Primary School, Croydon

Evacuation

As the train chuffs in,
My heart beats quickly,
The train door opens,
I feel very sickly.

As I get on
And wave goodbye,
I try to smile,
I try, I try.

The train smells dusty,
Looks old and battered,
The seats are comfy,
But ripped and tattered.

The train stops slowly,
Making a sound,
Creak the train
And my heart does pound.

When I get there,
I see my mum-to-be,
I really do hope
That she likes me.

Charlotte Hedley (10)
Purley Oaks Primary School, Croydon

Someone Was Being Evacuated

I saw a terrible thing today
Someone was being evacuated
A little child
A lot of little children
Someone was being evacuated
A little boy with blond hair
A lot of little boys with blond hair
Someone was being evacuated
A little girl crying her eyes out
A lot of little girls crying their eyes out
Someone was being evacuated.

The mums are there with their children
Someone is being evacuated
The mum is crying her eyes out
The mums are there crying their eyes out
Someone is being evacuated.

They are on the train now
Someone is being evacuated.

Ryan Steventon (11)
Purley Oaks Primary School, Croydon

Finally Leaving

She is finally leaving
Her tears flowing
As much as I try
To look at her my eyes just full of water
Her face as red
As the train
She looks at me in shame
I look around
I can see just the same
Children cling on to their mums
'Mummy, don't let me go'
I tried
I hugged her as I held my head down
My tears just fell
It hit her head
She looked at me
Don't cry
I will always write to you
The bell went
She's gone
My tears finally fell.

Colesia Carey-Ann Bogle (11)
Purley Oaks Primary School, Croydon

Home From School

Eating scrumptious pancakes with lemon on top
Eating squirmy spaghetti and lovely hot sauce
Eating smooth strawberry and chocolate ice cream with chocolate sauce.

Drinking cool sparkling apple juice.

Smelling warm, cosy air and the sweet smell of air freshener
Smelling flowers and my mum's perfume
Smelling mum cooking delicious cookies
Smelling lovely chocolate.

Hearing the cool computer play its games
Hearing the noisy telly shout and whisper
Hearing my mum singing to the radio
Hearing my brother play his PlayStation.

Paige Ell (8)
Purley Oaks Primary School, Croydon

Evacuation

Rivers of tears all around,
Children clinging to their mothers,
Like leeches on their skin.
The steam from the train,
Flying everywhere,
Children hugging their mothers,
Never letting go,
Shouting, screaming and wailing
Pierces my ears,
Children getting dragged
To the train
Letting go of their mother's hand
For the last time,
'Noooo!' A little boy cried,
The train door slammed shut
Like prison bars,
Mothers hiding their tears
Looking happy,
But really, tear crystals were forming,
As the train pulled out of the station
And all the noise
Disappeared.

Jade Billingham (10)
Purley Oaks Primary School, Croydon

Evacuation Poem

We pack our bags and leave home
Going to the station
No one knows, people rush, push, children cry, scream
People saying goodbye
Children saying, 'Mum, Mum,' in the station
And I try and try not to cry
My mum has to go to work
I write, write to try and try
And try and try not to cry.

Tamara Trimblett (10)
Purley Oaks Primary School, Croydon

Home From School

Eating mouth-watering lasagne, smothered in hot tomato sauce
Eating smooth chocolate ice cream with hot, hot chocolate sauce.

Drinking freezing cold Coke, freshly delivered to your home.

Smelling very hot shepherd's pie that has just come out of the oven
Smelling freshly squeezed orange juice into a glass
Smelling freshly chopped chicken with gravy.

Jamal Omar Nokoe (9)
Purley Oaks Primary School, Croydon

Emotion

It sounds like a dolphin jumping up and out of the water and back in
It feels like a dolphin's skin on its back
The colour of emotion is pink and green
It smells like red roses
Emotion looks like a princess.

Mica Wilkins (7)
Purley Oaks Primary School, Croydon

Home From School

Eating lovely macaroni with soft cheese
Eating smooth ice cream topped with sweeties.

Drinking freezing cold Coke, freshly delivered by the shop.

Smelling delicious chocolate
Smelling mouth-watering Chinese chicken
Smelling Domino's pizza coming out of the oven.

Hearing sweet birds, singing in the morning
Hearing footballs being kicked
Hearing people laugh at Christmas time.

Jed Moqaddem (8)
Purley Oaks Primary School, Croydon

Home From School

Eating crispy chicken with smooth sauce
Eating ice cream with vanilla and strawberry
Eating delicious coconut juice and lovely cheese pizza.

Smelling lovely Yorkshire pudding
And smelling the fresh smell of my mum
Shampoo smelling lovely
Food that makes my tummy rumble.

Hearing my dad snoring
And my mum singing while cooking.

Kojo Kankam (8)
Purley Oaks Primary School, Croydon

Home From School

Eating soft, fluffy mashed potatoes, with boiled egg and corned beef
Eating delicious smooth, sweet chocolate cake.

Drinking sweet, hot cocoa.

Smelling sweet, bright flowers
Smelling hot chocolate straight from the kettle
Dinner rising.

Hearing trains stopping every two seconds
Hearing sounds from my dad's computer.

Courtney Covington (8)
Purley Oaks Primary School, Croydon

Home From School

Eating delicious chicken burger with a dollop of ketchup
Eating smooth, rich chocolate that looks like a snowball.

Drinking freezing cold Coke.

Smelling the pizza coming from the shops
Smelling the chicken sandwiches for my dinner.

Hearing the cars and buses roar out from the road
Hearing my mum singing in her bedroom.

Nithin Rajanpandarathil (8)
Purley Oaks Primary School, Croydon

The River's Story

I was polluted
That was it,
The factories were growing,
I was boarded off and the children couldn't play with me anymore,
Now behind the derelict housing estates I lie,
The kingfishers no longer my secret agents.

I am now polluted and clogged with junk,
I hate it,
No skating bugs to skate on me,
No fish to keep me company,
No kingfishers as my secret agents.

Now I lie with depression and stress
With my friend, the mouth,
Who has also been polluted,
People come and throw their rubbish into me,
I meander along the track, doing the usual things,
Then I see the waterfall, bubbling and gurgling away, happily
No kingfishers as my secret agents.

This is my story,
The river's story,
I am now finding it hard to shilly-shally and gurgle
I am now like a rubbish bin and smell unpleasant and horrid,
No kingfishers as my secret agents.

Mirran Harper (8)
Rotherfield Primary School, Crowborough

Space

Space is as dark as black,
Debris floating around,
Like garbage,
Garbage eater.

Space is like billions of miles of air,
Planets floating everywhere,
As big as Mount Everest,
Planet maker.

Space is like hot lava
Blowing up spaceships
As cold as ice,
Rocket destroyer.

The planets are like circling balls,
Rocks floating everywhere,
Getting smaller and smaller,
Rock maker.

Robbie Ellis (8)
Rotherfield Primary School, Crowborough

Fire

Fire is a god,
Things run away from it,
Fire is destructive,
Fire is a dragon.

Crimson, mauve and gold,
Destroying everything in its path,
Fire is a star,
Spreading at the speed of light.

Bullets go right through it,
Swords will meet thin air,
Nobody can contain it,
Or stop it in its tracks.

Nobody can endure it,
It's impossible to resist it,
Without being reduced to ashes,
Fire is a sweep of death.

Its flames are reinforced,
It summons death within its claws,
Fire is like boiling rain,
With reversing effects.

Nothing can stand up to it,
It's only scared of one thing,
So scared it hides like a mouse,
One trickle will terrify it
And that is water.

Sun-stopper.

Max Bates (9)
Rotherfield Primary School, Crowborough

The Wind

The wind is like a fox catching its prey,
A dragon flapping its wings,
Like a house getting wrecked,
A night-time sky.

A river flooding in its flood plain,
An animal breathing on your hand,
It is a death shadow,
The wind is like a wave in the sea.

Like a firework going *bang!*
A ghost moving in the wind,
It is a night stalker in the night,
The wind is as fierce as a lion's *roar!*

Lucy Evans (9)
Rotherfield Primary School, Crowborough

Stars

Stars twinkle like shimmering clear drops of water
As though they are trying to talk
Shooting through the wide, open space of the sky
This is the night shiner at work.

The star shoots around at the speed of light
A portion of light in the dark grey sky
Piercing through spinning planets
This is the sky light.

The light of the world flies like a bird
A giant light bulb shiny and serene
Flying through the sky at break-neck speed
A source of light.

The stars are very special
They are another version of shooting stars
Twinkling yellow, white, yellow, white
A multicoloured dot.

Sophie Gray (8)
Rotherfield Primary School, Crowborough

The Iceberg

The iceberg is as tall as a mountain,
An elephant as clear as water,
In the snowy, cold air,
Human freezer.

The iceberg is as still as a statue,
A frozen volcano,
Right near the Antarctic,
Blue statue.

The iceberg is as blue as a pond,
A giant rock,
The sound of wind blowing around it,
Clear block.

The iceberg is as white as snow,
An animal frozen,
The sea trying to fetch it,
Water freezer.

Jake Tibbutt (9)
Rotherfield Primary School, Crowborough

Fire

Fire is like a rolling fireball
A burning phoenix flying about the forest,
In the pitch-black sky,
Tree burner.

Fire is like a mix of different colours,
A burning metal pole, melting as time goes by,
In its hot place,
Metal melter.

Fire is like a golden plate,
A burning rainbow,
In the dark green forest,
People killer.

Fire is like the sun but even hotter
A volcano just erupting,
In a choking, smoky sky,
Smoke strangler.

Fire is like a dragon,
Breathing boiling fire,
In the dark grey sky,
House destroyer.

Rebecca Ann Modjesch (9)
Rotherfield Primary School, Crowborough

Snow And Ice

Snow is icy cold but fun to play with,
Temperature dropping -6, setting slowly, freezing cold,
Fires crackling no flowers blossoming,
Tap water stuck in its icy case
Snowmen being made in the street,
Water freezer.

Wrapping up warm, enjoying themselves, the ice is causing trouble,
Skidding cars, no brakes are working,
Snow is madly falling, deeply setting,
Temperature dropping, -9,
Snowball.

The sun is coming melting the snow
Temperature making flowers brighter,
People more happy, more cars about,
Summer has come again.

Sam Osborne (8)
Rotherfield Primary School, Crowborough

The Forest

The forest,
Like a place covered in all different colours,
Like someone has thrown and splattered paint everywhere,
The colours shimmer in your eyes,
As when you look at the sun,
It's as big as the universe and as wide as the world, home giver.

The forest,
A place where someone has planted a tree that gives birth to all animals,
It sounds like there could be animals in everything,
Around every corner,
You see the toadstools shimmering in the sun,
The spring trickles down the cut in the ground,
Like a firework on its non-stop stage, peace lover.

The forest,
Like heaven to an animal,
With fresh green trees and small humps,
The backs of toads shiny and smooth,
The ants so busy at work,
Harvesting all different fungi,
The mice poking up and down out of their small holes, heaven bringer.

Dexter Gribble (9)
Rotherfield Primary School, Crowborough

The Wind

The wind is high, the wind is low
The wind is full of that frosty blow
The wind causes hurricanes
And blockages between lanes

The wind is high, the wind is low
The wind is full of that frosty blow
It blurs the sky
And aeroplanes that fly

The wind is high, the wind is low
The wind is full of that frosty blow
It nips at your bare faces
And unties your shoelaces

The wind is high, the wind is low
The wind is full of that frosty blow,
The wind is bitter, the wind is nice
The wind is full of freezing ice.

Taylor Beth Gillin (8)
St Cuthbert's CP School, Egham

My Mum And Dad Are Aliens

My mum and dad are aliens,
They come from outer space,
As they come from Mars,
They think that Earth is a funny place.

They wake up at six in the morning
And have their toast and tea,
They think that it is horrible,
But it tastes just fine to me.

They take me up to school,
In a solar-powered car,
But they're not that good at driving,
So we don't get very far.

We usually end up walking,
It is a funny sight,
As Mum's three legs go round and round,
The children run in fright.

I like it when I get to school,
The people there are sane,
But then it comes to home time
And Mum and Dad are there again.

When it comes to dinner,
The food can be quite odd,
I like proper English food
And they like bugs from a pod.

When they think I've gone to sleep,
All curled up in my bed,
My dreams will always tell me,
Aliens are inside my head.

David Andrews (10)
St Cuthbert's CP School, Egham

Stripes

I have stripes and claws
I have jaws and paws
I have meat to eat
I am a big cat, but I don't sleep on a mat!
If you get too close, I might pounce
I've got very sharp teeth,
As sharp as needles!

Who am I?

A: A tiger!

Isabella Samuels (7)
St Cuthbert's CP School, Egham

My Lazy Cat

Sitting in the midday sun,
Chasing mice, just for fun,
Balancing on walls and chasing birds.

Busy, busy, busy to my cat
Are just words,
It's all in his mind
My lazy cat.

He never moves more than one lazy eye,
Except when I tell him for tea
It's *fish pie!*

Clare Pike (10)
St Cuthbert's CP School, Egham

My Family

My dad is tall
And my mum is small,
I have a sister and a brother who are a really big bother
But we all stick together
And we will love one another forever.

Sean Mullan (8)
St Cuthbert's CP School, Egham

My Day

When the sunny sun comes out,
All I do is laugh and shout,
When it's breakfast I have toast,
But it's not as good as a Sunday roast.
When midday comes, I play lots of different games,
Some boys play with paper planes,
I sing and dance like Britney Spears,
My sister laughs so much it ends in tears
When it is dinner, I sometimes have pie,
Then I get undressed and take off my tie
When it's bedtime I go to sleep
And my dreams, I'll try to keep.

Lauren Rossiter (10)
St Cuthbert's CP School, Egham

What Am I?

I'm round and fat, short and pink,
I've got a curly tail
And you get pork from me.

Don't worry if you get it wrong,
Have a look some more,
Come, come along,
There are lots more friends
For you to meet.

I go, *'Oink, oink!'* have you got a clue?
I live on a farm
I'm normally in a barn,
My friends are a donkey, horses and a sheep,
Have you got the answer?
Have a look to see if it is right,
The answer is a *pig.*
If you got it right, guess another one
They're really fun.

Molly Molloy (7)
St Cuthbert's CP School, Egham

Football Fever

I like football, I play it and it's great
You can play it on your own
And also with your mates

I like to support Chelsea, just like my old dad
But when I see them lose a game
It makes me kind of sad

It's not just about winning
As my dad, the coach, would say
It's taking part that matters
And enjoying when you play

So come on footie lads, let's have some laughs today
Score some cracking goals
And have fun all the way!

Jack Grey (8)
St Cuthbert's CP School, Egham

Marmie

I have a cat called Marmie
And I must admit, he's a little barmy!
He used to sleep in washing machines,
Maybe he thought he'd have better dreams!
He also used to climb up trees,
This for most cats should be a breeze!
He could climb up all right,
But get down the tree? Oh, what a sight!
Most cats go down without a hitch,
But Marmie went down into a ditch.
He was lost for days, nowhere to be seen,
Until his wounds were nice and clean.
Marmie got into many fights,
This resulted in him receiving many bites.
The little devil got taken to the vets,
As you do with any loving pets.
Although he might be a little barmy,
I still love my little Marmie.

Celine Allaker (9)
St Cuthbert's CP School, Egham

I Want!

I want the sun to keep me warm,
I want the moon to keep me cool,
I want the sun to be very bright,
So I can see all day and early night.

I want the moon to glisten like water,
So I can see my face and it doesn't alter.

I want the sun to sparkle and dazzle,
I want the moon not to frazzle,
I want the moon to shine at night,
So I can see and not get a fright,
I want the world to stay alive,
Because it's beautiful and it should never die.

Katie Sharples (10)
St Cuthbert's CP School, Egham

My Dogs

My dogs of three,
Are precious to me.
There's Pudsey, Juno and Kgun too,
They'll come bounding up to slobber you!
Their big brown eyes,
It's no surprise,
Melt my heart,
Like a cupid's dart.
On a walk,
They like to stalk,
Squirrels and birds for their prey,
But cleverly, they stay away!
They will pounce
And then bounce,
On any finds,
Of any kinds.
They're so cute,
But sometimes I want to press their mute!
My dogs,
Aren't clever clogs.
They're always on the go,
But I love them so!

Beth-Anna Varley (10)
St Cuthbert's CP School, Egham

Red Is . . .

Red is a glossy rose petal,
Lying in the sun.

Red is a fire engine,
Putting out fires that have just begun.

Red is a ruby,
Sparkling and proud.

Red is a sunset,
Behind a fluffy cloud.

Red is your parents' lips,
Kissing you goodnight.

Red is a baby's cheeks,
Cuddled nice and tight.

Olivia Patton (9)
St Cuthbert's CP School, Egham

My Little Sister Kayin

I have a small sister, only four years old,
She doesn't speak many words, but she knows what she's told.
If she want to tell us something, if there's something on her mind,
She can tell us what it is, by using a special sign.
She makes lots of noises and we don't always understand,
So it's a pretty good thing that she can always use her hands!

She walks very fast, but doesn't quite run,
She has a trampoline and she thinks it's really fun.
It took two years for her to find her feet
And a little bit longer for her milestones to meet.
On her sports day she entered a little race,
She tried her best and she came in first place.

I could make this poem go on forever and ever,
But I'm nowhere near that clever.

Jaiye Maja (10)
St Cuthbert's CP School, Egham

The Final Journey

In moonlight, no faces were found,
Nor a gentle foot aground.
Though as the whining clock chimed ten,
The weary cat came out again.

Its paws had walked for many years,
Its conscience had not many fears,
But he was old and was distressed,
He had decided for the best.

The gentle cat found a place to lie,
A place where no man could look nor pry
And as the whining clock struck twelve,
The cat peacefully curled up and died.

Louisa Jane Reid (10)
St Cuthbert's CP School, Egham

The Beautiful Sight

They are strong, wild and free,
They will be where they want to be,
They will run till they can run no more,
With their hooves pounding on the floor.

They kick, they buck, they rear,
So be warned, don't go near,
They have run wild and free
Since times of old,
They have a thick fur coat
To protect them from the cold
And they remain brave
And a beautiful sight to behold.

Sian Jarvis (10)
St Cuthbert's CP School, Egham

The Jungle

The jungle is like a never-ending hike
It is filled with the sweet singing of the birds
It smells like fear is lurking in the shadows
Its trees feel as rough as their creepers
The addictive taste of sap filling the eternally growing trees
The colours of the berries standing out over the rest
The jungle is a palace of frenetic fun.

Rufus Roy (10)
St Edmund's School, Hindhead

The Blitz

T ing, tang, goes the bell, the Germans are coming
H itler has hit London, the Germans are coming
E xhausted in the shelter, the Germans are coming

B ombs are falling, the Germans are coming
L ighting the candle in the shelter, the Germans are coming
I feel sick, I'm going to throw up, the Germans are coming
T im, our warden, has died in the bombing, the Germans are coming
Z ing, tang, the siren goes, the Germans have left.

William Wright (9)
St Edmund's School, Hindhead

The Jungle

The jungle is like a towering skyscraper besieging me in its liveliness
The jungle sounds like bugs crackling the crisp leaves
The jungle smells like the aroma of fresh mangoes ripening in the tropical heat
The jungle feels like a moist enclosure
Scraping and biting me as I hike through the wilderness
The jungle looks like an erupting volcano spraying greenness everywhere
The jungle is an amazing green planet, grasping me in my dreams.

Jaye Tolervy-Suter & Bruno Broughton (11)
St Edmund's School, Hindhead

Jungle

J ungle is an amazing place
U nlike anywhere else
N ight falls, the moon is bright
G orillas eating through the night
L eopards prowling for their prey
E lephants tearing down trees

M onkeys hiding in my tent
A nd pandas chewing bamboo
N imble cats ripping up the tent
I guanas eating my food
A nnoying mosquitoes biting me.

Mark Czajkowski (9)
St Edmund's School, Hindhead

Mystery

Mysteries are everywhere as far as you can see
In the mistiness of the universe, you don't know what there could be.
A strange light on the other side of the field,
Or why they have thunderbolts on a Roman shield.
There were many mysteries for when I was young,
Like did we have a skeleton and only one lung?

These mysteries have all gone by
But I still wonder what's in the sky
I'm sure I don't know everything yet
I wonder if I know everything about this planet
It's best not to worry about these things
But I would like to know what's in Saturn's rings.

Jason Roy (9)
St Edmund's School, Hindhead

Jungle World Panic

J ungle has the colours of the rainbow
U nder the spell of the environment
N ever has been big, this is utterly huge
G reat trees bigger than buildings in cities
L ooking for animals? Here they are, swinging through the jungle
E dging jaguars setting up prey. There he goes, a meal for the day.

W eather is hot and steamy
O ther people have no luck, then you find them in the water
R ather like a volcano day
L ightning flashes in the rain
D eadly animals are water's prey

P anicking animals run around
A nd nailing rain stings the animals' fur
N ow animals try to escape as it comes hammering down
I n the darkness of their den
C rafty jaguars lie down to rest.

Douglas Hazell (10)
St Edmund's School, Hindhead

Jungle Fever

J aguars running through the trees
U nder and over, brown monkeys swing from tree to tree
N esting birds high in the trees
G rave grey wolves panting through the tangled trees
L ifeless corpses lie on the ground
E normous elephants raging through the dense jungle

F erocious black panthers moving slowly for their prey
E nergetic lions tearing through the tangled veins
V igorous birds pecking at the bugs
E ccentric tigers jumping up for food
R avenous, raging wolves howling through the night.

Benedict Philipp (10)
St Edmund's School, Hindhead

Jungle Poem

The jungle is as silky as a spider's web
It sounds like a hundred crickets croaking
It smells like a ton of fresh mangoes squeezed for ripeness and juice
It looks like a colossal city of trees
The jungle is the wild people's home.

Matthew Clark (11)
St Edmund's School, Hindhead

Jungle

J umping tigers ready to kill
U nited, strong and never defeated
N othing living over the mountains
G rass around completely calm
L iving animals may die today
E ating food and killing prey

D estructive claws coming today
E xterminating enemies attacking the pack
A t the trees the birds will fly
T igers kill and never die
H illtop sunsets never pass.

Josiah White (9)
St Edmund's School, Hindhead

The Jungle

The jungle is like a ghostly graveyard
The trees gaze down upon you like freaky gaping monsters
It sounds like a ruffled clashing orchestra
There's rustling here and there
The jungle smells like gloomy fear
It feels like creepy eyes observing you like a grumpy janitor
The jungle looks like a balmy army of rotten trees that have taken over half the world
The jungle is a never-ending ghost and will reign for evermore.

William McCreadie (10) & Anthony Metelekamp (11)
St Edmund's School, Hindhead

The Jungle

The jungle is like a crowded city
It sounds like a playground with children laughing and screaming
It smells like the winds that blow in every day
It feels like the rough bark of the colossal trees
It looks like spaghetti hanging in the branches
It tastes like sweet, mouth-watering melon
The jungle is an overgrown country in the middle of nowhere.

Ciaran Dougherty & Finnbarr Joynson (11)
St Edmund's School, Hindhead

The Jungle

The jungle is like a crazy parrot
The jungle sounds like a thousand rustling hedgehogs
The jungle smells like a massive sweet factory
The jungle feels like a tingly spider running across your hand
The jungle looks like an overgrown temple
The jungle is a roaring tiger.

William Adams (10)
St Edmund's School, Hindhead

The Jungle's Way

The jungle is like a green, impenetrable fortress with no way out
It sounds like a frantic city waking up
It looks like a massive prison
It smells like a tropical wild flower
It feels like a giant green blanket
The jungle is a winding labyrinth.

James Adams (10)
St Edmund's School, Hindhead

Jungle

J ungle, jungle, swing, swing
U nited, strong, apart, weak
N ever rest, too much fun
G oing crazy in the sun
L ike a jigsaw puzzle, they fit together
E xcited every day, for a day is another year

S trong, vicious, or so they seem
T hey're always on the move
R unning and eating bananas
E very day jumping around
N aughty, dangerous
G anging up, fun, fun, fun
T hough always hiding behind trees
H air or fur, do you know what it is?

Callum Kent (9)
St Edmund's School, Hindhead

Jungle Days

J ungle jaguars jump through the greenery
U nder the leaves, snakes slither
N ow it's nightfall and some go out to hunt
G rowling animals sneak all around
L ittle animals take a quick glance
E ndangered animals happily alive

D anger creeps in and the prey starts to shake
A nimals in the jungle sleep, unaware of peril approaching
Y awning, the animals wake
S tart of another jungle day.

Duncan Spears (10)
St Edmund's School, Hindhead

Hard To Please

I don't like schools with lots of rules,
I don't like butter or cheese, with lots and lots of peas,
I don't like saying please when I'm eating cheese
That's why they call me hard to please.

I don't like dogs, I don't like frogs,
I don't like honey sandwiches for lunch,
I don't like bees mixed with peas,
That's why they call me hard to please.

I don't like cups of tea mixed with leaves,
I don't like to sneeze with a plate of peas,
I don't like peas that smell of cheese,
That's why they call me hard to please.

Elena Symes (8)
St Faith's CE Primary School, Winchester

My Magic Box

(Based on 'Magic Box' by Kit Wright)

I will put in my box . . .
The world,
Doctors and nurses,
Sweets and chocolates.

I will put in my box . . .
Happiness and kindness,
The films of Narnia
And the Polar Express.

I will put in my box . . .
People's friendships,
Sparkling shoes,
Fruit and vegetables.

I will put in my box . . .
Heaven and angels,
Fun,
Myself and my family.

Haleema Ahmed (8)
St Faith's CE Primary School, Winchester

My Magic Box

(Based on 'Magic Box' by Kit Wright)

I will put in my box . . .
A kitten playing about,
God,
The snow witch.

I will put in my box . . .
Christmas,
When I was born
And Robby.

I will put in my box . . .
My little sister,
My friends,
My family and Miss Rabey.

Eleanor Roberts (7)
St Faith's CE Primary School, Winchester

Football

The team at home uses their stadium
If you get fouled it's a free kick
If it hits the net, it's a goal
Football is a sport which has professionals who play it
If the keeper gets it, it's a goal kick
I enjoy football, it's my favourite game
The funny, fat, fierce football laughed
At the fouling footballer who looked
Like a mental madman
Just then he got hit past the goalkeeper
As he hit the net, the referee's whistle blew
He realised it was a goal!

Daniel John Thompson (8)
St Faith's CE Primary School, Winchester

The School Kid

T hink before you do
H e graffitied the wall
E nd up in trouble

S crubbed the wall
C ouldn't get it off
H ad to go home
O ff he went
O n a bus
L ooked for his house, couldn't find it

K id's in trouble
I n deep
D eep trouble.

I hate the world!

Callum Laing (8)
St Faith's CE Primary School, Winchester

Hunger

It sounds like a silent room or growling across your tummy
It tastes like chocolate with no flavour
It smells like an empty perfume bottle with nothing in
It looks like a square in space with nothing in
It feels like a hole which you can't fill
It reminds me of an empty wrapper of chocolate.

Olivia Kenchington (9)
St Faith's CE Primary School, Winchester

Hard To Please

I don't like thunder and lightning,
I don't like a sting from a bee,
I don't like things that are frightening,
That's why they call me hard to please.

I don't like it when people die,
I don't like blueberry pie,
I don't like male sharks,
That's why they call me hard to please.

I don't like smelly cheese,
I don't like mushy peas,
I don't like rats or fleas,
That's why they call me hard to please.

Kayla Leeson (7)
St Faith's CE Primary School, Winchester

My Magic Box

(Based on 'Magic Box' by Kit Wright)

I will put in my box . . .
A field full of horses,
Rubies and diamonds
And kittens with their mothers.

I will put in my box . . .
A sun full of love,
Voices singing
And a kite full of hope.

I will put in my box . . .
The stars and the moon,
Dolphins and whales
And all my relations.

Mhairi Brannigan (7)
St Faith's CE Primary School, Winchester

Big Ben

Big Ben, a great building,
Giant, striking, golden-coloured carvings,
A beautiful clock face,
One of many houses of the great Houses of Parliament,
Big Ben stands tall in the middle of London
Next to a river as blue as the sky, the river Thames.

Elliot D'Souza (8)
St Faith's CE Primary School, Winchester

School In Silence

That night I went there, that night I did,
There were creaking floorboards
And the whistle of the wind
The white moon was shining when the fog appeared
And in the mist I saw . . .
The ice on the windows and the dark barn
Owl in the empty tree, down the hall and turn left
The empty classroom and I won't forget me
Everything is dark, everything is black,
Everything is coming, I can feel it on my back.
Don't forget the starlight
Don't forget the icy frost on the grass
If you look in the playground
There's quite a lot of moss
So listen to me carefully
And don't go there at night
Because if you do
You might get quite a . . .
Fright!

India Ayling (9)
St Faith's CE Primary School, Winchester

Friends

Friends should always be there for you
Whenever you need help!
Friends are kind, caring, generous and helpful
If you have a real best friend
You should never break up.
You have someone to play with
Someone to help when you are hurt.
Friends are great
They're always there for you when you have troubles.

Friends are the best!

Elizabeth Bunnage (8)
St Faith's CE Primary School, Winchester

Fear

Fear is a shrill scream suddenly being silenced,
Fear is like lemons taking over your mouth,
You're choking with all black-hearted things running down your throat.

Fear is the stench of evil filling you,
Knocking you over,
Fear is a cloud as white as a sheet,
Drifting creepily in an opaque mist,
Towards a silent, unprotected Earth.

Fear is cruel things squashing you,
Making you beg for mercy,
Fear is an enclosure,
Never letting you out.

Destruction,
Debris,
Death,
Fear,
That smell of fear is coming.

Annie Hazlitt (10)
St Faith's CE Primary School, Winchester

The Daredevil Penguin

The penguin
The frightless penguin
Is he going to jump?
He is going to jump!
It's not safe,
Diving for food,
Will he do anything for food?
Penguin the daredevil
To rule the world,
He dives fearfully
Squawks and squeaks
He made it!
Snatching the food he needed
Piercing the water's skin
Watching the fish frantically swim by
He survived his ordeal.

Jake Sylva (10)
St Faith's CE Primary School, Winchester

The Way God Wanted

War, war, war,
What's the point of shedding blood?
Suffer, suffer, suffer,
People are dying.
Hunt, hunt, hunt,
Why do we kill?
Greed, greed, greed,
All we do is want.
Steal, steal, steal,
Do we have to go this far?
Disaster, disaster, disaster,
The world does enough without us.
Murder, murder, murder,
What's the point?

I just wish
Joy, joy, joy,
We can have fun if we try.
Happiness, happiness,
We should get on together,
Help, help, help,
Help each other all the time.

Live happily and peacefully
The way God wanted.

Chris James (10)
St Faith's CE Primary School, Winchester

This Penguin

This penguin likes adventures
Roaming his habitats.
This penguin likes adventures
Diving like a daredevil.
This penguin likes adventures
Survival in Antarctica.
This penguin likes adventures
He and his group at feeding time
Grabbing fish in their beaks and dodging the sea lions.
This penguin is adventure.

Patrick Daly (9)
St Faith's CE Primary School, Winchester

How To Create Your Very Own Universe

Firstly, find your big bang,
It will look like a tiny speck of dust,
Twinkling like coloured stars,
This will help you recognise it.

Secondly, explode it (this will look like a wonderful firework display)
Take an exceedingly small pin and burst it
Tiny drawing pins work best.

Thirdly, cool your universe with super-cold,
Freezing, giant blocks of ice
Or other extremely cold substances.

Lastly, admire your wonderful creation,
(Oh, I forgot, find a way to prevent global warming!)

Niko Sollohub (10)
St Faith's CE Primary School, Winchester

My Magic Box

(Based on 'Magic Box' by Kit Wright)

I will put in my box . . .
A chocolate factory,
A vase of pretty flowers,
A lovely family.

I will put in my box . . .
A wishing well,
Some jewellery,
The snow and sun.

I will put in my box . . .
Friendship and a kitten,
Some pretty pens
And a pencil case.

Annie Parsons (8)
St Faith's CE Primary School, Winchester

Music

I've been listening to music since I was one and a half,
I've got a red mp3 player,
Smooth jazz, charming classical and all different types,
I play different instruments - piano, guitar, drums and violin,
Dancing's the best though,
Booming music rocks,
Yo! I'm in the house, so ya better watch out!
That's why I love music.

Boz Jack Martin-Jones (9)
St Faith's CE Primary School, Winchester

Easy To Please

I like honey from bees
I like butter and cheese
I like picking apples off our tree
That's why they call me easy to please.

I like honey sandwiches for lunch
And then I have an apple to crunch
I like dogs, I like frogs
That's why they call me easy to please.

Megan Tyler-Smith (8)
St Faith's CE Primary School, Winchester

Hard To Please

I don't like bees
I don't like my keys
I don't like Mum's cheese
That's why they call me hard to please.

I don't like friends who fight and tease
I don't like green teas
I don't like mushy peas
That's why they call me hard to please.

I don't like the sound of trees
I don't like thanks or please
I don't like knobbly knees
That's why they call me hard to please.

Issy Evans (8)
St Faith's CE Primary School, Winchester

Hard To Please

I don't like pink
I don't like stings from wasps or bees
I don't like spots you have to squeeze
I don't like tuna
That's why they call me hard to please.

I don't like mushy peas
I don't like sitting but I like to run around
I don't like smelly cheese
That's why they call me hard to please.

Daisy Jones (8)
St Faith's CE Primary School, Winchester

Winter

Winter's night
Frosted moon
Dead trees
Falling leaves
Snow falling
Fires glowing
Wind blowing
Trees swaying
Closed cocoon
Ice skating
Lights up
Wrapped up warm
Cold night
Robins singing
Animals hiding
People dancing
Trees decorated
People celebrating
In the breeze
In the tree
The cold
Decorated.

Madeleine Davis (9)
St Faith's CE Primary School, Winchester

My Magic Box

(Based on 'Magic Box' by Kit Wright)

I will put in my box . . .
Something soft
Something furry
And Joey, my teddy bear.

I will put in my box . . .
A plate of mash and chicken
The colour pink
My family.

Kelly Bendall (9)
St Faith's CE Primary School, Winchester

Music

When you're down, listen to music.

Music is very much like the sea,
Beats as the waves go up and down,
Notes as the tone of the sea creatures,
When you're down, listen to music.

I watch the TV,
On the news they're talking about Mozart's 250th birthday,
When you're down, listen to music.

I get tickets to a gig to see my favourite band,
There are thousands of people trying to get into the mosh pit,
When you're down, listen to music.

I'm really bored, so I listen to my iPod,
When you're down, listen to music.

M ighty
U nbelievable
S tylish
I nspiring
C lever!

Hugh Williams (9)
St Faith's CE Primary School, Winchester

My Magic Box

(Based on 'Magic Box' by Kit Wright)

I will put in my box . . .
My toy rabbit,
My mummy, daddy and family,
My dog.

I will put in my box . . .
Hope and love,
My friends,
God and Jesus.

Abigail Riem (8)
St Faith's CE Primary School, Winchester

Looking Through My Window

I'm looking through my window
I see a herd of horses
Stampeding towards me
They turn a sharp corner
Racing through the hot, misty day
Tails swishing high
Manes blowing wildly through the breeze.

The clattering of hooves
Dust and dirt vigorously flying up behind
Foals trying to keep up
Sweat dribbling down their long, elegant necks
From the baking, burning, blazing hot sun
The day is drawing to an end
Time to rest and a new day will begin.

Laura Outhwaite (10)
St Faith's CE Primary School, Winchester

Spring

Winter has gone, spring is here,
New flowers come blossoming out,
Animals are born on farms,
Fresh green grass is growing on the land,
People with smiles on their faces,
It's a new beginning,
Laughter spreads around the room
Like fire spreading quickly,
It's a new beginning,
I walk out of the door,
I take a deep breath,
Smelling the flowers that are growing,
I feel all strong,
When spring is here.

Alex Carswell (9)
St Faith's CE Primary School, Winchester

The Ice Tiger

Out he comes, out, out, out
One foot, two foot, eyes alight,
Slushing through the snow,
Breaking through ice,
For the tiger, no worries,
For the tiger, no foes
And always is striped
From his head to his toe,
If you ever do see him
Please let me know.

For tigers out there on the ice,
In the snow,
Looming ahead,
For ahead he goes,
In blizzards, in storms,
He keeps plodding till dawn.

The ice tiger
A fascinating beast,
Very different, very striking,
Every day,
Sweeping and swaying far into the day.

The ice tiger knows every step that he takes
With his eyes ablaze and tail swinging.

That's the last I ever saw
Of the fascinating beast.

Meg Honigmann (9)
St Faith's CE Primary School, Winchester

Elephant

The elephant is strong,
Elegant and fearless,
It will never stop going,
It has deep wrinkled skin all over its head,
Shining silver horns,
Big, huge ears, flapping in the warm air,
It never forgets anything, never, ever,
Not even its mother's soft voice,
Its long trunk swaying in the breeze
Splashing in the mud.

Calum Farwell (8)
St Faith's CE Primary School, Winchester

It's Coming

It's coming
What?
You'll see . . .
A meteorite
Hurtling through space like a ballbearing from a gun.

It's coming
What?
You'll see . . .
Ten million earthquakes
Making the world tremble like innocence under the destructive hand of an alien.

It's coming
What?
You'll see . . .
A tsunami with no charity or aid, just death.

It's coming
What?
You'll see . . .
The sun
Exploding like a firework in the sky.

It's coming
What?
You'll see . . .
The last congregation, then nothing.

This is God, the mighty
He has spoken.

Joe Smith (10)
St Faith's CE Primary School, Winchester

Monkeys

Monkeys are cute but cheeky little apes,
Monkeys are always out to get your bananas,
So I warn you, not to bring bananas to the jungle,
Monkeys are like furry kids with long arms,
A monkey's monkey nut is nice for a monkey,
A monkey can't resist a snowball fight.

Lucas Modiano (9)
St Faith's CE Primary School, Winchester

A Life Full Of Dreadful Lies

He peered through the icy window
Shivering, frozen
Watching the family like a hawk

He slid down the snowy wall in grief
His tears formed icicles around his eyelids
Cold and still
Sadness struck like a wave as he remembered

He knew there was no going back
A life of lies dissolved into nothing
Death was the result

As he wept, a child crawled up to him
Her eyes as large as an owl's
Hazel and deep

Her mother ran out of the house and slapped him
He fled, still remembering
He felt tense with anger

He crawled under a holly bush
Rip, tear
He scowled like a wolf ready to pounce

He stayed up half the night
Till at last he fell to the ground and never woke up

That is what a lifetime of lies brings
And he deserved it.

Olivia Rachel Stone (11)
St Faith's CE Primary School, Winchester

The Siberian Tiger

The Siberian tiger, a ferocious beast
Hunting in blizzards for a satisfying feast,
As it fights for survival out on the ice,
Give caution to its prey from his devastating bite.
The stripes in the snow are a deadly encounter
For the scream of the hunt gets louder and louder,
The Siberian tiger strides faster and faster,
For now fear comes and no more laughter,
As poachers arise on the brim of the mountain
And the tiger is shot, for its fur is of value.

Theo Williams (9)
St Faith's CE Primary School, Winchester

Trees

Weeping willow of the lands
Wave your young and noble hands
Drifting near and drifting there
Catching the eye of him who stares.

Royal oak bowing down
Ruling all, wearing the crown
Bark is brown, branches strong
Time has past, seasons gone.

Watchful walnut with shallow roots
Squirrels prosper with your fruits
If man chose not to preserve your woods
Nature's suffering surely could.

Pine of the forest standing proud
How far can you see from up in the clouds
Can you see the dwindling forest
Caused by man attracting tourists?

Silver birch shimmering white
Your bark is silver, extremely bright
Lighting up the passer-by
Putting the spark back into eyes.

Rory England (10)
St Faith's CE Primary School, Winchester

The Slow Snail

Slowly the snail creeps across the grass,
Like a cheetah creeping up on its prey,
Not noticing a bird's beady eyes,
Twinkling in the moonlight,
Watching down on him.
In the light of the moon
The brown and orange shell
Of the snail, shone,
Suddenly, the tree rustled
And down swooped the bird,
The snail hid in his shell . . .

But he was too late.

Harriet Billington (9)
St Faith's CE Primary School, Winchester

Families

Dad: the one who always goes mad
And punishes you when you've been bad.

Mum: thinks she's your supersonic chum,
But she feeds you, though not very nice
But at least you've got something in your tum.

Brother: always getting you into trouble
And give you cheeky ideas like, 'Go on, push her.'

Sister: if you want to know what she does
Just put tease in your head and reoccur.

Aunt: you can get cool ones but they're mostly embarrassing
They can do things others just can't.

Uncle: making up silly jokes all the time
And trying to make you giggle.

Grandpa: mostly into boring stuff
Like paintings and out-of-date cars.

Grandma: she gives you lots of sweets
And money, shame she lives so afar.

James Crowley (11)
St Faith's CE Primary School, Winchester

The Staring Monkey

There's a monkey who has no friends,
Hanging on a tree,
Staring at all the other wild animals playing,
Watching,
Eating fruit with wide eyes looking down at them triumphantly.
Staring at the lions playing,
Crocodiles swimming,
Birds flying.
There's a monkey hanging slated from a tree
On his own, sleeping softly,
While he's sleeping, he's dreaming strongly
About having some friends
And guess what?
It came true.

Emilie Vigneron (10)
St Faith's CE Primary School, Winchester

My First Day At School

OK I admit I was scared,
It was the first day of school,
I better sit at the back,
Apparently it was cool.

I saw my teacher,
Crouching on her chair,
Would I do well at maths?
But do I really care?

I looked to the left of me,
I looked to the right,
I saw Big Ben,
Who always gets into fights.

In front of me,
Was the class snitch,
I saw the girls,
Plotting to push him into a ditch.

Yes, finally it was lunch,
The teacher had stopped talking,
By the time I teased big Ben,
I was barely walking.

I got into class for maths,
I was chatting away,
The teacher asked me a question,
I didn't know what to say.

Finally, I packed to leave,
With relief, but also sorrow,
School is fun as well as scary,
So I'll be back tomorrow.

Jonathan Harwood-Yeo (11)
St Faith's CE Primary School, Winchester

The Creak

There was a creaky noise under the corridor
And the kitchen floor.
So I walked to where the creaking noises were coming from
And had a little peek
Creak!
It creaked again
So I shouted for my mum, who was called Glen
There was no reply, so I sprinted to my grandad's house
Without realising it was only a mouse.

Alex Armstrong (10)
St Faith's CE Primary School, Winchester

The Poem

When I write a poem, they're normally not that good
The teacher says, 'Write this poem, so I think I should.'
It's called 'The Poem' that's all I've got so far
I need an inspirational star
It might start me off on this thing
My dad's watching rugby, there's another player on the wing
How to end this, what should I do?
Oh yeah, got to go, here comes 'Doctor Who'!

Ben Cronan (10)
St Faith's CE Primary School, Winchester

Seasons

The trees waved to each other,
The wind whistling, calling my name,
Snow drifted down like confetti landing on a cushion of feathers,
Time changes into anger,
Fury throws leaves around landing on the mud bed,
Trees swing their arms frantically for help,
A bandage wraps its arms around the storm,
All is calm, time is back to summer.

Emma Forrester (10)
St Faith's CE Primary School, Winchester

Countryside Life

The perplexed trees sway in the morning breeze
Whilst simultaneous harks originate from the crows
Who swoop above the treetops,
Taking heed of their young ones.

The resplendent fox stands proud
Gloating over its slain prey
Tongue glistening and eyes gleaming.

The robust rabbits bound across the spruce green fields
To abscond from danger
And the moles clamber into their minute dwellings
For a good night's slumber.

Freddie Taylor (11)
St Faith's CE Primary School, Winchester

Heroes

I am a hero to my parents;
Combined and united
We make together
A grand union of our power to be.

As I share my powers
With people that I meet
I greet them like I am a man
Of my own kind.

What does a real man do I wonder?
I pretend to be one
I do not know
If even I am a hero, I wonder

As I hear the cries of people
I rush to their rescue
To save them
From great dangers of the world.

While I'm rewarded
By my grandma and grandpa
I share my powers with them
To show my kindness.

As I reach home
I'm greeted with respect
From my parents
To show their care for me.

I am all; all is one;
I share my powers with my family
To hopefully make them
Super too.

Huh! I wish I could be a powerful hero
Like Mum!

Jack Fifield (10)
St Faith's CE Primary School, Winchester

Froggy

I once saw a jumping frog,
Getting lost in the murky fog.

He loves to bound all day long,
To keep him company, he sings a song.

His big blue eyes sparkle in the sun,
He likes to eat the occasional bun.

From lily pad to lily pad, hippity, hippity, hop,
He jumped right through the air, but landed with a flop.

Froggy, froggy, jumps so high,
Will you be back when morning is nigh?

Lucy Dunn (11)
St Faith's CE Primary School, Winchester

At Work Today

At work today I thought it would be alright,
At least I thought at the office, it meant you didn't need to read or write,
But when I went up the hall that day and saw the pens and all,
I realised a terrible thing, I was back at school!
When they sat me down with pen and paper,
I was aware that I had fallen asleep 15 minutes later!
They sent me to the manager's office, where they told me I shouldn't have been hired,
Then (what rotten luck) I was fired!
When I went back home that day, I felt a bit of sorrow,
But the worst thing is, I've got to find another job tomorrow!

Holly Woodward (11)
St Faith's CE Primary School, Winchester

Hard To Please

I don't like mushy peas,
I don't like nasty fleas,
I don't like cold cheese,
I don't like people who tease,
That's why they call me hard to please.

I don't like red knees,
I don't like the sound of bees,
I don't like eyes that wheeze,
I don't like colds that sneeze,
That's why they call me hard to please.

Olivia Hazlitt (7)
St Faith's CE Primary School, Winchester

Haunted House

In the haunted house there is . . .
A ghost hunting in the night
A skeleton walking to find people
A gravestone thumping
A zombie ready for a fight.

In the haunted house there is . . .
A crackling door screeching
A rat climbing up the wall
A werewolf reaching for the sky
A statue ready to fall.

In the haunted house there is . . .
A crack in the roof
Blood cells dripping to the floor
A cracked chimney smoking out a tooth
A spooky servant waiting for children to eat more and more.

In the haunted house there are . . .
People shaking to death
And running out of breath.

Hannah Nabil (8)
St John's Primary School, Woking

My Friend Ryan

My friend Ryan
Has a smile as big as a whale.
My friend Ryan
Is as silly as a clown.
My friend Ryan
Is as fast as a cheetah.
My friend Ryan
Is as smart as a lawyer.
My friend Ryan
He is as brainy as a mastermind.

My friend Ryan
He has hair like a porcupine.

Michael Atkinson (9)
St John's Primary School, Woking

My Friend

My friend Aaron
Has ears as hard as stone.
My friend Aaron
Has eyes as glimmering as crystals.
My friend Aaron
Has cheeks as red as a rose.
My friend Aaron
Has muscles as big as a lion.
My friend Aaron
Has feet as big as an elephant.
My friend Aaron
Has hair as brown as a tree.
My friend Aaron
Smells as bad as a dump.
My friend Aaron
Has knees as stretchy as a monkey.
My friend Aaron
Has teeth as white as snow.

Thomas Pullen (8)
St John's Primary School, Woking

Haunted House

In the haunted house
Bats are hunting
Chimney smashed to bits

Bashed tiles like squidged leeches
Cobras waiting like hawks
Monsters eating berserkly

In the haunted house
Windows like bullet holes
The door is a monster-like beast

In the haunted house
Skeletons like spiders
Gravestones as gruesome as goo

In the haunted house
Frankenstein is fierce like a dragon
Dracula sucks blood like a monster.

Ryan Cree (9)
St John's Primary School, Woking

All About My Friend Charlotte

My friend Charlotte has hair that is as furry as a cheeky monkey
She has a smile like a monkey laughing
She has eyes like an ant
Her nose is tiny like a circle
She has eyebrows like brushes.

Abbey Palmer (9)
St John's Primary School, Woking

Emma

My friend Emma has hair as brown as wood
She has skin as bright as a peach
Her lips are as red as a rose
She is as smart as neat handwriting
Emma is kind and very friendly
She has lots of friends
Sometimes we break up, but we'll be friends the next day.

Fern Wilson (8)
St John's Primary School, Woking

Haunted Mansion

Smashed glass
Cracked walls
Worn-off slate
Cracked windows
Creaking floorboards
Smashed roof
Broken door
Blood dripping like a leaking tap
Pool of blood and pointy spikes
Dead men appearing from gravestones
Electrocuted men
Fire-breathing dragon
Spooky noises
Zombies fighting
Blood as cold as ice
Skeletons as wobbly as jelly
Zombies as fierce as dragons
Ghosts as big as ten bears.

David Westmacott (9)
St John's Primary School, Woking

My Poem About My Best Friend Abigail

She has hair as soft as fur
Cheeks as pink as a peach
Chin as hard as a rock
She has skin bright like a tulip
Shoes as high as the stalk of a flower
A smile like a red, bright rose
Eyelashes as dark as a bat.

Marina Lang (9)
St John's Primary School, Woking

Callum

My friend has hair like a pineapple
He has a mouth like an elephant's trunk
He has eyes like an elephant's
He's as cuddly as a teddy
He is funny like a monkey.

Nathan Barnett (10)
St John's Primary School, Woking

Untitled

Lips as red as a cherry
Cheeks are bright pink
Earrings as pretty as gold money
Her ears are as round as an apple
Her eyes are as green as a monster
Her hair is as brown as a tree.

Natasha Gent (9)
St John's Primary School, Woking

Monique

My friend Monique has hair as brown as chocolate
Her eyes are as brown as a dog's
Earrings are as bright as a crystal
Face shaped like an oval
Her cheeks are like Maltesers
Her voice is just like an angel's
Her nose is curved the same as a hill
Skin as soft as a cat.

Emma Cull (9)
St John's Primary School, Woking

Haunted House

Battered roof
Mouldy roof
Planks packing the roof
Very dirty roof

Man-eating trees
Blood on the walls
Blood dripping like a tap
Smashed windows

Battered door
Dead people
Blood as cold as ice
Zombies as fierce as ten mummies

Half-eaten zombies
Scary ghosts flying
Hungry vampires
A pool of blood as red as a devil

Soft bones since they've been in the ground for so long
Awakening skeletons
Planks on the letter box

Keep Out sign,
Stay out or else
Devil from the dead
Dancing gravestones.

Charlotte Lee (9)
St John's Primary School, Woking

Haunted House

Bats scattered in the attic
Green leaves like a dragon's skin
Blond hair dancing in the wind
Like ghosts floating in the air
Doors creak as they open
When midnight comes, you never know
It might be fun, ha, ha, ha!

Monique Gouws (8)
St John's Primary School, Woking

Horrible House

Outside the haunted house there are . . .
Bats flying to the attic
Bent chimney, broken window
Blood splattered on the roof
A big hole in the door.

Outside the haunted house there are . . .
Great big ponds of pouring blood
Gravestones with skeletons looking out
Zombies walking towards the fence
Wolves howling really loud
Trees catching children as they come in.

Outside the haunted house there are . . .
Birds pecking at skulls on the ground
A ghost flying around the house
The fence shaking, going to fall
No one dares go in again.

Ronnie Hack (8)
St John's Primary School, Woking

Haunted House

People walking past the haunted house
Screaming, screeching when drivers drive past
Bats nesting in the attic
Blood dripping down the drains
Dead people waking up from the dead
Ghosts as white as skeletons rising from the dead.

Chantelle Gibbs (9)
St John's Primary School, Woking

Haunted House

A three-headed dragon waiting to kill
A zombie as bent as a question mark
Bats flying inside holes that lead into the roof
Bats nesting inside the attic
Broken patches on the roof
Broken windows all over the house
Rats climbing up the walls
A sign saying *Keep Out Or You Will Die*
Swimming pool of blood
Thirty ghosts making noises
Thirty zombies trying to kill bats.

Aaron Martyn Wilson (9)
St John's Primary School, Woking

Kennings

Apple muncher
Nest nestler
Log wrestler
Cage-bar biter
Cat fighter
Finger nipper
Quiet sitter
Nose twitcher
Sawdust hitcher
Apple muncher
Cheese cruncher

Finger scratcher
Fly chaser
Dog facer
Finger scratcher
Trouble hatcher
Biscuit gobbler
Tree wobbler
Sick spewer
Loud mewer.

Francesca Crisante (10)
St Joseph's Primary School, Christchurch

Flying Through The Air

I climbed to the top of the six foot ramp
I looked out over the whole skate park
I put the board over the edge
And then I heard a dog bark.

I fell down the ramp
And landed on my leg
I hope it isn't broken
I beg, I beg, I beg.

I was rushed into hospital
And was lying on a bed
I sat up carefully and said a prayer
To find I had no head.

Ryan Watts (11)
St Joseph's Primary School, Christchurch

Bite Me - Haiku

His menacing jaws
Reach out to swallow his prey
And take his victim.

Daniel John Clark (10)
St Joseph's Primary School, Christchurch

The Sound Collector

(Based on 'The Sound Collector' by Roger McGough)

'A stranger called this morning
Dressed all in black and grey
Put every sound into a bag
And carried them away'

The crumple of the paper
The buzzing of the computer
The ringing of the bell
The hissing of the tutor

The running of the children
The screeching of the chalk
The zipping of the pencil case
The stomping of the walk

The clapping in assembly
The chanting of the times tables
The squelching of the mud
The sticking of the labels

The squeak of the violin
The banging of the drum
The burning of the candle
The chewing of the gum

'A stranger called this morning
He didn't leave his name
Left only silence
Life will never be the same'.

Tamara Hattab & Emily Gillard (10)
St Joseph's Primary School, Christchurch

The Sound Collector

(Based on 'The Sound Collector' by Roger McGough)

'A stranger called this morning
Dressed in black and grey
Put every sound into a bag
And carried them away'

The buzzing of the bell
The cry of the hurt kid
The talk of show and tell
The school council bid

The telling of detention
The parking of the school bus
Getting kids attention
The crunch of the school dinner's crust

The rustling of SATs papers
The stampede of playing at break time
The clicking of the staplers
The flushing of the toilet grime.

Alastair Buckle & Michael McDowell (11)
St Joseph's Primary School, Christchurch

The Sound Collector

(Based on 'The Sound Collector' by Roger McGough)

'A stranger called this morning
Dressed all in black and grey
Put every sound into a bag
And carried them away'

The screeching of the whistle'
The dripping of the pipes
The ticking of her watch
The squeaking of the bikes

The flickering of the light
The creaking of the playhouse
The ringing of the telephone
The squeaking of the mouse

'A stranger called this morning
He didn't leave his name
Left us only silence
Life will never be the same'.

Elliott Ray (11)
St Joseph's Primary School, Christchurch

Haikus

Happiness
Kind joy spreads within
Blossoming trees smile at you
The sun is beaming.

Sadness
Rain drips down your face
Trudging down an empty street
No, nobody cares.

Madeleine Bell (11)
St Joseph's Primary School, Christchurch

The Sound Collector

(Inspired by 'The Sound Collector' by Roger McGough)

A stranger called this morning,
Dressed in pink and blue,
Put every sound into a bag
And carried them to you!

The falling of the children
The laughing of Year 6,
The smiling of the young kids,
Playing with their sticks!

The rolling of the football,
The whistle coming soon,
The people playing on the grass,
Until the afternoon!

The squelch of the children's shoes,
Coming in from break,
The sound of the caretaker,
Pulling out her rake!

The groaning of the children,
As soon as they're inside,
They sit on their seats,
Then the feeling that you've died!

A stranger called this morning,
His name was something like Bob,
He said, 'I'll call ya later!'
Then never did, *the slob!*

Niamh Tickner & Libby Sandoe (10)
St Joseph's Primary School, Christchurch

The Sound Collector

(Inspired by 'The Sound Collector' by Roger McGough)

A stranger called this morning
Dressed in pink and blue
Put every sound into a bag
Will bring them all to you.

The shouting of the children
The ringing of the bell
The kicking of the football
The dripping of the well.

The yawning of the boys
The giggling of the girls
The falling of the receptionist
The singing of the birds.

The shouting of the teachers
Some screaming from the head
The shout of someone shrieking in pain
That was going round my head.

A stranger came this morning
Dressed in pink and blue
Put every sound into a bag
He'll bring them all to you.

Maria Camila Humphries (10)
St Joseph's Primary School, Christchurch

Spike

Spiky scratcher
Winter sleeper
Snail slurper
Christmas forgetter
Leaf sleeper
Road crosser
Flattened friend!

Rebecca Lancaster (10) & Meike Cook (11)
St Joseph's Primary School, Christchurch

The Sound Collector

(Based on 'The Sound Collector' by Roger McGough)

'A stranger called this morning
Dressed all in black and grey
Put every sound into a bag
And carried them all away'.

The ricochet of a football
The ringing of the bell
The sniff of the nose
The kid in the toilet putting on gel.

The sparkle of the water fountain
The smack of the school bully
The rolling of the skateboard
At the end of the day.

'A stranger called this morning
He didn't leave his name
Left us only silence
Life will never be the same'.

Daniel West (10) & Joe
St Joseph's Primary School, Christchurch

Fear - Haiku

It's your worst nightmare
Might scare you all the way home
'Cause it's your own fear.

Simon Morris (10) & Curtis Bussell (11)
St Joseph's Primary School, Christchurch

The Best Kennings In The World

Sweet smeller
Speller corrector
Lesson planner
Child carer
Whistle blower
Desk sitter
Homework giver
Lovely teacher!

Isobelle Cording (10)
St Joseph's Primary School, Christchurch

My Enchanted Treasure Chest

(Inspired by 'Magic Box' by Kit Wright)

I will put in my chest . . .
A miaowing dog
And a barking snake
The only hissing cat
In the solar system.

I will put in my chest . . .
A roaring drum
And a banging glass
A smashing drummer
Who beats like lightning.

I will put in my chest . . .
A shouting choir
And a clattering guitar
These are the only
Noises in the world.

My enchanted chest
Is made from the finest copper
Iron and steel
With planets on the lid.

I will journey around the world
In the chest
And surf across the sea
To different continents
And have fantasmaglorious fun!

Callum Russell (10)
The Mount Primary School, New Malden

The Magic Box

(Inspired by 'Magic Box' by Kit Wright)

I will put in the box . . .
The twist of a
Shining starfish.

The delicious taste
Of chocolate.

A bright
Silver diamond.

An enormous sweet
With spices.

A wonderful
Red dress.

Dip Kaurana (10)
The Mount Primary School, New Malden

My Magic Pen

(Inspired by 'Magic Box' by Kit Wright)

I will draw with my magic pen . . .
The first stripe of a baby tiger,
The world's biggest golden pyramid,
A lion that roars and makes the forest rumble
A queen's shiny crown made of rubies,
The eyes of a ghost filled with crystal,
A portrait of Guru Nanak,
To remember him forever.

I will draw with my magic pen . . .
An aeroplane that is remote control
So it can fly to India and bring me news of my brothers,
A bicycle with a jetpack so I can fly into space,
A magic machine that gives paper so I can never stop drawing.

I will fly with my magic pen . . .
All over India,
I will see the lovely palaces,
The glittering temples
And the beautiful Taj Mahal,
I will feel like we are a full family once again.

My magic pen is made of shimmering silver
That makes the whole world shine.

Monu Sachdeva (10)
The Mount Primary School, New Malden

Magic Dream

(Inspired by 'Magic Box' by Kit Wright)

In my dream is . . .
The fluffiest cloud
Floating in my mind.

The whistle from
A roaring wind.

A fresh, clean snowflake
Falling from the sky.

The pure smell
Of a newborn baby.

The crunch of footsteps
Through the snow.

The first drop of rain
Falling from the sky.

Mitta Kurana (10)
The Mount Primary School, New Malden

My Treasure

My treasure
Is my secret diary
To write my daily news.
Pirates' treasure
Is in a chest -
Diamonds, rubies, sparkling jewels.
A dog's treasure
Is his white bone
That he buries down deep.
A lady's treasure
Maybe her crystal-clear ring
That shows the symbol of her love.
Men's treasure
May be their gym equipment
To make them
Fit and strong.
Girls' treasure
Could be a locket
With a family photo.
Boys' treasure
Could be a great round football
To kick up high into the air.
My mum's treasure
Is me!

Hollie Fouracre (10)
The Mount Primary School, New Malden

Magic Chest

A shiny red rose
A gold and silver glittering star.
A magic kingdom
With a mermaid.
A dragon
With red spots and a green tongue.
A hot desert
Pirates on a ship
Baby clouds
And . . .
An enchanted unicorn.

Azra Mohammed Ali-Abbas (10)
The Mount Primary School, New Malden

The Magical Casket

(Inspired by 'Magic Box' by Kit Wright)

I will put in the casket . . .
The first spot of a baby leopard
A feather from a cooing lovebird
And the tear of a lonely maiden.

I will put in the casket . . .
The point of a Viking's spear
The shiny scale of a fish
And the first word of a baby.

I will put in the casket . . .
A glittering garnet
The crown of the last Tudor queen
And a broomstick made of gold.

I will put in the casket . . .
Shakespeare's first story
Bread from when Jesus shared his meal
And a slice from the world's largest pizza.

My casket is made
From bronze and plastic and copper
Its hinges are made from pterodactyl bones.

My casket is full of secrets
Known to me and no one else.

Zoe Wolff (9)
The Mount Primary School, New Malden

Magical Thoughts

A witch with a lasso
And a cowboy with a wand.

A rubber duck with a bark
And a dog with a quack.

A lion with a chatter-voice
And a monkey with a roar.

A warthog with a giggle
And a hyena with a snort.

A cat with a squeak
And a mouse with a purr.

A cow with a neigh
And a horse with a moo.

A pig with a cluck
And a hen with an oink!

Daniel Byrne (10)
The Mount Primary School, New Malden

The Mummy
(In the style of Brian Patten)

There is something in the museum
I wonder what it can be?
It has only just arrived
So I'd better go and see.

A coffin - magnificent and enormous,
I crept slowly towards it
And got a stick, made a hole
And looked in . . .
There I saw a slimy rotten head.

It started to make a noise
Like a man shivering
I raced back to the exit
I glanced back at the coffin -
It was open!

Something was hiding in the shadows,
It touched me with fingers
Like a witch's claws,
I touched it back
And it was cold and bandaged.

I grabbed it from the shadows
And saw it was an Ancient Egyptian
His eyes blank and scarlet . . .
Staring at me.

Mustak Miah (11)
The Mount Primary School, New Malden

Beneath My Bed
(Inspired by 'Magic Box' by Kit Wright)

I shall store beneath my bed . . .
The swish of a bird soaring overhead
A captain sailing the open seas
The sound of laughter from people
Runny jelly melting in my mouth
The smell of apple pie
The sound of water running down a pipe
The fresh smell of flowers.

My bed is made from chocolate
And sand and light
With ribbons on every side
And secrets
Never to be told.

Hayley Shaw (10)
The Mount Primary School, New Malden

The Mummy
(In the style of Brian Patten)

There is something in the pyramid
I wonder what it could be?
It has only just arrived
So I'd better go and see.

He hides inside the darkness
You see his golden eyes
Watching your every move . . .
For he is very wise.

Don't make a loud noise
Keep your body still
He is ready to pounce
He is waiting to kill!

Avoid his tomb
Or he'll mummify you
Stay with the group
For you don't know what he'll do.

Spring away quickly
Run away *now*
Glimpse those hieroglyphics
Escape *somehow.*

The mummy is approaching
See his golden eyes
Glowing in the darkness
Planning to surprise!

Ana Cheang (11)
The Mount Primary School, New Malden

The Commentator

. . . Aaaand here we are at
Stamford Bridge
Ready to kick off!
Miah is back
From his head injury
And the game begins!
Chelsea has the ball!
Carr is sprinting
Down the pitch
Ready to strike -
And it's Woods -
No, it's Guruwar -
And it's a foul!
O'Shea takes the ball
And on comes the ref
With a yellow card
The crowd's in shock!
They're going crazy!
It's a free kick -
Essenouni shoots . . .
The ball . . . flies . . . through . . .
The . . . air
Like . . . slow . . . motion -
And it's a goal!
The fifth of the season!
It looks like another victory
For the Blues!

Michael Carr, Usama Essenouni (11) & Harmeet Guruwar (10)
The Mount Primary School, New Malden

What's Cooking In The Kitchen?

(In the style of Brian Patten)

There is something in the kitchen
I wonder what it could be?
It has only just arrived
So I'd better go and see.

It's hairy pink and purple,
With lots and lots of eyes,
It wriggles very dangerously
And it's wearing many ties.

I peek through the keyhole
And inhale a terrible smell
The monster is cooking
And muttering a spell.

He's cooking bacon sandwiches,
To take home to his wife,
I'm feeling rather horrified,
As he brandishes the knife.

The monster's disappearing,
Leaving complete chaos,
I'd better tidy up now because . . .
No one will ever believe me!

Dominique Winterbourne (11)
The Mount Primary School, New Malden

Summer Scene

Butterflies flutter
In the blazing sun
Gliding downwards
Onto soft, silky
Sunflowers swaying
Silently in the breeze.
Scent of flowers
Drifts on the air
Like a fantasy
Of fragrance
Combined with
The constant
Buzzing and humming
Of the black
And golden
Honeybees.

Hannah Forshaw (11)
The Mount Primary School, New Malden

Twist In The Tail

(In the style of Brian Patten)

There is something in the garden
I wonder what it can be?
It has only just arrived
So I'd better go and see.

I stroll down the garden path
Move towards a box,
Then I realise . . .
It's approaching me!

It stares at me
With small, blue eyes
So I stare back
I wonder what it can be?

I open up the box
And guess what?
The diminutive green thing
Is observing me!

Maybe it is an image of me?
Maybe it is an alien?
Oh no, I see . . .
It's a dragon - just like me!

Bernadette Trayers (11)
The Mount Primary School, New Malden

The Magic Wardrobe

(Inspired by 'Magic Box' by Kit Wright)

I will put in the wardrobe . . .
A silent footstep
Plodding through a meadow.

Chocolate that melts
On the tip of my tongue.

A freezing snowflake
That *never* melts.

A world that
Never spins.

The bite of the blazing sun
On my back.

The resonance of people
Walking on the pavement.

The juice of an orange
As it's squeezed.

Jannath Zabed (10)
The Mount Primary School, New Malden

The Cheeky Monkey
(In the style of Brian Patten)

There is something in the bedroom
I wonder what it could be?
It has only just arrived
So I'd better go and see.

As I climb the stairs
To take a peek
It is jumping on the beds
And I'm certain I saw a beak.

It's munching big, brown bananas
Making lots of noise
It's dressed in my brother's pyjamas
And starts playing with the toys.

As day turns into night-time
And the stars come out to play
He snuggles up in the bed
And sleeps the night away.

I fall asleep
Till the morning comes
I creep into the room
And he is *gone!*

Hope O'Shea (10)
The Mount Primary School, New Malden

My Magic Box
(Based on 'Magic Box' by Kit Wright)

I will put in the box . . .
An ancient golden pyramid
From the hot Egyptian desert.

Some shiny silver crystals
From the icy Antarctic Ocean.

I will put in the box . . .
Some magical fairies
From the fairy kingdom.

And unicorns' horns
Purple and pink.

I will swim in my box
With grey, shiny dolphins
As I float through international waters.

Hersimran Kaur (10)
The Mount Primary School, New Malden

Letter To Hollywood

Dear Hollywood
I've heard about the auditions
For the re-make of the Wizard of Oz
And darling, there's no one like me.
I'm destines for stardom, can't you see?
You can't make this film without *me!*
I have learnt the script off by heart,
Every bit of it, every part.
I've got golden locks, turquoise eyes
And gorgeous glowing skin.
I sing like an angel, I dance like heaven;
I'm outrageously talented and spectacularly slim
And darling, there's no one like me.
I'm destined for stardom, can't you see?
There's *no one* like me,
I'm the one, *I'm the one!*

Yours sincerely

The one and only Sian (Dorothy)

PS: I even have my own ruby slippers.

Sian Hughes (11)
The Mount Primary School, New Malden

Something Strange

(In the style of Brian Patten)

There is something in the kitchen
I wonder what it can be?
It's only just arrived
So I'd better go and see.

As I walk towards the kitchen
Getting scared (more and more!)
I hear a loud *bang*
As I open the door.

And with a great big fright
But to my delight
I see something hanging
From the light.

It has black, silky skin
And a pair of long wings
Its eyes are like ruby fire bolts
Lighting up the room.

Oh my gosh -
It's a bat!

Kelly Holland (11)
The Mount Primary School, New Malden

Dreams

(Inspired by 'Magic Box' by Kit Wright)

I will see in my dreams . . .
Fairies fluttering about with excitement
A mermaid splashing her magnificent tail
And singing to the moon
A rainbow soaring with colour
God's laughter and a goddess singing
A unicorns galloping in a pink, fluffy sky
A newborn puppy sleeping in his bed.

My dreams are made of
Happiness, love and joy
They will defeat nightmares
With a little help from a dreamcatcher.

In my dreams I will
Fly and rest upon the pink, fluffy clouds
Swim with the mermaids in the purple Ari Sea,
Hear the gods and goddesses.

I will remember these dreams.

Jordan Brodie (10)
The Mount Primary School, New Malden

The Magic Garden

(Inspired by 'Magic Box' by Kit Wright)

I will put in the garden . . .
Juliet waiting for her winsome Romeo
On a steep balcony
The gift of mankind
Upon the world
The heart of an ancient mother
Caring for her child
The colour of love
A sun that dances
Through the sky
Fresh green grass
With plants on either side
And secret doors
That take you to
A world of the future.

Zahra El-Sekaifi (10)
The Mount Primary School, New Malden

What Can *It* be?

(In the style of Brian Patten)

There is something in the garden
I wonder what it can be?
It has only just arrived
So I'd better go and see.

I peep through the keyhole
I see him getting ready
Starting the motorbike
Holding it very steady.

He's conversing with his motorbike
In a strange and silly way
Uttering and muttering
What did he say?

'Go! Go! Motorbike!
You accelerate enough
You were brisk yesterday -
Are you feeling rough?'

Now, I peep through the keyhole
Suddenly . . . he's *gone!*
Now I'm all alone again,
Maybe the alien's moved on?

Somaya Sahara (10)
The Mount Primary School, New Malden

Snow Scene

Outside the snow
is sparkling on
The ground
Like a blanket
Of thousands
Of priceless
Precious diamonds.
Snowflakes drift
And float
Like silver
Crystals, creating
A winter
Wonderland of
The world.

Ryan Woods (11)
The Mount Primary School, New Malden

Locked In My Diary Is . . .

(Inspired by 'Magic Box' by Kit Wright)

The musty smell of a cat's fur,
The first sign of love,
The swaying mane on a horse's back.

The healing hands of a wicca,
The ferocious roar of a pouncing tiger,
The thumping of delicate rabbit feet.

The unknown silence of a deserted island,
A drop of uncontrolled Atlantic,
The malevolence of a scheming warlock.

A red ruby, as sharp as a Samurai sword,
The cackle of a malicious witch,
A golden ball the colour of the sun.

My diary is styled from crystals
From the great walls of fiery volcanoes
With gems on the cover and secrets on the pages
Its writing is the trust of cats.

I shall write in my diary
On the soft surface of my bed,
Then become a character from
The fairy folk stories that I write.

Tilly Fouracre (9)
The Mount Primary School, New Malden

The Stone Castle

(Inspired by 'Magic Box' by Kit Wright)

I will put in my stone castle . . .
The ghost of William Shakespeare
Floating in the air
The heart from a pirate's body
Beating on a rock
The spirit of Sir Francis Drake
Standing on his ship
The fantastic smell
Of sizzling pancakes

I shall surf in my stone castle
On colossal high rolling breakers
Of lava
Like fire on Bonfire Night.

Joshua Joseph (10)
The Mount Primary School, New Malden

My Mysterious Cupboard

(Inspired by 'Magic Box' by Kit Wright)

I shall store in my cupboard . . .
The cheerful laughter of my friends,
The cleansing breath of my mother,
The calm flapping of a sail
In the cool, fresh wind.

I shall store in my cupboard . . .
The white froth of spit on my tongue,
The triumphant smell
Of never-ceasing victory,
The height of Scottish mountains.

I shall store in my cupboard . . .
An avalanche of frosty snow,
The sweet song of a mermaid,
A delicious brown toffee
Sticking to my teeth.

I shall fly in my cupboard
Through the moonlit skies
Of the Himalayas,
Then land on the tip of a mountain
Slippery with snow the colour of paper.

Peter Bache (10)
The Mount Primary School, New Malden

Autumn Scene

Autumn leaves everywhere
Golden, hazel, ruby, bronze
Drifting down like fairies
Leaves the trees
Like faceless skeletons
Bony branches reaching
To the sky
Mysterious fog
Like layers of silk
Descends on the Earth
And like cobwebs
The mist creeps around
On sly, soft feet
Creating a lonesome feeling
Like you are the
Only one in the world.

Katie Wilson (11)
The Mount Primary School, New Malden

Locked In My Heart

(Inspired by 'Magic Box' by Kit Wright)

I will lock in my heart . . .
The aroma of a flower budding
The softness of Mrs Lewis' pencil case
The whoosh of wondrous waves
A melting Aero bar bubbling on my tongue
The memory of my daddy's wedding
When he cuddled me . . .
And the confetti showering
Through the raindrops.

I will lock in my heart . . .
My nanny's laugh as she sat on a boat
A doggy called Abigail
Snuggling in my bed
Baking cakes with Mummy
And licking the bowl
Getting excited when
I smelt the swimming pool!
Seeing white clouds float across the sun.

My heart is made from
Silk and sequins
With pink ribbons
Dangling from the edge.

I will have love in my heart
Keep treasure inside
Like a warm sun glowing gently
Forever and ever.

Morgan King (10)
The Mount Primary School, New Malden

Crazy Nightmare

Head on the pillow
Drifting into nowhere
Eyes closed sleepily . . .
As I fall asleep.

Floating from the distance
A secret mansion
Murky and gloomily spectral . . .
Coming nearer and nearer.

Imagination drives me crazy -
Candles flash and flicker
Creaky doors make me shiver.

Walking down the corridor
Trees cast shadows
Wooden floors groan.

Clock ticking like a bomb
Ticks float everywhere on the air
Spiders and cobwebs everywhere.

Cracks in the wall . . .
Wind thrashing, water dripping, dribbling
Damp odours oozing.

Goosebumps on my arms . . .
Lightning strikes! Reflects upon a
Ghost playing haunting tunes on a piano.

A crimson cat prickly
Like a hedgehog - wails!
A mouse - squeaks and squeals!

Black bats flap . . .
Owls hoot . . .
And I awake!

Tiffany Hughes (11)
The Mount Primary School, New Malden

The Pouncing Panther

Nobody knows
That me and Kevin
Aren't best friends.
He's a bully boy,
He pushes me,
He punches me
And tells me
He has done it as a joke.
Nobody ever listens to me
And I feel like a mouse,
Hiding in a hole.

Mum thinks
Kevin is a friendly boy
But to me he is a bully boy.
Inside I feel like a panther pouncing
But outside I am like a baby bird
Who can't fly,
Staying in the nest alone.
Mum says,
'Invite Kevin for tea,'
I shrug my shoulders.

At school I climbed
The sloping carpet
Down the hall
To the headmaster's enormous door.
My heart isn't letting me do it
But I must stand up
And try to solve my problem.
Knock, knock!

Pragash Rajalingam (11)
The Mount Primary School, New Malden

My Trinket Box

(Inspired by 'Magic Box' by Kit Wright)

My trinket box will hold . . .
The splash of a magical dolphin
Following a ship
The Golden Hind
Full of spices
Silver fish swimming
In a sapphire sea
On a calm, summer day
An ancient Egyptian scroll
Scribed by a pharaoh
A roaring polar bear
From the Antarctic
A sparkling jewel
From a queen's palace
A tooth from a T-rex
An icicle as clear
As a crystal
From the snowy mountains
Of Canada.

My trinket box is styled
From pottery and silver
With red rubies on the lid
And golden medallions
In the corners
Its hinges are the beaks of penguins
I shall run in my box
In the Olympics in 2012
Then reach the red line
And win a thunderous standing ovation.

Zahrah Vencatasamy (10)
The Mount Primary School, New Malden

My Perfect Friend!

I created my perfect friend
And here are the ingredients
Of my blend:

Shake in a sprinkle of fun,
Flip in a chunk of kindness,
Drop in a heartful of love
And a spray of loyalty.

Now . . .

Pour in a spoonful of understanding,
A fragment of respect,
Blend a slice of helpfulness
And a dollop of sharing.

Then . . .

Mix in a shower of smiles,
Toss in a kettleful of companionship,
Whisk in a scattering of compromise
And flick in a jugful of forgiveness

And . . .

You have the perfect friend!

Angelika Molas (10)
The Mount Primary School, New Malden

The Magic Box

(Based on 'Magic Box' by Kit Wright)

I will put in the box . . .
The last flower
In the world
Dying for
Some water
Bright colours
Floating in
The air
And a
Sparkling star
Falling from
The sky -
A sky that
Is never dull
And the
Pure smell
Of a
Red rose.

Tayyaba Khalid (10)
The Mount Primary School, New Malden

The Hound From Hell

When the clock strikes midnight
The hell hound comes to bite
And howls up to the sky above
Searching for a fight.

He howls like a demonic dog
As he creeps through thick night fog
And glares at the light of the moon
As he prances over a log.

A hound from the world of evil
A nasty piece of work
When he performs a dirty deed
It seems he always smirks.

His heart is filled with darkness
A deep and empty space
Like a long, hollow tunnel
As black as his dark days.

When the clock strikes midnight
The hell hound craves for a fight
He howls up to the stars above
Ready to scratch and bite.

Suyamba Kumaresan (10)
The Mount Primary School, New Malden

Secret Treasure Chest

(Inspired by 'Magic Box' by Kit Wright)

I put in my chest . . .
A sparkly star
From a baby-blue sky
A mermaid with a long tail
A candyfloss cloud
As white as snow
A teddy with a cherry velvet bow
A witch on a hockey stick
Drifting over the moon.

My secret treasure chest
Is brown and gold
With diamonds and sequins all over
And contains my dream
To sing with Girls Aloud
In a stadium with millions of people
Clapping their hands
In a standing ovation!

Amelia Fairchild (10)
The Mount Primary School, New Malden

The Secret Garden

(Inspired by 'Magic Box' by Kit Wright)

I shall hide in the secret garden . . .
The roundness of a hot, crispy pizza
Baking in the oven
The smoothest chocolate
Dissolving in my mouth
The crunch of crisps
Near my ears.

I shall hide in the secret garden . . .
The entertainment
Of a banana skin!
A mouth-watering cheeseburger
Digesting in my stomach
The enjoyment
Of my friend's laughter.

I shall hide in the secret garden . . .
The cheers of football fans
Singing forever!
Ants that flow
Through space
A statue that lives
In everlasting fire.

Jacques Kitenge (10)
The Mount Primary School, New Malden

Under My Bed!

(Inspired by 'Magic Box' by Kit Wright)

I will keep under my bed . . .
A snake swishing
Along the slippery floor
Snowy mountains walking
Along the beach
A river flowing
Through space
A baby elephant's footstep
And a secret garden
A monkey walking
On the Earth
And a human being
Hanging from a tree
The spirit of
Ancient Egypt
I shall rummage
Under my bed for all
These fanciful things . . .

Lauren Hardwick (10)
The Mount Primary School, New Malden

My Magic Chest

(Inspired by 'Magic Box' by Kit Wright)

I will put in my magic chest . . .
The sparkling wings of fairies
In the midnight sky
The bright sun shining above our heads
A unicorn's pink and purple horn.

Flames of dinosaurs
Stomping through the frightening woods
A spectacular safari
With animals playing.

Five magical wishes
Granted by a dream-making genie
Six friends sharing secrets
Under the moon and stars.

I shall fly on my magic chest
To the Great Wall of China
To the tower in Portsmouth
To a sandy beach . . .

. . . And splash all day in the aqua sea.

Nicole McDonnell (10)
The Mount Primary School, New Malden

My Magic Tin

(Inspired by 'Magic Box' by Kit Wright)

I will put in the tin . . .
The football used
When Chelsea beat Arsenal 2-0
In the Barclays Premiership.

I will put in the tin . . .
The goal scored by Steven Gerrard
The time when England
Won the World Cup in 1966.

I will put in the tin . . .
The fifteenth goal
Scored by Frank Lampard
When Liverpool won the Champions League.

My tin is made of metal
And fashioned of new football boots
It's magic will take me and my parents
To the Yankees Stadium.

Jack Fouracre (10)
The Mount Primary School, New Malden

My Magic Box
(Based on 'Magic Box' by Kit Wright)

I will put in my box . . .
The first birthday of baby Jesus
The first autograph of a famous sportsman
And the first ship to set sail.

I will put in my box . . .
The Last Supper with Jesus
The Declaration of Independence
And the first stripe of a zebra.

I will put in my box . . .
The captain of a football team
The crown of a king and queen
And the first play written by William Shakespeare.

I will put in my box . . .
The first pyramid ever built
A sunken treasure chest
The voodoo of an ancient curse.

My box is fashioned with pirates' treasure
With chains around it
So nobody . . . can hear . . . my
Secrets . . .
Sshhh!

Rhiannon Lewis (10)
The Mount Primary School, New Malden

My Secret Garden
(Inspired by 'Magic Box' by Kit Wright)

I will put in my secret garden . . .
The fear of a blazing dragon
A snowman playing on a beach
The Statue of Liberty
Walking through New York
The president of the USA
And snow on a boiling day.

Talha Mahmood (10)
The Mount Primary School, New Malden

Roses

When I look out of the window
And I'm feeling down
The flowers make me happy
Especially the roses.

Pink roses make me feel thoughtful
And I can picture them
In a beautiful park
In the summer.

Roses make me think
Of my mum and dad together again
And if they could speak
They would have a soft, lady's voice.

They would sing happy songs
And there would be a harp
A piano and a violin playing
Roses are bright and wonderful.

Elizabeth O'Connell (11)
The Mount Primary School, New Malden

Friendship Poem

I have a best friend
And this is how she's made:

Take a chunk of co-operation,
A heartful of love,
A kettleful of fun
And a whisk of care.

Pour this mixture into a bowl
And stir till light and fluffy
Blend for ten minutes
Then pour into a baking pan
And bake until golden -
And top with friendship sprinkles -
There - perfect!

Victoria Westlake (10)
The Mount Primary School, New Malden

Travelling To Madeira

Fluffy white clouds
Surround the plane,
Tilt your head,
Use your imagination,
Turn them into
Different shapes.
Worried the landing
Might be bumpy
But feeling happy
As I see
My family
Waving at me
In bright coloured clothes.
The sun is shining
As my godmother
Drives us home
To our pink house.
I see orange trees
Through the window
And water trickling
Down the brown mountains.
Figos green like watermelon
But squishier and sweet.
On the veranda
We play with puppies
And when the priest
In the church next door
Rings the bells at 7 o'clock
He *wakes us up.*
The sea is blue and the shells are curly.

Kelly Neves (11)
The Mount Primary School, New Malden

The Useless Fairy

Once upon a rhyme,
Long ago in time,
There was a fairy,
Long and hairy,
She loved blue,
But hadn't a clue,
On being a fairy.

She was really tall,
Her feet were quite small,
She loved all cats
And liked cool hats,
But wasn't any good,
At being a fairy.

When she cast a spell,
It never went well,
Dogs turned into bats,
Hogs changed into rats,
Frogs turned to cats,
She wasn't any good,
At being a fairy.

She loved fluffy moles
And liked digging holes,
She wasn't that cool,
She was a fool,
Her name was Jess
And take a wild guess,
She was really stupid.

Sarah Pierce (9)
St Katharine's CE (VA) Primary School, Bournemouth

All About Me

I am a dolphin, gentle and caring
I am a rose, loving and bright
I am a cushion, soft and squishy
I am a limo, sleek and smooth
I am the colour lilac, helpful and loveable
I am Coke, bubbly and fizzy
I am a T-shirt, cool and flowing
I am a hotel, expensive and slick.

Olivia Thompson (9)
St Katharine's CE (VA) Primary School, Bournemouth

Someone Came This Morning

(Inspired by 'The Sound Collector' by Roger McGough)

Someone came this morning
Through the open door
Came to the office window
And fainted on the floor

The clicking of the light switch
The footsteps in the corridors
The pressing from the computer room
The coughing from Year 4s

The tweeting from the birds outside
The singing from Miss Parker
The shouting of the babies
The scribbling of the marker

The cutting of the scissors
The stapler, stapling onto the wall
The weeping from the first aid room
The singing from the hall.

Natasha Handscomb (9)
St Katharine's CE (VA) Primary School, Bournemouth

Dazzling Dad

He is the colour green,
Alive and energetic.

He is a light switch,
Changing by the minute.

He is Tango,
Bubbly and fit.

He is a pair of jeans,
Funky and always on the go.

He is a Springer spaniel
Fun and bouncy.

He is an apple,
Fresh and round.

He is the wind,
Always there to protect me like a shield.

He is my dad,
Cool and *mine!*

Hannah Partridge (10)
St Katharine's CE (VA) Primary School, Bournemouth

Who Am I?

I am a sunflower, happy and bright
I am a sister to my brother and sister
I am a daughter to my mum and dad
I am a mini, small and colourful.

I am a sun, warm and cuddly
I am a glass of Coke, fizzy and wizzy
I am a sofa, comfy and warm
I am a young girl, wanting a long life.

I am a bath, hot and bubbly
I am a horse, trotting everywhere
I am an owner of dogs, cats and a rabbit
I am a knife, sharp and pointy.

I am a bike, waiting to be rode
I am a bookcase, doing nothing
I am a chair, waiting to be squashed
I am a table, being leant on.

Shannon Sherar (9)
St Katharine's CE (VA) Primary School, Bournemouth

Who Is Behind Me?

I walked in a room
Empty and bare
I shouted out loud
'Is anyone there?'

All I heard back
Was an echo of me
I looked around
But there was nothing to see.

I stood in silence
Waiting for sound
I heard some footsteps
Someone's around.

I said to myself
'This must be a dream'
As I turned round
I wanted to scream.

I ran and ran
As fast as I could
'Shall I lock myself up?
Maybe I should!'

Annabelle Williams (10)
St Katharine's CE (VA) Primary School, Bournemouth

Dancing With Stars

She is a snow leopard, strong but elegant
Dancing, prancing, spinning and jumping
Starting as something else.
She is a rose, sweet and mothering
Dashing, diving, dancing, such a busy life
With two young girls but still coping.
She is a stage, bold and bright
Performing, practising, showing off.
She is a rubber, bendy but never breaks
How did she get so flexible?
Just is a mystery to me, is how rubber is made.
The star is getting tired, I think it's time to go to bed
But don't give up, don't waste your life,
Carry on, keep going
There are more challenges ahead.

Elisa Jacobs (10)
St Katharine's CE (VA) Primary School, Bournemouth

Happiness Poem

Happiness is a hug, very warm and welcome
Happiness is a bedtime book, before you sleep
Happiness is a bath, warm and bubbly
Happiness is a piece of cake (eat the icing first)
Happiness is missing homework (so you can relax)
Happiness is making friends, so you're not alone
Happiness is brothers and sisters, so you can play
Happiness is having pets, they always understand
Happiness is mums and dads, they help us every day.

What's your happiness?

Ella Josey (10)
St Katharine's CE (VA) Primary School, Bournemouth

Who Am I?

I am a panda, friendly and lazy
I am a lily, beautiful and attractive
I am a bed, cuddly and relaxed
I am a lawnmower, slow and wondrous
I am the colour yellow, calm and bouncy
I am a hamburger, big and strong
I am a pair of jeans, well-dressed and pretty
I am a house, short and steady
I am the clouds, floating and drifting away.

Charlotte Hawtrey-Coombs (10)
St Katharine's CE (VA) Primary School, Bournemouth

About Me

I am like a dolphin, gentle and caring
I am the colour purple, lively and bold
I am a sunflower, smiley and bright
I am a bed, cuddly and warm
I am a scooter, fast and smooth
I am chocolate, smooth and nice
I am a sofa, new and soft
I am a church, kind and loyal to God
I am a hot summer's day, warm and fun
I am a good friend, understanding and trusting
I am the youngest to my brother and sister
I am a daughter to my mum and dad.

Ashley Reedman (9)
St Katharine's CE (VA) Primary School, Bournemouth

What Is Happiness?

Happiness is a bath, hot and bubbly
Happiness is a bed, comfy and cosy
Happiness is a present, to show someone cares
Happiness is a pet, always loyal
Happiness is old toys, reassuring
Happiness is teamwork, to make something better
Happiness is friends and family!

Happiness is lots of things
What's your happiness?

Heather Smith (9)
St Katharine's CE (VA) Primary School, Bournemouth

I Am . . .

I am the colour blue, joyful and bouncy
I am a bluebell, swaying in the breeze
I am a cat, lively and happy
I am a chair, new and soft
I am Coke, sizzling with laughter
I am pyjamas, loose and funky
I am the wind, always on the go
I am a house, strong and tall.

Lauren Dingley (10)
St Katharine's CE (VA) Primary School, Bournemouth

Forever?

I was like an old toy, lonely and forgotten,
I had been thrown away too many times, lost,
My tears, they fell,
The ripples circled round,
Some hit the water, some on the ground,
Mangled corpses draped themselves round my legs,
Tugging effortlessly,
I pull, struggling, fighting,
Fighting for life that I was going to waste?
I trek through the filthy leaves,
Leave my life and memories that should not be forgotten?
Someone crying in the dark,
Someone laughing in the light,
I am a ship, sailing through the storm,
Or wind, never sun,
Sunshine has been forgotten,
Forgotten with lots of others,
What more to life is there? I have been given the chance for a good life,
But it has not come,
I feel frozen, as I sink into the cold water
And then I flee my life forever.

Alice Massey (9)
St Katharine's CE (VA) Primary School, Bournemouth

I Love Dogs!

I love dogs,
But what should I choose?
Floppy ears?
Spotty ears?
Funny ears?
Silly ears?

I think I'll choose a . . .
Floppy-eared,
Spotty-eared,
Funny-eared,
Silly-eared,
Dog!

Laura Tarrant (9)
St Katharine's CE (VA) Primary School, Bournemouth

I Am . . .

I am a star, glitzy and pretty
I am a cherry, with a lovely smell
I am the colour purple, girly and bright
I am a puppy, playful and fun
I am a jungle who loves animals
I am a rose, pink or red
I am a limousine, posh and clean
I am a party dress, gorgeous and stylish
I am a hill, high and green
I am a letter, understandable and new
I am a pair of disco boots, black and fashionable
I am a bed, comfy and neat
I am a sleepover, cool and funny
I am laughter, friendly and giggly
I am sensible, brainy and awake
I am a person, nice and quiet
I am a friend, comforting and kind
I am a portrait, real and beautiful and without any mistakes at all
I am a flower, free and different
I am me and me is wonderful!

Kimberley Stone (9)
St Katharine's CE (VA) Primary School, Bournemouth

When I Think Of A Poem

When I think of a poem, I think of fun,
A poem is a sunflower shining in the sun,
So listen to this in a happy mood,
And by the end of it, you'll be a cool dude.

When I think of a poem, I think of magic,
Like James Bond with all his gadgets,
He drives around in his nice sports car
And stops for a pint at the local bar.

But when I think of a poem, I think of doom,
War, explosions and bombs that go *boom!*
The army is hiding in big, deep trenches,
On the old radio, tanks were mentioned.

When I think of a poem, I think of death,
People dying and losing their breath,
As I walk around in my tough gang,
I can only hope it will end in a *bang!*

James Ryan (9)
St Katharine's CE (VA) Primary School, Bournemouth

I Would Win The Gold

I would win the gold if these were Olympic sports:

Rubber flicking
Pencil snapping
Noodle eating
Non-stop talking
Goal scoring
Late morning snoring
Long distance race
Same sock wearing
Gogglebox watching
GameBoy playing
Money spending
Bogey picking
Tennis ball lobbing
Class skipping
Homework blotching

Recognise all these sports?
Then meet me!
The champ: a pathetic athlete!

Felix Granell (9)
St Katharine's CE (VA) Primary School, Bournemouth

A Question Of War

What is a bomb?
Your last moment.

What is a gun?
The weapon from Hell.

Who is Hitler?
The Devil's best man.

What is a tank?
The dragon's death machine.

What is a soldier?
The blood of our country.

What is a ship?
A floating bullet.

What is war?
The worst night!

Tom Wilson (9)
St Katharine's CE (VA) Primary School, Bournemouth

Which Pet Shall I Get?

Rabbits like to cuddle up,
But dogs like to play,
Hamsters like to scuttle around,
But cats like to sleep all day.

Mice like to nibble on cheese,
Horses like to jump,
Parrots talk when you're lonely,
But snails have a shell lump.

Snakes like to slyly slither,
Turtles like to swim,
Rats like to munch on litter,
Stick insects are really thin!

I'm not too sure what to get,
Should I get a bat?
Shall I get a guinea pig?
I'm happy to stick with that!

Alice Kent (10)
St Katharine's CE (VA) Primary School, Bournemouth

The Four Seasons

Spring is very cool
The rabbits are hopping now
Chicks are coming too

Summer is coming
Sun in the pale blue sky
People enjoy fun

Autumn's colourful
Playing with coloured leaves
Lots of joy is shared

Winter is now here
Children make lots of snowmen
Snow is falling down.

Bryher McCabe (10)
St Katharine's CE (VA) Primary School, Bournemouth

Pirate Pete

There was an old pirate called Pete
Who captured a whole fishing fleet
He said, 'Don't be scared
All your lives will be spared
I only want something to eat!'

Braden Elcock (9)
St Katharine's CE (VA) Primary School, Bournemouth

What Pet Shall I Get?

These are the pets that I might get . . .
A rabbit and I'll give it cuddles,
A dog which would jump in muddy puddles

A cat which would nap on my bed,
A snake which wouldn't usually be fed

A rat which would nibble on cheese,
A fluffy hamster which would make me sneeze

But I think I'll get a horse and I'll meet it every day
And when it's feeling very happy, it will neigh!

Megan Proctor (10)
St Katharine's CE (VA) Primary School, Bournemouth

My Mum's An Alien

Do you like your mum?
I think mine's from Mars!
Or maybe even Jupiter,
Definitely from the stars!
My mum's gone crazy,
It's from living in outer space
Is your mum an alien?

Do you like your mum?
My mum's really weird!
She's not acting normal at all,
I think she's feared!
She doesn't fit in,
She's an embarrassment!
Is your mum an alien?

Asha Gilbert (9)
St Katharine's CE (VA) Primary School, Bournemouth

Who Am I?

I am a cheetah, as fast as lightning
I am the colour black, as dark as a rain cloud
I am a dripping tap that will never stop
I am a poppy, as red as fire
I am spare ribs, as tender as gold
I am the sky, sending gales that will blow you away
I am a star, as bright as the sun
I am a picture, as quiet as a mouse
I am a clock, *tick-tocking* away!

Brendan Kirkton (10)
St Katharine's CE (VA) Primary School, Bournemouth

I Don't Mind What Pet I Get!

Pets are all different,
Some are large and some are tiny,
Some are soft, others are rough,
But I don't really mind.

Pets are all different,
Some jump and others crawl,
Some are long-haired, some are short-haired,
But I don't really mind.

Pets are all different,
Some are playful, some are cuddly
And they are all different colours,
But I don't really mind.

All pets are fun whatever kind!

Leah Rockett (9)
St Katharine's CE (VA) Primary School, Bournemouth

The Four Seasons

Red leaves and yellow,
The autumn leaves are falling,
Leaves are everywhere.

Summer is just great,
The sun is shining brightly,
No clouds in the sky.

The snow is falling,
Winter is just fantastic,
Christmas is coming.

Some leaves are tiny,
Leaves are growing everywhere,
They are just green.

Amber Colston (9)
St Katharine's CE (VA) Primary School, Bournemouth

As Swift As An Arrow - Haikus

Peregrine falcon
The master of speed and sky
A killer on wings

Peregrine falcon
Feather as smooth as cotton
Swift as an arrow.

Alex Peek (9)
St Katharine's CE (VA) Primary School, Bournemouth

The Twelve Seasons

January starts freezing cold,
Wind hits you as you've been told,
February rain, hands frozen,
How long do you wait for March?

March better but still bad,
I am starting to get mad,
April fine with some rainy days,
May soon have a cheer!

May, great for a walk,
Or a holiday to New York,
June lovely with the beach,
August soon - can't wait!

July the end of school,
Let's go in the pool,
August fantastic
Please don't go too quick.

September still hot,
Let's go on a yacht,
October getting worse,
But soon it's Christmas!

November ice-cold,
You feel like you're very old,
December have a snow fight,
25th, Christmas Day!

Adam Carter (9)
St Katharine's CE (VA) Primary School, Bournemouth

Weather Is Lovely

The sun is shining,
Pretty things are growing now,
Leaves are falling now.

Hot sand burning feet,
Children splashing all around,
Lovely cool water.

Leaves are falling down,
Children playing happily,
Autumn is so fun.

Fresh snow is falling,
Snowmen are being built,
Wintry scenes now.

Isobel Nunn (10)
St Katharine's CE (VA) Primary School, Bournemouth

Pets, Pets And More Pets

When I was a toddler,
I bought a little hamster,
Who stood as still as a statue.

Later on, I got bored with it,
So I bought a lizard,
Now I had a hamster and a lizard.

But I got bored with them,
So I bought a rat
And now I had a hamster, a lizard and a rat.

But I took it a step further and bought a yellow paper,
I checked up on the pets section and bought a fish,
A dog, a cat, parrot, a guinea pig, a snake,
A horse and obviously a stick insect,
But what I didn't think about was,
That I don't have any money left for food!

Kiyavash Kandar (9)
St Katharine's CE (VA) Primary School, Bournemouth

Different Pets

I would love to have a pet
Which one shall I get?
Should it be a hamster?
Or one that I can pamper?

Some pets are cute
Some pets are cuddly
Some pets are really, really funny.

Some can be big
Some can be small
But I don't think it matters at all

They can have long hair
They can have short hair
But I do not think it matters at all

Some pets are fat
Some pets are skinny
But their size does not matter at all.

Lucy Allen (10)
St Katharine's CE (VA) Primary School, Bournemouth

When I Lost My Shoe

Once, when I lost my shoe
I really couldn't find it
I searched the house and garden looking everywhere

Under the sofa and the chair
I knew it really was not fair
But even so, I carried on looking everywhere

I looked under the bed
And behind my enormous ted
I was getting tired from looking everywhere

I was battered by now
But I'd got to clean the dog
So I went to the kennel -
And there he was, nibbling my shoe!

Tom Dow (9)
St Katharine's CE (VA) Primary School, Bournemouth

I Don't Like Winter!

Bitterly cold winter,
I don't like it at all,
I got hit by a cold snowball
And ended up on the floor.

Colourful, windy autumn,
I don't like it at all,
Last time I got blown off my feet
And landed a mile away or more.

Cheerful, flowery spring,
I don't like it at all,
Last time the flowers grew so much,
I couldn't get out of my door.

Dry, sizzling summer,
I love it, it's great!
Seven fantastic weeks off
And on the beach with my mates!

Kieran Cheesman (10)
St Katharine's CE (VA) Primary School, Bournemouth

The Dog Of The World

My dog is playful, my dog is fun
Whenever he's awake
He will always run.

His name is Bob and he's my dog
Also I love him lots
And he wears my socks.

And when he's nice to my hamster
He gets very pampered
He loves going on walks.

He cuddles up on my mum and dad's bed
And he falls asleep
With his teddy, Ted.

James Webb (10)
St Katharine's CE (VA) Primary School, Bournemouth

Happy House

Chorus:
We've got a happy house,
A clappy, slappy house,
A laughing, crying, happy house.

We've got . . .
Brave brothers
Sloppy sisters
Annoying aunties
Devastating dogs
Crazy cats
Tiny toys
Boring books
Conquered clocks

We've got . . .
Great grandads
Gripping grandmas
Loopy sister Lauren
Bouncing babies
Oliver eating olives
Hungry hoovers
Vicious vacuums
Angry Alex.

Chorus.

Andrew Harley (8)
St Martin's School, Bournemouth

My Alien

My alien goes wobbling where the lamp post hangs,
He chomps it very hard with his dripping fangs,
My alien goes wobbling where the strange things are,
When he comes home, he says he's been to a bar!

I go swimming with my alien friend,
When we go swimming, we swim to the end.
When we come home I have some tea,
But my alien friend has a big, juicy flea!

Jessica Mae Stalley (8)
St Martin's School, Bournemouth

Pet Shop Rap

We've got a pet shop,
A dangerous pet shop,
A snappin', flappin' pet shop.
We've got a pet shop,
A dangerous pet shop,
A howling, growling pet shop.

We've got . . .
Howling hounds,
Creepy cats,
Crazy crocs,
Rummaging rats,
Bashing bunnies,
Snapping sharks,
Mangy mice
Angry aardvarks.

We've got a pet shop . . .

We've got . . .
Prowling Persians,
Scary snakes,
Terrible tigers,
Swimming in lakes,
Spooky spiders,
Slimy swans,
Charging cheetahs,
Eating scones.

We've got a pet shop . . .

Lauren Hennessy (9)
St Martin's School, Bournemouth

Padget The Cat

Padget goes running in the dark, black wood
Padget goes swimming where she really should
Padget goes walking with a black, smelly rat,
Padget meets a dog and stops for a chat.

Padget talks about the dog's unusual name
'Wellieboots' sounds like a silly game
He's good at fetching boots for his young friend
Padget runs off and that is the end.

Alicia Morgan (8)
St Martin's School, Bournemouth

Super Class

We've got a super class
A noisy super class
A laughing, crazy super class
We've got a super class
A noisy super class
A madly, laughing super class.

We've got . . .
Arguing Andrew
Burping Ben
Deadly Daniel
Kicking Katy
Jumping Jodie
Running Reece
Silly Sandie
And never any peace.

Chorus

We've got . . .
Laughing Lauren
Joking Jess
Giggling Gabby
Angry Andy
Acting Alexander
Action Alex
And never any quiet.

Chorus.

Louise Katie Garner (8)
St Martin's School, Bournemouth

The Rubber Duckie Rock

Rubber duckies are so cool!
They're a buddy for the pool.
Different sizes, different shapes,
Some are purple, just like grapes.

I collect them, any kind,
Ducks to blow away your mind:
An astronaut, a street duck,
A glow-in-the-dark duck.

I also have a set of lights;
When the wind blows they fly like kites.
Of course, they're shaped like rubber ducks,
Don't try to eat them, they're just yuck!

I get new ducks day after day,
Even though I have to pay.
My collection will grow and grow,
Some bright green and some with bows!

Rubber duckies are my friends,
Even though they break and bend.
No duck is too boring for me,
Soon I'll have 103!

Lottie Martin (11)
St Martin's School, Bournemouth

I Wish I Had A Dog

I wish I had a dog,
I've got two fish,
But they're rather boring,
They just do a lot of swimming!

Not a big or fierce dog,
But a small, furry, happy dog,
We'd go for walks, I'd throw a stick,
It will wag its tail and give me a lick.

I know I'd have to look after it,
To brush its fur, clean its paws,
Feed it and take it to the vets,
But a dog really is the greatest pet.

Someday soon I'll get my dog,
He'll bound around and chase his tail,
He'll woof with joy when I come home,
He'll always be there when I'm alone.

David Appleton (11)
St Martin's School, Bournemouth

Poor Little Whale!

Swimming with his family
Swimming deep within the sea
He took a turn and swam towards
The coast of England and its shores.

He could not see his family
He could not see his friends
But up ahead he saw a ship
And followed in the end.

He didn't know the place he was
The water was all dirty
And ended up at Westminster
As Big Ben struck 2.30.

A man came to save him
And helped him out the river
They put him on a boat
And then he died forever.

Anouska Emery (11)
St Martin's School, Bournemouth

My Cat

My cat is called Charlie,
He is black, white and furry,
He is cute and small
And loves to play with a ball,
You'd better watch out,
If you wander about
He'll creep up behind you and pounce!

By day he sleeps,
By night he creeps,
He's wild and brave and not afraid,
Small creatures beware
Because Charlie is there.

When I go to school
Charlie stays at home.
When he is older he can go outside and roam.
When the school day is done
I know that Charlie and I will have some fun.

James Errington (9)
St Martin's School, Bournemouth

Football Crazy!

On Saturdays I'm in Dallas,
No, not the USA,
Dallas is my football team,
A serious game we play!

Alex plays up front
And I am a defender,
Rebecca is the goalie,
Team rules we must remember.

Manager Justin calls the shots,
Dad is the referee,
He blows the whistle on and off,
Shouting frantically.

Our aim, the league we want to win,
Our tactics we deliver,
But really how we play the game,
Depends on the cold and shiver!

I take a shot and hit the post,
From Declan it rebounds,
We really hope to score the most
And cheer the winning sound.

I want to score the final goal,
More than I can tell,
From deep down within my soul,
'We've won, we've won!' I'll yell.

It happens all so very fast,
The ball, it comes to me,
I leap and head it to the goal,
Instant victory!

The team are cheering, smiles all round,
I laugh and dance away,
The fun of football we have found,
Hip, hip, hip, hooray!

Toby Sharer (10)
St Martin's School, Bournemouth

Crazy Cat

I saw a crazy cat,
Eating a flapping bat,
She likes to lick her head
She sleeps on my bed
With a red hat on her head.

The crazy cat wears a jacket
She plays with a tennis racket
She wears a gold collar
That cost her a shiny dollar.

She chases all the cats away
Because she never likes to play
And tells them not to come back
When she is eating her snack.

She puts her paw in a dish
So she can eat all her fish
Then when she's eating it all up
She puts all her bones in a cup.

She runs after her ball
When it goes into the hall
She catches all the mice
Then she puts them in some rice.

When it's rainy she's inside
Then when it's sunny she goes outside
She comes and sleeps on my bed
With a red hat on her head.

Gage Davies (10)
St Martin's School, Bournemouth

Mav

Maverick goes prowling where the wild things roam,
He stays in the garden, but never goes home,
Maverick goes hunting for a pigeon or a mouse,
But never, never dares to go near the house!

He lies in the road, right under the sun
And if a car or lorry comes, off he'll run,
Maverick grooms his puffy fur whilst sitting on the mat
And Maverick eats his breakfast, a furry, fat rat!

Jodie Forbes (9)
St Martin's School, Bournemouth

School Fashions

The fashion of collecting cards,
Is something I've found rather hard.
For other things I find quite easy,
But sometimes they are rather cheesy!

For football cards the boys go mad,
I just find it very sad!
They love to get loads of five stars,
But they always go way too far!

Scoobies were the fashion once
And at it I was quite a dunce.
As soon as they went out of fashion,
I could do it with a passion!

Then there was Yu-Gi-Oh and Pokémon,
But it was Pokémon that carried on.
The duels were planned quite carefully,
But we girls were quite carefree!

It's cool to stand by the school gate
And never ever to be late!
I must say our school is very cool,
We even have fashions at the swimming pool!

Hannah Jones (10)
St Martin's School, Bournemouth

The Creature In The Pool

No one wants to go to school,
Because there is a creature in the pool.

Every Monday children run,
Before the day has begun.

The pool is a threat,
In it is the teacher's pet.

Everyone wants to see,
What is it that's swimming free?

One day it jumped right out,
With lots of water splashing about.

Then I knew it and dived straight in,
Yes, I was right, it was a dolphin!

Lizzie Jones (9)
St Martin's School, Bournemouth

Sweet Shop Rap

We've got a sweet shop,
A yummy sweet shop,
A gummy, scrummy sweet shop.

We've got . . .
Lollipop liquorice
Goofy gum
Moon Maltesers
Phooey fudge
Football yummies
Stupid sherberts
Tarantula tots
Apple crumbs

We've got a sweet shop,
A yummy sweet shop,
A gummy, scrummy sweet shop.

We've got . . .
Toothy toffee
Stroppy Starbursts
Burning bonbons
Fantastic elastic
Take-away taffy
Infesting invisibles
Whistling Wonka bars

We've got a sweet shop,
A yummy sweet shop,
A gummy, scrummy sweet shop.

Alexander Robert Jon Moneypenny (8)
St Martin's School, Bournemouth

The Eagle's Day

He perches in his nest,
Wearing a golden vest.

He sits proud,
Away from the crowd.

With his beady eyes and pointy beak,
He sits and searches for the weak.

Flying over the mountains so high,
Soaring through the silky sky.

He goes searching for his prey,
Hoping that he'll find some before the end of the day.

He sits down for his evening dish,
Yummy, yummy, lovely fish!

Georgia Rose Stalley (10)
St Martin's School, Bournemouth

Animals!

I love animals,
Animals of any kind
Especially mammals,
So many species you shall find.

Cats, monkeys, whales and more,
So many creatures that you can adore,
Cute and cuddly, I love them all,
They're all God's creatures, big or small!

The amazing sea,
A place of wonder,
Thousands of fish swimming free.

The mysterious jungle,
A great place to be,
Charging elephants make a loud rumble,
Scaring monkeys into the tallest tree.

Way up high in the beautiful sky,
Soars the powerful eagle,
Making its victims cry.

Ants, caterpillars, bees and flies,
Worms and beetles, what a surprise!
Creepy-crawlies in the wood,
Most of them misunderstood.

That's what animals are all about,
Definitely, without a doubt,
The best things in the world are free,
God made them just for you and me.

Tiah Charlotte Lily Oates (9)
St Martin's School, Bournemouth

Snow

Cold and bright
Crisp and white
The snow is so deep
I must run and leap.
I mustn't stumble
I might take a tumble.
It's still falling
The warmth is calling
It's time to go
And leave the snow.
Now I go to sleep
With my cuddly toy sheep.

Zelie Batchelor (7)
St Martin's School, Bournemouth

A Day Out With My Dad

When I go out with my mum all we do is shop,
But I would rather be with my dad in the spying Kop.
The Kop is at Anfield, the place of my dreams,
That is why Liverpool are my favourite team.
When we look round the stands you see nothing but red
Flags in the air and hats on heads.
The kick-off is near
The crowd begin to cheer.
As the teams come out, I jump on my seat,
Another match begins, a new team to beat.
I'm full of excitement, a smile on my face
As Gerrard and Carragher take their place.
I hope we win, if we lose I'll be sad,
I don't want to spoil my day out with my dad.

Kai Wilkinson (9)
St Martin's School, Bournemouth

Winter

What's the reason
For the seasons?
There are four,
Why not more?

Digging paths,
Sitting by hearths.
Roaring fires burn,
While tractor tyres turn.

Logs being sold,
People are cold.
The trees are bare,
Frost is in the air.

Bells are ringing,
As people are singing.
Christmas is here,
Children full of cheer.

Sleet or snow,
We do not know.
The wind will blow,
Our noses will glow.

Soon springtime will start,
As bulbs do their part.
Birds will be full of song,
When the days are long.

Charlotte Luther (10)
St Martin's School, Bournemouth

Countryside

(Inspired by 'Cats Sleep Anywhere' by Eleanor Farjean)

Moles dig everywhere
On the golf courses
In the fields
Anywhere
They don't care
Moles dig everywhere.

Hares run anywhere
In the garden
In the woods
Anywhere
They don't care
Hares run anywhere.

Owls fly anywhere
In the forest
Over fields
Anywhere
They don't care
Owls fly anywhere.

Goerge Brewster (8)
St Martin's School, Bournemouth

The Jungle

The jungle is so big and scary,
Most of the creatures are fast and hairy.
Some are scaly and bite,
Most would give you a massive fright.

Big cats that would love to eat you,
Crocodiles and alligators would eat you too.
Snakes that can bite and squeeze,
Would swallow you whole and not say please!

In the water, piranhas like drinking blood,
Dangerous hippos hiding in the mud.
Monkeys in trees that screech and swing,
Wasps and hornets that can really sting.

Frightening sounds are everywhere,
Step very carefully and take care.
The jungle is so dark and black,
Don't go alone, you might not come back!

Tom Newcombe (10)
St Martin's School, Bournemouth

Pets

Some are sweet,
Some are sour
And some need to take a shower.

Some pets growl,
Some pets talk
And some you need to take for a walk.

Pets can be ill,
But are normally well
And when upset you can usually tell.

Like a tiger,
Pets can be very, very wild,
Or like a puppy, they can be very, very mild.

Do you like cats?
Do you like dogs?
If you do you'll especially like frogs!

I love my pets,
Hope you do too,
Cuddle them lots and they will love you.

Beth Wilson (9)
St Martin's School, Bournemouth

Why Not?

Why not take a crazy chance?
Why not do a crazy dance?

Why not take me to school?
Why not take me to the swimming pool?

Why not take me to the shops?
Why not let me eat lamb chops?

Why not let me ride my bike?
Why not let me call my dad, Mike?

Why not bring my bag upstairs?
Why not let me eat some pears?

Why not spread your wings and fly?
Why not fly high above the sky?

Why not?
Because!

Reanne Soraya Emery (11)
St Martin's School, Bournemouth

Dogs

(Inspired by 'Cats Sleep Anywhere' by Eleanor Farjean)

Dogs run anywhere
Any playground, any field
Dogs growl everywhere
In the kitchen, on the stair
Dogs bite everything
Any table, any toy
Dogs sleep anywhere
Any garden, any mat
Anywhere they don't care
Dogs, run, growl, bite, sleep
Anywhere.

Nick Howell (7)
St Martin's School, Bournemouth

My Bedroom

Purple, gold curtains,
Blue-coloured floor,
Purple, pink wall.

Bunk bed.

Jewellery, book, DVD player,
CD player, video player.

Safe, happy, cosy,
Exciting.

Laura Uffindell (7)
St Martin's Primary School, Dorking

My Bedroom

White curtains
Lovely patterned rug
Furry tigers
Heaps of medals
Football poster
Beanbags everywhere
Army models set up
Theo's coming up the stairs.

Theo Grant (7)
St Martin's Primary School, Dorking

My Bedroom

Dark blue curtains,
Light blue carpet,
One boiling bed,
My messy heaven.

Toys are everywhere,
On my bed,
On the floor,
Why so messy?

Wardrobe so old,
Bookcase so new,
Walls glossy pink,
My own bedroom.

Gemma Nicholson (7)
St Martin's Primary School, Dorking

My Bedroom

Purple coloured curtains
Pink carpet
My bedroom Narnia
Giant unicorn, horse.

My bedroom rainbow
My own world
My own safety
At night
I hug my toys
It makes me warm.

Izzy McCaskill (7)
St Martin's Primary School, Dorking

My Bedroom

Brightly coloured duvet
Fluffy white carpet
Comfy on my bed
Purple walls
Curtains to match.

Lots of teddies
A CD player
So many books
And loads of toys
I love my bedroom!

Millie Wallace (7)
St Martin's Primary School, Dorking

My Bedroom

Crayon sea curtains,
Bright blue carpet,
My bedroom heaven.

I feel as if
I'm in Wonderland,
just like the sea.

Can you feel the
warmth? Come
follow me.

It's always blue
or pink or
green - like sunset.

The waves of my
bed bash against
the walls.

The rainbow blows
me through, to
To touch coral shells.

Have you followed
me through the
magic bedroom rainbow?

Tessa Harding (7)
St Martin's Primary School, Dorking

My Bedroom

My bedroom
Is a wonderland
Lots of toys
I lock my door.

By the time I come in
It feels like my own little home.

Light off,
Stars glow in the dark.

Lovely
It feels like I'm in Narnia
I hide sweets
Under my bed!

Alasdair Rodgers (7)
St Martin's Primary School, Dorking

St Martin's Counting Rhyme

One by one, one by one,
At St Martin's we have fun.
Two by two, two by two,
I saw someone do up their shoe.

Three by three, three by three,
I like playing near the tree.
Four by four, four by four,
We have new carpets on the floor.

Five by five, five by five,
I see people just arrive.
Six by six, six by six,
I see someone lick their lips.

Seven by seven, seven by seven,
I think school is just like Heaven.
Eight by eight, eight by eight,
I think school is great.

Nine by nine, nine by nine,
We all stand straight in the line.
Ten by ten, ten by ten,
I wish school would start again.

Olivia Masters (7)
St Martin's Primary School, Dorking

My Bedroom

In my bedroom
All my things
Are special.
My sticker album
My small giraffe.

I feel safe
When I'm there,
By the stairs.
It's the best!
Oh, the best
Of all the
Places on Earth.

Caitlin O'Carroll (7)
St Martin's Primary School, Dorking

Clouds

The fire-breathing dragon as tall as the mountain.

The pink candyfloss floating in the sky
A white parachute flying in the sky,
It's like a helicopter speeding by,
A piece of cotton passing by.

A ball of snow coming closer,
It's like a mermaid swimming by.

A never-ending line through the sky
A fast tiger sprinting across the valley
Like a white smoke in the sky
A small swordfish darting through the sky.

Megum Muhic (8)
St Michael's Primary School, Bournemouth

Clouds

The white crown of the kingdom floating away
The snowflakes are falling from the sky
They can't reach the ground so they try to fly
The enormous white, soft blanket drifting in the sky
A little picture has formed in the sky
Now that picture has hidden the sun.

Simona Boncheva (8)
St Michael's Primary School, Bournemouth

Clouds

Silky hair flying by
White rabbits
Round and plump
Creamy whirls
Of fluffy ice cream
Cotton wool
White and fluffy
A pillow
Floating in the air
White sheep
Passing by
White coat
Flying up high
White, cold
And shiny ice.

Georgia Vailes (8)
St Michael's Primary School, Bournemouth

Clouds

A soft, white sea spreads over the sky
Soft candyfloss for the sunset to eat
A shape you have never seen before
A long, white, whispy streak,
A big white mouse ready to squeak
A bright blue boat set sail at sea
A large scoop of ice cream
A helicopter flying very high
Lots of snow falling from the sky
A snowy white cat sitting on a cloud.

Sophie Chandler (9)
St Michael's Primary School, Bournemouth

The Pretty White River

The pretty white river on top of the sky
The white flowers are growing rather high
A big, white fluffy feather flying like a plane
A tiny bag of cotton wool
And a big piece of candyfloss
A little, white tiny star lying on a bed of snow
Floating ever so low.

Chloe Hanham (8)
St Michael's Primary School, Bournemouth

Clouds

White marshmallows
Floating in the air
The soft sunset candyfloss
Flying in the sky
The fluffy cotton wool
Floating by
A misty aeroplane
Drifting high
A tiger behind
So don't look back
Layers of soft ice cream
Flying by
A big surprise
So look up high.

Olivia Povey (9)
St Michael's Primary School, Bournemouth

The Clouds

The clouds as soft as a feather,
So curved as a letter . . .

The lovely pictures in the air
While the wind moves side to side . . .

The soft water splashing so very high
A fluffy sheep sailing in the sky . . .

A white dragon blazing fire
And he moves higher and higher.

Smoke coming from the chimney,
So dark like a thunderstorm . . .

A helicopter flying through the air
A plane reaching his wings out wide.

As white as foam going down the river
White as PVA glue moving slower and slower . . .

Jonathan Evans (9)
St Michael's Primary School, Bournemouth

Cloud Poem

A floating pillow swishing in the air.
Flakes of snow flowing in pairs.

The moon shines up as the candles
Say goodbye.

The brightness of the moon
Comes through the clouds
And lights up the sky.

A crowd of people storming
Across the breezy air.

Fluffy marshmallows hanging
Out of nowhere.

Ben Povey (9)
St Michael's Primary School, Bournemouth

Spiky Creature

As hard and spiky as a chestnut shell.
It eats slugs and worms.
It has a button nose.
As prickly as a rose bush.
When under attack rolls up like a football.

Sam Parsons (9)
St Nicolas CE Primary School, Cranleigh

Centaurs

Centaurs, centaurs, never knew the dinosaurs,
Centaurs, centaurs, killing all the minotaurs,
Centaurs, centaurs, getting arrowed now,
Centaurs, centaurs, lying on the ground,
Centaurs, centaurs, going up to Heaven,
Centaurs, centaurs, can now count to seven,
Centaurs, centaurs, standing on the clouds,
Centaurs, centaurs, falling into the crowds,
Centaurs, centaurs, letting out groans,
Centaurs, centaurs, are turned into stone,
Centaurs, centaurs, Aslan's coming,
Centaurs, centaurs, better start running,
Centaurs, centaurs, badly injured,
Centaurs, centaurs, now are ninjas,
Centaurs, centaurs, are centaurs again,
Centaurs, centaurs, are now making friends,
Centaurs!

Daniel de Silva Jones (8)
St Nicolas CE Primary School, Cranleigh

Teddy Bear

Teddy bear, teddy bear, touch your nose
Teddy bear, teddy bear, touch your toes.

Teddy bear, teddy bear, touch your paws
Teddy bear, teddy bear, you've loud roars!

Teddy bear, teddy bear, pull your tail
Teddy bear, teddy bear, hear you wail!

Sebastian Pickworth (8)
St Nicolas CE Primary School, Cranleigh

Sea

As wet as the kitchen sink
As rough as a shark
As fun as football
As salty as a chip
As wavy as a pool
As deep as a tunnel
As long as a boat
As good as a car
As big as a house.

Ben Bates (8)
St Nicolas CE Primary School, Cranleigh

Alice Bettell

Imaginative, short
Long hair
Two sisters
One big
The other
Small
Very friendly
Nice attitude
Cares for others
Green eyes
Dark brown hair
St Nicolas
Lives in Cranleigh
Hates maths
Loves street dancing
Couple of dogs
American bulldog
Cross collie
Jack Russell
Year 5
Nine years old
That is
Alice Bettell.

Alice Bettell (9)
St Nicolas CE Primary School, Cranleigh

Milly Burge

Very sporty
Good-looking
Quite tall
Has brother
Gold hair
Blue eyes
Bad reader
Great friends
Mum, Dad
Nice house
St Nicolas School.

Millie Burge (9)
St Nicolas CE Primary School, Cranleigh

Why Are Parents Soooo Embarrassing?

Why are parents soooo embarrassing?
They drive me absolutely crazy,
When I'm shopping with my mum
She drags me out of the changing rooms
And asks an assistant's opinion.
(I'm 15 for goodness sake!)

Why are parents so embarrassing?
They really aren't cool,
When I see my friends down the road,
She'll run over there and say, 'Hi,
I'm Becca's mum.'
(How embarrassing is that!)

Why are parents soooo embarrassing?
They make me very mad,
Don't like to be mean,
But they're a bit on the big side
And well, at the beach, she wears a bikini.
(It's really not a pleasant sight!)

Why, why, why are parents soooo *embarrassing?*

Rhiannon Thomas (10)
St Nicolas CE Primary School, Cranleigh

Georgia Griffin

Georgia Griffin
Lives in
Shamley Green
Likes school
Watches TV
Reads lots
Cooks mad
Loves cakes
Has friends
Crazy together
Does dancing
PlayStation good
Georgia Griffin.

Georgia Griffin (9)
St Nicolas CE Primary School, Cranleigh

Beach

B linding sea sparkling but the rumble of the motoring skies
E choing sands from the marvellous crab's shell
A ir gliders barely touching the edge of the crystal-blue tide by the rich, golden sand
C lashing waves smashing like dynamite hitting the gold
H iding behind an umbrella from the beaming, blazing sun.

Oliver Whitton Richardson (10)
St Nicolas CE Primary School, Cranleigh

School Dinners

'Hey, there are gloodles in my noodles
Tautages in my sausages
Blice in my rice
Letchup in my ketchup
Snashed blatoe in my mashed potato
Snocklet nake in my chocolate cake
Snustard in my custard
Lizzy nop in my fizzy pop
Oh! that's the dog's dinner!

Nyssa Staniforth (9)
St Nicolas CE Primary School, Cranleigh

Jake Silvester

Blue eyes
Blond hair
Going brown
Very intelligent
Likes maths
Quite small
Brilliant parents
Very popular
Wants a motorbike
Can't drive
One sister
Sometimes loving
Loves chocolate
Cool cat
Name spooky
Age nine
Jake Silvester.

Jake Silvester (9)
St Nicolas CE Primary School, Cranleigh

Dragon Of Hell

Dragon, dragon, as large as mountains
Dragon, dragon, breathing fire
Dragon, dragon, as fast as the wind
Dragon, dragon, its scales as gold as a golden nugget
Dragon, dragon, its jaws as sharp as a sword
Dragon, dragon, its claws as sharp as a dagger
Dragon, dragon, flying over.

Ryuta Ogawa (8)
St Nicolas CE Primary School, Cranleigh

Rosie Payne

Rosie Payne
Blonde hair
Green eyes
Quite tall
Year 5
One brother
And a sister
English parents
Great friends
Pet hamster
Called Galaxy
Fantastic swimmer
OK runner
Loves fashion
Very friendly
Enjoys sport
Hates maths
Adores animals
Amazing family
Fairly fit
I am
Rosie Payne.

Rosie Payne (10)
St Nicolas CE Primary School, Cranleigh

Winter

Snowdrops falling all around
Snowdrops melting on the ground
Winter comes and winter goes
I think my snowman's lost his nose!

Danielle Ferry (11)
St Nicolas CE Primary School, Cranleigh

Rosie Lucas

Rosie Lucas
Blue eyes
Lovely family
Brilliant friends
Brown hair
Quite tall
Bit shy
Very quiet
Little giggly
Likes art
Giggly friends
Good school
Dislikes PE
Curly hair
Loves animals
Age nine
No brothers
Or sisters
Rosie Lucas.

Rosie Lucas (9)
St Nicolas CE Primary School, Cranleigh

Joshua Liddicott

Joshua Liddicott
Enjoys rugby
Brown eyes
Short hair
Quite small
Likes chocolate
One brother
Good parents
Walks to school
Can't drive
Excellent swimmer
Nice cousins
Very bad
Age nine
Joshua Liddicott.

Joshua Liddicott (9)
St Nicolas CE Primary School, Cranleigh

Connor Ferry

Connor Ferry
Really fast
Slow walker
Blue eyes
One sister
And a brother
Very sporty
Brown hair
Extremely bad
Likes football
Enjoys basketball
Hates maths
Two mice
Cute hamster
Quite strong
Mum, Dad
Brilliant friends
A bit lazy
Connor Ferry.

Connor Ferry (9)
St Nicolas CE Primary School, Cranleigh

Adam Brown

Adam Brown
Lazy child
Likes breeze
Flies plane
Into tree
Drives cars
Tampers them
Trips sister
Gets pinched
Tells Mum
Cries tears
Crocodile tears
Tricks Mum
Blames Ellie
Gets away
Trips up,
Her fault,
I win,
Adam Brown.

Adam Brown (9)
St Nicolas CE Primary School, Cranleigh

James Newman

Black hair
Brown eyes
Freckles
Long legs
Quite tall
Thin
Likes rugby
Adores sweets
Does skating
Great parents
James Newman.

James Newman (9)
St Nicolas CE Primary School, Cranleigh

Asya Andreeva

Asya Andreeva
Very sleepy
Gets dressed
Has breakfast
Watches TV
Changes channels
Likes chocolate
Loves cakes
Asya Andreeva.

Asya Andreeva (9)
St Nicolas CE Primary School, Cranleigh

Michaella Sparkes

Michaella Sparkes
In Cranleigh
Likes TV
Big food
Many friends
Likes chocolate
Brown hair
Has rabbit
Good dog
Doesn't snore.

Michaella Sparkes (9)
St Nicolas CE Primary School, Cranleigh

I Wish I Was Free

Every night I long to find my family in the sky.
Soaring, gliding and looking for a way out,
I spend my day trying to fit through bars,
I just wish I were free.
I want to know what the jungle is like.
I don't have any memories of the jungle.
I don't know what my family looks like.
All I can remember is hearing my mum squawking,
And then fading in the mist.
'Help me,' she seemed to say.
'Help me, help me please!'
And me wishing I could do something . . .
But I was only a baby.

Joe McMillan (10)
St Nicolas CE Primary School, Cranleigh

Bardy Kerr

Bardy Kerr
Blonde hair
Blue eyes
Quite tall
One sister
Two brothers
Likes hockey
Dislikes England
Good skater
Hates school
Especially English
Grumpy sometimes
Bardy Kerr.

Bardolph Kerr (9)
St Nicolas CE Primary School, Cranleigh

My Sister

She's caring
She's loving
She's ever so kind
She's always there for me
She's pretty and fine
She's my sister.

Natalie Skates (9)
St Nicolas CE Primary School, Cranleigh

Can You Guess What I Am?

Bigger than a mouse,
But smaller than a house,
Smarter than a bee,
But not as smart as you and me.

Flies like the wind
And never can be heard,
Sleeps in the morning,
But does not in the night.

Can you guess what it is ?
That's right.

Answer: owl.

Helena Victoria Burke (9)
St Nicolas CE Primary School, Cranleigh

Cheetah

Fast, fearless, fascinating
Cheetah
Leaping and climbing across the plain
Peacefully
Powerfully
It moves like the clouds drifting across the sky
Cheetah
Wondrous cheetah.

Sophie Evans (9)
St Nicolas CE Primary School, Cranleigh

Flutter In The Night

Bigger than a bee
But smaller than a house.
Deep sea-green eyes but shiny feet
As square as a dice and as round as a ball
Catches his food, maybe mouse
All year round.

Watches his mouse but mouse runs around
And stares at him all year round
Flutters in the night
Brown feathers flutter
In the night.

Mollie Hearn (8)
St Nicolas CE Primary School, Cranleigh

A Rugby Match

Great game
Tries being scored
Crowd are going wild
Teams are going off for half-time

Chips, yum
Crowd are cheering
Men betting on their team
Team merchandise being sold out

Burgers
Crowd are wild
Commentators talking
The home team have won the match.

Will Brook-Jones (10)
St Nicolas CE Primary School, Cranleigh

Puppy

Lively puppy sitting on the kitchen floor
Noisy puppy barking at the door
Excitable puppy waiting for a walk
Silly puppy found some chalk.

Little puppy six months old
Cute puppy so, so cold
Lovely puppy colour so, so black
Angry person gave her a smack.

Rosie Jones (9)
St Nicolas CE Primary School, Cranleigh

Puppies

Quick
Furry
Jumpy
Puppies
Running
Quickly
Fluffy
Barks louder than a bear
Playful
Puppies
Furry.

Victoria Lanni (8)
St Nicolas CE Primary School, Cranleigh

My Puppy

Hungry puppy just like me
'Come on Mum, where's our tea?'

Tiny puppy waiting for a walk
I'm teaching my puppy to eat with a fork.

She runs so fast in the cold, misty wood
I wish I had brought a coat with a hood.

Tiny puppy gone to sleep
I am too, but I'm counting sheep.

Georgia Lindsay (9)
St Nicolas CE Primary School, Cranleigh

Penguin

Penguin, penguin, on the ice
White and black
And very nice.
In the snow I see you go
A black shiny beak with a white tummy
Black shining eyes in the snow.
I wonder where it's going to go
It's like a dove when it swims
But although it has wings
It cannot fly.

Jessica Sellwood (8)
St Nicolas CE Primary School, Cranleigh

Shark

A shark is as deadly as a razor
They're as big as a boat
Sharks are as heavy as a four-ton truck
They're as fast as a speedboat
As beautiful as a painting.

Thomas Barker (9)
St Nicolas CE Primary School, Cranleigh

Whale

Whales live all over the world
A whale can eat a lot of plankton and krill
It is bigger than a coach
A lot of whales live in the Pacific Ocean.

Patrick Woodward (8)
St Nicolas CE Primary School, Cranleigh

Whale

A whale is like the deep blue sea
It sways through the sea like the calm sea

A whale sparkles like a sapphire
When the moon reflects on the whale

A whale is like a torpedo
Exploding through the sea

A whale dashes through the sea like a submarine
A whale is as sparkling as a diamond.

Jake Howick
St Nicolas CE Primary School, Cranleigh

Beautiful Whale

A whale is beautiful
Like a dove it floats like an angel in the sky
It spins in the air
And in the deep blue sea
It waggles its tail behind him
Its colour is black
And it flips in the water
And laughs.

Vicky Pibworth (9)
St Nicolas CE Primary School, Cranleigh

Falcon

Moves faster than a rocket.
Its talons are sharper than a razor.
Shaped like a plane, high up in the sky.
It sounds like a bullet shot from a gun.

Rifat Chowdhury (9)
St Nicolas CE Primary School, Cranleigh

Snail

Sluggish and slimy is the snail
Nothing is as slow as it
As sad as a baby
It is like a slug but it has a shell
Like a very slow school bus.

Joe Williams (8)
St Nicolas CE Primary School, Cranleigh

Sean Richardson

Sean Richardson
In Cranleigh
Ice skates
Inside rink
Never ponds
Not safe
Always sleeps
Very lazy
Hates girls
Likes dogs
Especially Holly
His dog
Loves her
She licks
Him
On the cheek
The dog
Is cute
Sean Richardson.

Sean Richardson (10)
St Nicolas CE Primary School, Cranleigh

Chickenpox

Spots, spots, spots, I've got the chickenpox,
I start to stare they're everywhere
I've got so many spots!

Red, itchy, bulgy things,
I start to scratch them, then they sting!

My spots are going one by one,
My brother's now got them on his tum!

Spots, spots, spots my brother's got the chickenpox!

Gemma West (10)
St Nicolas CE Primary School, Cranleigh

Love

Love is bright red like strawberries freshly picked from a field.
It tastes like creamy chocolates.
It smells like rich perfume.
It feels like soft silk.
It sounds like pianos playing music.
It looks like flowers in a bow.

Ellen Ambrose (7)
St Nicolas CE Primary School, Cranleigh

Things You Could Find In Obi Wan Kenobi's Pocket

A light sabre in case someone gets in his way
A chicken sandwich in case he's hungry
A bomb if someone is chasing him
Some sleeping tablets if he want to send his enemies to sleep
New boots because his old ones have ripped
A gun to shoot his enemies
A piece of rope to climb high walls
A compass if he is lost
Mini computer to track people down
A CD player if he is bored.

Michael Shevlin (7)
St Nicolas CE Primary School, Cranleigh

Dominic McKenna

Dominic McKenna
In Cranleigh
Loves football
Runs well
Likes dogs
Goes on
Walks with
His aunty
And her dog
Goes to
Winterfold
And walks
The dog
Climbs trees
In there
Likes Galaxy
And beans
Dominic McKenna.

Dominic McKenna (9)
St Nicolas CE Primary School, Cranleigh

Excitement

Excitement is the colour of yellow
It tastes like cold ice cream in your tummy
It smells of a big soft pillow
It looks like a butterfly flying in eights everywhere
It sounds like a person laughing
It feels like a yellow sun.

Polly Jacobs (7)
St Nicolas CE Primary School, Cranleigh

Five Things You Could Find In Mr Willy Wonka's Pocket

A recipe for whipple-scrumptious-fudgemellow-delight
Instructions for flying the great glass elevator
Extra nuts for the nut-case-taking-off-squirrels
A melting chocolate bar which is a whipple-scrumptious-fudge-mellow-delight
A dog-eared, chocolate-splattered photograph of the factory.

Oliver Morris (8)
St Nicolas CE Primary School, Cranleigh

Happiness

Happiness is red like a sword of red-hot hope.
Happiness tastes like hot pork ribs in the oven.
Happiness smells like my cute kitten with eyes like my dreams.
Happiness looks like the sun in the sky with rays so bright.
Happiness sounds like songbirds flying high, while singing a song of joy.
Happiness feels like love in my mind.

Clementine Bridges (8)
St Nicolas CE Primary School, Cranleigh

Lonely At Silverstone Race Course

I can see racing cars speeding round Silverstone race course
I can hear the revs of powerful engines
I can smell the burning rubber of skidding tires
I wish I had someone to share my excitement with.

Christopher Thompson (10)
St Nicolas CE Primary School, Cranleigh

Boredom

Boredom is the colour of grey
It tastes of toast with nothing on top
It smells of a soulless room
It looks like a grey rainy day
It sounds like a person talking about nothing
It feels like a cold, smooth slate

Anna Holcombe (9)
St Nicolas CE Primary School, Cranleigh

Puppies

Puppies are cute and cuddly,
They're a man's best friend,
They come in different types of breeds,
And enjoy their daily feeds.

Sometimes they sneak up onto your bed,
Just so you can stroke their head,
Two puppies are never the same,
They love to play a different game.

Puppies are full of fun and mischief,
They're bouncy and fluffy too,
Everyone would love a puppy,
Including you.

Lisa Holmes (10)
St Nicolas CE Primary School, Cranleigh

If People . . .

If people got much taller
The world would seem much smaller.
If people go more wide
The Earth would tip on its side.
If people turned into cats
There would be no more rats.
If people got really mad
All the animals would be sad.
If people never stood up
Then who would walk the cute pup?
If people stayed as they are now
Then no one would ever have a row.

Alice Morgan (11)
St Nicolas CE Primary School, Cranleigh

Bertie

Bertie twitters all day long,
And sometimes he sings a song.
His favourite food is a seed called Trill,
Other seeds may make him ill.
He flicks feathers from his cage
And when he does Mum's in a rage.

Lauren Madgwick (10)
St Nicolas CE Primary School, Cranleigh

Night-Time

It's dark and cold, it's late at night
The moon is out the stars are bright.
As you listen carefully you will hear
The tu-whit tu-whooing of owls and the snoring of deer.
In the street where the lampposts are on
The choir are practising the church's special song.
The countryside is peaceful with no motorbikes and cars
Where you find some flowers to be put in a vase.
In my bed where it's cosy and soft
I hear the creaking of Dad in the loft.
Sometimes at night the things that I hear
Is the ticking of my clock or the silence I fear.

Joe Coode (11)
St Nicolas CE Primary School, Cranleigh

Rusty The Horse

My favourite horse is Rusty
I see him every day
His favourite food is Polo Mints
And lots and lots of hay.

We normally go riding
At the weekends
I never can find him
Because he is hiding.

His stable is next to Poppy
She knocks about and plays
She always nicks my toffee
And jumps around in silly ways.

Natasha Haycraft (11)
St Nicolas CE Primary School, Cranleigh

In The Bath

In the bath I can see a fin,
I can hear quiet slices and swishes,
I can feel a sharp tooth in my leg
I wish my mum had never bought me a pet shark.

Ben Williams (11)
St Nicolas CE Primary School, Cranleigh

Funny Dreams

When I went to bed one night
Everything went black and white.
It must have been a weird dream
'Cause I was seeing whippy cream.
Then my hand started moving,
I was doing disco grooving.
Along came a big baboon and
Said to me, 'I'll see you soon.'
I closed my eyes to think it through
To find myself in a witch's brew.
Then I began to understand
How important it was to live on land.
For under my feet was nothing but air
This was really, really rare.
And before I knew it I was back
In my room, *just like that!*

Slavi Sarbeva (11)
St Nicolas CE Primary School, Cranleigh

Happiness

It's yellow like the shining sun.
It feels like someone hugging you.
It smells lovely like bright red roses.
It sounds like a busy bee humming away.
It tastes like a crunchy red apple.
It looks like a cat by the fire.

Jack Moseley (9)
St Nicolas CE Primary School, Cranleigh

Monkey

Cheeky
Cute
Jumping from tree to tree
So fast
Small
Quickly
Smaller than a gorilla.

Reece Placzek (8)
St Nicolas CE Primary School, Cranleigh

Who Am I?

I'm in the largest tank in the world,
I have a twin on land,
I swim ever so fast,
But I could bite your hand,
I move through the water smoothly.
Who am I?

Sophie Watkins (9)
St Nicolas CE Primary School, Cranleigh

Happiness

Happiness is blue like the salty sea.
It tastes like melting ice cream.
It smells like newly cut grass.
It feels like fluffy white clouds.
It sounds like happy laughter.
It looks like a newborn kitten.

Jo Holmes (8)
St Nicolas CE Primary School, Cranleigh

Whale

A whale is as beautiful as the blue sea
A whale is as enormous as an elephant
Bigger than a classroom.

A whale is larger than a lion
A whale is as fascinating as an artist's painting
A whale is as long as a limo.

Kieran Hargreaves (8)
St Nicolas CE Primary School, Cranleigh

Elephant

Elephant, elephant oh so big,
His huge feet stomp across the sand
Ears as flat as pancakes,
A nose as long as a sausage.

Lara Carey (8)
St Nicolas CE Primary School, Cranleigh

Shark

Hunts fish, moves fast.
The shark might hunt other sharks.
They don't need to come up for air.

Oliver Parrington (9)
St Nicolas CE Primary School, Cranleigh

Untitled

A heavy, ancient, string-covered, brown vase with no water in it.
As rough as the bark of a tree.
Friendless, lonely, no water inside.
An eyeless, rough, one-eared, noseless bear with a rough face.
As old as time going along the world.

Haqeeb Khan (11)
Sythwood Primary School, Woking

My Poem

A cosy, cute, soft, bald bear with only one ear.
As soft as a knitted blanket.
He feels happy as he is loved.
A patterned, bumpy, rough, dusty pot with a lovely woven pattern.
As bumpy as a camel's hump
And shy whenever someone looks at it.

Emily Anderson (11)
Sythwood Primary School, Woking

Objects

A thatched, cramped, shiny, rough vase
With patterns on the outside.
As elegant as a swan.
Feels aggravated at people feeling him.
A mouldy, manky, dirty, scruffy boot
With laces long and lean.
As well used as a pen
Feels excited about meeting human children.

Alex Emmerson (10)
Sythwood Primary School, Woking

My Teddy Bear And Pot

A cuddly, soft, old, scruffy bear with one ear on his head.
As cute as a baby.
This bear is feeling very happy that he's been looked after.

A woven, soft, beautiful, elegant vase.
It's woven and wavy.
As wonderful as a swan.
The vase is very sad, it's left on its own.

Kimberley Barnes (11)
Sythwood Primary School, Woking

Teddy Bear

A well loved soft, cuddly old teddy bear with stuffing poking out of the toe.
As cute as a newborn puppy,
Feels poorly and sore.
A muddy, dirty, hard, battered walking boot with a leather tongue.
As rough as stormy seas, feels grumpy as it stomps through mud.

Jane Salmon (11)
Sythwood Primary School, Woking

Untitled

A fluffy, old, one-eared scruffy bear with no eyes.
As battered as a rusty crashed car, heartbroken, not played with.
An old, muddy, useful, rough boot, well-used.
As scruffy as an old newspaper, sad, it's muddy.

Jamie Rowan (10)
Sythwood Primary School, Woking

Ancient Pot

The pot is ancient, chipped, dull grey.
Standing up by its ancient chipped base.
As aged as an ancient temple.
It feels like it's going to be shattered.

Jack Dunphy (11)
Sythwood Primary School, Woking

The Shattered Boot

Foul, mucky, vulnerable, weak,
Still holding onto its laces.
As dull as the brown bark from a willow tree.
Prehistoric as the dinosaurs, worthless, lifeless and is gone, thrown away.

Chloe Poore (11)
Sythwood Primary School, Woking

Ted

A delicate, abandoned, townie bear
With a sad, heartbroken face.
As brown as a cupboard that he looks at all day.
He is melancholy and tearful because he wasn't looked after.

Kirsty Jones (10)
Sythwood Primary School, Woking

Teddy Bear, Teddy Bear

A comfortable, new, attached, peaceful bear
With its soft, old, furry jumper.
As flexible as an elastic band pulling and pulling.
It feels unhappy and all alone with its old yellow jumper.

Hina Khan (11)
Sythwood Primary School, Woking

The Used Boot

It's an ancient, grubby, shabby weak boot
Tangled in its manky laces.
As rusty as the oldest object ever made.
It feels lifeless and used as it gets thrown away.

Tauheed Raza (11)
Sythwood Primary School, Woking

The Teddy

A saggy, old, rough, ugly bear.
A prehistoric Brittany Ferry yellow jumper.
As jagged as a mountain.
A lonely, lonesome bear.

Sunmbal Mazar (10)
Sythwood Primary School, Woking

Boot

An old, dilapidated, muddy, saggy boot,
Bravely being kept together by a single lace.
As worn out as a tyre on a bike.
Depressed, decrepit raggy boot.

Ellie O'Sullivan (11)
Sythwood Primary School, Woking

Musical ABC

Accordions being played in the street
Bugles being blown through
Cymbals crashing together
Drums beaten loudly
Enormous instruments being played
French horns loud and clear
Gorgeous sounds all around
Harmonicas making strange sounds
Imps dancing to the music
Join in and have fun
Keyboards keeping the rhythm going
Leaping all around
Music ringing in your ears
Noisy instruments making lots of sounds
Oboes occasionally sounding
Peaceful and then loud
Quavers, crotchets and semibreves
Rustling leaves in the background
Singers singing joyfully
Tambourines shaking and rattling
Unexpected sounds
Violins suddenly make a noise
Wind blowing more noise
Xylophones being hit softly
Young people going to sleep
Zzzzzzz.

Miranda Payne (8)
The Kings Primary School, Southampton

ABC Poem

Ants are moving about
Bugs are going to their homes
Crunching caterpillars eating leaves
Diving ducks swimming away
Evil elephants stamping their feet
Flying flamingos standing about
Goats eating green grass
Hopping horses jumping about
Igloos in my fridge
Jets are flying away
Koalas climbing up trees
Lemmings scattering around
Monkeys jumping on trees
Nuts that are yummy
Octopuses long arms
Parrots talking to my dad
Queen ants laying eggs
Rabbits eating carrots
Snakes sliding through the grass
Tigers trying to pounce
Ugly grubs sliding through the mud
Very fast cheetahs running
Wriggly worms sliding
X-ray of animals
Yetis are big and white
Zebras zipping up things.

Mike Toomer (8)
The Kings Primary School, Southampton

The Sea

What is blue?
What is gentle?
The sea
What is rough?
What is heartless?
The sea.
What rises up
Then comes crashing down?
The sea
The sea
The sea.

Keziah Collett (8)
The Kings Primary School, Southampton

The ABC Poem

Antidioxide gas spreading all around.
Beyond the stars and space.
Carbon dioxide went smash.
Deadly smoke fills the lab.
Electricity kills us.
Fire kills you and me.
Galaxies from far away.
Hint, do not touch acid.
Ingredients makes green acid.
Jellyfish poison kills you.
Kaleidoscope spins your eyes.
Microscope to see small bugs.
Nitro from exhaust pipes.
Oil causes explosions.
Power plants over the world.
Quicksand swallows trees.
Radar communications.
Solar panels on motorways.
Technology is great.
UFOs are getting discovered.
Vapour drips from the ceiling.
Waterfalls are dangerous.
X-Rays are scientific.
Yeast makes bread rise.
Zoology, the study of animals.

Angus Hartnett (8)
The Kings Primary School, Southampton

The Wonderful Poetry Of Art

Art begins lesson starts
Brushes swift like a cart
Colours brighten, come to life
Dogs have been painted and so have knives
Elephants stand on the children's paper
Floats are painted in the beautiful lake
Goats are standing on the countryside
Hummingbirds fly in the clear blue sky
Ink on pens has all run out
Jake wets his brush right near the spout
Kind children paint each other well
Lunches have been painted then children then tell
Monsters have been painted from the boys
Noise has been made while I've been painting wing toys
Octopus sway as the brush moves around
Popcorn for cinemas, the noise has a sound
Queens and kings have been painted for bridges
Roman soldiers have been fighting on edges
Statues are still, brushes don't move
The dog brushes the picture has a groove
Underwater animals are going to bed
Violets and colours the colour spread
Wet paintbrushes are now being dried
X-Rays from fishes are on the paper laid
Yachts and boats both have fish in
Zebras and animals the fish's fin.

Priyanka Arora (8)
The Kings Primary School, Southampton

Autumn

Autumn is here the wind is blowing.
Birds are vanishing from the sky.
Clouds are waving in the air.
Dogs are barking in the park.
Excited children can't wait till Christmas.
Flowers are gone and leaves are falling.
Girls and boys are bored.
Hedgehogs are hibernating in the leaves.
Inside people are shouting loudly.
Jelly sitting on the side.
Kittens miaowing loudly at the door.
Leaves cracking under people's feet.
Mice running across the floor.
Nests abandoned by the birds.
Orange leaves are falling from trees.
People buying Christmas presents.
Quails flying away.
Rustling leaves are everywhere.
Squirrels are collecting acorns.
Trees are blowing in the wind.
Uncles and aunts are coming to stay.
Villages are decorating houses.
Wild winds are blowing.
Xmas is coming, everyone's excited.
Yellow leaves are getting trampled on.
Zebras shivering in the zoos.

Rebekah Robinson (9)
The Kings Primary School, Southampton

Food And Drink

Apples being eaten by hungry children
Bacon being fried for breakfast
Chocolate being melted into a hot drink
Drinking adults are thirsty
Eggs for the frying pan
Fruit is being paid for at the shops
Grapes purple and green in separate bags
Honey going in the kids' sandwiches
Ice lollies are melting in the sun
Jelly with ice cream at the party
KitKats are being put in lunch boxes
Lemons are being squeezed into puddings
Meat in the oven cooking for the roast
Noodles getting twirled around the fork
Orange juice getting poured for breakfast
Pineapple pizza is eaten for dinner
Quality raspberries are being picked from the bushes
Rice pudding is ready to be bought in the shops
Strawberry smoothie being made
Toast being buttered to eat soon
Upmarket food is being sold
Vegetables ready to eat for lunch
Water is being poured into the glass
Xmas food is here for lunch
Yoghurt is being bought
Zebras being eaten by lions.

Jessica Hughes (9)
The Kings Primary School, Southampton

Jim

There once was a boy called Jim,
Whose mother thought he was terribly slim.
He tried getting fat,
By eating his cat.
But instead his cat ate him!

Josiah Lyon (8)
The Kings Primary School, Southampton

The Swop-Smop

In da forest of good
A swop-smop stood
A swop-smop
With colours a lot
And always stole some pud.

A tiger stood
In da forest of good
Her name was Kim
She lost her ring
And the swop-smop took it for good.

He gave it colours
And to his mother
For all of his days
Were sadness and dismay
And his colour was given to his brother.

Thomas Ellis (9)
The Kings Primary School, Southampton

Ben The Tiger

There was a tiger called Ben
Who was caught chasing a hen
He tried to jump over the chair
Rolling head over hills in his lair
And then he got chased by ten men.

Toby Blake (8)
The Kings Primary School, Southampton

Arbeit Macht Frei

Going to a better place,
A place where our lives would be fruitful, alluring.
A place where we would live in tranquillity,
Deep in my heart I felt fear, rock solid fear.

We were packed onto cattle wagons and sent to work.
I saw a boy nearly dying of fear, separated from his family.
I clinched my father's arm with all my might.
We walked through a gate headed, Arbeit Macht Frei
A promise I knew was false.

Louie Mackee (11)
The Queens CE Primary School, Richmond

Child In The Ghetto

I can hear people shouting, screaming,
I'm getting pushed on the train now.
I am filled with fear,
I don't know where I'm going.

I can see children on their own,
No mother or father, no sister or brother.
I am filled with fear,
I don't know where I'm going.

The Star of David is sewn tightly around my arm,
I may lose my life because of it.
I am filled with fear,
I don't know where I'm going.

Daisy Bairamian (10)
The Queens CE Primary School, Richmond

Fear

You cannot run away from fear,
Fear comes and finds you.
You cannot hide from fear,
If it's there, it's there.

Fear is a peculiar feeling,
You cannot explain it.
Sometimes you keep fear to yourself
But sometimes you share it.

Lucy Jackson (11)
The Queens CE Primary School, Richmond

Fear

I see everyone's faces
Afraid and scared
Hoping they're not picked.
Some carry on, some get shot,
Fear comes faster and faster
Nazis feeling anger.
More people getting upset
Hope my father is still alive
I hope it's over by Christmas.
The ghetto is darkness not light
My last few words are
Don't have fear!

Miles Copland (11)
The Queens CE Primary School, Richmond

Being Evacuated

I'm getting on the train to be evacuated,
My mum is waving to me and weeping.
I know that I will not be with my mum,
It's just making the experience more frightening
Will my mum be safe without me, will she get bombed?

I'm trembling with fear because I'm going to live somewhere
That I don't know about!
I'm not going to have my mother near me.
She was always there to answer my questions or go to for help.

I'm going to be living with someone I don't know.
This whole experience is making me terrified.
I can feel a tear drip down my cheek.
There is now a soaked patch on the seat because I have been weeping so much.

Joseph Konstam (10)
The Queens CE Primary School, Richmond

A Child In The Ghetto

Hungry, I trudge through mud and filth
Surrounded by Germans who are armed
With guns and beating sticks,
Ready to fight and hurt.
Surrounded by people speaking different languages,
As I stand alone.
Mother, father, brothers, sisters gone to a new world,
With me here alone.
Tired, weak and hungry,
Standing in the mud and filth.
I want to fly over the barbed wire like a bird.
Away from fear.

Rosie Thomas (11)
The Queens CE Primary School, Richmond

Fear

I know fear,
The fear in the faces,
The yell of the dying,
The cold look of the Nazis,
The scream of my parents,
You have never known this fear
Or, do you know fear?

Sam Crane (10)
The Queens CE Primary School, Richmond

Death In The Ghetto

In a ghetto the chances of living seem like a million to one.
The ghetto can tear your soul in two.
The ghetto is no place of love and joy.
In the ghetto, love never exists.
In the ghetto sadness is always in action.
The ghetto is death and fear but worse than you expected.
Happiness is always exterminated in the ghetto.
The ghetto is not a place of love and joy but death and sorrow.
Death is fear but this fear is worse than you ever expected.
You can never feel safe in the ghetto.
When you are picked out of the crowd, you know you have seconds to live.
A ghetto is a dark place.
A ghetto can rip your family in half.
You will never hear a bird.
In a ghetto there is only the sound of people dying.
The ghetto will fill your heart with darkness not light.
In the ghetto there is no food, there is no water.
There is always hunger in the ghetto.

Matthew Carney (10)
The Queens CE Primary School, Richmond

Fear Of The Ghetto

Around me I see mothers and children crying,
Knowing they are going to be separated.
Every minute the sound of a shotgun, then a deadly cry.
Children clinging onto their mothers, dying of thirst and hunger.
I look to my left and see the Star of David, wondering if He is letting us down.
I see people getting whipped, crying in pain.
I look down and pray.

Emma Crampton (10)
The Queens CE Primary School, Richmond

Child In The Ghetto

People facing the wall,
Hands above their heads
Silently waiting.
I run, my feet aching and cut.
An officer blocks the pavement
And I sprint into the road.
Into the city, men chasing me.
I stand still, guns pointing at me.
The crack of a single gunshot
Then silence.

Joseff Morgan (11)
The Queens CE Primary School, Richmond

Evacuated

Bang! Down goes the door,
I am being taken away,
To be safer from War,
Bags are grabbed and parents scream for me,
I was dragged out,
To be evacuated,
To be gone and safe.

The station was crowded with children in despair,
There is no going back,
The train had one space left, for me only.
Mother and Father were pushed back,
Way back into the distance,
Until they were nowhere to be seen.
This is the most frightened I have ever been.
My stomach tightened,
My power was drained,
My movements were useless.
The train started to move.
A picture spun through the window,
A picture of my parents and I on the beach.
Glistening tears fell onto the picture,
I was out of the station,
What will happen?
Who am I going to live with?
When will it be normal with no war and happy faces?

Oliver Taylor (10)
The Queens CE Primary School, Richmond

Fear In The Ghetto

No food, no family, why must it be this way?
My family has gone away, why am I left by myself with no food or shelter?
The German guards show no compassion,
Their eyes show hate and contempt,
They slap me and push me over and spit on me,
They call me horrible names.
Will I ever be free or will this be my place of death?
Will I die unloved, scared and lonely?
I am so scared, so scared of the guards.
I am so scared, so scared for my family.
But I am petrified, so petrified for me.
Will I ever be free or will this be my place of death?
Oh will I ever be free or will I die unloved,
Scared, scared and lonely.

Luke Hammett (11)
The Queens CE Primary School, Richmond

The Escape

I knew where we were going,
I glanced at my parents and looked at my bear.
I didn't want to die,
I needed to escape.

Looking at the escape I did it.
I ran in a frenzy,
People began joining in.

One bullet hit my teddy bear,
I knew they were gaining on me.
I reached the end with my mother
I did not see my father.

I slipped under the wire, gradually reaching the end, with only a few scratches.
I lingered with my teddy to find Mother.
Stuck in the wire she was dragged away.
Giant drops of tears clung to my eyes,
I walked away.
I thought I would find freedom,
I didn't.

Armen Bodossian (11)
The Queens CE Primary School, Richmond

Child In A Ghetto

One way in
No way out.
Three sides wired
All sides armed.

One way in
No way out.
Mothers gone away
Don't know where.

One way in
No way out.
Father's gone away
I'm breaking out.

One way in
Some way out.
Run for my life
Now the time has come.

One way in
No way out.
I've been found
One way out.

Matthew Judge (10)
The Queens CE Primary School, Richmond

Ghetto

A gust of wind and icy, cold weather
Blew the air, silencing us all.
Only the haunting murmurs of frightened children could be heard,
Parents wept and prayed, including mine.

Babies cried, I held my ears,
I couldn't bear the noise.
The guards eyed us up if we even moved at all.
The result was a slap of the face and a curse.
Desperate screams were heard from new arrivals when they entered the ghetto,
Crowding, reaching out towards loved ones, torn away from their grasp.
I was confused and terribly frightened,
Where were we?
I couldn't think, my mind was blank.
I was too afraid, I closed my eyes.
My hands were frozen and painfully bruised,
Tears from my eyes dropped to the ground,
I wanted to escape; I wanted to shout for help,
But I was in a ghetto and there was no way out.

Chloe Narey (10)
The Queens CE Primary School, Richmond

Child In The Ghetto

Heads down, bodies cramped,
Trudging along the dusty road to Umschlangplatz for the selection.
Weeping mothers, confused and bewildered children
With the Star of David attached to a banded arm.
All of us, together as one.
Elderly to the left,
Men to the right,
Women and children to the left,
Young workers to the right.
Fear of being left alone is excruciating.
First my father, then my mother, lastly my sister.
I was left alone.
Pushed viciously onto a train,
Shaking with fear and anger,
Hot with perspiration.
Melancholy, choking, smothering,
Uncontrollable fear increasing.
We all were the fooled victims of that old lie,
Arbeit Macht Frei.

Ophelia Pressley (10)
The Queens CE Primary School, Richmond

Child In The Ghetto

There's a child in the ghetto,
He's about to die.
There's a child in the ghetto,
He's about to cry.

There's a child in the ghetto,
He can't see his dad.
There's a child in the ghetto,
His face shows he's very sad.

There's a child in the ghetto,
He's starving for a bun.
There's a child in the ghetto,
He's desperate to run.

There's a child in the ghetto,
His life is coming to an end.
There's a child in the ghetto,
He doesn't have a friend.

There's a child in the ghetto,
He has to work.
There's a child in the ghetto,
He's going berserk.

There's a child in the ghetto,
He's crying with fear.
There's a child in the ghetto,
You can see it with every tear.

Areya Konjkav-Dana (11)
The Queens CE Primary School, Richmond

Child In The Ghetto

A new fear hangs low
I started crying, haven't stopped.
I hardly notice my own tears now.

Separation feared the worst,
I survived, I survived
Wish I hadn't.

The emotion that cannot be conquered,
The pain that never ceases to exist.
Fear, I remember.

Gala Wesson (11)
The Queens CE Primary School, Richmond

The Girl In The Ghetto

I wear my Star of David with pride,
Even though my body is covered in bruises,
To show where I have been beaten.
But it is twelve o'clock I fear,
For I will leave my home, my friends,
My pride and possessions for Umschlangplatz
Where they decide my life.
If I shall live or die.
I am a Jude and I believe in that too,
But the Nazis think differently.
We walk in the gutters,
Or we're pushed out of the way and drown in our tears.
With my father gone
And my mother too
As an only child
I believe I am next, don't you?
I heard my mother cry last night,
As I went to bed she said,
'We were doomed and this is the end,
For all hope has vanished into the fire
With my father too.'

Florence Sandford-Richardson (11)
The Queens CE Primary School, Richmond

Surviving In The Ghetto

The sound of death echoes in the streets,
I cannot hear it.
The Star of David blazes on my arm,
Singling me out, leaving me by myself,
I will survive.

The smell of decaying bodies fills the gutter,
I will not inhale it.
My mother's death is enough for me,
I must never give in to this endless battle,
I will survive.

The sight of deceased Jews litter the ghetto,
I must not look.
A dark blanket now covers the world,
Leaving me cold and fearful,
But I will survive.

Polly Mackintosh (10)
The Queens CE Primary School, Richmond

Fear From The Ghetto

I have no food, I have no food
In this ghetto no one is happy
So many come every day
So many die every day.

The Nazis are so cruel
They torture us, kill us
Then more come the next day
The guards show no mercy.

I had my family with me
But they have been taken away
This was happening to everyone
We were on our own.

Now it is my turn to go
I wanted to go to a good place
But I knew we were not
We were going to die
I was full of fear.

Alexander Tippett (10)
The Queens CE Primary School, Richmond

In A Ghetto

I've been pushed suddenly in a ghetto
I have been separated from my family and friends,
The icy wind is blowing in my face
As guards look at me with hate in their eyes.

The Star of David labels me
But that does not suppress me, but makes me proud.
I know I am not really alone in this dreadful place,
Although I can't turn off the dread and fear.

I hear children screaming in fear
Looking to their parents for help,
But they just stare back with helpless eyes
They are powerless.

Coughing and choking from adults and children
People dying from different diseases,
I hope I'm not one of them.

Lina Tsontzos (10)
The Queens CE Primary School, Richmond

Fear

In the ghetto
I saw people lying on the floor drowning in their sorrow
Nazis were killing the Star of David
Jews losing the will to live.

In Umschlangplatz
It seemed every second was lasting an hour
All you heard was the noise of death.
We waited anxiously to know our fate as the guards read out,
With no compassion, the names of the death camps where our journey would end.

At Auschwitz, others and I prayed not to be the next victim.
We watched the smoke of death rising from beyond our view,
All our hopes and dreams lost.

Freya McGrath (10)
The Queens CE Primary School, Richmond

My Fears

I fear,
I fear a loved relative dying,
I see myself crying,
I will never be able to see them again,
I see their faces as a distant memory,
I feel so sorrowful still.

I fear having to be sent away from my family,
I will miss them every day,
What if I never see them again?
I fear getting lost somewhere I don't know,
What will I do? Where will I go?
I fear.

Dominic Simpson Vanner (11)
The Queens CE Primary School, Richmond

Hospital

How could this happen?
One minute he's fine, now he's here in this, this terrible place.
Just sitting on the hospital bed, with him not moving.
Not knowing whether he's going to be alright.
Listening to the soft beating of the machines.
Wondering if they might suddenly *stop!*
Bang! There it goes, certainty, routine, security, so quickly, so sudden.
What will happen?
I don't know, all I can do is wait, wait and hope.

Claudia Quayle (10)
The Queens CE Primary School, Richmond

Evacuee

I have to be sent away to someone,
I fear that something bad may happen,
I'm away from my parents
I know that my dad may be dead in the war.

I've been sent to an old man,
He's grumpy and mean.
Fortunately they say the war will be over by Christmas.

I'm having a tough life with the man,
He doesn't like me much.
I wish the war was over and the world declared peace.

I fear my parents are dead,
I fear the war may be on forever.

I fear that my dad has been killed,
So it would only be me and Mum.

James Whittaker (11)
The Queens CE Primary School, Richmond

Fear The Ghetto

When I entered I knew my life was over.
The walls were big, dark, grey things with barbed wire on them.
Split from your mum and dad is like being cut in half.
At night all I can hear is the screaming of others being tortured in a violent way.
We all have to sleep in small beds full of dust.
I cannot bring myself to walk the streets of disease and decay.
My own thought is that the black gate is the black gate of Death.
I feared the ghetto but now I fear the concentration camp.
My life is over but others can still live.

Thomas Jones (10)
The Queens CE Primary School, Richmond

My Fears

My fears are sad, ghostly and always bad.
I have fears of people dying.
Mum and Dad are always sad.
I have a fear of blood.
If my mum and dad die I will not stop crying.
One fear of mine is people screaming down the road.
I don't know where I am but I know I am in the middle.
I am still screaming and sad.
But I will get all of this out of my mind.

Kunal Patel (10)
The Queens CE Primary School, Richmond

Evacuee

I'm leaving my mother,
I'm fleeing away.
She's in grave danger
But I'm far away.

My father may be dead,
I dearly hope he's not.
He's freezing, starving
But I'm far away.

It'll be over by Christmas
That's what they say,
It's now late April
And I'm far away.

I don't like my guardian
He doesn't like me,
My mother's not met him
But she's far away.

I've not heard from Mother
I fear the worst.
I'm miles from anywhere
I'm an evacuee.

Ben Lewis-Clare (10)
The Queens CE Primary School, Richmond

Time

Time whizzes fast,
Time slows down,
Time will run out one day.

Time is there,
Time is everywhere,
Time we cannot see,
Time will run out one day.

We have no choice about time,
Time is free,
Time will run out one day.

Time is near, time is far,
Time is lurking around corners,
Time will run out one day.

Will we ever exit this place?
Time knows,
Time knows everything,
Time will run out one day.

Pippa Wallace (10)
The Queens CE Primary School, Richmond

Child In A Death Camp

They're going to set me free,
Away from this terrible enclosed space
Or so I thought.

We arrive at the Umschlagplatz
Finally our liberty back
Or so I thought.

Onto the train
The journey to freedom
Or so I thought.

We arrive at Auschwitz
Our belongings taken away
I thought we'd be happy here.

I am sent away from my family
Off to the gas chambers
The cursed Germans killing us.

I will not breathe, I cannot breathe,
I must not breathe, *bang!*
The door is blown to smithereens!

We flee like cowards to the Russians that stand outside
The war is over, the Germans are defeated.

Rusheb Shah (10)
The Queens CE Primary School, Richmond

Child In The Camp

Hitting and beating I can see,
Being lead into the crammed train,
The heavy steam rising above clouds,
Wheels screeching as the train moves,
People screaming, children crying,
Auschwitz awaits me and my family.
Slapping and whipping that is here,
Being led through gates with the title, *Arbeit Macht Frei.*
This is Auschwitz, the Holocaust.
Crammed into one man bunkers by the twenty,
I am separated from my brother and father.

Nazi man winding me,
My mother is half dead and so am I,
I can see a building, it smells of gas,
This is it, my destiny, my death,
My teeth trembling towards torture,
Just me and my mother, I can't breathe.

Charles Fisher (11)
The Queens CE Primary School, Richmond

Fear Of The Evacuation

Looking into my mum's eyes, blue, twinkling in the sun,
Glistening tears running down our cheeks with laughter,
Staring at my dad's open arms,
Running to jump in them,
Laughing with Mum and Dad, playing games over tea.
Now it's all gone.
I'm here straining with all my might, pulling carts down through bumpy roads,
Rummaging through old dirty bins
With blood dripping down my knees into my new socks that Mum and Dad gave me.
Wondering if I will ever see them again.

Charlotte Jenkins (11)
The Queens CE Primary School, Richmond

Fear Poem

Will he live?
Will he live?
Trying to keep my sister calm is harder than I thought.
Toys lying around us in the hospital waiting room, but we don't care.
All we want to know is whether he has survived.
Time is ticking and still no news.
When we last saw him, he had tubes and wires all over him and
An oxygen mask covering his face.
We looked up hopefully as Mum entered the room,
Tears were trickling down her face,
'Your uncle is dead girls . . . I'm sorry.'

Nicola Lennard (11)
The Queens CE Primary School, Richmond

Some Fears Of Mine

I have fears all around,
Up and down but sometimes up and sometimes down,
Some fears are noises in the front room,
In the kitchen, in my bedroom.

I fear people screaming and shouting down the road,
Spiders crawling up the wall,
Someone crying but that is a different story in all.

With all of these fears I feel different
One day I want them gone.
I would rather be happy than have fears all night long.

Sophie Lamb (10)
The Queens CE Primary School, Richmond

Child In The Ghetto

People died around me, one by one.
I was wondering when it would be my turn.
I was pushed to one side,
My mother and father to the other.
A soldier pulled out his gun, he made me watch
When he shot my parents in the head.
They fell to the ground like flies.
I knew it was my turn soon,
I ran for freedom,
The fear was indescribable,
It was too late, I fell to the ground, I was gone.

Oliver Weeks (11)
The Queens CE Primary School, Richmond

Child In The Ghetto

I wander up to the gates,
All I see is fear,
All I hear is fear
And all I fear is death.

Young and old clutter round the trains.
Screaming and crying is all I hear,
Beating and shooting is all I see.

The Star of David,
My proud possession.
I will keep it safe
On my way through life.
Hope is not yet over
Many still believe in freedom.

Joshua Denington (10)
The Queens CE Primary School, Richmond

A Child In Treblinka

Tired, hungry, working endlessly,
The screams of my dead parents still haunt me,
Every day I wonder if it will be my last,
I had some hope but now it has been thwarted.
Now it is over,
My name is called,
It is the end.

Marc Oppenheimer (11)
The Queens CE Primary School, Richmond

The Armenian Genocide

In 1915, innocent Armenians were pointlessly massacred,
The Turks made guiltless, just unlucky Armenians rapidly fall to the ground.
Poor little children were marched into the desert, many of them died.
Men were made to do hard labour,
Their fate unclear, indescribable, they were not saved.
Women were sent straight to the death.
They were also sent into the desert.
What angers me the most is that now,
While the Germans have apologised a million times for what they did,
We are still waiting for an apology.
And another thing that is sheer agony for us,
No one here recognises the Armenian genocide, no one knows where Armenia even is!
But I am only glad that now, while we were weak in 1915, almost ninety-one years later
We are still standing, *stronger than ever!*

Maral Bodossian (11)
The Queens CE Primary School, Richmond

Child In The Ghetto

Death surrounds me,
I am alone in the middle of it,
My star is red, soaked in blood,
Bodies lie everywhere, the sign of a ghetto.

It won't go away, I'm not scared - I'm fearful.
Fear of death, of being alone,
Of them, the creators of the fear.

No one here left, they left on the train,
The huge, dark, stinking train,
More people coming in, fearful too.

They're coming to get me,
To make the horrible fear go away.
Everything's going black, sounds are distant . . .
It is over.

Robbie Wood (10)
The Queens CE Primary School, Richmond

Death Camp

Blood fills the place from people beaten,
I stand watching them dying and vomiting
People being shoved and hit.
The fear on people's faces
Like standing face to face with a tiger,
I wonder if I will live.

Jordan Pamment-Gayle (11)
The Queens CE Primary School, Richmond

The Dangerous Drive

(Story: On safari in Botswana our guide had two hours sleep the night before. That day he had no food (breakfast or lunch). It is about how he drove for the five hours journey)

No sleep, no food from which our guide had none.
Speeding down the motorway like an old timid man.
Sober all round, falling asleep at the wheel.
All the passengers shaking like rattles, terrified.
Slipping and sliding all along and off the grass.
Shivering as we screeched onto the horrible bumpy motorway.
Crashing through the invisible wall in front of us.
Closer and closer, rattling into trees every time.
At last, after five hours torture, we are relieved, we arrive at our destination.

Sam Rowley (11)
The Queens CE Primary School, Richmond

Ghetto

Some people thought
We would get better lives,
But no.

The star we had to wear
People wanted to rip it off,
But no.

The fear of being left alone,
People wanted to run,
But no.

Everyone knew now
They would die,
But yes.

Brittany Borkan (10)
The Queens CE Primary School, Richmond

Deportee

Herded in our excited masses,
Each family together, walking car chassis,
Ahead a Jew crashes to the ground,
Round him German hired Jews circling round and round.
What! And now they're dragging him away,
Hope fading, maybe he had seen a better day?
No! No! No! Father's going with them.

'No, Mother where did Father go?'
This train is too packed!
The train stops, open doors,
I look out . . . to see the truth.

Joe Morris-Bray (11)
The Queens CE Primary School, Richmond

Fear The Evacuation

When I go what will I do?
I will have to start a new school and have new friends.
Go somewhere new.
Will they hit me or kill me?
Will they adopt me?
They might not like me.

Will I have to work?
They're going to see my cut.
What are they going to say about that?
Will they still take me or hate me?

I really do not want to pass out.
Will I like the supper?
I can't swallow food or drink.
I think I will be fine.
Will my family be thinking of me?
I hope I will be happy where I am sent to.

Sian Redman (11)
The Queens CE Primary School, Richmond

Fear Of The Evacuation

I was saying goodbye to my mother,
I heard a bang, the sound of a gunshot,
Then the short but sharp scream.

I looked over to the place where my mother stood,
I saw nothing but a crowd of people.

I rushed over to them but was dragged back by someone,
I turned to face them and to my disgust found a soldier pulling me back
Then throwing me onto the train.
The train started to move,
It was then that I realised the bang and scream was my mother.
I tried to hide the fear on my face
But really I was scared.
Where was I going to go and what was going to happen to me?

Gemma Hanvey (10)
The Queens CE Primary School, Richmond

Evacuation

Crouching down in the corner,
Of the gloomy village town hall,
A bear of a man strode towards me,
Lifted me up and took me away.

Like a rushing river came,
The next days of my horrific life,
I only knew of the measly portions of food,
And the regular chores that the bear avoided.

I wet the tattered old bed tonight,
He treated me as vermin,
Striding towards me, I shrank into the shadows,
He loomed over me, lifted me up and threw me down.

I received a letter from home today,
Bad news, bad news about Mum,
Bombing of the Blitz had burnt her to a cinder,
Oh no! I'm stuck with the bear forever.

Anthony Boyle (10)
The Queens CE Primary School, Richmond

Boy In Camp

Slap, punch, my nose bleeding and numb,
My face exasperatingly painful,
Shoving me to one side, I pushed off.
'You there, get moving or you'll end up worse than him.'
Digging, my back throbbing with pain, I was whipped for stopping,
My bones as weak as lead.
Gasping for breath through the dusty, clammy air
My heart slowing down a beat each day.
Removing decaying gassed bodies from the rotting death chamber,
My feet dragging me down,
My rags draping down, my body barely covered by them,
The bitter winds freezing me, I couldn't feel anything.
My Star of David torn on what was left of my sleeve,
Slowing down, I was pushed against the wall . . .
And shot.

Miranda Willott (11)
The Queens CE Primary School, Richmond

The Child In The Ghetto

The sound of retching fills my head,
Filling the streets, the gutter where I sleep.
Typhoid spreads, brutally killing
I must live but I don't know how.

The Star of David brands me a Jew,
Jude, this word is like a curse,
My religion it may kill me,
I must live but I don't know how.

Mother, Father keep away the fear,
We soon will be separated,
It may be starvation or the gas,
I must live but I don't know how.

Olivia Davies (10)
The Queens CE Primary School, Richmond

The Similes Of Nature

As cruel as a bramble,
As confusing as a tangle,
As robust as a bridge,
As sneaky as a midge,
As murky as a pond,
As unbreakable as a bond,
As unknowable as an ancient tree,
As peaceful as a unthreatened bee,
As silky as a cobweb,
As easy as said,
As magical as a blade of frosty grass,
As old as the past,
As rhythmic as a bird in flight,
As horrible as a fight,
As rusty as an old gate,
As loving as a mate,
As muddy as an old log pile,
As beautiful as a smile.

Charlie Newton (8)
Tillingbourne Junior School, Guildford

The Little White Men

I went out to sea
On November the twelfth
And saw an island
But kept it to myself.

Little white men
With little white hats
Sat on the island
In little white shacks.

With little white coats
And little white eyes
They skipped to the shore
With their little white ties.

Their little white shoes
Twinkled with light
And their little white lips
Smiled with delight.

Rachel Nugent (10)
Tillingbourne Junior School, Guildford

Blue

Blue, blue, blue is a colour - a colour of ice and cold.
A colour of sadness - a devastating colour
Blue is like a land of ice, tree, grass, cars and rivers covered in blue.
Foggy, gloomy, thick mist, all blue.

Blue is a colour that has a destination.
Blue is a colour that shows in every nation.
Blue is a colour that never gets eliminated.
Blue is the colour of my grandpa's transportation.
Blue is the colour of the underwater city.
Blue is the colour of a sensation.
Blue is the colour of the night in the morning.
Blue is the colour for evaporation, of icy winds and quivering people.
Blue is the colour of frost, snow and shivering rivers.

Rebecca Lewis (9)
Tillingbourne Junior School, Guildford

Morning Madness

7.00am - Alarm goes off, wake up really slow.
7.15am - Mum shouts, 'Time to get up now, come on, let's go!'
7.30am - Get up and go straight downstairs.
7.31am - I've forgotten my slippers again, oh well who cares!
7.32am - Now what shall I have this morning to eat?
7.33am - This kitchen floor really is so cold on my feet!
7.34am - Hot porridge for breakfast, my favourite hooray!
7.34am - What a great way to start a school day.
7.44am - Time to go upstairs and start to get ready.
7.45am - Say, 'Good morning' to my little brother who is still clutching his teddy.
7.46am - Begin by brushing my teeth and then by washing my face.
7.50am - My mum is calling, 'Hurry up' she's always on my case.
7.55am - Go downstairs and put on my coat and shoes.
7.57am - An apple or a banana for break today, which one should I choose?
7.59am - Oh bother, I forgot my homework back upstairs, oh what a pain!
8.00am - Bang on time, ready to leave and tomorrow I will do it all over again!

Natalie Thompson (10)
Tillingbourne Junior School, Guildford

Books

The introduction is the start of a book
It's the part that makes you want to look
The middle makes you want to read on
Some are scary and some are long
And then the epilogue gives you glory
It tells you the end of the story.

Gideon Brennan (8)
Tillingbourne Junior School, Guildford

My Dad

My dad's as meek as a mouse
As brave as a knight,
As swift as a kite.
He's as hard as iron,
Yet as fearless as a lion.
But he's very, very mad
And he's my dad.

Samuel Jelley (9)
Tillingbourne Junior School, Guildford

Silence

Silence is the colour of green, green grass waving in the wind.
Silence tastes like delicious gold plums in the air.
Silence feels like thin soft fabric slowly drifting across the sky.
Silence reminds me of Harry Potter and the Prison of Azakban.
Silence sounds like nothing, like the moon in the night sky.
Silence looks like a star in the sky with a black background.
Silence smells like a sweet strawberry giant lollipop.

Tom Winchester (7)
Vinehall School, Robertsbridge

What Is A Rainbow?

A rainbow is like clown's hair.
A rainbow could be a shark's mouth grinning in different colours.
A rainbow could be a glass bowl thrown up in the sky.
A rainbow is like 'The Simpson' in yellow, red and green.

Daniel Hotz (8)
Vinehall School, Robertsbridge

What Is A Hurricane?

A hurricane is a dragon blowing up
It is a lorry of glitter burnt in an oven
It is magical fairy wings exploding here and there
The smoke is fluffy sheep's skin puffing on top
It is clouds coming down from Heaven
It's goat's skin and cow's skin shaved off,
that's why there are some black parts
It is steam from a train
It's twisting and turning flames washing about
What do you think it is?

Tobin Cleary (7)
Vinehall School, Robertsbridge

What Is Fun?

Fun is bright like turquoise
It smells like the fresh air
Fun tastes like chocolate brownies
It looks like an obstacle course
Fun reminds me of fort fun
It sounds like laughter in the park.

Libby Hodgson (7)
Vinehall School, Robertsbridge

Happiness

Happiness is yellow like the sun after a storm.
Happiness feels like winning the biggest race in the world.
Happiness tastes like fresh ice cream on a hot summer's day.
Happiness smells like Mum's best perfume.
Happiness sounds like loving laughter.
Happiness looks like joyful people dancing on the horizon.
Happiness reminds me of all my lovely birthdays.

Alice Whaley (7)
Vinehall School, Robertsbridge

Happiness

Happiness is the colour of golden yellow like the huge round sun.
Happiness tastes like mouth-watering salty chips.
Happiness looks like a birthday cake with candles on top.
Happiness smells like the strawberry scent of a rose.
Happiness reminds me of my best friend Georgia.

Lucy Brown (7)
Vinehall School, Robertsbridge

Silence

Silence is white like a ghost.
It sounds like the gloomy sky.
It tastes like quiet air.
It looks like a big, white, empty box.
Silence smells like cold air.
Silence feels like a touch of nothing.
It reminds me of my silent bedtime.

Florence Williams (7)
Vinehall School, Robertsbridge

What Is Love?

Love is a ruby poppy in the summer breeze.
It feels like a smooth rose.
Love looks like a heart.
It tastes like a red sweet.
Love smells like sugar.
It reminds me of a glittering sunset in Heaven.

Maria Angele (7)
Vinehall School, Robertsbridge

Darkness

Darkness is as black as a bin bag.
Darkness looks like ten thousand bulls coming to attack you.
Darkness feels like a snail.
Darkness sounds like one million rhino on your head.
Darkness smells like a burning bonfire.
Darkness tastes like burnt bacon.
Darkness reminds me of my old fish.

George Birrell (7)
Vinehall School, Robertsbridge

Darkness

Darkness is black like a black, black night.
Darkness tastes like dark chocolate.
Darkness looks like brown crispy leaves.
Darkness feels like I am lonely.
Darkness sounds like people getting ready for bed.
Darkness smells like chocolate cake with chocolate sauce.
Darkness reminds me of me cuddling Benji, my bear, in bed.

Reboert Bensted-Smith (7)
Vinehall School, Robertsbridge

Anger

Anger is like red-hot fury.
It sounds like noisy loathfulness.
It tastes like sour prawns and rotten cheese.
It looks like mouldy bread.
It smells like red-hot blood.
It feels like someone turned to stone.
It reminds you of an earthquake.

Ethan Archer (7)
Vinehall School, Robertsbridge

Darkness

Darkness is black like a panther going to pounce on you.
It sounds like bats' wings attacking you.
It tastes like eating my worst food.
It looks like dragons surrounding you.
It feels like I'm lost forever.
It sounds like there's so much noise.
It reminds me of Herbert dying.

Jemima Acock (8)
Vinehall School, Robertsbridge

What Is The Night?

The night is the gloom of the day.
It is when the night drops down from Heaven and the day is pulled up to Heaven.
The moon twizzles through it with its silver moonlight.
Night is navy blue, when the lights are off darkness comes weaving up.

Ivo Elliott (7)
Vinehall School, Robertsbridge

Fear

Fear is green like werewolf eyes.
It looks like red eyes looking back at me.
It sounds like a twig snapping suddenly.
It smells like rotten eggs that have been left for weeks.
It tastes like blood and makes my mouth water.
It feels cold like a knife in the ice.
It reminds me of being lost.

Archie Ridpath (7)
Vinehall School, Robertsbridge

Princess Poseana

I am a prince who lives in a castle
Yesterday my mail man delivered a parcel
Inside there was a princess beauty
Who was a little cutie, cutie
She looked at me with sparkling eyes
Then she made a thousand sighs
And then I said, 'Oh why? Oh why?'
Then she said, 'Goodbye, goodbye.'

Ruby Russell (8)
Vinehall School, Robertsbridge

What Is Love?

Love is the colour of a rich violet rose.
It looks like a giant ruby heart.
Love reminds me of all my fun friends.
It sounds like an orchestra of angels.
Love smells like a pool of lavender.
It feels like a foamy sponge.

Jasper Piper (8)
Vinehall School, Robertsbridge

Happiness

Happiness is blue like the calm, calm sea.
It sounds like the splashing of water.
It tastes like ham, avocado, mayonnaise, prawns and bread.
It looks like food in two slices of bread.
It smells like it is grilled bacon sandwich.
It feels like me hugging my dad.
It reminds me of amazing Legoland.

Fred Holt (8)
Vinehall School, Robertsbridge

Who Am I?

I'm spotty, I'm nasty, I look very ugly,
I'm eighty; my name could be Katy,
I am a biz size
I would win the winning prize
I make lots of potions
I would dare to make some oceans
I would say, 'Shut up!'
Come on people, buckle up
Who am I?

James Moug (7)
Vinehall School, Robertsbridge

Anger

Anger is the colour red.
It looks like a steaming hot, red, fiery volcano.
It sounds like loud, shouting, barking dogs.
It feels like cold wind hitting your face.
It smells like burning wood.
It tastes like a bitter lemon.
It reminds me of being annoyed.

Ryan McWilliams (8)
Vinehall School, Robertsbridge

What Is Fun?

Fun feels tickly, like grass in summer,
Fun looks like Mickey Mouse in Disneyland,
Fun sounds like my piano,
Fun tastes like chocolate spread,
Fun reminds me of watching 'The great escape'.

Oliver Flood (7)
Vinehall School, Robertsbridge

What Is A Rainbow?

A rainbow is lots of colours like red, blue, yellow, gold, silver, green, orange and pink.
A rainbow is half a coloured apricot.
A rainbow is very beautiful, it shines very light in the summer sky.
A rainbow is a coloured archway to a land of gold,
When the sun is shining and the rain is pouring a rainbow will appear.

Anthony Dunn (7)
Vinehall School, Robertsbridge

What Is The Moon?

The moon is a silver plate popped out of a dark cupboard,
It is a giant ghost's head in the dark blue sky,
It is an enormous white ball thrown into the calm sea,
It is a yellow beach ball bouncing in the park.

Anna Winter (7)
Vinehall School, Robertsbridge

What Am I?

I used to be a rock.
I'm as round as a clock.
I was a ball of fire.
Some people think I'm as flat as a wire.
I'm sort of spotty.
I'll give you a clue if you want me to.
I have fluffy white things around me.
Some parts of me are as hot as tea.
Some parts of me are as cold as ice.
So what am I?

Freddy Condon (7)
Vinehall School, Robertsbridge

Love

Love is like a rose.
It sounds like a cat purring when you tickle its chin.
It tastes like rich red lipstick.
It looks like a heart pounding.
It smells like a beautiful perfume.
It feels like a soft pillow.
It reminds me of my loving family.

Lydia Butler (7)
Vinehall School, Robertsbridge

What Is Love?

Love is red like the colour of your heart.
Love is peace waiting to be found.
Love looks like mistletoe hanging from the ceiling.
Love sounds like a lullaby rocking you to sleep.
Love smells like romantic perfume.
Love tastes like melted Galaxy chocolate on the aga.
Love feels like strong arms around you.
Love reminds you of your best friend and somebody in love.

India Condon (7)
Vinehall School, Robertsbridge

Fun

Fun is a yellow beach ball.
It smells like a big chocolate cake baking in the oven.
Fun looks like reading a book with my friends.
It sounds like people laughing.
Fun feels like squidgy Play-Doh.
It reminds me of playing with my friends.
It tastes like a birthday cake.

Saffia Dalton (7)
Vinehall School, Robertsbridge

What Are Stars?

They are yellow pieces of sweetcorn on a dark blue plate.
They are little grains of gold from the Queen's crown.
They are royal subjects bowing to the moon.
They are the fizzy bubbles in yellow lemonade.
They are tiny chicks chirping in the sky.
They are like blobs of honey.

Ursula Horton (7)
Vinehall School, Robertsbridge

What Is Happiness?

Happiness is gold like the sun.
It looks like fireworks.
It sounds like cracking.
It smells like seawater.
It tastes like pepper.
It feels like burning fire.

Jack Clayton (7)
Vinehall School, Robertsbridge

What Is Happiness?

Happiness is gold like some toffee dangling above your mouth.
It looks like a delicious banana.
It sounds like sweet music.
It tastes like melted chocolate.
It feels like a warm electric blanket.
It reminds me of my holiday in France.

Georgiana Knight (7)
Vinehall School, Robertsbridge

What Is Love?

Love is red like a juicy shiny apple.
Love is joy that is waiting to be found.
Love looks like a sunny day on the beach.
Love sounds like birds singing on a spring day.
Love smells like chocolate by a warm fire.
Love tastes like a roast dinner on a winter's day.
Love feels like a warm hug you've been given.
Love reminds you of your family.

Lucy Everist (8)
Vinehall School, Robertsbridge

What Is Happiness?

Happiness is gold like a block of cheese.
It looks like bananas.
It sounds like peaceful music.
It smells like roast chicken.
It tastes like chocolate.
It feels like Play-Doh.
It reminds me of going on holiday.

Henry Long (7)
Vinehall School, Robertsbridge

What Is A Banana?

Bananas are mini golf clubs in a kitchen.
Bananas are like a smiley face.
Bananas are like a half-moon floating in the sky.
Bananas are like chocolate to a monkey.

Oliver Crawford (7)
Vinehall School, Robertsbridge

What Is The Moon?

The moon is the home of the man on the moon.
The moon is a big huge light that has come from nowhere.
The moon is a big ball of cheese dangling on an invisible string.
The moon is a big disco ball hanging over the world.

Yolanda Morley (7)
Vinehall School, Robertsbridge

What Is Sadness?

It is the colour of grey tapping on the window.
It looks like wars with people drying and people crying.
It sounds like people chanting names.
It smells like overdone porridge.
It tastes like too much vinegar on chips.
It feels like a waterfall coming down your cheeks.
It reminds me of dead flowers.

Jesse O'Shaughnessy (8)
Vinehall School, Robertsbridge

What Is Amazement?

Amazement is the colour blue.
It tastes like delicious blueberries.
It is like a hundred children at the funfair.
It sounds like a big bang.
It feels like exploding fireworks.
It reminds me of having everything I want.

Max Olujobi (7)
Vinehall School, Robertsbridge

What Is Anger?

Anger is the colour red like a volcano exploding.
It sounds like a steam train's whistle.
It smells like a smoky bonfire.
It tastes like a hot chilli.
It feels like a fireball.
It reminds me of nasty people kicking me.

Alexander McAlister (7)
Vinehall School, Robertsbridge

What Is Home?

Home is the colour maroon like a fresh mushroom.
It looks like a raging fire, warm and cosy.
It is a tub of Belgian chocolate ice cream
And watching TV about the jungle and the environment around us.
It sounds like a train's whistle tooting away.
Home smells like burnt ashes and rose perfume.
Home feels like love.

Gemma Robinson (8)
Vinehall School, Robertsbridge

Hunger

Hunger is pale pink like lips.
It looks like an empty plate.
It sounds like a baby wailing for food.
It feels like an empty tummy rumbling.
It tastes like nothing at all.
It smells like something you like but can't get at.
It reminds me of my cooking party.

Anna Campbell (8)
Vinehall School, Robertsbridge

What Is Love?

Love is the colour pink, like a big heart.
It is my family all together.
It smells like my dogs by a hot, hot fire.
It sounds like my brother's laugh when he's in the bath.

Celia Fraser (7)
Vinehall School, Robertsbridge

I Am . . .

As cold as the night
An amazing sight
The gold of the sun
And I love having fun
A mind of my own
Encased in stone.

Philip Jarczyk (9)
Westbourne Primary School, Emsworth

I Am . . .

I am as hot as flame
I am purple and plain
I have a mind of my own
I am as rough as stone
I am as clear as ice
I am dark and light
I am the Queen's delight
I am an only child
I am bright and wild
I am the gold of the sun
I am forbidden to fun
I am the colours of the world
I am a friend of a girl
I have a dark soul
I am . . .

Victoria Kelly (10)
Westbourne Primary School, Emsworth

A Dream

A dream is when your heart flies
It ends when your thoughts land
Your mind disappears into a different world
It flies into other people's spirit and wakes them
The very next minute, you're in Heaven in the skies
Meeting others, free to fly
To find the future, to live for those out there
Your mind goes to another world
And you turn into a star
And your spirit will shine.

William Reed (8)
Westbourne Primary School, Emsworth

I Am An Unknown Creature

I have a rule but my ice is still cool
My ice is sharp but I play like a harp
I shimmer in the light, I glow quite bright
I shine like a moon, I'll come out soon
I am a guitar of a flame, I'm always the same
My heart beats are slower; I'm going lower and lower
I am Blue John.

Kit Steely (9)
Westbourne Primary School, Emsworth

I Am The Darkness Of Light

I am the darkness of light
I am clear as glass
I am a burning flame
I am rigid like a stone
I am purple and plain
I am lively and rough
I am never the same
I sparkle like a jewel
I have a mind of my own
I shimmer in the light
I am sad and alone
I have a heart of my own
My world never ends
My heart can never mend.

Rumena Begum (10)
Westbourne Primary School, Emsworth

Wishes

The stars wish they were the moon
The great ruler of the night shining, shining.
The Moon wishes it were the Earth
Looking down at the people of the world.
The Earth wishes it were a rainbow
With all the colours of the world.
The stars wish they were the Moon
The great ruler of the night shining, shining.

Edward McPhee (8)
Westbourne Primary School, Emsworth

My Friend

My friend is like ice cream on a hot sunny day.
She warms like a snugly coat on a cold winter's day.
She is in the hugs and kisses from my nan
My friend is like laughter on a sad day.
She is my friend and I am hers.

Shanie Barnes (9)
Westbourne Primary School, Emsworth

My Magic Poem

Queen's delight
Forbidden sight
Floating in the air
I stop and stare
Golden hair
Silver glare
Crystal-shaped stone
Sparkle on its own
I'm warm like spice
But cold as ice
Queen's crying
I think I'm dying
Cold as ice
That's the price.

Tamsin Robinson (9)
Westbourne Primary School, Emsworth

I Am . . .

I am a colourful sight
I am a sparkling gem
I am longing for light
I am freezing like ice
I am like a razor
I am dancing like a champ
I am a delicate creature
I am a person's treasure
I am . . .

James Biggin (9)
Westbourne Primary School, Emsworth

Crystal Clear

Queen's delight, blazing sight
Crystal clear, like a tear
On the ground it was found
Kind of its own, I was alone.

Connor Stenning (10)
Westbourne Primary School, Emsworth

Night

Dark night, shining stars
Grey thoughts
Ghostly night, stars shining
Grey thoughts.

Glowing night, bright stars
Midnight dancers
Angel night, stars bright
Midnight dancers

Hidden creature, glowing stars
Fixed eyes
Red fur, stars glowing
Fixed eyes.

Tabitha Peel (8)
Westbourne Primary School, Emsworth

Glowing Night

Blue, pink, purple
Sparkling all night
Glowing bright
Shining light.

Shining bright night
Sparkling stars
Sparkling lights
Glowing bright.

Blue, pink, purple
Colours shining
Oh so bright
Sssh, sleep tight.

Amie Ayling (9)
Westbourne Primary School, Emsworth

Fly

Fly, buzzing round my head
I pick up the swatter to make you dead.
And then you land upon my nose
Why you did that no one knows.
Finally from my face you hop
I squash you - you go *slop!*

Matthew Cowen (11)
Westbourne Primary School, Emsworth

Wishes Of The World

The moon wishes it were the trees
Swaying and singing in the wind.

The trees wish they were the rainbow
All the colours of the world.

The rainbow wishes it were the rocks
Never going always staying forever.

The rocks wish they were in Heaven
Free in flight.

Heaven wishes it were angels,
Flying in the night.

Harry Foster (9)
Westbourne Primary School, Emsworth

I Am . . .

I am blue and yellow
I am clear as ice
I am hot like the flame
I am precious as a gem
I am patterned all over
I am light like the sun
I am rough and rigid
I am shiny and fine
I am a jewel
I am . . .

Abby Hunter (10)
Westbourne Primary School, Emsworth

I Am . . .

Queen's delight
Limited sight
Precious worth
Glittering birth
Golden stone
Deep dark home
Golden yellow
My mother's fellow
Textured home
Colourful bones
I love my home
I'm made of stone.

Becky Smith (9)
Westbourne Primary School, Emsworth

My Family

My sister is gorgeous,
My sister is great,
She's perfect now
But wait till she's eight.

My brother's a disaster
Although he's only two,
He got my sister by the arm
And hit her with a shoe.

My mum is such a killjoy,
She always spoils my fun,
She makes me do my homework
Before a nice cream bun.

My dad is such a joker,
He always thinks he's cool,
You should see him playing cricket;
He cannot catch the ball.

Now since we've wrote this poem
I've got a problem too,
I'm not wanted here anymore,
So can I live with you?

Harry Dinnage (9)
Westbourne Primary School, Emsworth

I Am As . . .

I am as cold as ice
I am as hot as spice
I am as fragile as old bone
I am as strong as a stone
I am a jewel-like creature
I have a dark-coloured feature
I am a crystal embedded in rock
I am Blue John.

Connor P Bowen (9)
Westbourne Primary School, Emsworth

I Am . . .

I am as hard as rock
I am like a sparkling glee
I burn like a white flame
I am the shivering cold
I am as pure as fresh ice.

Tom McPhee (10)
Westbourne Primary School, Emsworth

This Stone

This stone sparkles in the light,
I am sparkly like a jewel.

This stone has a mind of its own,
I am delicate and fragile,
This stone is glittery as ice.

I am textured with colour,
This stone has indefinite tones,
I am patterned with ice.

This stone is clear and precious,
I am crystal embedded in stone.

This stone is as sharp as teeth,
I am the shadow of darkness.
This stone is rigid and lively.

I am my own light.

Sophie Atkinson (10)
Westbourne Primary School, Emsworth

I Am . . .

I am flickering red heat
I am cold clear blue
I am hard unfeeling rock
I am a gentle child
I am as huge as a mountain
I am as small as a stone
I am as red as a robin
I am as blue as the sea
I am as ugly as a boulder
I am as beautiful as a diamond.

Adam Millard (9)
Westbourne Primary School, Emsworth

I Am . . .

Queen's delight
Forbidden light
Precious worth
Amazing birth
Slowly growing
Quietly knowing
Disappearing to stone
Always alone.

Emily Jeffery (9)
Westbourne Primary School, Emsworth

Blue John

Queen's delight
Forbidden sight
Precious worth
Amazing birth
Golden stone
Left alone
Beautiful sight
Glorious night
Slowly glowing
Nobody knowing
Always shiny
Never tiny
Flickering flame
Never plain.

Scott Davis (9)
Westbourne Primary School, Emsworth

I Am . . .

As cold as the night
My queen's delight
I shimmer like a jewel
All amongst the icy pools
I dance amidst the burning flame
And shiver with an icy mane
I dance inside with light
I glitter with my might
I go outside into the warm heat
And feel my mother's angry sleep.

Molly Peel (10)
Westbourne Primary School, Emsworth

Clouds And Rainbows

Clouds wish they were rainbows multicoloured
Rainbows wish they were clouds floating in the air
Swaying trees bend in the wind
Castle haunted by myths, ghosts
Singing grass whispers to the sea.

Peter Moore (9)
Westbourne Primary School, Emsworth

Imagine

Imagine a cave where no one goes
Imagine a queen no one knows
Imagine an indigo flame
Imagine a boy who couldn't be tamed
Imagine a world embedded in ice
Imagine the scorching sun, hot as spice
Imagine the burning moon, it'll be out soon
Imagine the Queen crying
Imagine the boy dying
Imagine a dark world of sadness
Imagine . . .

Holly Caird (10)
Westbourne Primary School, Emsworth

Swooping Bird

Swooping bird is like
A wave surrounding a village
A friend giving you faith.
Swooping bird is like
A siren warning of danger
A friend giving you a chance.
Swooping bird is like
A star that guides you
A sign to show the way.
Swooping bird is like
A blessing from God
A dove to pray for you each day.

Ella Roberts (8)
Westbourne Primary School, Emsworth

The Crystal

Queen's delight
Silent night
Burning star
Nearly done
Brownish-yellow
Purple mellow
Amazing birth
Precious worth
Hummed a song
Anger strong
On the ground
It was found.

Thomas Ludlow (9)
Westbourne Primary School, Emsworth

I Am . . .

I am a flame of the golden moon
I am the shadow of the glacier
I am the jewel of the shining star
I am a glimmer in the darkest cave
I am the loneliest heartbeat
I am curious and inquisitive
I am the queen of darkness precious
I am as stern as a glittering diamond blue
I am rigid like a rock's face
I am the heart of the lonely mountains
I lie forever still.

Harry Crocker (10)
Westbourne Primary School, Emsworth

I Am . . .

Queen's delight
Silent night
Boys are worth
Amazing birth
Golden stone
Glittery tones
Mind of it own
Very dark home
Textured bone
Always alone
Clear as ice
Very dark price.

Davin Haskett (10)
Westbourne Primary School, Emsworth

Flames Of Ice

Flaming heat
Icy sheet
Golden stone
All alone
Twinkling jewel
Soaking pool
Endless dark
Purple mark
Blinding light
Shattered night
Growing stone
Skeletal bone.

Robert Alder (10)
Westbourne Primary School, Emsworth

Angels Flying

Your dreams are a part of your heart
An angel shielding you from nightmares
Trying is best but dreams can come true.

Dreams guide you to a place,
A place with a heart,
A place with a soul,
A magical place with a pitch-black room, angels flying.

They can see, can see anything without a person
And help each person
The higher their new magical feeling, then your dreams come true.

Craig Newson (8)
Westbourne Primary School, Emsworth

Ice Of Glacier, Gold Of Sun

Banished from light
Queen's delight
Precious stone
Always alone
Icy cold
Blazing gold
Candle flicker
Heartbeat quicker
Peaceful dancing
Cave enhancing
Freedom growing
Queen moaning
Limbs weak
Lay down to sleep.

Ruby Conlon (10)
Westbourne Primary School, Emsworth

Night-Time Owl

Owls, flying, fighting, feasting.
Trees, spooky, scary, silent.
Moon, shining, shimmering, shadowy.

Owls, phantom, furious, fabulous.
Badgers, biting, beastly, black.
Moon, bare, black, bad.

Owls, flying, fast, fighting.
Mice, scavenge, scuttling, silent.
Moon, singing, shadowy, shimmering.

Ben Parker (8)
Westbourne Primary School, Emsworth

Brother Mouse

When we first saw it, it was spiralling,
Down and down.
It looks like a jet-black shadow,
Shadow of the night.
It came swooping down to seek its prey,
Grey owl of the night.
Night's owl spiralled, hovered and tore through the air,
Devil of the night.
It saw me and my brother, scurrying,
Under the cover of night.
A silent swoop.
He was gone and I was all alone.

Jude Conlon (8)
Westbourne Primary School, Emsworth

In The Night

Twinkling stars in the night
Slowly, scary in the sky
Trees are swaying in the wind
Animals whispering like a deer in danger.

Scary, spooky in the night
Hooting of an owl in the night.

Spooky, scary, silent night
Trees sway, dark, menacing
Animals, whisper
Owls hoot.

Scary spooky in the night
Hooting of an owl in the night.

Katie Sanderson (8)
Westbourne Primary School, Emsworth

My Friend

My friend is like a warm cosy bed.
She is like a bouncy trampoline.
She has a voice like an owl hooting.
Her friendship means the world to me.
She is my family and I am hers too.

Cody Hamilton (8)
Westbourne Primary School, Emsworth

Me And It

I never saw it
But it saw me.
I never heard it
But it heard me.

I never saw it
But it saw me.
I never missed it
But it missed me.

I never saw it
But it saw me.
I never mentioned it
But it mentioned me.

I always saw it
And it saw me.
I was it
It was me.

Toby Smith (8)
Westbourne Primary School, Emsworth

My Friend

My friend is like a warm cosy bed.
He's like cocoa with chocolate cream.
My friend is the strong brick protecting my house.
He warms me, like hugs from my family.
He is my baby brother and my best friend.

Ryan Lintott (9)
Westbourne Primary School, Emsworth

He's Gone

Fiery red fur
Hopes not to be seen
One pounce and he's gone
So quick, so sly
And he's gone.

Bushy red tail
White tips on his toes
In the mist of the moon
He fades
He's gone.

Leanne Rule (9)
Westbourne Primary School, Emsworth

The Power Of My Heart

My heart is the love of good
My heart is my true power
That keeps on going and never stops.
My heart is the power of a hundred eyes
My heart is the power of a thousand suns
That keeps on going and never stops.
My heart is the power of a hundred stars
My heart is the power of a thousand moons
That gets bigger and bigger.
My heart is like a machine
My heart is a burning ambition that never stops.

Jai Carter (8)
Westbourne Primary School, Emsworth

My Friend

My friend is like a strawberry milkshake.
My friend is like a warm bed.
My friend is like a nice day.
My friend is like my dad telling jokes.
He is my friend and I am his.

Billy Reed (8)
Westbourne Primary School, Emsworth

My Friend

My friend is like sausage, mash and onion gravy.
He is fun, like sliding down a slide.
On a cold winter's day he's like a fire and always there for me.
He helps me in anyway.
He is my friend and I am his.

Charlie Gallear (8)
Westbourne Primary School, Emsworth

The Night Is . . .

The night is somewhere your dreams take flight,
The most important part of each day, is when you have love in your grasp.
The night is a teleporter, which takes you away from a world of glittery joy.
People are in despair with hope all gone.
A dream is someplace where you can do anything for anyone.

Russell Hesketh (8)
Westbourne Primary School, Emsworth

Animals Of The Night

Ferocious fox in the dead of night,
Boastful badger in the dead of night,
Running rabbit as fast as light
Fleeing vole in the dark of night.

Owls eyes like fire in the dark of night,
Glamorous moon in the dead of night,
Dangerous dogs as dark as the night,
Horrendous hunters harass at night.

Grey owl like a fluttering thought,
Silent seeker looking for prey,
Powerful predator in the dead of night,
Fearsome fox creeps at night,
Friends and foes in the dead of night.

Harry Pescott (8)
Westbourne Primary School, Emsworth

My Friend

My friend is a friend.
He is close, we are close.
Friends are friends,
We are always close together.
My friend is very, very kind
And very, very delicate.
And as powerful as anything.
That's my friend.
God is my friend.
He is kind, I am kind.
I have friends, He has friends, we are always friends.

Jack Guillen (8)
Westbourne Primary School, Emsworth

The Gazing Bird

There was a full moon
It gave shadows to the gazing owl.
The owl softly flew down and snatched a worm.
It was morning
The lark was flying high in the sky.
The lark gazes into clouds.
The lark was wishing it were a cloud,
The cloud was wishing it were a bird.

Abbie Drinkwater (9)
Westbourne Primary School, Emsworth

Sunlight

Sunlight is a light
It moves in the daylight
Sunlight is like a moon
In the day, not night
Like a star, but not at night.

The night is like a star
The night shines when you're asleep.

A dream is an angel
What is a star?
An angel lives in Heaven
God made the stars into angels.
A dream is a star which lights up the night.

Ella Stubbs (8)
Westbourne Primary School, Emsworth

Football

F unniest game in the world
O n the field you need to play your best
O rganisation
T eamwork
B all smacked in the back of the net
A ce performance is what you need
L ift the cup at the end of the season
L ampard is the man who can do that job.

Jordan Kane (9)
West Byfleet Junior School, West Byfleet

Football

F ootball is interesting and cool
O ut of the ordinary
O ught to win the World Cup for England
T o kick the football in the net
B egging for the Premiership
A rsenal for the Champion's League
L obbing the ball in the air
L oving the *sport!*

Simon Hack (8)
West Byfleet Junior School, West Byfleet

Sport

S uccess winning or losing is still very fun
P laying enthusiastically with your friends is so enjoyable
O f all the possibilities sport is the best game
R unning hard, sprinting fast
T rying hard is the only way to succeed!

F or four-hundred years I've played this sport
O bviously I've had injuries
O f course I enjoy playing the funny game
T he players always laugh at me
B ut I don't really mind
A t the game I score lots of goals
L ots of lovely memorable moments
L oads of the team really want me to play now.

Megan Wordingham (9)
West Byfleet Junior School, West Byfleet

Monkey

M ad monkey on the loose
O penly swinging amongst the glistening treetops
N aughty monkey climbing on the shining green trees
K nowing a monkey is a wonderful thing
E xcited monkeys lying in the tall branches of the trees
Y ellow bananas are the favourite food.

Anna Rickards (8)
West Byfleet Junior School, West Byfleet

My Kitten

My kitten is called Sausage
He speaks a different language
He made a hole in my school shirt
I told him to do it to my sister's skirt
Even though he is very little
His bones are not at all brittle
He's black all over with one white spot
He likes to bathe in my brother's cot
And when he's resting or in other words asleep
I think he looks like a baby sheep.

Izzy Hamilton (9)
West Byfleet Junior School, West Byfleet

Love Is . . .

Love is a waterfall.
Love is like a rose.
Love is like cuddles.
Love is happiness.
Love is a great big heart.
Love is a tingling feeling in your tummy.
Love is when you show friendship.
Love is cream.
Love is blossom.
Love is care.
Love is a bowl of strawberries.

Katrina Francis (8)
West Byfleet Junior School, West Byfleet

Life

L ife is nice, you've got to make the most of it
I nteresting things happen throughout it
F orever I'll like it
E verything will feel great!

Oliver Holland (8)
West Byfleet Junior School, West Byfleet

Love Is . . .

Love is good.
Love is happiness.
Love is good and joyful.
Love is cream.
Love is roses and blossom.
Love is happy thoughts.
Love is lipstick.

Sophie U'Dell (8)
West Byfleet Junior School, West Byfleet

Love

Love is like a bowl of berries.
Love is friendship.
Love is like a petal.
Love is like a juicy apple.
Love is like bright red cake.

Euan Watt (7)
West Byfleet Junior School, West Byfleet

Football

F ootball is an excellent way to relax
O bserving the match from the stand
O ver the top football players
T -shirts thrown out to the supporters
B eautiful save by the goalkeeper
A mazing goal by number eleven
L azy legwork by number five
L ively crowd around them.

Kerry Russell (8)
West Byfleet Junior School, West Byfleet

Love

Love is a juicy red apple.
Love is like a red rose.
Love is happiness.
Love is as nice as a juicy apple.
Love is fun.
Love is an exciting feeling.
Love is a wonderful feeling.
Love is when I kiss my mum.
Love is brilliant!

Ben Kidgell (7)
West Byfleet Junior School, West Byfleet

Giraffe

G iraffes eat juicy leaves
I n the grasslands
R eally tall thin necks
A giraffe has brown spots
F unny clumsy giraffes
F ast running giraffes
E ating with flexible tongues.

Sophie Vaughan (9)
West Byfleet Junior School, West Byfleet

Class

C lever in what we do
L earning good things
A mazing work being achieved
S uper in the things we say
S porty when we have fun.

Michael Catton (8)
West Byfleet Junior School, West Byfleet

Goodbye

Children cry for their mums and dads,
Babies, toddlers, girls and lads,
They clutch their belongings in each hand,
In their best clothes looking so grand,
Some children cry their eyes out,
Some children scream and shout.

Finally they get on the train,
In their hearts they all feel pain,
Brothers and sisters stay close by,
The little ones are starting to cry.

Teachers take kids to a big hall,
Couples choosing children short and all,
Children think it's just a game,
But it seems real all the same.

When they realise it's not a game,
The siblings shout each others names,
Not all siblings can stay together,
They think they'll be split forever and ever.
When they get to their new home,
They cry even more and start to moan.

Molly Hutchins (9)
West Byfleet Junior School, West Byfleet

Monkeys

Monkeys swing from here to there
People like to stop and stare
They have a toffee-coloured tummy
They think bananas are yummy
Monkeys are very cheeky
They are a little bit sleepy
They hate apes
But they love grapes
They like to dangle
But they get in a tangle!

Lucy Hutchins (8)
West Byfleet Junior School, West Byfleet

Opposites

Fear
Fear smells like a decomposing body.
Fear tastes like rotten egg soup.
Fear looks like body parts rotting away.
Fear feels like a spear going through you.
Fear sounds like a pack of hungry wolves.

Security
Security smells like a home-cooked meal.
Security tastes like shepherd's pie.
Security looks like home.
Security feels like love.
Security sounds like children playing.

Darian Nel (11)
West Byfleet Junior School, West Byfleet

Love Is . . .

Love is holding hands
Love is caring for friends and family.
Love is caring for people all around the world.
Love is being thoughtful to family.
Love is like a big juicy cherry.
Love is like pink bubblegum.
Love is like a big, giant lollipop.
Love is like a big chocolate heart with marshmallow inside.
Love is brilliant!

Poppy Ryder (7)
West Byfleet Junior School, West Byfleet

Love

When you get that warming feeling
You know that someone loves you
When you get that tingly feeling
You know that you love someone too
When you see a rose growing
You know that love is around
When you see the sun come out
You know some love is coming.

Sarah Cole (7)
West Byfleet Junior School, West Byfleet

Dolphin

D olphins jumping in the glistening sea under the sunlight
O pen your eyes and see the wonderful dolphins
L ovely dolphins splashing in the shimmering sea
P layful animals under the sea waiting to pounce with glee
H urry up and don't miss the spectacular dolphins
I nside the incredible sea lots of extraordinary fish, not to mention the wonderful dolphins
N ot the world's worst animal, the best!

Chloe Jones (8)
West Byfleet Junior School, West Byfleet

Sports

S hiny racket sparkling in the sun
P owerful swimmers, swim, swim and swim
O pen your eyes to see the wonderful sports from Heaven
R unning so fast multicoloured smoke will come out of your feet
T ennis is fun, fun and fun
S ports will race you to the finish line and you will win.

Chloe Spencer (9)
West Byfleet Junior School, West Byfleet

Trains Poem

The quickest train in the world
Moving so fast
Rain and shine no matter what the weather
Watch it fly past
People consuming food
In the buffet car
Into a city out of a town
Travelling so far
Train, train
How great you are!

Liam Grant (9)
West Byfleet Junior School, West Byfleet

Swimming

S wimming is good exercise
W aving water swiftly moving
I open my eyes under the sea
M oving water in the sea
M oving people in the sea
I can swim like them because the sea likes me
N ice water comes to me
G oing mad in the water.

Aiysha Laborde (8)
West Byfleet Junior School, West Byfleet

Tigers

T igers are sly and have stripes of black
I n the jungle hear the eerie sound of tigers roaring!
G etting ready to pounce on its prey
E verybody likes tigers
R isky but beautiful
S o incredible, so clever.

Fenella Hughes (8)
West Byfleet Junior School, West Byfleet

School

My friends like school but I don't,
My friends do the work but I won't.
The rules are nasty
And the dinners are ghastly.
The punishments are horrible
And the playground is terrible.
Although I've made outrageous remarks,
Secretly I like . . . *school!*

Jenny Jarman (9)
West Byfleet Junior School, West Byfleet

Love Is . . .

Love is happiness.
Love is a tingly feeling in my tummy.
Love is beauty.
Love is a great big heart.
Love is the land of Narnia.
Love is when you show friendship.
Love is brilliant!

Shannon Guett (8)
West Byfleet Junior School, West Byfleet

Bombings

I felt the bomb beneath my feet.
My shelter was shaking like a herd of elephants rushing past.
I was scared.
I was in the shelter all alone.
I could hear the planes.
They were here.
I could smell the burning buildings and gas masks.
I suddenly tasted blood then I realised it was mine.
When will the war be over?

Bethan Ford (10)
West Byfleet Junior School, West Byfleet

A Summer's Afternoon

In the afternoon
The sun shines bright
I feel all tingly
And that should be right.
All the pretty flowers smiling at me
And all the little children singing happily.
The people are sunbathing in the bright summer sky
I love being happy in the sun.

Darcy Brenna Fox-Williams (7)
West Byfleet Junior School, West Byfleet

A Cousin Is . . .

A cousin is a caring person.
A cousin is a loving person.
A cousin is a magical person.
A cousin is a calm person.
A cousin is an understanding person.
A cousin is everyone's dream.
My cousin is Christie.

Georgia Page (8)
West Byfleet Junior School, West Byfleet

Horses

Horses in the stable
Having their cosy sleep.
I snuggled up in their shavings.

Paris Kyriakides (8)
West Byfleet Junior School, West Byfleet

Hitler's War

I can see dried blood everywhere like a red blur.
I can see tear-stained faces.
I can smell smoke and rotting bodies.
I can feel sweat from the hot air of the fire.
I feel depression from the war.
I can feel rubble falling off tumbling houses.
I can hear screaming as people run for their lives.
I can hear explosions and German soldiers laughing.
Why? Why? Why?

Charlotte Hambly (10)
West Byfleet Junior School, West Byfleet

Class

C lever in what we do
L earning different things every day
A mazing work being achieved
S uper is the work we do
S mart in what we say.

Peter Hawkings (8)
West Byfleet Junior School, West Byfleet

Cousins Are . . .

Cousins are the best.
Cousins are cool.
Cousins are loving.
Cousins are fun.
Cousins are good.
Cousins are lovely.
My cousin is Georgia.

Christie Tillett (8)
West Byfleet Junior School, West Byfleet

When It Happened

It feels like I'm falling into pieces.
I can see the sadness and the weeping.
I can hear death upon me.
I can smell the breath of gas.
I can taste the rich blood.

Emily Stott (10)
West Byfleet Junior School, West Byfleet

Terror

I hear screaming and bombs bang everywhere and the crashing of buildings.
I feel sadness as the bombs go *boom!*
I can feel the crushed homes.
I can feel the holes in the path where the bombs have missed buildings.
I can taste the toxic smoke and the blood on my arm.
I can see crushed buildings and people running and black skies with fire.
I can smell fumes.
Not a nice time, not at all.

Daniel Vanhinsbergh (9)
West Byfleet Junior School, West Byfleet

The Bombings

I could just see fire and fire.
I saw people with gas masks, people were crawling.
I felt pain like a giant stamping on me and people grabbing me.
I could taste the smoke going into my mouth.
I smelt death.

Connor Barrett (10)
West Byfleet Junior School, West Byfleet

The War

All I could see were people running like headless chickens.
All I could smell was gas going through my nose and mouth.
All I could feel was dead, slimy bodies.
All I could smell were explosions, screaming and death.

Abdurr Rehman (10)
West Byfleet Junior School, West Byfleet

Bombs

B ombs are dropping on me
O ur army is strong
M y mum is crying
B ang! Crash! People being killed
S mash, the glass has gone.

Maxine Guyett (9)
West Byfleet Junior School, West Byfleet

World War II

I can hear people screaming and bombs shattering homes like a bulldozer.
I can see children being evacuated but having no idea what is happening.
I can smell gas, fire and blood of the unfortunate.

Megan Hawkins (9)
West Byfleet Junior School, West Byfleet

World War II

As I heard the sirens ring
I felt as if my whole life was going to end.
When I got to my shelter, I felt safe in my mother's arms.
I looked out of the window to see the fire slashing like ravenous tigers.
As the people ran through the streets,
They were like a herd of elephants running in the jungle.
I could smell the ashes of burnt wood.
As I was evacuated I tasted the bitterness of war.

Chris Schmitz (10)
West Byfleet Junior School, West Byfleet

Bombs

Bombs are horrific, especially the Blitz.
I see houses burn into bits.
Planes dropping bombs, everyone runs.
I hear screaming and exploding.
I smell gas and fires burning.
I feel nervous and the shaking of the greyish shelters.
I taste the gas and smoke in my mouth.

Helayna Saunders (9)
West Byfleet Junior School, West Byfleet

The Air Raid

Bombs, bombs, I hate bombs
They hurt people like you and me.
Every day and every night
All I can hear is *bang! Bang! Bang!*
People are running as fast as a tiger
People are running to the air raid shelter.

Katie Gosham (10)
West Byfleet Junior School, West Byfleet

The Killing War

I could smell the gas around me.
The sirens kept going off.
There were people crying, the noise was deafening.
I stood on a baby bloodstained gas mask as I ran into the shelter.
I couldn't stop crying when I was informed my best friend had been killed
in an explosion.

Lauren Hillier (10)
West Byfleet Junior School, West Byfleet

Football

F un is the main thing in football
O n the field is where you need to try
O rganisation
T eamwork
B all smacks in the back of the net
A ce performance is what you need
L ift the cup
L ampard's the man.

Alexander Waddell (8)
West Byfleet Junior School, West Byfleet

Flowers

F antastic for a lovely present
L ovely like family
O range blue and green
W onderful like life is
E xtreme is the shape of the petals
R ed, purple and yellow
S uper looking at the colours.

Edan Fox-Williams (9)
West Byfleet Junior School, West Byfleet

Fire

F lames set alight
I ce melting
R oaring fire
E xploring's unsafe
S moke, don't choke.

Eleanor Reid (10)
West Byfleet Junior School, West Byfleet

I'm Not A Well Monster

I'm not a well monster
I'm hardly green at all
My warts are pale and pasty
My hair is almost clean
My horns are weak and wobbly
I think I need a doctor
I'm not a well monster
Hurray, here comes the medicine
Its whirling on my plate
I'll soon be well again
And I can hardly wait!

Georgina Murrin (8)
West Byfleet Junior School, West Byfleet

Narnia

Narnia is Aslan's kingdom
Narnia is a big enchantment
Narnia is where four children sit
Narnia is a giant dream
Narnia is an icy adventure
Narnia is a wonderful place
Narnia is where the white witch dies
Narnia is magical.

Lara Mills (8)
West Byfleet Junior School, West Byfleet

From A Bus

Slower than a train,
Slower than a train,
Duck when you go under a bridge!

Feel the bus shake as if it is going down a hill,
Feels like it will topple over.

Hear the engine shake
As if an army of soldiers are thundering past.

Julius Lewis (7)
West Dene School, Purley

From A Plane

Longer than a marathon
Faster than a runner
Houses smaller than toys
Passing West Dene School.

Feeling the wind breeze
Gliding in the rain
Rocking in the turbulence
Scared of heights.

People chatting
Daddy's snoring
Mummy's angry
Nanny's calm.

Soon we land
People shout, *'Hooray!'*
Some people are upset
But I'm OK!

Neha Maini (7)
West Dene School, Purley

From A Speedboat

Faster than a jet ski,
Faster than a rocket,
Twice as fast than sound,
Faster than a jet launching into the sky.

Gliding on the waves,
Charging like a marathon runner,
Hovering on the sea,
People shouting, *'Hello!'*

Passing ships that glide,
Passing harbours along the ride,
Passing dolphins that leap in the air,
Passing seagulls that cry in the sky above.

Nathaniel Aloshias (8)
West Dene School, Purley

From A Helicopter

Faster than a marathon runner
And schools are passing by
Faster than a frisbee.

Zooming past a speedboat
Drifting down the sea.

I'm nearly at land now
And can see a rubber dinghy.

I can hear the propellers roar
Slowing down.

As I land upon the golden sand
I see people swimming gently.

I see some trees
Swaying in the breeze.

Sonam Shah (8)
West Dene School, Purley

From A Bus

The bus is slower than a snail,
Slower than a worm,
Passing under low bridges,
Crouching down,
Bubbling like an apple in cold water.

When I see a low branch
It feels like
It's going to
Scrape the bus,
But it doesn't.

Max Roberts (7)
West Dene School, Purley

YOUNG WRITERS INFORMATION

We hope you have enjoyed reading this book - and that you will continue to enjoy it in the coming years.

If you like reading and writing poetry drop us a line, or give us a call, and we'll send you a free information pack.

Alternatively, if you would like to order further copies of this book or any of our other titles, then please give us a call.

Young Writers,
Remus House,
Coltsfoot Drive,
Peterborough
PE2 9JX

Tel: 01733 890066

Email: youngwriters@forwardpress.co.uk

Website: www.youngwriters.co.uk